A Jewish Renaissance in Fifteenth-Century Spain

JEWS, CHRISTIANS, AND MUSLIMS
FROM THE ANCIENT TO THE MODERN WORLD

SERIES EDITORS
R. STEPHEN HUMPHREYS, WILLIAM CHESTER JORDAN, AND PETER SCHÄFER

A Jewish Renaissance
in Fifteenth-Century Spain

Mark D. Meyerson

PRINCETON UNIVERSITY PRESS

PRINCETON AND OXFORD

Copyright © 2004 by Princeton University Press
Published by Princeton University Press,
41 William Street, Princeton, New Jersey 08540
In the United Kingdom: Princeton University Press,
3 Market Place, Woodstock, Oxfordshire OX20 1SY

Library of Congress Cataloging-in-Publication Data

Meyerson, Mark D.
   A Jewish renaissance in fifteenth-century Spain / Mark D.
   Meyerson
      p.   cm.   — (Jews, Christians, and Muslims
from the ancient to the modern world)
      Includes bibliographical references and index.
      ISBN 0-691-11749-7 (cl : alk. paper)
      1. Jews — Spain — Civilization.   2. Jews — Spain — Valencia
(Region) — Civilization.   3. Spain — Civilization — 711–1516.
4. Spain — Civilization — Jewish influences.   5. Spain —
Ethnic relations.   6. Valencia (Spain : Region) — Ethnic
relations.   I. Title.   II. Series.
DS135.S7M485 2004
946'.004924 — dc21

                                                    2003056329

British Library Cataloging-in-Publication Data is available
This book has been composed in Electra
Printed on acid-free paper. ∞
pup.princeton.edu
Printed in the United States of America
1   3   5   7   9   10   8   6   4   2

For Jill, Benjamin, and Samuel
my life

———————————————

CONTENTS

FIGURES AND MAPS

Figures

Maps

ACKNOWLEDGMENTS

This book was a long time in the making. I have incurred many debts along the way. Yom Tov Assis of the Hebrew University first suggested the project to me, though it acquired dimensions neither of us had foreseen. José Ramon Magdalena Nom de Déu of the Universitat de Barcelona offered helpful advice when the project was in its early stages. Stephen Humphreys, David Nirenberg, Jeff Paul, and Derek Penslar read the manuscript at various stages and made many useful suggestions, especially in helping me decide which parts of the archival iceberg to leave submerged. Larry Simon saved the day with the two-volume solution. The directors and staffs of the Arxiu de la Corona d'Aragó, the Arxiu del Regne de València, the Arxiu Municipal de València, the Archivo de Protocolos del Patriarca de Valencia, and the Archivo Histórico Nacional were all kind and helpful. Through the years of archival research I have enjoyed the friendship and collegiality of many scholars: Larry Simon, David Nirenberg, Steph Bensch, Kathryn Miller, Debra Blumenthal, Elka Klein, Brian Catlos, Gemma Escribà Bonastre, José Ramon Magdalena Nom de Déu, Manuel Sánchez Martínez, Vicent Giménez Chornet, Luisa Tolosa Robledo, Rafael Narbona Vizcaíno, Germano Navarro. I owe special thanks to my *mudejarista* friend Manuel Ruzafa García for his many insights and hospitality. None of this, I am sure, would have been possible without Lluís To Figueras, Silvia Gassiot — and now Emma and Enric. They have opened their home and hearts to me these many years and have become like family, an immeasurable boon when I was so far from my own.

Research for this book has been generously supported by the Institute for Scholarship in the Liberal Arts at the University of Notre Dame, the National Endowment for the Humanities, the Memorial Foundation for Jewish Culture, and the Social Sciences and Humanities Research Council of Canada.

My embarking on this study of Valencian Jewry was, I know, somehow bound up with what one might call "identity issues." Though the exploration of Spain's Jewish past has not resolved them, the home and life I have made with my wife, Jill, and my boys, Ben and Sam, have. Without Jill I could not have grappled with my own past, much less Spain's. My sons were born while this project was in progress. Nothing matches the power and joy of simply being their father.

NOTE ON NAMES AND MONEY

Since the Jewish and Christian inhabitants of the kingdom of Valencia were Catalan-speaking, I have used the Catalan forms of their names whenever possible. I have done the same for toponyms (e.g., Morvedre instead of Murviedro, Xàtiva rather than Játiva). For Castilian or Aragonese persons or places, I have used the Castilian or Aragonese forms.

In order to enable readers to follow Valencian Jewish individuals and families over the course of many years or generations, I have regularized their surnames, using the forms that most commonly appear in the documents (e.g., Avincanes instead of Abencanyes or Hincanes, Asseyo rather than Asseu or Asseo). I have also regularized the spelling of their given names for the sake of consistency and identification (Jahudà instead of Jaffuda, Isaac rather than Içach). Adhering to the inconsistent and variable orthography of the documents would only confuse readers.

Again, for the sake of clarity, I have used the Catalan names and numeration of the rulers of the kingdom of Valencia. Even Valencian scholars writing in Catalan use the Catalan rather than the Valencian numeration. Hence, I refer to Pere the Ceremonious as Pere III, not as the Aragonese Pedro IV or the Valencian Pere II. However, I have used the Castilian forms of the names of the kings of the Castilian Trastámara dynasty — the names by which they were commonly recognized: Fernando I, Alfonso IV, Juan II, and Fernando II.

All monetary sums mentioned in this study are in the currency of the kingdom of Valencia, except when specifically indicated by "sous b." for the sous of Barcelona, the currency of Catalonia. Throughout the Crown of Aragon, 1 lliura (or pound) = 20 sous; and 1 sous = 12 diners.

ABBREVIATIONS

ACA	Arxiu de la Corona d'Aragó
AHN	Archivo Histórico Nacional
AMC	Arxiu Municipal de Castelló de la Plana
AMV	Arxiu Municipal de València
AMVil	Arxiu Municipal de Vila-real
APPV	Archivo de Protocolos del Patriarca de Valencia
ARV	Arxiu del Regne de València
B	Bailia
C	Cancilleria Reial
CR	Cartes Reiales
G	Gobernació
Inq.	Inquisición
JC	Justicia Criminal
JCivil	Justicia Civil
leg.	legajo
LM	Lletres Missives
M.	Manus (=quire)
MC	Manuals de Consell
MR	Maestre Racional
P	Protocolos

A Jewish Renaissance in Fifteenth-Century Spain

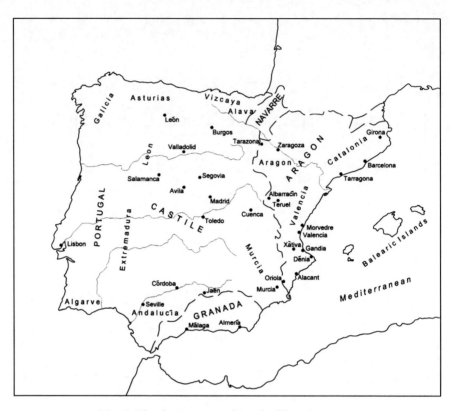

Map 1. The Iberian peninsula in the fifteenth century.
Map prepared by Steven Sanford.

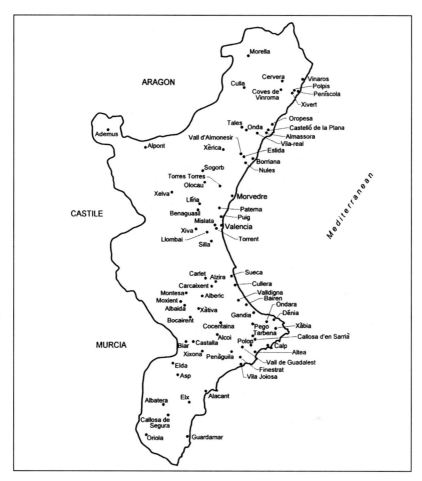

Map 2. The kingdom of Valencia. Map prepared by Steven Sanford.

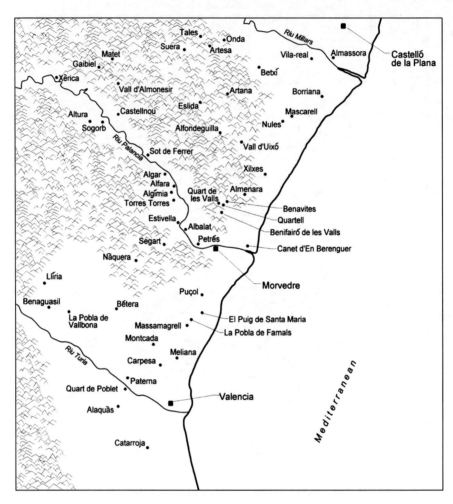

Map 3. The main area of activity of the Jews of Morvedre.
Map prepared by Steven Sanford.

Introduction

This book focuses on the final century of the history of the Jewish community of Morvedre, a town located in the kingdom of Valencia, itself part of the federated Crown of Aragon. The story of the Jews of Morvedre begins in 1248, with Jewish settlers' convergence on the town in the wake of King Jaume I's conquest of the region from the Muslims. The story ends as do all histories of the Jews of medieval Spain: with the Jews abandoning their homes and departing for new lands in the summer of 1492, in compliance with the edict of expulsion.[1] Morvedre's old Jewish quarter still stands in mute testimony to the Jews' previous existence and exile. The town itself, however, is no longer called Morvedre but Sagunto. In 1868 it reverted to a form of its old Roman name, Saguntum, as if to draw attention to its Roman antiquity at the expense of its medieval past, when the town was peopled by Muslims and Jews. Indeed, while the stark and magnificent Roman arena readily brings the town's ancient glories to mind, the rather ordinary architecture of the former Jewish quarter can almost make one forget that Jews ever lived there at all.

Yet for a historian intent on recovering the Jews of medieval Morvedre from oblivion, the narrow streets of the Jewish quarter do resound with Jewish voices — or at least they can be made to do so through careful archival reconstruction and with a healthy dose of imagination. The Jewish voices and bodies must be, as it were, conjured, for in merely viewing the streets and houses of the Jewish quarter the visitor can hardly believe that in the century prior to 1492 it was the home and hub of a vital and flourishing Jewish community. The closed quarter with its narrow streets might suggest restriction and oppression, a harried and degrading Jewish existence for which the expulsion was the natural conclusion, the emphatic punctuation to decades of despair. Such an impression, however, would be far from the truth.

The architectural remains of present-day Sagunto belie the history of a Jewish community that runs against the grain of the master narrative of Sephardic history, a narrative mainly fashioned by Yitzhak Baer and perpetuated in more recent syntheses.[2] According to this narrative, the Jews of the Christian realms

---

[1] Hinojosa Montalvo 1983; Beinart 1994, 226–231.

[2] Baer 1961. Assis 1997 is, like Baer, a magisterial work that, despite its more limited chronological scope, nonetheless implies that the post-1327 era was one of universal decline. Gerber 1992, 110–144, is a more popular work that seems to regard the fourteenth and fifteenth centuries as hardly worthy of consideration, except to explain the Spanish Inquisition and the expulsion. Foa 2000, 74–107, offers the most recent summary of the master narrative. Beinart 1994, 13, argues,

of Castile and the Crown of Aragon experienced, from roughly the end of the twelfth century until the second quarter of the fourteenth, a kind of golden age, analogous to the one their ancestors had enjoyed in Muslim Spain prior to the Almohad persecutions. During this second golden age Christian monarchs were solicitous of their Jewish subjects, Jewish courtiers and officials were powerful and influential, Jewish communities were prosperous and contributed greatly to the economic development of the Christian kingdoms and to the treasuries of Christian kings, and Jewish intellectual and religious life remained vigorous and creative. The period following the golden age is presented as one of inexorable Jewish decline, right until the expulsion. Kings favored and protected the Jews less consistently, while the Christian masses, moved increasingly by religious zeal and agitated by plague, political upheaval, and economic dislocation, reacted with growing vehemence and violence against Jewish power, Jewish usury, and Jewish infidelity. Internally Jewish communities were racked by problems already evident in the golden age: social and political strife as well as ideological controversies between worldly, philosophically minded elites and upright pietists, conflicts that corroded the cohesion of the Jewish community and the commitment and identity of individual Jews. All this came to a head in the summer of 1391, when Christian mobs attacked Jewish communities throughout Castile and the Crown of Aragon, killing many Jews and forcibly baptizing thousands. The final century between 1391 and 1492 was, according to the master narrative, one of almost unmitigated Jewish despair; Jews, for the most part, simply endured.[3] In this narrative the Jews themselves recede into the background, with the baptized Jews and their descendants — the *conversos* — taking center stage. The history of Spanish Jewry in the fifteenth century thus becomes largely a history of the conversos, the Spanish Inquisition, and the expulsion. The Jews return to center stage only when they are on their way out of Spain; for the entire previous

---

in line with Baer, that the Jews of the Crown of Aragon were unable to revive in the fifteenth century.

[3] However, Gutwirth 1992, 52, points out that "paradoxical as it may seem, the period which begins with pogroms and ends with expulsions need not be seen as one of unmitigated decline." Still, Gutwirth does not explain *why* a given community might have experienced something different—in the case of Morvedre, something dramatically different—from "decline." Gampel, 1989 and 1998, paints a picture of Navarrese Jewry at the end of the fifteenth century that would seem to challenge the master narrative and suggest that the experience of Morvedre's Jews was not an anomaly. Yet his work views the post-1391 period as an era of "decline for the Jews of Castile and Aragon," with only Navarre, and perhaps Portugal, salvaging his notion of *convivencia*. In any case, Gampel treats only the final years of the fifteenth century, which makes it difficult to see how the situation of Navarrese Jewry might have changed over the later Middle Ages. He does demonstrate, though, that it was mainly the pressure exerted by Fernando and Isabel on Navarre's rulers and cities that brought about the downfall of Navarre's Jews. This accords with my discussion in chapter 7 of the transformation of Valencian Jewry after the Castilian-run Spanish Inquisition began to operate in the kingdom.

century they are merely preparing for—or being prepared for—that last, painful journey.

For the Jews of Morvedre, however, the century between 1391 and 1492 was not simply a gloom-filled parenthesis; it was instead an era of remarkable resurgence. Yet the community's early history does not easily fit the golden age paradigm. During this period the kingdom of Valencia underwent rapid social, religious, and institutional changes that were as problematic for the Jews of Morvedre as the calamities of the fifteenth century.[4] Despite the impression lent by much historical scholarship, and by all the "Jew-free" Jewish quarters in contemporary Spain, the Jewish experience in medieval Spain was not uniform, neither in the fifteenth century nor earlier. This is not to say that the history of the Jews in Christian Spain defies generalization, but that any revised master narrative, if such is a desideratum, must take into account the variety of Jewish experience. My research on the history of the Jews of Morvedre has resulted in the writing of a counternarrative, a narrative that challenges the prevailing master narrative. There is no reason to think that the historical experience of the Jews of Morvedre was a complete anomaly; whether it was can be determined only through additional local studies.[5] Even if it was anomalous, it is still crucial to know why. But if Morvedre was not unique—and it probably was not—then the master narrative of Sephardic history, as well as that of Christian-Muslim-Jewish relations in medieval Spain, requires serious rethinking.

This book grows out of my ongoing concern to contribute to the understanding of the dynamics of Christian-Muslim-Jewish coexistence in medieval Christian Spain and of the social, religious, and political processes resulting in its breakdown. These are not minor, esoteric issues. The ethnic conflicts and "cleansings" plaguing the modern world compel one to try to make sense of how a country like Spain could have been transformed from a land of three religions into one wholly Catholic, at least superficially, by 1526, and to determine the impact of this transformation on individuals, families, communities, and kingdoms. In some regions, I am convinced, the transformation was not internally generated; it did not result from popular Christian pressure and local intergroup conflict. External movements, ideologies, and institutions were far more important for effecting dramatic socioreligious change.[6]

In the case of the Jews, comprehension of the causes behind the violence of 1391 or the expulsion of 1492, especially the relation of these critical events to

[4] I treat the pre-1391 period in a separate volume, *Jews in an Iberian Frontier Kingdom* (Meyerson 2004a).

[5] The Jews of the kingdom of Aragon, for instance, warrant further consideration in this regard, but the relevant scholarship, such as that of the prolific Motis Dolader (e.g., 1996 and 1997a), does not even broach, much less answer, the sorts of questions I pose in this book, particularly those concerning the evolution of Jewish-Christian relations.

[6] Meyerson 1991, for the case of the Muslim population.

the previous decades of Jewish-Christian interaction in particular locales, can be achieved only through highly contextualized local or regional studies over the *longue durée*. Yet for the history of Spanish Jewry such studies have still not been undertaken. I propose to fill this historiographical lacuna with my work on the Jews of Morvedre. In this book and in a separate volume on the earlier period,[7] I treat the entire history of the community from the time of its establishment, after the Christian conquest of the Valencian region from the Muslims, until the final expulsion. By taking the long view of the history of a particular Jewish community, one can trace with far greater clarity the changing position of the Jews within the shifting constellation of religious and social groups, and identify the factors — social, religious, economic, and political — shaping or sometimes distorting intergroup as well as intragroup relations. In such a history events become as important as social and economic structures, individual personalities and families at least as crucial as social classes or essentialized "Jews," "Christians," and "Muslims." The world thus recreated is particular to Morvedre and environs between 1248 and 1492 and yet is in certain respects more representative of Jewish life in medieval Iberia than any pancommunity study.

The result of such a focus is, as suggested above, utterly at odds with the master narrative of Sephardic history. In the volume that deals with the 1248–1391 period, I locate the decisive downturn in the fortunes of the Jews of Morvedre between, roughly, 1280 and 1325, and so take much of the luster off the golden age. The Jews' difficulties resulted in part from the very success of a colonization process in which they themselves had played a vital role. The Christian rulers and subjects of the new kingdom relegated the Jews to a markedly inferior position. The Jews' seemingly inescapable dual function as royal fiscal serfs and primary purveyors of credit produced conflict within the Jewish community while poisoning relations with Christians. This early downturn, however, was not the beginning of an inexorable decline for the Jews. They effectively adapted to the changed conditions, weathered the violent upheavals of the mid–fourteenth century, and entered the 1390s with considerable vigor and optimism.

This book takes as its point of departure the horrific summer of 1391, when Christian violence irrevocably transformed the world of Spanish Jews. The ensuing century of Jewish life thus warrants serious consideration in itself. Instead of viewing it as simply a long prelude to the expulsion, I treat it as a period of adjustment, reorganization, and creativity for Jews, conversos, and Old Christians. I demonstrate why the Jews of Morvedre enjoyed a renaissance after a difficult period of transition (1391–1416). Favorable royal policies were, of course, crucial, as was the welcome extended to the Jews by the town fathers of Morvedre. But what emerges most strikingly, especially in light of the Jews'

[7] Meyerson 2004a.

circumstances prior to 1391, is how the combination of a new royal fiscal regime and new credit mechanisms brought about a restructuring of the kingdom's credit markets; a significant modification, if not a complete reversal, of the credit relationship between Jews and Christians; a marked amelioration of Christian attitudes toward Jews; new investment strategies and greater economic diversification on the part of the Jews; and a reorientation of class relations and politics within the Jewish community. Besides these political and economic factors, and just as critical, was the Jews' sense of identity and commitment to the wider Jewish community, as evinced, perhaps surprisingly, in their spiritually rewarding relationship with the Judaizing conversos of Valencia.

The counternarrative I have fashioned is also at variance with a newer and largely uncontested narrative propounded by Spanish and non-Spanish scholars working outside the area of Jewish studies that emphasizes the persecution and exclusion of the religious minorities and firmly links the religious homogenization of Castile and the Crown of Aragon to the rise of the early modern state.[8] For the non-Spanish scholars especially, the forced baptisms, inquisitorial persecutions, and expulsions appear as a kind of prelude to the evils perpetrated by Spaniards and other Europeans on the colonized peoples of America, Africa, and Asia. For the Spanish scholars, who are products of — and perhaps victims of — this very history of religious homogenization, it is difficult to imagine a medieval world in which the conquest, subordination, persecution, and elimination of Muslims and Jews were not, for good or ill, almost destined steps leading to the Spain they presently inhabit. Hence, they too, also with the best liberal intentions, have seized on this narrative of religious hatred, persecution, and colonialism.[9]

The teleology inherent in this narrative has been cogently challenged by David Nirenberg.[10] Nirenberg's work, however, stops in 1348 and therefore leaves unanswered many key questions concerning Spain's dramatic socioreligious transformation in subsequent decades. It obviously cannot contribute to any understanding of the complex converso issue, nor does it address the implications of the emergence of new state institutions and ideologies for the religious minorities. Yet, as this study will show, grappling with both questions is integral to a full comprehension of the somewhat paradoxical history of the Jews of Morvedre in the fifteenth century. On one hand, the institutions and officialdom of a stronger monarchical state protected Jews (and Muslims) more effectively and, as suggested above, helped create a context for improved Jewish-Christian relations — at least in the lands of the Crown of Aragon. On

---

[8] E.g., Motis Dolader 1997b.

[9] The subtitle of Hinojosa Montalvo's documentary collection (1993a), *From Persecution to Expulsion*, is typical of this perspective.

[10] Nirenberg 1996.

the other hand, the fate of the Jews of Morvedre was tied to that of the conversos of Valencia, for, in the end, the perceived necessity of resolving the religious and social problems surrounding the conversos determined the policies
of Fernando and Isabel toward the Jews, and even the Muslims. The state,
then, did ultimately intervene to effect the religious homogenization of both
Castile and the Crown of Aragon, but for religious purposes that contradicted
its concurrent political and economic objectives.[11]

In constructing a narrative that runs against the grain of these two other dominant narratives I do not mean to imply that all other Jewish communities in
the Crown of Aragon and Castile had the same experience in the fifteenth century as the Jews of Morvedre, or that those communities that also enjoyed stability and prosperity did so for the same reasons. By explaining why the Jews of
Morvedre flourished after 1391 and by pinpointing the factors crucial for this
community's success, I hope to move other scholars to raise similar questions
with regard to other Jewish communities, to explore why they did or did not
prosper in the fifteenth or earlier centuries. The historiographical problem, as
I see it, is that such questions are rarely asked, much less answered, about the
Jews of Spain in the later fourteenth and fifteenth centuries. Studies of Jewish
communities, whether individually or in the aggregate, tend to be written from
the perspective of 1492, as so many postmortems or as collections of data about
what the Jews owned, where they lived, and so on before their expulsion. Furthermore, the chronological scope of such studies is often too limited to allow
for any sense of how Jewish-Christian relations, Jewish economic strategies, or
Jewish communal politics evolved. I am, in other words, making a strong
methodological argument for reconstructing and rethinking the history of
Christian-Jewish relations in medieval Spain on the basis of contextualized
local and regional studies, through which patterns of interaction can be compared and analyzed and the direction of fundamental changes charted. Morvedre was not the only town, the kingdom of Valencia not the only region where
Jews and Christians experienced the mob violence of 1391, the actions of the
Castilian-run Spanish Inquisition, and the proclamation of the edict of expulsion as unexpected and unwanted disruptions of decades of fruitful interaction.
The Valencian region clearly was not the same as New Castile or Andalucía,
whence so much religious violence and momentous change seem to have originated, but it was not so different either. The distinctions are fine; they must be
located and analyzed. Only then will it be possible to comprehend the meaning of the Jewish expulsion for local societies and for all of Spain.

My work on the Jews of Morvedre stands at the confluence of three overlapping historiographical traditions: the Jewish, the Spanish, and the local. It
benefits greatly from all three — indeed it would have been impossible without
them — but also departs from each to some degree. For the social historian aim-

---

[11] Meyerson 1991 and 1995a.

ing to produce a contextualized local study, the Jewish historiographical tradition has certain shortcomings in terms of both perspective and sources utilized. With regard to the latter, a history that privileges philosophical, theosophical, and polemical texts often overlooks crucial details of Jewish socioeconomic life and the complexities of Jewish coexistence and conflict with non-Jews. Non-Jews appear for the most part as essentialized "others" and the encounters between them and Jews often as the discussions or debates of clergymen, of so many talking heads. Even when scholars like Baer and Assis, drawing on archival as well as Hebrew literary sources, have striven for a "well-grounded historical perspective" and a contextualized treatment of Spanish Jews,[12] they have not gone much beyond indicating the parallels between Jewish and Christian social and institutional structures while tracing the evolution of royal Jewish policy. Lacking in such work is a deep familiarity with Christian society and politics and attention to the social, economic, political, and religious changes affecting Christians in their daily lives and therefore sometimes shaping their interaction with the Jewish population.

There is, moreover, a tendency in this historiographical tradition to regard Spanish Jews as a homogeneous unity. This position has considerable cogency if one considers, for instance, that Aragonese and Castilian monarchs usually made policy decisions with all their Jewish communities in mind, that Jewish communal authorities throughout Iberia grappled with similar sets of problems, or that Jews wherever they were parried the arguments of Christian missionaries in a relatively consistent manner. Still, this assumption of a unity of experience at the expense of local context can limit our understanding of precisely how changes in royal policy affected Jewish communities and families, or why the social and intellectual conflicts upsetting some Jewish communities did not disturb others. Even within the Crown of Aragon alone Valencian Jews had a history distinct from that of Catalan and Aragonese Jews.[13] The beginnings of the Valencian communities were different, as were the Jews' memories of these beginnings, which continued to inform their views of the present and hopes for the future until the expulsion. Valencian Jews, especially the Jews of Morvedre, were as much affected by the vagaries of Valencian (Christian) politics, whether the revolt of the Union (1347–48), the Castilian invasion of the kingdom and occupation of Morvedre (1363–66), or the long-standing conflict between Valencia, the capital city, and Morvedre.[14] The crisis of Morvedre's Jews in the fourteenth century and their remarkable revival in the fifteenth are incomprehensible without a thorough grasp of regional society and politics.

If an essential Jewish trait emerges from the study of the Jews of Morvedre,

---

[12] Myers 1995, 100, and 109–128 for his treatment of Baer.

[13] This is not clear in Assis 1997, which, in any case, gives minimal coverage to Valencian Jewry.

[14] See Meyerson 2002 and 2004a, and further in this volume.

it is the Jews' ability to adapt to new and at times trying conditions to survive or even prosper. Here too, with regard to this nearly stereotypical Jewish mutability and knack for survival, a detailed knowledge of the regional context is crucial. Without it I could not have reconstructed the Jews' social, political, and economic strategies and thereby achieved one of the aims of this study: to give the Jews greater historical agency and to make them the subjects of their own history.[15]

A work that evaluates the success and revival of a Jewish community on the bases of its demographic expansion, prosperity, social stability, and mutually beneficial relations with non-Jews will not be convincing to everyone in the field of Jewish studies, especially as far as the fifteenth century is concerned. In a field where the well-being and achievement of a Jewish community are often correlated to the productivity and brilliance of religious scholars, philosophers, and poets, Valencian Jews in general and the Jews of Morvedre in particular are bound to be found wanting.[16] Throughout their history the Jews of the kingdom of Valencia could boast of very few intellectual lights and noteworthy religious leaders, and none came from the Jewish quarter in Morvedre.[17] There were nonetheless rabbis and judges in Morvedre who struggled to uphold Jewish legal autonomy and to see to it that the community lived in conformity to halakhic standards, even if they tended, rather unimaginatively, to make their decisions in accordance with the *Mishneh Torah* of Maimonides. For this community, philosophy and mysticism do not seem to have been pressing concerns. Given the sources available on the Jews of Morvedre — almost all documents generated by the royal bureaucracy or, toward the end of their history, by the Spanish Inquisition — it is practically impossible to determine whether the dichotomy posited by Baer between a worldly, "Averroistic," courtier class and the mass of poor, pious Jews led by scholars with a mystical bent is applicable to the Morvedre community. Although there were, before

[15] In this sense my work can perhaps be read as a subtle rejoinder to the Zionist critique of diaspora Jews, who were deemed passive objects of persecution living outside history as long as they lived outside their national homeland (Myers 1995, 4). Yet in underlining Jewish agency my intention was actually to remedy certain deficiencies in the treatment of Jews in the scholarship on medieval Spanish society (see below).

[16] Indicative of the tendency in Jewish historiography to assess the relative well-being and achievement of Spanish Jews without any reference at all to economic and social criteria is Shmueli 1986, 169–171, who criticizes Baer for his tendency to "Ashkenize" Spanish Jews and to downgrade them for their philosophical pursuits, and then himself lauds "the special qualities of the extraordinarily gifted community that created the brilliant 'Poetic-Philosophic' culture."

[17] This is not to say that the Jews of the kingdom of Valencia were completely impoverished intellectually. The great rabbi Isaac ben Sheshet Perfet made Valencia his home between 1385 and 1391; see Hershman 1943. Fifteenth-century Xàtiva, moreover, could boast of the Kabbalist Yosef Alcastiel — see Scholem 1955 — and the chronicler Isaac ben Hayim Ha-Kohen. From the work of Idel 1999, it is clear that Valencian Jews could obtain an education in philosophy and Kabbalah as well as in biblical and talmudic studies.

and after 1391, Jews in Morvedre who had connections at the royal court, they
were not philosophers.

Perhaps more importantly, with respect to the fifteenth century, there is a
lack of sources that would enable one to establish whether the Jews of Morvedre experienced the sort of spiritual malaise or espoused the same neo-
Platonic, antinomian philosophy as did the Jewish thinkers discussed by scholars like Joseph Hacker, Dov Schwartz, Frank Talmage, and Eric Lawee.[18]
Although I do not necessarily think that the actions of ordinary Jews speak more
loudly than the written words of the intellectual elite, an examination of the
regular interaction of the Jews of Morvedre with the conversos of Valencia over
the course of the fifteenth century does shed a different light on the religious
outlook of the Jews. Historians who have touched on Jewish-converso relations
have treated the matter as subsidiary to the central question in a polemical historiography on the converso problem: were the conversos adherents of Judaism?[19] For those like Benzion Netanyahu and Norman Roth who would answer in the negative, the very existence of so many conversos after 1391–1416
testifies to the spiritual apathy or crisis of the Jews prior to these decades of persecution; the steadfast Jews who clung to Judaism, they argue, wanted little to
do with the conversos and regarded them with increasing disdain.[20] Those who
have argued to the contrary, most notably Yitzhak Baer and Haim Beinart, have
cited all known examples of Jewish contact with conversos as indications of the
conversos' deep sense of affiliation to the Jewish people.[21] Both schools have
tended to argue in rather extreme terms: either practically all conversos were
assimilating or almost all of them were Judaizing. Yet neither school has given
sustained attention to the Jewish parties involved in the Jewish-converso relationship, except when considering the opinions of rabbis who were frequently
far from the scene.[22] In this book, rather than treating converso life per se, I

[18] Hacker 1992, esp. 264–274; Schwartz 1991a, esp. 102–107; Talmage 1985; Lawee 1996.
These authors, however, do not regard demoralization or nearly heretical philosophizing as universal among Sephardic Jewish intellectuals during the fifteenth century. Hacker, for instance,
sees demoralization — insofar as it is reflected in interpretations of Psalm 44 — setting in only a
decade or so before the expulsion. Schwartz (1991b) finds that as the fifteenth century progressed
radical philosophy waned while the "moderate school" of philosophy predominated.

[19] Gitlitz 1996 provides a useful overview of the debate.

[20] Netanyahu 1973 and 1995; N. Roth 1995. Their contention — the foundation on which their
main argument about converso assimilation rests — that inquisition records are wholly unreliable
sources, fabricated by the conversos' racist, political enemies, is untenable and has been countered
elsewhere (e.g., Yerushalmi 1971, 21–31; Pullan 1983, 201–210; Gitlitz 1996, 76–82). It reflects
their unfamiliarity with archival records, especially judicial records, and the modus operandi of
the institutions that produced them.

[21] Baer 1961, 2:244–443; Beinart 1981. I do lean more toward this school, particularly because
these scholars regard inquisition records as valid historical sources. The principal problem with
Baer and Beinart is that they tend not to take other records into account and thus ignore the existence of a substantial number of assimilating conversos.

[22] Especially Netanyahu 1973; cf. G. D. Cohen 1967.

view the conversos from the perspective of one Jewish community. I undertake
the first extended analysis of Jewish-converso relations at the local level between 1391 and 1492. The relationship changed in significant ways over the
years, as will be seen, but evident throughout the fifteenth century is the endeavor of the Jews of Morvedre to provide the conversos of Valencia, at least
the committed Judaizers and some of the vacillators, with religious instruction
and inspiration as well as *kasher* foodstuffs. This consistent effort, which at
times amounted to a proselytizing enterprise, reflects a level of spiritual vitality and commitment and belief in the redemption of the Jewish people (including Judaizing conversos) such as would lead one to think that the demographic and economic expansion of the Jews of Morvedre in the fifteenth
century was linked to — though not the cause or the effect of — spiritual well-
being and optimism. It was probably no mere coincidence that the Jewish community leader Salamó Çaporta, who was a very successful entrepreneur and
royal favorite, also actively abetted Judaizing conversos. Toward the end of the
fifteenth century, the Jews of Morvedre expressed their self-confidence and
manifested their religious identity in various meaningful ways, even if no intellectual giants numbered among them.

The use of the term "renaissance" to describe Jewish revival in fifteenth-
century Morvedre naturally draws one's gaze across the Mediterranean to the
Jews of Renaissance Italy and again raises questions about the criteria by which
a Jewish renaissance in this period should be evaluated. Historians of the Jews
in fifteenth-century Italy have focused on Jewish intellectual life, the degree
to which it was influenced by (Christian) Renaissance humanism, and the interaction of Jewish and Christian scholars. An older school of historians, daz-
zled by evidence of the collaboration of Jewish and Christian intellectuals, espoused the idyllic view that the more open ambience of Renaissance Italy
fostered an Italian Jewish Renaissance.[23] A newer, revisionist school has called
this interpretation into question. Though not denying Jewish interest in humanism, these historians have emphasized the Jews' selective adoption of humanist ideas and their adaptation of them for their own (Jewish) purposes.
They have also pointed to the proselytizing agenda of Christian Hebraists and
Kabbalists, and to the resultant apostasy of some Jewish intellectuals involved
in their circles.[24] If the notion of a Jewish renaissance in fifteenth-century Italy
is problematic from the perspective of intellectual and (high) cultural history,
it is even more in socioeconomic terms. The often tiny Jewish communities of
northern and central Italy were quite insecure. Italian municipalities granted
them short-term residence permits (*condotte*) primarily for the purpose of giving Christians, especially poorer Christians, access to needed Jewish credit.

---

[23] E.g., C. Roth 1959.
[24] Especially Bonfil 1984 and 1994, 1–15, 101–124, 145–177. Also Ruderman 1981, 43–56;
Lesley 1988; Tirosh-Rothschild 1991.

The Jews' particular function not surprisingly earned them Christian resentment and made them the targets of vicious Franciscan preachers who complained about Jewish exploitation of the Christian poor and urged municipal
authorities, sometimes successfully, to eject the Jews.[25] As stated above, the
quality of the intellectual life of the Jews of Morvedre cannot be ascertained,
but, as will be seen, there can be no doubt about the revival of this Jewish community in socioeconomic terms, including the amelioration of its relations
with Christians.[26] The point here is not to engage in endless speculation about
what does or does not constitute a Jewish renaissance but to suggest that just
as one need not view Jewish life in Renaissance Italy as halcyon and splendid,
one need not regard Jewish life in fifteenth-century Spain as bleak and painful.
"Renaissance" and "expulsion," the two buzzwords that seem to define the histories of Italian and Spanish Jews, respectively, were by no means diametrically
opposite aspects of Jewish experience in this period.

Although this book may well be regarded as a work of Jewish studies, or at
least a work of Jewish studies of a particular kind, it is primarily, by virtue of
the training, methodology, and intentions of its author, a work of medieval
Spanish history, or, more specifically, a study of a plural society in Christian
Spain from the perspective of one of its constituent communities. Just as the
book has profited greatly from the labors of scholars in the field of Jewish studies and Jewish history per se, it also owes much to the work of Spanish and
non-Spanish historians of medieval Spain. The highly contextualized history
of a Jewish community I present here would scarcely have been possible were
it not for the explosion, in recent decades, of local and regional studies. I am
particularly indebted to historians of the medieval kingdom of Valencia who
have been producing, especially since the late 1980s, first-rate studies of peasants, seigneurs, urban folk, and royal and municipal institutions — in other
words, of the people and structures shaping the world within which the Jews
of Morvedre lived.[27]

The Jews have long had a place in the narratives of Spanish history, whether
of the "national," regional, or local variety. At one time, their place in the master narrative of Spanish history, like that of the Muslims, was hotly debated, especially by Claudio Sánchez Albornoz, who viewed the Jews for the most part
as usurious bloodsuckers responsible for many of the ills of later medieval
Spain, and by Américo Castro, who emphasized the importance of Jews and
Jewish influences for the development of Spanish literature, science, and in-

[25] Bonfil 1994, 19–59, 83–93; Toaff 1979, 39–71, and 1996, 234–253; Pullan 1971, 431–475.
[26] This is not to say that Jews elsewhere in fifteenth-century Iberia did not productively inter-
act with Christian scholars or that they were not open to humanist influences. See, e.g., Lawee
1995; Fellous 1998.
[27] Indicative of the recent explosion in Valencian historiography is the publication, since 1989,
of the excellent *Revista d'Història Medieval* by the Universitat de València.

stitutions.[28] As noted above, the Jews now, like the Muslims, occupy a secure place in the uncontested teleological narrative, or narratives, of persecution.

There are, however, methodological problems with the treatment of the Jews in these newer national, regional, and local narratives and studies. They deprive the Jews — and Muslims — of agency. Like the Muslims, the Jews are categorized as a minority or as a marginal group, and are often quite literally placed in the margins, or in small subchapters of historical works. Jews rarely appear as subjects of their own history. They do so only in monographs devoted specifically to such-and-such Jewish *aljama*. Yet such works treat the Jews in an oddly decontextualized, at times taxonomic fashion, as if the socioeconomic and institutional changes to which Christians were subject somehow did not affect them. The Jews are usually presented as industrious, moneylending objects of persecution and are scarcely given a role in local or regional histories; they somehow reside outside history. Insofar as their interaction with the Jews is concerned, Christians often come off as little better than hate-filled, persecuting automatons. As a result, Jews and Christians are both essentialized, and the histories of their relations acquire a uniformity and predictability that do justice to neither group.

Thus I have attempted in my work to treat the Jews as actors and to place them on the center stage of Valencian history along with Christian and Muslim actors. I have endeavored to show how the social origins, personality, and ambitions of individual Jews affected their relations, and their community's relations, with Christians and Muslims. The non-Jews are presented not as essentialized others but as individuals whose views and treatment of the Jews were shaped by their social class, political alliances, economic interests, and religious sentiments. I show how the attitudes of Christians and Muslims toward the Jews changed over time, though by no means in the expected direction. Rather than offering a neat and linear narrative of persecution, my work tells a story full of contradiction and ambiguity, a counternarrative that will make readers think differently about 1492 and the preceding centuries of Jewish life in Morvedre and elsewhere in Christian Spain. The story of the Jews of Morvedre ends where all histories of Spain's Jews must, but the road on which the Jews were traveling in the years preceding the expulsion seems to have been leading in another direction. We can only imagine where.

Early History of the Morvedre Community

Jews dwelt in Morvedre from the beginning of the Valencian region's history as a medieval Christian kingdom and part of the Crown of Aragon.[29] Of late

---

[28] Glick 1979, 6–13; Hillgarth 1985.

[29] For a detailed treatment, with sources, of the 1248–1391 period, see Meyerson 2004a.

foundation by western European standards, the new kingdom of Valencia changed rapidly and dramatically in a relatively short time. King Jaume I of Aragon-Catalonia carved it out of Muslim al-Andalus between 1233 and 1245. Yet by the 1460s the kingdom had become the monarchy's most reliable source of financial support, and its capital, Valencia, the Crown of Aragon's most important port and one of Christian Spain's most populous cities. In these two and a half centuries of remarkable development, the Jews of Morvedre were no mere bystanders but full participants in the kingdom's history. Like other Jews in the kingdom, they soon became just as "Valencian" as the Christian settlers and the indigenous Muslims, contributing to and being shaped by the kingdom's peculiar history.

In no period of the telescoped medieval history of the kingdom of Valencia were changes as fast and as consequential as in the first one hundred years. The kingdom's metamorphosis is most clearly evinced in the tumultuous political relationship and shifting demographic weight of its Muslim and Christian populations. A product of crusade and conquest, the kingdom began as a colonial regime, in which Christian kings and lords, aided by Christian and Jewish administrators, ruled over a restive Muslim population while fostering the settlement of Christians and Jews, and sometimes even of foreign Muslims. Comprising approximately 80 percent of the kingdom's population, the indigenous Muslims, or Mudejars, revolted unsuccessfully several times between 1247 and 1277. The upheaval and fluidity of the decades of colonization gave way to greater calm and the consolidation of Christian authority in the fourteenth century. As a result of Christian and Jewish immigration and Muslim emigration, by midcentury the Mudejars constituted only one-half of the realm's population. By this time the kingdom was no longer precariously colonial but securely part of the Crown of Aragon and unmistakably Christian in its public character, despite the still considerable Muslim presence. Indeed, serious threats to the kingdom's stability and survival came not from rebellious Mudejars or foreign Muslim princes, but first, in 1347–48, from local Christians who formed the Valencian Union and revolted against royal authority, and then, in the 1350s and 1360s, from invading Castilian armies.

By the time the Union raised the standard of rebellion, the Jews of the kingdom had already fallen from the lofty position they occupied in the thirteenth century. Streaming into the new kingdom along with Christian settlers in the wake of Jaume I's conquest, Jews from Catalonia and Aragon settled in key urban centers. The most important families among them became cogs in the Crown's colonial machinery. Jewish officials and administrators in the kingdom attained a level of power and privilege rivaled only by that of their counterparts in the regions the Castilian monarchs had wrested from the Muslims.

In Morvedre Jewish bailiffs played a key role in organizing the colonization of the town and its wider district (*terme*). Situated on rich alluvial lands near the mouth of the Palancia River and located less than twenty-five kilometers to the north of the capital city, Morvedre offered Jewish and Christian immigrants great agricultural and commercial opportunities. Town walls and the formidable royal castle promised security in the event of Muslim uprisings. The Jewish settlers quickly diversified economically. Jewish proprietors, who sometimes owned sizable estates farmed by Muslim tenants, developed an important kasher wine industry paralleling the Christians' production of non-kasher wine. Ensconcing themselves in regional trade networks, Morvedre's mobile Jewish merchants dealt in agricultural products, including local wine, and manufactures, such as the silverware and shoes made by the town's Jewish artisans. Like Jews elsewhere in the new kingdom, the Jews of Morvedre were established as the main purveyors of credit in their area and thus were authorized by the Crown to lend money at the rate of interest already set for Catalan and Aragonese Jews — 20 percent of the principal. Often the members of leading Jewish families, Morvedre's lenders made loans to Christian and Muslim farmers and artisans as well as to Christian knights and nobles in a wide region extending from Valencia in the south to Castelló in the north. They also invested their capital in the farming of royal and seigneurial taxes. By around 1325, the end of the era of colonization, the Jews of Morvedre formed a medium-sized aljama of perhaps sixty families, approximately 250–300 individuals. It was dwarfed by the great aljama in Valencia, whose population was five times larger. The Christians of Morvedre numbered some six thousand souls; hence the Jews comprised roughly 3 percent of the town's population.

During this colonization period the existence of Jewish communities in Morvedre and other urban centers was never put in doubt; what Christians did question was the Jews' high status. The Jews of the kingdom were, after all, *Jews*, their power and influence incongruous with the vision of a Christian society articulated and promoted by reforming popes, monks, and friars, and shared increasingly by laypersons and princes in thirteenth-century Europe. Though new, the kingdom of Valencia did not develop in a vacuum, impervious to the currents of Christian reform and anti-Judaism then leaving their mark on societies north of the Pyrenees and even in the northern realms of Christian Spain. Its Jews could not be allowed to hold the reins of power too long. From the 1280s through the 1320s Valencian Christians managed, in various ways, to put the Jews in their proper, inferior place. Newly confident in their authority over the Muslims, whose last major revolt Pere II crushed in 1277, and resentful of the power of Jewish bailiffs, tax collectors, and proprietors, Christians pressured King Pere to remove Jews from office in 1283. In the ensuing years Jews wisely divested themselves of the ownership of large estates, which, to many Christians, smacked of Jewish lordship. Christians, moreover, were increasingly inspired by their identification with and sense of belonging to the Corpus Christi — a metaphorical socioreligious body that excluded the Jews and a physical body that the Jews had allegedly crucified — and they used religious rituals to humiliate and, occasionally, to terrorize Jews.

At the same time, the monarchs enserfed Valencian Jewry to the royal treasury, a policy that complemented their licensing of Jewish usury. Kings expected that revenue, in the form of interest on loans, would flow steadily from
Christian or Muslim borrowers, through the hands of taxpaying Jewish lenders,
into the royal treasury. Power in the Jewish community, in Morvedre and other
towns, therefore inhered to an unusual extent in the manipulation and amass-
ing of monetary resources. The major taxpayers won social prestige and dominated aljama government. The wealthy oligarchs, however, walked a fine line
between fulfilling their fiscal responsibilities to the community, thereby maintaining their elite and honored status, and prudently concealing enough assets
to avoid a severe economic setback and consequent social demotion. This was
no easy balancing act; fiscal politics were thus intense and bitter. On one hand,
lower- and middle-class Jews frequently complained to the Crown that the oligarchs were not paying enough taxes. They channeled their discontent into demands for electoral reform that would give them some role in communal government and tax assessment. The oligarchs, on the other hand, engaged in
vicious intraclass warfare, which was more threatening than the protests of the
lower classes. The weapons they usually wielded against each other were fiscal. As annual elections kept them rotating in and out of communal government, they used their time in office to tax their enemies heavily and their allies lightly, knowing full well that their rivals would soon be wreaking fiscal
vengeance on them.

The monarchy's incessant and exorbitant fiscal demands locked the Jews
into a perpetual cycle of lending money and then dangerously squeezing
Christian debtors in order to subsidize the king. The bishops of Valencia, who
opposed usury of any kind, ably fanned the resultant ill will of the debtors,
which sometimes manifested itself in particularly nasty Holy Week violence.
Until the later fourteenth century this troubled triangular relationship among
royal tax collector, Jewish creditor, and Christian debtor was inescapable. It
was, however, not the only factor shaping relations between Jews and Christians, for many Jews had other forms of livelihood and did not lend money
while many Christians did practice usury. Still, the perception of Jewish usury
was often just as, if not more, important than the reality. With the right amount
of clerical agitation, or in times of agrarian crisis, the phenomenon of Jewish
usury could become the source of considerable tension.

The decline of the Jews of Morvedre after 1283 was neither absolute nor
endless. The Jews effectively compensated for their loss of public authority by
cultivating mutually beneficial relations with Christian elites—the knights
and lesser lords of Morvedre and its terme, and the great lords of domains farther afield. They adjusted to the difficulties of their fiscal servitude by devising
new economic strategies. In order to evade at least some of the requirements
of an insatiable royal treasury, they dispersed their assets and investments
widely, in other royal towns and, most importantly, on the estates of their

knightly and noble patrons. Fourteenth-century monarchs — Jaume II (1291–1327), Alfons III (1327–36), and Pere III (1336–87) — nonetheless continued to regard the Jews as an asset, for their own purses and for the local and regional economy.

In fact, during the rebellion and warfare that rocked the kingdom in the middle decades of the fourteenth century, the Jews of Morvedre suffered violence and displacement precisely because of the firm bonds tying them to the monarchy and to Christian notables. When the hosts of the rebel Union of Valencia attacked Morvedre in November 1348, they made a point of looting the homes of royalist nobles and sacking the Jewish quarter. In 1365, two years after the invading army of Pedro I of Castile captured and occupied Morvedre, the local Castilian commander expelled from the town a number of Christians and the whole Jewish community, all deemed loyal to King Pere. Neither action resulted from popular Christian animosity in Morvedre toward local Jews; each one was a matter of political contingency. Hence after King Pere recaptured Morvedre in September 1365 and began to rebuild and repopulate the shattered town, the remaining and returning Christian inhabitants did not in any way resist the return of the Jews. They needed Jewish bodies and Jewish resources. But more important than the views of local Christians was the Jews' own stubborn will to endure as a community in a town and a region they had made their own.

The process of postbellum reconstruction was, in several respects, a new beginning for the Jews and Christians of Morvedre. Having lost some families during the war years, the Jewish aljama got some new blood and saw a changing of the guard in its oligarchy. Three families in particular emerged as the dominant force in aljama politics by the 1380s: the el Raus, in the person of David, who earned his fortune with investments in credit operations, tax farming, and maritime commerce; the Legems, headed by the tax farmer Jahudà and his son Samuel; and the Façans, a new family whose patriarch Jacob was a wealthy lender who had come to the kingdom of Valencia from Teruel (Aragon) in the service of King Pere and Prince Joan. These and other affluent families tightened their grip on the reins of aljama government throughout the reconstruction era, denying to the lower classes the role they had played, through their representatives, since the 1320s. In 1390, however, King Joan I (1387–96) altered the electoral regime in response to lower-class protests. Now a council of twelve, composed of four members from each class, would advise the executive officials (*adelantats*) and treasurer (*clavari*) and, along with the outgoing adelantats and clavari, choose the new executives. Government remained oligarchic but the lower classes again had a voice, and their leading members the possibility of climbing into the ranks of the ruling elite.

The aljama's relationship with the municipality of Morvedre was put on a new footing through the modification of the aljama's responsibilities in a matter of great import to both corporations: taxation. By virtue of an agreement reached between the two on 22 September 1370, the Jews would henceforth pay all sales taxes (*cises*), utility fees, and other levies the municipality collected from local Christians. Previously the Jews had paid all their taxes directly to the Crown; municipal officials had always resented the fiscal autonomy of "the king's Jews." With the Jews contributing to municipal revenue as a result of the 1370 accord, the repopulation of the Jewish quarter became essential to the reconstruction of Morvedre and, in the long term, to the solvency of the town's government.

The new taxation plan in Morvedre was linked to the development, over the later fourteenth century, of a new fiscal regime for the kingdom in which the Corts (representative assembly) and its permanent administrative body, the Generalitat, new forms of taxation, and new credit mechanisms became central. In the changing configuration of royal finances the Jews assumed a different and progressively less significant position. The community in Morvedre consequently carried a lighter and more reasonable tax burden, a factor that facilitated its growth in the postwar years. The new regime, moreover, was beginning to reshape the triangular relationship among revenue-hungry kings, taxpaying Jewish creditors, and taxpaying Christian debtors.

At the Corts of Monzón in 1362–63 a new and more efficient system of royal finance was established. Previously, when the Corts conceded taxes — or "donations," as they called them — to the Crown, the funds were collected in two ways: through the assignment of specific quantities to each estate, which were then divided up among and collected from the households within it, and through indirect taxes, mainly on foodstuffs. Now, in addition to these sources, a new series of general taxes was created — the *generalitats* — which were levied on textile production and on external commerce, the most dynamic sectors of the Valencian economy. The newly created delegation of the Corts, the Generalitat, administered and controlled these vast fiscal resources. It had more money under its control than the royal treasury.

At the same time, the kingdom's cities and towns gained greater financial autonomy. Although since 1321 towns (and aljamas) had been granted the right to impose indirect taxes temporarily to meet the Crown's fiscal demands, in 1363 King Pere made it a permanent right for all the towns.

These developments coincided with the widespread and increasing use of the new credit mechanisms, the *censal* and the *violari*. The censal was a loan that took the form of a contract of sale (*carregament*), in which the borrower, or vendor, sold to the lender, or buyer, the right to receive annually a pension (or *pension de censal*) for a certain price, that is, the capital loaned. The rate of interest on the capital borrowed through the censal was 7.69 percent in the latter half of the fourteenth century. With the debtor rendering annuities to the creditor, the censal contract could be maintained indefinitely until the debtor, or his or her heirs, reimbursed the creditor for the capital borrowed. A variant of the censal, the violari was limited to a set period, usually one or two life-times, after which the pension was automatically extinguished. Because of its limited temporal scope, the loan contracted through the violari carried a rate of interest twice as high as that of the censal.

Since they need not liquidate the debts acquired through the sale of censals until they chose to do so, or could gradually repay the money borrowed through the sale of violaris over a long period, municipalities and aljamas found these credit mechanisms ideal for raising funds quickly to meet their im-mediate necessities, such as rendering subsidies to the king. Over the course of the 1340s the aljama of Morvedre had begun to use the censal, or the vio-lari, as a means of financing its public debt. The aljama's adoption of this credit mechanism was roughly contemporaneous with its rapid and widespread dif-fusion among the municipalities of the kingdom. Municipalities and aljamas both requited their *censalista* creditors with funds drawn from the cises they now had the right to levy.

The censalistas who invested their capital in the purchase of censals or vio-laris saw it as a fairly secure form of investment yielding moderate and regular returns. These *rentiers* were mainly affluent urban citizens — honored citizens, merchants, professionals, and some artisans — and members of the lesser no-bility. While each town had its own local censalistas investing in the munici-pal debt, or in that of the local aljama, citizens and nobles from the capital con-stituted a significant portion, and frequently the majority, of the creditors of many municipalities in the kingdom. Through purchasing the censals sold by municipalities, and later by seigneuries, the moneyed classes in Valencia came to dominate the credit networks of the kingdom. They were among the cen-salistas who invested in the public debt of the aljama of Morvedre.

A new credit market was gradually coming into existence; as a result, the alignment of money and power in the kingdom was beginning to change. The censalistas were in a position to displace the Jews as the principal purveyors of credit and to free them from their peculiar form of thralldom — to the royal treasury and to the necessity of practicing usury. The violence of 1391 would, as will be seen, temporarily interrupt these ameliorative developments but would not bring them to a halt.

Such continuity would be possible in Morvedre because between 1365 and 1391 the town had not seen a deterioration of Jewish-Christian relations. The wave of anti-Jewish violence that engulfed the kingdom of Valencia, and much of the Crown of Aragon, in 1391 originated outside Crown territories, in Castile. The Christian elites of Morvedre, moreover, did not allow it to swamp their town. The attacks on Jewish communities in the kingdom of Valencia and elsewhere in the Crown of Aragon were not, in other words, the product of years of escalating Christian animus toward the Jews. In the lands of the Crown of Aragon the violence of 1391 was unexpected and more of an anomaly, whereas in Castile the violence was the end result of years of vicious anti-Jewish activity. This was not because Castilian Christians were inherently more anti-Jewish than their counterparts in the Crown of Aragon, but because the distinctive political traditions and institutions of Castile had made anti-Judaism a fixture in this realm's public discourse.

In Castile the nobility exercised a preponderant influence on political life, dominating both town and countryside. Since the realm's representative assembly, the Cortes, had proved unable to challenge the monarchy effectively on constitutional grounds, the nobles, through a combination of brute force and chicanery, became the main check on the monarchy's centralizing pretensions. The Jews were an obvious and easy target for the monarchy's noble opposition because some of them performed for the royal government administrative and fiscal functions deprecated by ambitious nobles as well as townspeople, whose views the nobility's knightly ethos had shaped. Thus when Enrique de Trastámara led the nobility in an ultimately successful revolt against Pedro I, he was able to provoke popular outrage against the king and the Jews, and to inspire attacks on the latter, by excoriating the king and his Jewish advisors for their alleged rapacity and cruelty.[30] Enrique had thereby created an expectation among Castilians that he would have no Jews in his government. Yet when he seized the crown in 1369, he too found that he needed Jewish advisors and financiers, as did his successors. This, and the perennial issue of Jewish usury, remained a sore point with Castilians, as the protests of the Cortes and sermons reveal. The incessant anti-Jewish preaching of Ferrant Martínez, the archdeacon of Ecija, from 1378 on caused the first explosion of violence in Seville in 1391. The politics of the previous years, which had fixed anti-Judaism in the public discourse, explains why the violence spread so rapidly throughout Castile.

In the Crown of Aragon high politics worked differently. There the rural nobility exercised minimal influence in cities and towns, which were dominated by oligarchies of bourgeois background. Urban and rural elites had joined with ecclesiastical notables to form assertive representative assemblies that demanded that kings respect regional laws and redress their subjects' grievances. Whatever the motives of the monarchy's domestic enemies, opposition to the monarchy was constitutional and couched in constitutionalist terms.

The urban elites, who did not view financial and administrative activity as incompatible with their status, were willing and able to serve in the royal government in positions once held by Jews. While the Jews had suffered some loss in political and economic status since 1283, they were also less open to attack by antimonarchical forces. This alone, however, does not explain why opponents of the Crown did not utilize anti-Jewish propaganda, for there were still enough influential Jews in royal circles, such as Jahudà Alatzar of Valencia, for

---

[30] Gutwirth 1999, 164–168, for a discussion of the account of the violence by the contemporary Jewish chronicler Samuel Çarça.

them to have pilloried the king for using Jewish servants.[31] They did not do so because it was far more effective to beat the king over the head with their regional laws and liberties.

The revolt of the Aragonese and Valencian Unions against Pere III in 1347–48 is a case in point. The Unionists did not resort to anti-Jewish propaganda during their rebellion; they focused on constitutional issues. True, Unionists from the capital did sack the *jueria* of Morvedre, but this attack was due to the Jews' real alliances with royalist nobles. It was not caused by indiscriminate anti-Jewish propaganda, nor did the violence spread to other parts of the kingdom. After 1283 the Jews were not a subject of intense political discussion.

Politics too would determine the stance Morvedre's elite Christian families took when Christian pillagers from Valencia moved on their town's Jewish quarter in July 1391. Relations between Morvedre and the capital during the preceding quarter century had been hostile, as a consequence of the new authority Valencia exercised over its smaller neighbor. In 1365 a vindictive King Pere punished the people of Morvedre for having surrendered to the Castilians by depriving the town of its autonomy and placing it under the jurisdiction of Valencia. Although Morvedre still had its own government and officials, it now fell under Valencia's civil and criminal jurisdiction and paid certain taxes and extraordinary subventions along with the capital. The municipality naturally bristled at its loss of complete autonomy and often contested the legitimacy and size of the fiscal exactions made by Valencia's officials, who proved to be hard and aggressive taskmasters. At times mutual animosity brought city and town to the brink of armed confrontation. When another armed horde marched from the capital toward their town in the summer of 1391, Morvedre's political elites would almost instinctively leap to protect their Jews.

Despite this history of political conflict, and despite the fact that after 1391 Valencia would no longer house a Jewish community and professing Jews would be permitted only brief visits there, the city would continue to be a major factor in the lives of Morvedre's Jews and Christians throughout the fifteenth century. This century was Valencia's golden age both culturally and economically. Its industries, especially textiles, developed prodigiously; it became one of the great Mediterranean emporia, superseding Barcelona as the Crown of Aragon's main commercial and financial center. The economic engine of the kingdom, Valencia was also a magnet for immigrants; by the 1480s it had some seventy thousand intramural and extramural inhabitants. Holding nearly one-quarter of the kingdom's population, it dominated the kingdom in every way. Morvedre, in fact, remained unwillingly part of Valencia's fiscal "contribution" and was in other respects subject to it.

So, oddly enough, while Valencia, in 1397, would be granted the royal "privilege" of never again having to house a jueria, a town under its very jurisdic-

---

[31] Romano 1991, 410–412; Riera i Sans 1993a.

tion and almost in its shadows would have a thriving Jewish community. The Jews of Morvedre could never become Jews of Valencia, but they could make the short trip to the capital, conduct business with its merchants and artisans, and, in one way or another, deal with its large converso population. By proximity and paradox, the history of the Jews of Morvedre would continue to be closely linked to the history of Valencia. In its Jew-free golden age the capital would help give the Jews of Morvedre a new lease on life.

Chapter One

ON THE EDGE OF DESOLATION

FOR JEWISH COMMUNITIES throughout Castile and the Crown of Aragon the quarter century between 1391 and 1416 was a period of heightened persecution. For a few communities the explosion of violence in 1391 was, by itself, the coup de grâce; for others the 1391 violence and subsequent difficulties were the beginning of the end, the start of a seemingly inexorable slide to the 1492 expulsion. Yet for other communities, like the one in Morvedre, the years from 1391 to 1416 constituted a period of painful transition to a new era of growth and good fortune. Of course after 1416 the Jews of Morvedre would flourish in a markedly altered socioreligious landscape. Those Jews who in the 1470s might have smiled contentedly about their affluence and relative security did so in an environment they must have recognized was only superficially similar to that before 1391. They knew that their grandparents and great-grandparents had experienced years of uncertainty and even terror, that they had lived through the time of the great conversions, back when their own world was born.

JOAN I

That world came into being on 9 July 1391, when a band of some forty to fifty Christian youths, carrying a blue banner on which a white cross was stitched and several bamboo crosses, marched to one of the gates of Valencia's jueria "shouting that the archdeacon of Castile is coming with his cross and that all the Jews should be baptized or die."[1] Ferrant Martínez, the archdeacon of Ecija, never appeared in Valencia but events unfolded much as the youths had foreseen. By the end of the day a Christian mob, composed of "vagabonds and foreigners and people of lesser and poor condition" as well as "men of the Order of Montesa and . . . mendicants . . . knights . . . and men of peerage and squires," had killed perhaps 230 Jews and forced most of the rest to receive baptism. Of the approximately twenty-five hundred members of Valencia's Jewish community only some two hundred escaped baptism or death.[2]

News of events in Castile triggered the anti-Jewish violence in Valencia. The

---

[1] AMV: LM g3–5:19r–20r [Hinojosa Montalvo 1993a, no. 6].

[2] AMV: MC A-19: 241r–245r (1391/7/10) [Hinojosa Montalvo 1993a, no. 7]; LM g3–5: 37r–v (1391/8/5) [Hinojosa Montalvo 1993a, no. 36]. There are numerous accounts of the violence in Valencia: Baer, 1961, 2: 99–102; Danvila 1886; Wolff 1971, 9–10, 16–18; Riera i Sans 1977, 217–225; Vidal Beltrán 1974, 53–70; Hinojosa Montalvo 1993a, 21–46.

harangues and agitation of Ferrant Martínez had provoked the first attack on
Castilian Jews, in Seville on 4 June; the violence then spread rapidly throughout
Andalucía and New and Old Castile.[3] By 3 July King Joan was writing his brother
Prince Martí, governor general of the kingdom of Valencia, advising him to take
precautions because "some unbridled and incorrigible persons," having heard of
the uprisings in Castile, were speaking ill of his Jewish subjects.[4] The presence
of rabble-rousers from Castile in the capital did not help matters much.[5]

Prior to the arrival of news and people from Castile there had been, over the
previous decade, the usual tensions and anxieties surrounding the Jews, which,
without the Castilian example conveying the sense that a new world without
Jews was in the offing, were not likely to have led to the explosion of 9 July. Annual Holy Week rituals; measures of the city Consell in 1383 to prevent Christians from sinning with Jews as a means of escaping divine wrath in the form
of bubonic plague; the stoning of Jews who crossed the path of a Corpus Christi
procession in 1385; Crown action against alleged excessive Jewish usury in
1389; the Christians of the Xerea quarter, upset that the enclosure of the newly
expanded jueria would inconvenience them, agitating against the Jews at the
beginning of 1391 — none of this, except the disgruntlement of the residents
of the Xerea, was new.[6] But the transformative violence that had taken place
in Castile in June 1391 was indeed unprecedented; it moved Christians in Valencia and elsewhere in the Crown of Aragon to consider the possibility of
using chrism and sword to effect a new socioreligious order.[7]

The fact that Joan I wore the crown was not likely to have quieted their imag-
inations; it may even have served to encourage their radical thoughts. True,
like his predecessors, Joan valued the Jews for the contributions they could
make to the royal treasury, and while a prince he had availed himself of Jewish subsidies, including some from the aljama of Morvedre. But as prince he
had also displayed a tendency to believe the fantastic charges of papal inquisitors and others against Jews. He had, for instance, zealously tortured and executed Catalan and Aragonese Jews for alleged host desecration despite his father's disapproval.[8] As king he had not prevented the inquisitor from jailing
Mossé Mahir Suxen of Xàtiva on charges of fashioning and worshiping an

---

[3] On these events and their background in Castile, see Valdeón Baruque 1968; Monsalvo Antón
1985, 207–276; Mitre Fernández 1994.

[4] ACA: C 1878: 54r (1391/7/3) [Riera i Sans 1977, 218].

[5] Riera i Sans 1980, 578–579.

[6] Hinojosa Montalvo 1981, 51–53; Vidal Beltrán 1974, 17–19, 51–52. For earlier ritual violence and measures taken by the municipalities to inhibit intimacy among Christians, Muslims,
and Jews in order to prevent outbreaks of plague, see Meyerson 2004a; for usury, see n. 15.

[7] Riera i Sans 1987, 114–135, emphasizes the circulation of rumors that the kings of Castile
and Aragon were in favor of baptizing the Jews and destroying the Jewish quarters. It is useful to
compare the unprecedented nature of the 1391 violence in the kingdom of Valencia, in terms of
both objectives and scope, to the violence perpetrated by the Union on the Jews of Morvedre in
1348. See Meyerson 2002.

[8] Miret y Sans 1911–12; Baer 1961, 2: 85–92; Rubin 1999, 109–115.

image of metal and mandrake. Joan ultimately challenged the inquisitor, not because of the absurdity of the charges, but on jurisdictional grounds, so that he could secure a share of the inheritance of the wealthy Suxen, who died in prison in the fall of 1390.[9] Given King Joan's record, officials, including Prince Martí, perhaps received with raised eyebrows and a hint of insouciance his instructions to protect the Jews. In any case, the measures they took in Valencia proved insufficient.

Word of the extraordinary happenings in the capital quickly spread to Christians and Jews in the rest of the kingdom. In almost every town with a Jewish population some form of intimidation or outright violence by Christians resulted in the baptism of many if not most terrorized Jews. Alzira and Xàtiva on 10 July, and Castelló and Borriana on 18 and 20 July, respectively, were all scenes of Jewish conversion.[10] The waves of religious violence swept over even smaller communities, like Llíria.[11]

Given Morvedre's proximity to Valencia, its Jews faced perhaps the greatest danger from the anti-Jewish hysteria bursting forth from the capital. Within a week of the destruction of Valencia's jueria, "a large group of people" marched from Valencia to Morvedre and attempted, with some success, to spark a riot against the Jews there. The prompt action of the local bailiff and castellan, Bonafonat de Sant Feliu, saved the Jews. He moved them into the well fortified castle and out of harm's way.[12] The *jurats* and *prohomens*, perennially disgruntled by their town's subjection to Valencia's authority, were not about to follow the lead of agitators from the capital; hence they assisted Sant Feliu. Local "knights and men of peerage," traditional allies of the Jews of Morvedre, offered Sant Feliu, one of their own circle, the most decisive support. Looking back a few years later on the events of 1391, King Joan reminded members of the Munyós, Vives, Aguiló, and other knightly families that the Jews had been protected "in great part through your effort, diligence, and care."[13]

The agitators from Valencia, however, managed to incite other townspeople to take up arms and chrismals against the Jews.[14] It would have been remarkable had not some of the Christians of Morvedre been caught up in the religious exaltation of the moment, in the belief that they could be the creators of a new, divinely sanctioned order. Others could hardly have resisted the opportunity to plunder the jueria, especially the homes of Jewish creditors.

Over the two previous years, hostility toward Jewish lenders may well have

[9] Küchler 1963; Vincke 1941, 135–136, nos. 126–127; Simonsohn 1988–91, 1: 502–504, no. 472.
[10] Hinojosa Montalvo 1993a, 50–62; Doñate Sebastià and Magdalena Nom de Déu 1990, 41–44, 174–175, 259–261; Furió 1993b, 155–160.
[11] Riera i Sans 1977, 224.
[12] ACA: C 1961: 41v–42v (1391/7/16) [Baer 1929–36, 1: nos. 409–410]; ACA: C 2093: 119r–120r (1391/7/20) [Riera i Sans 1977, 222–224].
[13] ACA: C 1862: 158v–159r (1395/2/25) [Hinojosa Montalvo 1993a, no. 240].
[14] ACA: C 1961: 41v (1391/7/16) [Baer 1929–36, 1: no. 410].

heightened, attributable in no small measure to the king's actions. In September 1389, in an alleged effort to curb the "usurious voracity" of the Jews of his realms and to prevent his Christian subjects from being "despoiled" and left beggars, King Joan commanded each aljama to choose one notary who would enregister all the loans its members made to Christians as well as the pawns the latter left with their creditors. Through this one notary, the king maintained, royal authorities could more easily control Jewish lending practices, lest the Jews collect interest beyond the established royal rate (*ultra cotum*), and more effectively handle debt litigation. But the king gave this single notary a much broader function: he was to record the wills, codicils, and contracts of all local Jews. By instituting these communal notaries, then, Joan was not so much limiting the damage done through the Jews' "insatiable" greed as creating a mechanism through which his fiscal officers could be kept apprised of the assets of each and every Jew.[15] However ill-disguised the king's real intentions would have seemed to Jews, among Christians the rhetoric about Jewish "usurious voracity," probably proclaimed publicly as local officials established the new lending arrangements, would have aroused indignation. According to a complaint registered by the Jews on 15 January 1391, unscrupulous notaries, likely from among those who had lost the Jews' business as a result of the king's provision, had indeed been inspired to blackmail Jewish lenders by "maliciously and cunningly" accusing them of illicit usury.[16] The king's immediate response, a five-year suspension of special royal investigations into illicit Jewish usury, would only have confirmed Christians' suspicions that the notaries were right and the Jewish usurers guilty.[17] The knowledge that truly culpable Jewish lenders could always be sued in regular civil courts would have made less of an impression. It is in any case likely that the Jews sustained some material losses in July.[18]

After the initial defense of the Jews of Morvedre sometime before 16 July, news of further outbreaks of violence against other Jewish communities, such as Castelló and Borriana, continued to stimulate the religious and material ambitions of some local Christians. Moreover, the influx of numerous Jewish refugees from "divers parts and places" in the kingdom had turned Morvedre, in the minds of some zealots, into the site of the Jews' last stand. Thus on 19 July the king placed all Jews in Morvedre, native and refugee, under his special protection and ordered the bailiff to make public proclamations to that effect.[19] On 5 August Joan wrote to Sant Feliu of his intention to stop briefly in

[15] ACA: C 1882: 37r–38v (1395/11/2) [Hinojosa Montalvo 1993a, no. 106], which includes the 1389 letter. Compared to other royal letters regarding alleged Jewish usury *ultra cotum* (see Meyerson 2004a), its language was strong.

[16] ACA: C 1847: 103r-v (1391/1/15): "eosdem frequenter callide et maliciose accusant."

[17] ACA: C 1899: 96v–97r (1391/1/16) [Hinojosa Montalvo 1993a, no. 3].

[18] Chabret Fraga 1979, 2: 338–339.

[19] ACA: C 1961: 41v–42v (1391/7/16) [Baer 1929–36; 1: no. 409]; C 1849: 117r-v (7/19); C 1961: 46r (7/20) [Hinojosa Montalvo 1993a, nos. 23, 27].

Morvedre en route to Valencia in order to punctuate his orders with the royal presence.[20] A royal visit would have helped, for without it "evil persons," inspired by news of the devastation of the Jewish communities of Palma de Mallorca and Barcelona in early August, were again plotting to "rise up, rob, and damage" the aljama of Morvedre. As in July, local officials and knights prevented serious violence.[21] In the process, the Jews' defenders earned the ill will of the troublemakers, who then began to conspire against them. King Joan authorized the local justice to boot these men out of town.[22]

Bonafonat de Sant Feliu and his colleagues thus had their hands full protecting the Jewish population throughout the summer of 1391. By mid-October the bailiff deemed Morvedre sufficiently quiet for him to leave for a while. The Jews, however, were less confident, and at their request, the king ordered Sant Feliu to stay put.[23] The Jews continued to live inside the walls of Morvedre's impressive castle into the winter of 1392.[24]

Although the Jews of Morvedre escaped the violence and forced baptism inflicted on Jews elsewhere in the kingdom, their community did not emerge from the dreadful summer of 1391 completely intact. Fear seems to have gotten the better of some Jews who, despite the bailiff's energy and the strength of the castle's walls, voluntarily descended from the castle and accepted baptism. During the first uprising prior to 16 July one Jewish child sought baptism, according to a letter of the Valencia jurats to Ramon Soler and Pere Marrades, the city's messengers at the royal court. Anxious to rebut the claims of Morvedre's troublesome officials that people from Valencia had sparked this uprising, the jurats gave the story of the boy's conversion a curious and spiteful twist. In Valencia, by the jurats' account, the chrismals were miraculously refilled after the baptism of so many Jews had exhausted the holy oil. This miracle sacralized the anti-Jewish violence that the municipality of Valencia had proven unable to control; it was a sign of divine approval of the forced baptism of the Jews.[25] However, in Morvedre, where municipal officials effectively defended the Jews, a kind of antimiracle occurred, indicating divine displeasure. When the boy came to receive the sacrament the townspeople found that the chrismal was strangely "dry . . . although they did not use up [the holy oil] in the baptism of Jews." The boy then had to be taken to Puçol for baptism.[26] Hence, even if King Joan criticized the municipality of Valencia for not preventing the destruction of the Jewish community and heaped praise on Morvedre's officials for their performance, God at least was on Valencia's side.

---

[20] ACA: C 1961: 60r [Chabret Fraga 1979, 2: 339 n. 2].

[21] ACA: C 1878: 139v–140r (1391/8/25) [Hinojosa Montalvo 1993a, nos. 47–48].

[22] ACA: C 1961: 108v–109r (1391/9/16).

[23] ACA: C 1961: 134r (1391/10/15) [Baer 1929–36, 1: no. 436].

[24] ACA: C 1852: seventh quire, 63r-v (1392/2/18) [Hinojosa Montalvo 1993a, no. 64].

[25] AMV: LM g3–5: 20v–22v (1391/7/14) [Hinojosa Montalvo 1993a, no. 11].

[26] AMV: LM g3–5: 29v (1391/7/22) [Chabret Fraga 1979, 2: 337–338 n. 2]; Piles Ros 1957, 359.

The boy was not alone. At least five other Jews of Morvedre converted. Perhaps the jurats of Valencia did not mention them because the baptism of these Jews did not fit well in their version of the antimiracle in Morvedre, where the impious people protecting the Jews during the first riot were rewarded with an empty chrismal. Yet it is possible that prior to 16 July the boy was the only convert, and that not until late July or August did the other converts decided to abandon Morvedre's castle and Judaism. Hearing the stories of Jewish refugees and news of the tragic events in Palma de Mallorca and Barcelona, and well aware of the continual plotting and agitation of some local Christians against them, they probably felt that the conversion or murder of all Jews was inevitable. After all, they could not remain in the castle forever; better to accept baptism voluntarily before a mob of Christian zealots somehow got their hands on them.

Fiscal records from 1393 partially identify these converts: Na Bella, who still had a Jewish daughter; Pere Català; Manuel de Villafrancha, the son of Sol, the widow of Meora Avinaçara; the son of David el Rau; and Vidal Abenganí, who became Guillem de Blanes.[27] The baptism of the son of David el Rau, however, was apparently involuntary, or, at the very least, performed against the wishes of his father, who subsequently shipped him off to North Africa, where he could return to Judaism.[28] One Jew of Morvedre, David Façan, the son of Jacob Façan, was in fact forced to convert, but this took place while he was visiting Gandia in the southern part of the kingdom. He too soon boarded ship for North Africa.[29] However willing their baptism, even the other converts would find it difficult to cut all ties with Jews and Judaism. The decisions they had made in the summer of 1391, when Jews and Christians alike had reason to believe that the world as they knew it was coming to an end, would seem rash several months later when order was being restored.

For all his credulity regarding alleged Jewish necromancy and host desecration, Joan I was sensible to the importance of the Jews for the royal treasury and therefore was disturbed and angered by what had transpired in July and August 1391. While he did little to punish the offenders, he expended considerable effort in salvaging what he could of Jewish persons and property, and made the best of an awful situation. In the kingdom of Valencia he focused his energies on Morvedre, the only aljama that emerged from the carnage relatively unscathed. For much of the remainder of his reign, which ended with his death in May 1396, Joan placed the Jews of Morvedre under special royal protection and encouraged municipal officials to carry out these orders. They did not fail him.[30]

[27] ACA: MR 393 (January-June 1393): 36v—Na Bella; 38r—Pere Català; 38v—Sol and her converso son, who, in ACA: C 2330: 58v (1396/12/1), is identified as Manuel de Villafrancha. Visitas pastorales, 242, for Blanes.

[28] ACA: MR 393: 39r.

[29] ACA: MR 393: 46v.

[30] Hinojosa Montalvo 1993a, nos. 51 (1391/9/15), 87 (1392/10/2), 110–111 (1392/11/25), 130 (1393/1/7), 168 (1393/5/15), 192 (1393/10/2).

Beyond providing for the basic physical defense of the Jews, other measures had to be taken to ensure their survival during the year or so following July 1391. The aljama and its members were in financial straits. Until February 1392 many Jews perforce resided in the local fortress and could not conduct their usual business affairs. The resultant dramatic decrease in income was potentially catastrophic for the aljama since it coincided with new and unusual expenses. In 1392 the aljama paid 1,080 sous for the castle guards' salary.[31] Far heavier were the expenses the aljama incurred while providing for the needs of the Jewish refugees who flooded into Morvedre throughout the summer of 1391. On 16 July and again on 1 August the king enjoined Prince Martí to transfer all surviving Jews in Valencia to the castle of Morvedre or some other safe place; on 19 August the jurats of Valencia informed the king of their plan to send the roughly two hundred Jews then living among the city's "new Christians" to the same castle.[32] Since there were not many safe places for Jews in the kingdom that summer, most of the Jews remaining in Valencia were probably taken to Morvedre. These refugees, and those coming from other towns, no doubt put an incredible strain on the resources of their brethren in Morvedre.[33] Living conditions in the castle must have been, to say the least, dismal.

In September the king took initiatives to help the Jews of Morvedre deal with these unprecedented circumstances. Since Jewish creditors could not very well travel about seeking payment from Christians and Muslims in the area, he instructed the justice of Morvedre and his counterparts in other towns to collect the debts owed the Jews of Morvedre, once the latter showed the appropriate documents.[34] Joan also prevailed on the noble widow Sibilia Boïl, to whom the aljama paid a 1,000-sous annuity each August as one-half of its 2,000-sous royal *servicio*, to allow the aljama to postpone its 1391 payment to her.[35]

Still, such measures did not leave the Jews of Morvedre the wherewithal to meet all the demands placed on them by the refugees. During the winter of 1391–92 it was necessary to transfer to Morvedre 150 gold florins from the property refugees had abandoned in the capital in order to provide for the "sustenance of their life."[36]

Through much of 1392 the Jews living in Morvedre experienced hardship and near anarchy. On 18 July the king learned that the sixteen posts in the aljama's government could not be filled owing to the diminution in the number

[31] ARV: MR 3986: 5r-v.

[32] ACA: C 1961: 41v–42v [Baer 1929–36, 1: no. 409]; C 1878: 91r-v [Hinojosa Montalvo 1993a, no. 35]; AMV: LM g3–5: 44r [Hinojosa Montalvo 1993a, no. 42].

[33] ACA: C 1961: 46r (1391/7/20) [Hinojosa Montalvo 1993a, no. 27].

[34] ACA: C 1878: 171v–172r (1391/9/18) [Hinojosa Montalvo 1993a, no. 52].

[35] ACA: C 1878: 173v (1391/9/19) [Hinojosa Montalvo 1993a, no. 53].

[36] ACA: C 1879: 93r (1391/12/4) [Hinojosa Montalvo 1993a, no. 59]; C 1963: 58r (1392/3/21).

of members suitable for holding office.[37] This lack of qualified Jews was a surprising development, for during the summer of 1391 perhaps ten Jews at most had converted and none had died at the hands of Christian rioters. In fact the very next day Joan praised Morvedre's officials for their defense of the Jews and urged them to keep up the good work; a year later he noted, with slight exaggeration, how the Jews of the town and their refugee brethren had been "wholly saved" (*omnino preservati*) from violence through the good offices of the bailiff.[38] The bailiff, however, had not been equipped to deal with the illness that resulted from privation, overcrowding, and poor sanitation in the castle. According to the king's letter, members of the aljama had succumbed to "past mortalities," which likely afflicted the Jewish population from late in the summer of 1391 through the winter of 1392.[39]

Even so, the death of so many leading members of the aljama is improbable. King Joan attributed their paucity also to "other chance happenings." They were not dead but "they could by no means be found."[40] At this juncture they could not have moved to other Jewish communities. However, given the Jews' long-standing connections with the knights and seigneurs of the region, and the outstanding role played by local knights and lesser lords in defending the Jews, the potential aljama officials could have removed themselves to the villages and fortresses controlled by their traditional allies.[41] Aljama elections could not be properly held because these Jews were not in town. The refugee crisis and the fear of Christian violence, then, were impeding the normal conduct of communal government; a makeshift administration had to be formed. Difficulties in holding elections notwithstanding, the Jewish community of Morvedre still suffered more from a surfeit of Jewish bodies than from a lack thereof.

The precise number of Jews from the capital and other towns who sought refuge in, or who were transferred to, Morvedre in the summer and fall of 1391

[37] ACA: C 1852: 149r (1392/7/18) [Hinojosa Montalvo 1993a, no. 78].

[38] ACA: C 1963: 122r-v (1392/7/19); C 1855: 140r-v (1393/7/16) [Hinojosa Montalvo 1993a, no. 188].

[39] ACA: C 1852: 149r: "occasione mortalitatum preteritas [*sic*] quam aliorum casuum foruitorum." Rubio Vela 1979, 43, notes that although the bubonic plague afflicted Barcelona in 1392, it did not reach Valencia. It is therefore unlikely to have struck Morvedre. Bubonic plague, of course, was by no means the only illness to which the Jews might have succumbed.

[40] ACA: C 1852: 149r.

[41] In fact, a few months later King Joan ordered all barons, knights, and prelates who had Jews residing on their estates to appear before his counselor and treasurer, Julian Garrius, to show "quo titulo sive jure vos iamdictos judeos sive judeorum aljamas tenetis seu habetis et tenere vel habere potestis in villis et locis ac castris" (ACA: C 1949: 163v [1392/12/3]). The king himself had, in the brighter days before July 1391, licensed certain nobles to establish small Jewish communities on their lands. Carroç de Vilaragut, the lord of Albaida, was permitted fifteen Jewish households, and Jacme Castellani, the lord of Navarres, ten households (respectively, ACA: C 1892: 88r [1387/11/6] and C 1897: 212v–213r [1390/4/20]).

is impossible to know. The Valencia jurats' plan to relocate "some two hundred" to Morvedre gives some sense of the magnitude of the phenomenon, although there is no firm evidence as to the extent to which this plan was carried out. A number of unbaptized Jews did linger on in Valencia until Martí I finally dissolved the Jewish community of Valencia, such as it was, in 1397. Yet some of these Jews perhaps first moved to Morvedre's castle and then, when conditions appeared favorable, say in 1394, returned to live in the capital for a few years.[42]

A comparison of the list of Jewish households in Morvedre compiled by collectors of the *morabatí* tax in 1379 with the list compiled in 1409 gives a rough idea of the long-term impact of the 1391 riots and the resultant refugee problem on the composition of the town's Jewish population. In 1379 there were twenty-eight distinct lineages, according to surname, living in forty-one separate households.[43] By 1409 the population had increased to thirty-eight lineages apportioned among fifty-three separate households. Of these thirty-eight surnames, twenty-six, distributed among twenty-nine households, were "new," or at least had not been recorded in 1379.[44] Other sources dating from 1393 to 1404 yield thirteen other family names listed neither in 1379, and therefore perhaps "new," nor in 1409.[45] Altogether, then, there lived in Morvedre between 1391 and 1409 thirty-nine Jewish lineages bearing surnames the morabatí collectors had not recorded in 1379. The great majority of these lineages must have fled to Morvedre from other places in 1391 and stayed on, though four or five of the new households moved to Morvedre only after the final dissolution of the aljama of Valencia in 1397.[46] Yet it is possible, considering the geographical mobility of the kingdom's Jews prior to 1391, that some Jewish

[42] See n. 32 for the *jurats'* plan to transfer the two hundred Jews. ACA: C 1905: 89v–91r (1393/12/31) [Hinojosa Montalvo 1993a, no. 196] is Joan I's order calling for the creation of a new Jewish quarter in Valencia. After this date, some Valencian refugees may well have left Morvedre and returned to Valencia. On the final dissolution of the jueria of Valencia, see below.

[43] Meyerson 2004a; Hinojosa Montalvo 1995, 282–283.

[44] ARV: MR 11800 (1409). The twenty-nine "new" householders: [Jamila], the widow of En [Samuel] Suxen; Astruc Çaporta; Abraham Gallego; Salamó Mateix; Levi Bilam; Abraham Rodrich; Menahem Gallego; Saltiel Caxo; Cresques Nati (probably Nasci); Jahudà Saladi; Salamó Arron; Jahudà Arrami; Mossé Abenlambut; Samuel Columbri; Mossé Levi; Isaac Ruben; the wife of Isaac Gallego, and two daughters; the wife of Jucef Avenresch; Abraham Huisqui; Jucef Abençema; Salamó Fanduix; Samuel Corquoz; Haim Vinaig; Salamó Vinaig; Salamó Tarfon; Samuel Afla; Mossé Letesi [Alateffi?]; Astruch Addet; Jahudà Leó and Na Regina.

[45] The thirteen family names: Isaac Xamblell, Curçani, and Jahudà Cap (all mentioned in ACA: C 1906: 64r–66r [1393/5/10]); Mossé and Soli Alateffi (ACA: C 1905: 80v–81r [1393/5/15]); Maymó Feraig (ACA: C 2335: 81v–82r [1398/5/18]); Astruc Abenpelx (ARV: P 1445, B. de la Mata [1399/1/14]); Bonjuha and Astruga Bonafos (ARV: P 1445, B. de la Mata [1399/1/20]); Isaac Morcat (ARV: P 1446, B. de la Mata [1401/2/8]); Jucef Mardahay (ACA: C 2338: 73v [1402/4/24]); Vidal Cerraig and Maymó Pardo (ACA: C 2339: 160r–161r [1404/8/28]); Mossé Vidal (ACA: C 2340: 30r [1404/12/1]); and Astruga, the widow of Salamó Abenmarvez (see below).

[46] ACA: C 2116: 16r-v (1398/3/1).

families absent from Morvedre in 1379 were residing there in July 1391 and later in 1409. Nevertheless, the evidence dating from almost twenty years after 1391 leaves little doubt that the influx of refugees significantly altered the composition of Morvedre's Jewish community. Moreover, some of the refugees who flooded Morvedre in 1391 had moved elsewhere by 1409, as the thirteen new surnames recorded between 1393 and 1404, but not in 1409, suggest. Once the royal towns were pacified and Jewish communities reestablished in several of them, there were alternatives to Morvedre's crowded jueria.[47]

Thus one year after the first explosion of violence in the capital, the situation of the Jews of Morvedre remained precarious. They were harboring a large number of Jewish refugees who stretched their resources to the limit, earnings were only trickling in, and their communal government was barely functional. They required further assistance from King Joan, particularly if they were ever to provide him with the funds he desperately needed. Royal finances were in a parlous state, owing in no small part to Joan's own mismanagement.[48]

Joan's policy toward the Jewish community in Morvedre in the final four years of his reign consisted of ensuring its physical security and economic recovery while grabbing revenue from it whenever possible. In most respects his policy was not much of a departure from that of his predecessors, but at this juncture, just after the debacle of 1391, fiscal rapacity was quite risky.

The king took several steps to create a context within which the Jews of Morvedre could do business with relatively little interference from royal and local officials. He began, on 22 November 1392, by revoking the provision he had made in 1389 instituting one notary to enregister all the wills and contracts, including loans, of every Jew in the aljama.[49] Three days later Joan afforded the Jews even more economic freedom by suspending all lawsuits and civil and criminal procedures that might have been initiated against them until that time. The pardon excepted certain heinous crimes, like sex with Christian women and sodomy as well as, significantly, sorcery and abetting Christian or Jewish heretics.[50] Joan reissued this blanket pardon in May 1393 and

---

[47] See chap. 2 on relations between the aljama of Morvedre and the other Valencian aljamas in the fifteenth century. The mobility of Valencian Jews before and after 1391 also helps explain why fifteen Jewish family names recorded in 1379 did not find their way onto the 1409 morabatí list (Jucef, Abendara, Tello, Tauell, Toledano, Far, Coffe, Lobell, Passarell, Maymado, Ballester, Bubo, Azamel, Axauarqui, Porporer). Most probably departed after 1391, trying their luck in towns whose Jewish quarters had been left nearly vacant by rioting. Indeed, from other sources it can be established that families bearing three of the fifteen names in question resided in Morvedre in 1391 but not in 1409: Coffe (ACA: MR 393: 31v [May 1393]; C 2339: 160r–161r [1404/8/28]); Passarell (ARV: P 1445, B. de la Mata: 174v [1399/6/30]); Tello (ACA: C 1905: 80v–81r [1393/5/15] [Hinojosa Montalvo 1993a, no. 167]).

[48] Hillgarth 1976–78, 2: 217–218, 224–225.

[49] ACA: C 1882: 37r–38v [Hinojosa Montalvo 1993a, no. 106].

[50] ACA: C 1899: 102v–103r; C 1904: 102v–103r (both 1392/11/25) [Hinojosa Montalvo 1993a, nos. 109, 112].

March 1394, until he was satisfied that the community was getting back on its feet economically.[51] These pardons protected Jews from undue judicial harassment and obviated unnecessary legal expenses, but they also gave unscrupulous Jews carte blanche to pursue shady business practices. This unusual degree of freedom ended, however, on 24 March 1394, the *terminus ante quem* of the final pardon.

The pardons coincided, moreover, with a stay on all special royal investigations into illicit Jewish usury, which had been in effect since January 1391, and thus for a couple of years afforded Jewish lenders considerable leeway as to the rate of interest they might charge.[52] Yet until 1393, if even then, conditions were hardly propitious for business, particularly moneylending, which for Morvedre's lenders involved a good amount of travel. Furthermore, having only recently ventured out of the castle or other hideouts, lenders would have been especially chary about provoking Christians by charging illegally high interest. On 1 March 1394 Joan extended the suspension of all royal inquiries into usury ultra cotum for another five years, although after 24 March borrowers could sue Jewish lenders in civil court.[53]

The Jews had to show the king that all the attention he was lavishing on them was worth his while. This they did first of all by rendering each year their ordinary tribute, or *peita*, of 2,000 sous, one-half of which went directly to the gracious Sibilia Boïl. The community managed to scrape the money together even in 1392, when it did not have a proper set of officials.[54] It also coughed up a further 550 sous for the king's "necessities" and 440 sous for expenses related to the marriage of his daughter Violant to Louis of Anjou, claimant to the throne of Naples. But the makeshift communal government had reached its limit; thus in December Joan forgave it the second 440-sous *auxilium* for Violant's nuptials.[55] At the same time, he promised the Jews that he would not make further extraordinary "demands" for the next five years.[56]

The Jews soon discovered, confirming what must by then have been popular Jewish wisdom, that royal promises were made to be broken. In June 1392 Joan had decided to lead a naval expedition to Sardinia, where there was yet another rebellion against Catalan rule. The expedition to Sardinia, which was

[51] ACA: C 1905: 81v–82v (1393/5/25); C 1909: 61r–62r (1394/3/24) [Hinojosa Montalvo 1993a, nos. 169, 215].

[52] ACA: C 1899: 96v–97r (1391/1/16) [Hinojosa Montalvo 1993a, no. 3].

[53] ACA: C 1906: 213r-v (1394/3/1) [Hinojosa Montalvo 1993a, no. 208]. Still, ACA: MR 393: 38v (1393) records a fine of 50 florins paid by Vidal Sibili, Jew of Morvedre, "que havia prestat a usura prenent ne mes de cot contra ordinacions Reyals." Sibili, however, had been a resident of Valencia until July 1391. The royal pardons would not have applied to the loans he had made in Valencia prior to his flight to Morvedre.

[54] ARV: MR 3986: 4v–5r (1392), 6v (1393), 9r (1394), 12r (1395); MR 3987: 3v–4r (1396).

[55] ACA: MR 392: 35r (November 1392); C 1904: 101r-v (1392/12/2) [Hinojosa Montalvo 1993a, no. 118].

[56] ACA: C 1903: 105r (1393/12/2) [Hinojosa Montalvo 1993a, no. 119].

to have departed in 1393, never materialized. When an armada finally set sail in 1394 it was diverted to Sicily, then in revolt against Prince Martí and his son, Martí the Younger, who had only recently conquered the island. All the same, Joan needed to raise money.[57] By the end of February 1393 he had already exacted "certain quantities of money" from the Jews and promises of further donations for the Sardinian expedition.[58]

Besides contributing to the illusory Sardinian expedition, the Jews had to pay a tidy sum of 1,980 sous for the general pardon of 1393.[59] Unfortunately the pardon did not cover the crime of proffering aid to heretics, for that same year King Joan heavily fined the two wealthiest Jews in the community, David el Rau and Jacob Façan, for sending their baptized sons to North Africa to live openly as Jews. El Rau paid 13,200 sous and Façan 8,800 sous.[60] Since the personal fortunes of the two biggest taxpayers were now seriously depleted, aljama officials had to adjust their tax rates accordingly and make radical changes in how they apportioned fiscal responsibilities among the rest of the community's members. Façan, who had several enemies in the community, emerged from this particular round of negotiations extremely disgruntled. He later left Morvedre, with royal permission, and settled in the capital.[61]

With the two wealthiest families either absent or financially crippled, the aljama was greatly hampered in dealing efficiently with its considerable expenses. These consisted not just of ordinary and extraordinary renders to the Crown but also of financing a large debt burden. The aljama had had to borrow widely to deal with effects of the 1391 violence, especially the influx of refugees. Many refugees of course were still in Morvedre and it could not have been entirely clear, either to aljama officials or to the refugees themselves, which ones regarded themselves as members of the aljama and therefore liable to pay taxes and shoulder part of the debt burden. Since they had left and lost property in other towns or in the capital, even those refugees desirous of staying on and making a contribution would have found it difficult to do so. The aljama was "almost on the point of desolation."

King Joan responded to the aljama's pleas by licensing it to institute a set of internal sales taxes (cises), covering practically all transactions, for ten years.

[57] He also alienated portions of the royal patrimony and collected substantial sums from the city of Valencia. See Rubio Vela 1989, 258; Vidal Beltrán 1974, 266–272.

[58] ACA: C 1940: 183r-v (1393/2/25). The Jews found it hard to deal with these new obligations because royal recruiters had been granting several men indebted to Jews moratoria on repayment. The king declared that only those recruits who swore to accompany him personally to Sardinia could get such relief.

[59] ACA: MR 393: 53v (June 1393); C 1905: 81v–82v (1393/5/25) [Hinojosa Montalvo 1993a, no. 169].

[60] ACA: CR Joan I, caixa 7, no. 715 (1393/4/15); MR 393: 39r, 46v; C 1855: 85v (1393/5/15) [Hinojosa Montalvo 1993a, no. 166].

[61] See chap. 5.

Aljama officials could farm out the cises to whomever they wished, for the entire ten years or for shorter periods. This latter clause would enable the aljama to raise large amounts of money quickly from the tax farmers. Officials could also modify the rates of the cises prior to each leasing period in accordance with communal necessities. As with past internal sales taxes, both established residents of Morvedre (*judei privati*) as well as "foreign" Jews (*judei extranei*) coming to trade would be liable. With so many refugees in town, however, this stipulation took on unusual importance; it was a way of shifting some of the financial responsibilities onto them. The king gave the aljama discretion to use the proceeds for the exoneration of its debts or for other purposes. Also, to put its officers at ease, he assured them that they would not be required to provide the Crown with an accounting of their disposition of cisa revenues.[62] Even so, Joan expected that some of this revenue would eventually come his way. Hence he demanded that the aljama use the "license" immediately. The representatives of the three social classes chosen to work out the details of the tax plan were to be confined in a house by the bailiff until they reached an agreement.[63]

Aljama officials must have farmed out the internal taxes right away, for less than two months after issuing the license Joan noted the "maximum" subventions he had exacted from the aljama to finance, among other things, the Sardinian expedition. Since the king had not allowed the aljama to benefit much from the sums advanced it by the farmers of the cises, it remained in "poverty." He therefore exempted it for three years from any further extraordinary *demanda*.[64] The exemption did not include, however, the fee the community owed the king for the services he had rendered it, namely the general pardon, the stay on inquiries into illegal usury, and protection from the papal inquisitors. The price of these services was another 3,300 sous.[65]

Joan kept true to his word for the remainder of his reign. But this was no great feat since by the end of August 1394 he no longer controlled the aljama's assets. He had ceded them, along with those of other aljamas, to the Genoese financier Luigi Scarampo in order to secure the Crown's vast debts to him. Joan consequently forbade all Jews to transfer their residence from Morvedre for a period of five years, lest the community lose its utility as a pledge.[66] He also required Jacob Façan to return to Morvedre. Without his wealth, the other Jews in Morvedre feared that they would be unable to meet their obligations and be forced to take to their heels.[67]

The fiscal imperative that drove Joan, after the conflagration of 1391, to at-

[62] ACA: C 1906: 212r-v (1394/1/7) [Hinojosa Montalvo 1993a, no. 198].

[63] ACA: C 1906: 212v–213r (1394/1/7) [Hinojosa Montalvo 1993a, no. 199].

[64] ACA: C 1908: 21v–22r (1394/3/1) [Hinojosa Montalvo 1993a, no. 210].

[65] ACA: C 1861: 26v–27r (1394/4/18) [Hinojosa Montalvo 1993a, no. 222].

[66] ACA: C 1927: 182r-v (1394/8/31) [Hinojosa Montalvo 1993a, no. 230]; Hillgarth 1976–78, 2: 225.

[67] ACA: C 1862: 159v (1395/2/25) [Hinojosa Montalvo 1993a, no. 239]; chap. 5.

tempt to resuscitate devastated Jewish communities, like those in the capital and Borriana, or to protect largely intact communities, like those in Morvedre and the kingdom of Aragon, largely guided his handling of the religious problems emerging from the coexistence of Jews with conversos and papal inquisitors' efforts to investigate them.[68] On one hand, this sometimes benefited Jews, since Joan preferred to keep the inquisitors, and the church in general, at arm's length from his Jewish "treasure."[69] On the other hand, harboring few illusions as to the sincerity with which many neophytes had received baptism in 1391, Joan seized the opportunity to profit from the punishment of Judaizing conversos and their Jewish accomplices.

For Joan the Jewish practices of New Christians were not the only cause for concern. Being of "an extraordinarily unstable and superstitious" nature, he could never quite allay his suspicions that Jews were the allies of Satan, and perhaps of foreign Muslim enemies as well.[70] These suspicions occasionally clouded the king's judgment and gave him additional reasons for investigating and penalizing Jews. Still, even in these instances the Crown's near bankruptcy checked the worst excesses, moving Joan to fine rather than burn the accused.

The conversos and Jews, wondering how King Joan would react to the Jewish practices of the newly baptized and whether he would give free rein to the inquisitors, had good reason for trepidation. His actions before ascending the throne and in the early years of his reign had been inconsistent; there was no predicting what he would do. Besides his brutal prosecution of Catalan and Aragonese Jews accused of host desecration, Joan had supported and protected the inquisitor Nicolau Eimeric, the most vociferous proponent of the view that papal inquisitors could prosecute Jews for the crimes and heresies they committed against their own faith as well as for those they committed against the Catholic faith. In supporting Eimeric he had opposed his father, Pere, who, disgusted by the inquisitor's methods, had ejected him from Crown territories in 1375. In Valencia, moreover, Joan had urged another inquisitor and the bishop in 1384 to continue their investigation of the "adorations of devils" and other "abominable excesses" in the home of a local Jew, Salamies Nasci.[71]

Yet the responsibilities of rule, and the realization that there were limited

---

[68] For Valencia, ACA: C 1905: 89v–91r (1393/12/31); C 1909: 49r-v (1394/5/26); C 1862: 42v–43r (1394/9/15); for Borriana, C 1910: 150v–151r (1395/10/16) [Hinojosa Montalvo 1993a, nos. 196, 227, 233, 246].

[69] E.g., ACA: C 2023: 11v–12r (1394/3/1). The pope had appointed the archbishop of Zaragoza his judge in the Crown of Aragon for treating matters pertaining to usury and the disposition of pious legacies possibly threatened by creditors of the deceased. The king admonished the archbishop's commissioners, who were snooping around Morvedre, to keep a healthy distance from the Jews, lest they incur a fine of 1,000 florins. The pope, he asserted, had no jurisdiction over the Jews; they were the royal treasure.

[70] Roca 1929, 166, 169.

[71] Vincke 1941, 123, no. 112 (ACA: C 1662: 35r [1384/9/30]).

funds for fulfilling them, sobered Joan somewhat. When he succeeded his father in 1387, he moved quickly to hamstring the inquisitors. Taking advantage
of the Great Schism and his leverage with the Avignon papacy, Joan demanded
that Pope Clement VII recognize the Crown's exclusive jurisdiction in cases
involving its valuable Jewish and Muslim subjects. Clement's negative response did not overly trouble Joan, for he was sympathetic to the aims of the
papal inquisitors when they did not threaten his patrimony. In fact Joan returned Eimeric to his post in 1387. Eimeric's procedure against allegedly
heretical Llullists and Beguines in Valencia so antagonized the citizens that
they drove him out of the city in 1388; Joan, too, then turned against him. Even
when inquisitors tried Joan's Jewish subjects for "heresy," both Pope Clement's
stance and his own credulity dissuaded him from firm opposition. His primary
concern was to secure the heretic's property for the royal treasury.[72]

The occasional Jewish necromancer was one thing, the mass of new converts baptized in the violence of 1391 another. With so many conversos, and
so many Jews around to encourage their backsliding, the potential field of investigation for the papal inquisition expanded dramatically. King Joan concurred with the inquisitors on the necessity of preventing the conversos from
returning to Judaism, whether in the kingdom or abroad. Yet, since the inquisitors could do so much harm to his Jewish and formerly Jewish treasure in
the course of their investigations, and since there was so much property and so
many monetary penalties possibly at stake, Joan exerted greater effort than he
had before 1391 to have cases involving Jews and baptized Jews tried in secular rather than ecclesiastical courts.

The king's most immediate concern was to prevent conversos from fleeing
his realms to North Africa or even Palestine in order to return to Judaism.[73]
Such flight could not be permitted for two reasons. First, since the sacrament
of baptism was ineffaceable, allowing conversos to live as Jews elsewhere was
tantamount to promoting heresy. Second, the affluence and economic potential of some converso families suggested to Joan that it would be folly to let
them flourish in the lands of another prince, especially a Muslim prince. Only
the Crown possessed the officials and ships to patrol the coastline; the inquisitors played a minimal role here.

Throughout 1392 and into 1393 many conversos were apprehended attempting to escape from Valencia, Catalonia, and Mallorca. Some, however,
slipped through the dragnet. Those captured usually paid substantial sums in
exchange for a royal pardon. The business of inhibiting heresy proved to be
fairly lucrative for the Crown.[74]

---

[72] Perarnau i Espelt 1982, 80–92; Puig i Oliver 1980 and 1982, 133–137; see above at n. 9.

[73] Dinur 1967; cf. Hacker 1985, 114–125; Hirschberg 1974–81, 1: 384–388.

[74] ACA: C 1877: 89v–90r (1392/6/5); C 1881: 40r–41r (9/20); C 1902: 36v–37r (9/20); C 1880: 164r–165r (10/16); C 1902: 79r–80r (12/14); C 1907: 240r-v (1393/2/14) [Hinojosa Mon-

Yet by the spring of 1393 the king was already easing restrictions on converso travel and indeed was permitting Valencian conversos to circulate throughout his realms and even to travel abroad as long as they left their families behind and substantial securities with the bailiff general.[75] Fostering converso mercantile activity would profit king and kingdom. Joan, however, distinguished between temporary absence for commercial purposes and permanent displacement outside his realms. He expressly forbade the latter to conversos, Jews, and Muslims in January 1394.[76] This portion of the royal patrimony had to be retained, at the very least so that he could pledge it to Genoese financiers.

The endeavor to prevent conversos from returning to Judaism outside Crown lands coincided with the prosecution of conversos for Judaizing within them. The papal inquisitors naturally assumed a much larger role in procedures against the Judaizers and the Jews who encouraged them in their heresy. Although Joan did not wish to cross the pope by challenging the inquisition's jurisdiction in these cases, he objected, in 1392, to the methods of the current inquisitor, the Dominican Pere d'Aguiló. Aguiló and his men were arresting and extorting money from conversos who had returned to their "Jewish blindness." Joan preferred that they draw the conversos back to the Catholic faith through teaching, gentle persuasion, and light penance.[77] He also preferred that any monies obtained from penalizing heretical converts go to the royal coffers, not to church officials. Joan therefore was more than happy to allow lay officials to take action against Judaizers and their Jewish accomplices without inquisitorial involvement. The inquisition was by no means omnipresent and lacked the larger personnel at the disposal of the Crown.

As the one Jewish community in the kingdom to come through the summer of 1391 more or less intact, and wedged as it was between the large concentration of neophytes in Valencia and the smaller groups of conversos in Castelló, Borriana, and Morvedre itself, the community in Morvedre became a focus for royal and inquisitorial attention. The first investigations into Judaizing in Morvedre, however, were undertaken by royal officials alone, almost

---

talvo 1993a, nos. 72, 82, 83, 94, 122, 152]. ACA: MR 392: 32v (November 1392): 100 florins collected from Manuel Martorell and other conversos of Valencia; MR 393: 39v–40r (April 1393): 16,417 sous 7 diners collected from various conversos of Barcelona for attempted flight to North Africa; MR 394: 4r (July 1393): 20 florins collected from Pere Fuster, ship patron, "per ço com fo inculpat que havia trets alcuns conversos de la ciutat de Mallorches per portar los en Berberia"; 8r–9r (July 1394): 370 florins earned from the sale of the property belonging to conversos of Barcelona that had been found on a ship the conversos were intending to embark for "terra de moros" where they could "tornarse a la ley judaica."

[75] ACA: C 1905: 82v–83r (1393/5/26); C 1907: 48r–49r (1393/6/23) [Hinojosa Montalvo 1993a, nos. 171, 185].

[76] ACA: C 1927: 89r (1394/1/15) [Hinojosa Montalvo 1993a, no. 205].

[77] ACA: C 1862: 43r–44r (1394/9/10) [Hinojosa Montalvo 1993a, no. 232]. The letter to Aguiló (1392/9/30) is included in this letter, which reiterates the command to the inquisitor Barthomeu Gaçó.

as if Joan desired to keep the inquisitors out of the kingdom's main Jewish center for as long as possible. The king's men could go to work because the general pardon granted the Jews did not cover the crimes of heresy and sorcery.

Royal prosecutors made their first move in 1393. They shrewdly chose to swoop down on the Jewish quarter during Passover, a time when the newly converted could hardly have resisted the temptation to gather with their Jewish relatives to remember divine redemption of the Jewish people from past bondage and to pray for their own redemption in the future. The tactic paid off, but not so handsomely, as there were very few converts in Morvedre. Officials collected a fine of 330 sous from the conversa Na Bella for having "had the *pascha judahica* with her one Jewish daughter," and another 253 sous from the converso Pere Català for having done the same with a female cousin.[78] These were not insignificant sums for the individuals penalized, and it seems that the officials fined them in accordance with an evaluation of their assets. Thus when they crashed the Passover seder of a wealthier family, that of the deceased Meora Avinaçara, they exacted a much larger fine. Meora's widow, Sol, and their baptized son handed over 1,650 sous.[79] The treasurer, however, recorded the fine as having been paid by Sol. Perhaps the son still lived at home and she was head of the household. In any case, it is striking that the royal authorities scarcely distinguished between the heretical conversos and their Jewish relatives. They were equally culpable. Thus penalized, they would perhaps remain apart on future Passovers.

Yet the big money came not from the conversos and Jews celebrating Passover together but from those Jews whose converso children were noticeably absent from the seder, from those Jews who had spirited their baptized sons to North Africa and effected their redemption. Luckily for King Joan the two perpetrators of this crime were by far the richest Jews in Morvedre, David el Rau and Jacob Façan. He could convict them and then charge them exorbitant sums for a royal pardon. Granting them pardons was no small matter, for they had committed a serious crime against the Catholic faith and had assisted their sons in violating royal prohibitions against converso emigration. In fact, in the letter of pardon he issued to Jacob Façan, Joan listed a whole series of crimes Jacob had allegedly committed. In doing so, the king expressed his growing uneasiness regarding the mixing of Jews and conversos and its dire implications for church and even state.

The main charge laid against Jacob by the royal prosecutor, Pere d'Anglesola, was, of course, that he, along with his wife, Ceti, daughter Jamila, and son-in-law Isaac Xamblell, induced his son David, who had received baptism in a church in Gandia, to return to Judaism. In various houses owned by Jacob

---

[78] ACA: MR 393: 36v for Bella, who "composa ab la Cort per ço com fo inculpada que havia tenguda pascha judahica ab .I. sua filla juhia," and 38r for Català.
[79] ACA: MR 393: 38v.

in Morvedre, the Vall d'Uixó, and other places, they convinced David — if he really needed convincing — that "the Hebrew law is worth more than the Catholic faith," and, having accomplished this, put him on a ship bound for North Africa, where he could live openly as a Jew. They bribed the Christian crew to deliver David and the many other converso men and women on board safely to "the parts of Barbary and of the Saracens, enemies of our faith."

Joan and Anglesola easily transformed Jacob's crime against the Catholic faith into a crime of treason. Since Jacob had sent his son to Muslim North Africa, it took no great leap of the imagination to claim that Jacob had sent money and arms to the Muslims and revealed royal secrets to them.[80] Although Joan did not possess firm evidence of the Façans' treasonable activities, the phenomenon of newly baptized Jews fleeing the Catholic faith and his kingdom in droves disquieted him. He could not grasp why Jews like David Façan, once baptized and exposed to Christian truth, would ever leave the church; hence, it stood to reason that his family had held him in hiding and had worn him down with their relentless arguments. Nor could he imagine why the baptized would abandon the lands of a Christian king for those of a Muslim prince, unless of course they were traitors. Joan and Anglesola, however, had no need to justify Jacob's conviction and punishment with further wild accusations, for the Jew was undoubtedly guilty of abetting the clandestine flight of his son. What Joan needed to do, and did in this pardon, was to articulate his incomprehension and the profound anxiety that his thousands of baptized Jewish subjects aroused.

If the flight of conversos abroad evoked unsettling fantasies of Jewish-Muslim conspiracy, the backsliding of conversos at home elicited visions of a church infected by Judaism and deviltry. Such visions were concretely expressed in the additional charges listed in Jacob Façan's letter of pardon. Besides sending his son to return to Judaism abroad, Jacob was undermining the Catholic faith of conversos in the kingdom. He was accused of making *matzah* and delivering it to Sogorb, so that the conversos there could observe Passover properly,[81] and of calling a converso of Morvedre a "renegade," thus expressing his opinion of a Jew who perhaps had sincerely embraced Christianity. Furthermore, according to the prosecutor's charges, Jacob was a "bad Jew," and the king referred to him as such in his pardon. Jacob, it was said, had worked on the Jewish Sabbath and had abused his power while an adelantat in the aljama. Jacob's Jewish enemies in Morvedre no doubt provided the prosecutor

[80] As ARV: B 1431: n.f. (1491/8/17) [Hinojosa Montalvo 1993a, no. 835] shows, Joan's imagination tended to leap farther than his father's had. This letter contains Pere III's 1386 ruling that Valencian Jews could ransom North African Jewish captives, and that Jews "from whatever place" should not be detained as prisoners of war, "since the Jews are persons of great simplicity and live under such subjection that they make neither war nor peace nor any practice of arms." The Jews, in other words, were politically and militarily neutral.

[81] Given Jacob's lending activities in and around Sogorb, this charge was plausible.

with some of the more plausible details of these accusations, but their inherent plausibility was not the point.[82] Joan, and his prosecutor, wanted to imply that only a "bad Jew" would defy royal authority and ecclesiastical prohibitions against conversos returning to Judaism; only a "bad Jew" would try to undo what God and king had ordained.

Finally, the prosecutor charged — and King Joan took pains to repeat — that when Jacob's daughter Jamila had fallen ill, he and his wife and son-in-law had congregated with Jewish, Muslim, and Christian sorcerers in order to discover, through "diabolic art," what malady was afflicting her. This last charge, in its presentation of an imaginary worst case scenario, lays bare the essence of royal fears. The return to Judaism of the newly baptized would blur the once clear boundaries between Judaism and Christianity. Bad Christians would become secret Jews and bad Jews would aid them in their Judaizing enterprise. It would become less and less certain what being a Jew or being a Christian meant and what the sacrament of baptism signified. The blurring of boundaries and the mixing of faiths would lead to no faith at all or to an antireligion, to a world where Christians, Jews, and Muslims would come out of their clearly identifiable churches, synagogues, and mosques and gather together in a murky underworld of diabolic sorcery.

In the letter of pardon the king pointed out that the prosecutor, possibly through his own "lack of skill or negligence," had not been able to substantiate the additional charges against Jacob and his family. Nevertheless, just in case they were later proven guilty of any of the alleged crimes, he was absolving them of all penalties they might incur.[83] Joan had a nagging doubt that there was something to these charges but Jacob had made it worth his while, in the form of an 800-florin payment, not to pursue them further.[84] After all, Joan could not bring David Façan back to Morvedre and Christianity. Since he desired to revitalize the Jewish communities after the devastation of 1391, it was better to keep a wealthy and enterprising Jew like Jacob Façan alive and in the kingdom.

Still, the case of Façan, brought to Joan's attention in April 1393, and others like it, affected the king, in whose mind Judaism and diabolic sorcery had long tended to converge. He began to regard the inquisition's activities more favorably. In November 1393 he commanded all his officials and subjects in the kingdom to cooperate with the inquisitor general, Barthomeu Gaçó, in his procedures against "wicked conversos who hold the erroneous sect [Judaism] in their depraved heart[s] . . . and . . . against some other wicked persons

---

[82] See chap. 5 on aljama politics.

[83] ACA: C 1906: 64r–66r (1393/5/10) [Baer 1929–36, 1: no. 451; Hinojosa Montalvo 1993a, no. 164]; Meyerson 1997, 132–133.

[84] Samuel Cabrit, a Jew of Tortosa, helped effect the remission of penalties King Joan granted to Jacob Façan and his son-in-law Isaac Xamblell, probably by contributing to the large fine Jacob had to pay. ACA: C 2332: 4v (1397/3/14), C 2114: 149r (1397/12/5) treat subsequent litigation.

touched by heretical depravity who . . . invoke evil spirits and adore and per-
fume them."[85] Joan did not identify the "other wicked persons" but he seems
to have linked the adherence of some conversos to Judaism to the spread of
necromancy.

Yet by the following spring fiscal pragmatism had gotten the better of the
king and dampened his imagination somewhat. It was all well and good for the
inquisitor to prosecute heretical conversos, especially if the Crown was getting
its share of the fines. For this purpose Joan had seen to it that his treasurer
Arnau Porta accompanied Gaçó when the latter proceeded against conversos
in Valencia.[86] But there would be no revenue coming from conversos, neither
from monetary penalties nor from taxes and tariffs, if there were no conversos
on royal lands. Through his brutal tactics Gaçó was creating just such a scenario. In Borriana the inquisitor and his colleagues had been jailing converso
women and forcing their families to ransom them. Almost the entire converso
population had fled the area.[87] In the capital similar molestations and extor-
tions had prompted more than fifty converso households to take refuge on the
lands of prelates and nobles. The king commanded Gaçó to cease these actions.[88] The issue was not whether the conversos were guilty of heresy — for
presumably most were only three years after their forced baptism — but how
they were to be punished and who would profit, one way or another, from the
converso presence.

Although Joan could rebuke the inquisitors for their unnecessarily harsh
methods, he could not challenge their jurisdiction in the cases of conversos,
who were, after all, Christians. Their jurisdiction in cases involving Jews and
Muslims, however, was more debatable.[89] Despite Pope Clement's denial of
his request, made at the outset of his reign, to grant the Crown exclusive jurisdiction in such cases, Joan was now, seven years later, prepared to clash with
the inquisition, if not the papacy, on the issue. The events of 1391 had changed
things considerably. There were now far fewer sizable Jewish communities;
those that remained had to be protected.

Joan had been giving special attention to the Morvedre community since
July 1391, and he had, until the end of 1393, shielded it from the inquisition.
As the scope of Gaçó's activities widened, however, he and his men were bound
to target Morvedre, whose population of "native" Jews and Jewish refugees
from Valencia made it the headquarters for abettors of heresy. In the winter of
1394 the inquisitors and episcopal officials were "daily" investigating the ac-

---

   [85] ACA: C 1927: 101r-v (1393/11/7) [Vincke 1941, no. 144].

   [86] ACA: C 1964: 99r; C 1950: 98r (both 1393/7/11) [Vincke 1941, nos. 140–141].

   [87] ACA: C 1861: 34r-v (1394/4/7) [Hinojosa Montalvo 1993a, no. 219].

   [88] ACA: C 1862: 43r–44r (1394/9/10) [Hinojosa Montalvo 1993a, no. 232].

   [89] Cohen 1982, 96–99; Simonsohn 1991, 343–366, treat papal claims of jurisdiction over Jews
for the heresies and crimes they committed against their own faith. Regarding similar claims of the
inquisitor Eimeric, see Perarnau i Espelt 1982; Eimeric and Peña 1983, 88–94.

tivities of its Jewish population. The Jews were so vexed and burdened by the expenses stemming from inquisitorial inquiries that they threatened to move to "other parts," presumably seigneurial lands. The king responded swiftly and reminded municipal and royal officials that ecclesiastical judges had no right to meddle with the "royal treasure." He commanded them not to cooperate with the inquisitors in procedures against the Jews, which, as far as he was concerned, were null and void.[90]

For the remaining two years of Joan's reign the inquisition apparently left the Jews in Morvedre alone. The Jews and their converso brethren, however, were not free to do as they liked. The king himself continued to be concerned about converso Judaizing. In 1396 he learned that conversos in Morvedre were still living with the Jews just as they had before their baptism, and that since Old Christians, conversos, and Jews all dressed alike, the Old Christians were confused as to who were the Jews and who the converts. The danger of this state of affairs for the conversos and even for the Old Christians was patent. Joan therefore issued prohibitions against the conversos' living with Jews, or eating, drinking, and praying with them. Since it was necessary that the Jews be easily identifiable, he required them to wear a red badge on their clothing.[91] This last measure was intended not to harass the Jews, whose recovery and prosperity the Crown encouraged, but to inhibit the backsliding of conversos. Significantly, the king had lay officials implement these regulations.

MARTÍ I AND MARÍA DE LUNA

Martí I (d. 1410) ascended the throne after his brother Joan's death on 10 May 1396. A more able king than Joan, Martí succeeded in recovering for the royal patrimony some Valencian lands and towns alienated by his father and brother. The new king, as conversos and Jews would quickly discover, was deeply religious, though given less to fantasy than his predecessor.[92]

Having been on the scene in Valencia in the summer of 1391, Martí was well aware of the origins and size of the converso population in the city and in the kingdom at large. Even if he had been inclined to lend credence to the "miracle of the chrismals," he recognized that the problematic manner of their baptism had not left the conversos with much opportunity or desire to receive proper instruction in the Catholic faith, and that they were consequently all too susceptible to the persuasions of their Jewish friends and relatives. Just the same, ambassadors from the capital, who reached the king before he returned to the

---

[90] ACA: CR Joan I, caixa 7, no. 797 (1394/3/1); C 1906: 213v–214v [Hinojosa Montalvo 1993a, no. 209].

[91] ACA: C 1911: 46r (1396/4/4) [Chabret Fraga 1979, 2: 341–342 n. 1].

[92] Ferrer i Mallol 1970–71; Tasis i Marca 1980, 195–241.

Iberian peninsula from Sicily, reminded him of the problem while entreating him not to allow the Jews remaining in the city to reestablish a Jewish quarter. The pious Martí could not have been unmoved by the argument that the co-existence of Jews with the city's numerous conversos would result in "grave scandals and errors." On 22 February 1397, three months prior to his arrival in Spain, he granted the municipality the "privilege" forbidding the reconstruction of a jueria in the capital and the residence of Jews there. All Jews had to exit the city within twenty days and settle in Morvedre or other royal towns.[93]

Removing Jews from the capital, however, did not address the problem of contact between conversos and Jews in the rest of the kingdom. It did not even impede converso residents of Valencia intent on practicing Judaism in the company of Jews. Moreover, as only a few years had passed since their baptism, all but the youngest conversos were capable of leading a full Jewish life with little or no Jewish assistance. With Judaizing pervasive among the kingdom's conversos, the king recognized the need for a more aggressive approach.

On 4 February 1398 Martí commanded an official of the royal household, Guillem de Feriaria, to work *viriliter* with the papal inquisitor to "extirpate" converso Judaizing and to inhibit the conversos "totally" from consorting with Jews.[94] In the diocese of Valencia the bishop and his underlings seconded the inquisitors in their campaign against converso heresy.[95] Thus in the course of his visitation of Morvedre the following summer, the episcopal vicar threatened the converso Guillem de Blanes with a fine of 200 sous if he did not exit the Jewish quarter and find a house in a Christian neighborhood.[96] The vicar also prohibited all local Christians, but particularly conversos, from buying and eating kasher meat, attending Jewish or Muslim weddings, and lighting candles and preparing food in the homes of Jews on the Jewish Sabbath.[97]

King Martí was, for a time, so zealous about preventing and punishing converso backsliding that he could even find the inquisitors wanting. He learned, in July 1400, that the inquisition in Xàtiva was ceasing its prosecution of a num-

---

[93] ACA: C 2209: 149r–150r (1397/2/22): "unde inconvenientia quamplurima proveniunt aliasque scandala gravia et errores evenire proculdubio sperantur." The same letter is in C 2303: 74v–75v. C 2239: 124v (1398/2/20) treats the Crown's confiscation of the Jewish cemetery in Valencia.

[94] ACA: C 2229: 60r (1398/2/4): "ad extirpandum errores predictos . . . totaliter, quod ipsi conversi abstracti et totaliter separati a consortio et conversacione judeorum." The errors in question were the conversos' meetings with Jews "in observatione sabbati et serimoniarum ebrayce cecitatis" and "quamplurimum frequentius judaytzant."

[95] Such was not the case in the diocese of Barcelona. The king called for the revocation of all procedures initiated by the papal inquisitor there, because the inquisitor had acted without the consent and in violation of the jurisdiction of the bishop (ACA: C 2170: 74r [1399/1/27]).

[96] *Visitas pastorales*, no. 242 (1398/7/15).

[97] *Visitas pastorales*, nos. 227, 231. The vicar seems to have had the odd impression that Judaizing conversos would perform labors on the Sabbath that Jews would not perform. A Judaizer would have "abstained from all work," just like the "perfidious Jews."

ber of prominent conversos, because its officials had been thus persuaded by
some local notables and had received a bribe of 500 florins from the defen-
dants themselves. The conversos, moreover, were busily converting all their
property into portable silver and jewelry so that they could escape with their
families to North Africa. Martí responded by sending Guillem Martorell, another member of the royal household, to seize the persons and property of the
conversos and to admonish the inquisition to get on with the case.[98]

Realizing that inquisitors might be sidetracked by financial considerations
and that in any case there were not enough inquisitorial officials to handle such
a widespread problem properly, the king issued the next month a special royal
pragmatica prohibiting the public or secret observance of any Jewish fast or
holiday, including the Sabbath, by the neophytes. Royal officials everywhere
were to make proclamations to this effect and were to punish offenders with a
fine of 100 sous. The royal treasury would receive two-thirds of the fine; the remaining one-third would go to the accuser.[99] The Crown thus encouraged spy-
ing and informing on converso neighbors and acquaintances.

The final dissolution of what was left of the Jewish community in the capital and the new monarch's vigorous efforts to extirpate Judaizing prompted
some conversos, like the aforementioned residents of Xàtiva, to attempt flight
to North Africa. Like his brother, King Martí took action against such clandestine emigration. He also called for an inquiry into the communication of
converso merchants with Maghriban Jewish merchants visiting the kingdom,
some of whom, Martí believed, were former Valencian conversos who had re-
neged on the Catholic faith abroad.[100]

Still, conversos' efforts to emigrate after 1397 seem not to have been nearly
as extensive as they had been under Joan I. During Martí's reign, in fact, there
was movement in the opposite direction as some conversos, finding conditions
in North Africa disagreeable, returned to Valencia.[101] Moved by piety, Martí
was pleased to receive them back into the fold of the church. Moved by economic interests, he was content to have them back in Valencia expanding its
commerce with North Africa.[102] After his initial misgivings, Martí, like his
brother, permitted conversos to travel abroad for trade, under the same conditions Joan had stipulated.[103]

---

[98] ACA: C 2233: 9r-v; C 2253: 48r-v (both 1400/7/11).

[99] ACA: C 2173: 115r (1400/8/12).

[100] ACA: C 2240: 27v (1398/1/8), 68r (3/15).

[101] ACA: C 2194: 62r-v (1399/9/16), C 2125: 58r (1399/10/7) concern the converso Roger de
Montcada; C 2193: 123r–124r (1400/1/20) [Hinojosa Montalvo 1993a, no. 258] concerns the
converso Pau Maçana.

[102] ACA: C 2264: 139v–140r, 143v–144r (1399/8/20) concern royal efforts to promote the
trade of North African Muslims and Jews with Valencia and Mallorca. The key role of conversos
as factors of North African Jewish merchants trading in Valencia is patent in Piles Ros 1984, 234–
237.

[103] ACA: C 2203: 156v–157v (1406/12/4), basically a confirmation of ACA: C 1909: 29v
(1394/4/14) [Hinojosa Montalvo 1993a, no. 221].

Also like his brother, Martí remained perplexed by the phenomenon of so many conversos adhering to Judaism almost a decade after their baptism. He, too, could not fully understand their stubborn denial of Christian truth. Yet whereas Joan had looked to the allegedly common attachment of Jews and conversos to diabolic sorcery as a possible explanation, Martí's thoughts were rather more conventional and wandered dangerously toward the Talmud. He pondered the rulings of Popes Gregory IX and Innocent IV, who had regarded the doctrinal errors and the blasphemies against Christ and the Virgin Mary contained in the postbiblical text as responsible for the Jews' rejection of Christian teaching. The Talmud, the king concluded, still rendered the Jews blind to the scriptural evidence of Jesus's messianic status; it was having the same effect on conversos who consorted with talmudic Jews. In almost a postscript to his pragmatica of August 1400 prohibiting the conversos' Jewish practices, Martí called on his officials to see that the sentences of Gregory and Innocent concerning the Talmud were observed. The king presumably had in mind the confiscation and examination — and perhaps even the burning — of talmudic texts.

Martí pointed out that the popes had commanded burning the Talmud, "in which many and varied heresies are contained," and punishing "those who teach or observe the said heresies."[104] He did not, however, elaborate on his understanding of what these talmudic "heresies" entailed. Whether he was thinking of heresies against biblical Judaism or heresies against Christianity, both, to his mind, would have led baptized and unbaptized Jews astray. More importantly, the king decided that since Jews were probably disseminating talmudic heresies among conversos, the papal inquisition should prosecute the guilty Jews. Little more than a month after issuing his pragmatica, Martí instructed all officials to cooperate in the investigation "begun or about to begin against Jews and Saracens by the inquisitors . . . or their agents."[105]

King Martí had, then, put in motion a thoroughgoing offensive against the Judaizing converts and their Jewish accomplices and teachers. Now set loose on the Jews by royal mandate, the inquisitors in Valencia set their sights on Morvedre. Yet they do not seem ever to have confiscated any rabbinic texts from the local Jews. They were otherwise occupied, but not with activities the king had had in mind. By the end of 1401 Martí had reason to believe that he had acted too hastily in September 1400. Once unleashed, however, the inquisitors proved difficult to control. Fortunately for the Jews of Morvedre Martí was assisted by his able and energetic queen, María de Luna.

[104] ACA: C 2173: 115r (1400/8/12): "Ceterum quia bone memorie pape Gregorius IX et Innocentius IIII in sacro consistorio sententialiter ordinarunt et mandarunt comburi librum quem judei vocant Talmut in quo multe et varie hereses continentur et puniri illos qui docerent dictas hereses vel servarent . . . disponimus et jubemus quod huiusmodi sententia inviolabiliter observetur."

[105] ACA: C 2195: 68v (1400/9/15): "inquisitionis officium contra judeos et sarracenos inceptum seu etiam incipiendum per inquisitores heretice pravitatis seu comissarios eorundem." See J. Cohen 1982, 77–99; Rembaum 1982; Baer 1961, 2: 391–393, on the papacy and the Talmud.

María emerged as the most resolute protector of Morvedre's Jews. She had a vested interest in the survival and prosperity of this aljama: in January 1398 it and several other Jewish and Muslim aljamas became attached to her treasury and remained so until her death on 29 December 1406.[106] With the expressed hope of augmenting the community's population, María confirmed all the privileges it had been granted by Pere III and his predecessors.[107] She took other steps on the aljama's behalf, such as empowering it to establish confraternities for caring for the sick, burying the dead, and teaching poor boys, as had been the custom before 1391.[108] These were all rather traditional measures, though after 1391 a consistent and familiar royal policy meant a great deal to the Jews.

Under the careful administration of King Martí and Queen María the financial situation of the aljama of Morvedre improved. They taxed it more lightly than King Joan had and were prepared to forgive some of its ordinary fiscal obligations, if aljama officials could make a good case. Extraordinary taxation was not too burdensome and was intermittent. The queen made the largest request in 1398, asking the aljama to pay her 3,135 sous for all the provisions she had made that year on the Jews' behalf. The money came directly out of the pocket of Jacob Façan, who seems by then to have become something of a favorite of the queen, probably because his pockets were so deep. She had in fact taken some care to ensure that Jacob's pockets stayed full, instructing, for instance, the justice of Sogorb and other officials to proceed against individuals indebted to him.[109] The king demanded less of the Jews.[110]

By the time Martí succeeded his brother, the aljama had amassed large debts, mostly in the form of censals and violaris it had sold to defray the expenses stemming from the emergency of 1391–92 or to finance royal subsidies. The aljama was only gradually liquidating its debts through the payment of annuities to its creditors.[111] On 20 July 1401 the royal couple licensed the

---

[106] ACA: C 2311: 10r–14r, 16v–17r (1398/1/26). Queen Elionor of Sicily, the wife of Pere III, had similar authority over the whole town of Morvedre and played a decisive role in the reconstruction of its Jewish and Christian communities. For a more detailed account of the actions of both queens, see Meyerson 2004c.

[107] ACA: C 2335: 91v (1398/5/18); reconfirmed by King Martí — C 2191: 26v.

[108] ACA: C 2338: 157v (1402/12/9) [Hinojosa Montalvo 1993a, no. 269].

[109] ACA: C 2335: 90r (1398/5/18). In her capacity as Martí's lieutenant, María had acted on Jacob's behalf even before the aljama of Morvedre was attached to her treasury — C 2330: 131v–132r (1397/2/23). Also, Meyerson 2004c, on this and the forgiving of fiscal obligations.

[110] ACA: C 2317: 171r-v (1400/7/22): 150 florins toward the expenses of Queen María's coronation; the following December 30 florins were still outstanding (C 2341: 39v). In 1402 the king requested that all Crown aljamas contribute unspecified amounts to the aid package he had promised to send the Byzantine emperor for his struggle against the Turks (C 2211: 174v; Hillgarth 1976–78, 2: 227–228). It is not clear that anything was ever collected.

[111] In order to avoid paying their portion of the pensions de censals that the aljama had contracted while they were resident in Morvedre, some Jews emigrated to other towns, especially Bor-

aljama of Morvedre to borrow, through the sale of additional censals, up to
15,000 sous so that it might redeem some of the censals and violaris already
burdening it. The aljama could sell the censals to whichever persons or corporations it saw fit; the annuities would be secured on the movable and im-
movable property of the Jews.[112] Due to the monarchs' fiscal restraint, in 1404
the aljama needed to sell only censals worth 5,000 sous for the purpose of liquidating its debts; by 1409 2,000 sous were sufficient.[113] To further assist aljama officials in their task, Martí and María upheld the system of internal sales
taxes established by King Joan in 1393 and renewed the license for another ten
years in 1403.[114]

The efforts of King Martí and especially of Queen María to foster the aljama
of Morvedre, and other aljamas, might well have come to naught had the inquisitors had their way. Within a year of having ordered the inquisitors to investigate Jews as well as Judaizing conversos, Martí came to the uncomfortable
realization that, as far as the Jews in particular were concerned, he and the inquisitors were working at cross-purposes. María probably helped open his eyes.
A pugnacious defender of her patrimony, the queen had from the start viewed
all clerical meddling in the affairs of her Jews as a threat. When she learned,
in 1398, that the bishop of Sogorb had indicted Jacob Façan "concerning certain things touching the Catholic faith," she asked the bishop to release him,
accepting Jacob's claim that the charges were false and the opinion of "trustworthy individuals" that the bishop's initiatives savored more of vexation than
of correction. She chose to disregard the fact that five years earlier Jacob had
been accused of delivering matzah to the conversos of Sogorb and convicted
for sending his baptized son to North Africa. It mattered less to María that Jacob
might possibly have encouraged conversos to Judaize than that "our rights and
our vassals . . . will remain whole."[115]

The bishop of Sogorb's procedure against Jacob Façan was trifling compared
to the torments that the inquisitor Barthomeu Gaçó and his colleagues inflict-

---

riana, whose nearly vacant Jewish quarters the Crown was resuscitating. King Martí saw to it that
they fulfilled their responsibilities to the aljama of Morvedre — ACA: C 2112: 42r (1397/7/11); C
2116: 16v–17r (1398/3/7); C 2126: 97v (1399/7/25). Some of the Jews therefore decided to return to Morvedre (C 2189: 181v–182r).

[112] ACA: C 2341: 123v–124r; C 2175: 11v–12r. ARV: P 1446, B. de la Mata: n.f. (1401/8/29)
records the aljama's payment of 300 sous to the noble Joan Roïs de Corella, which it owed him
annually "de violario ad vitam."

[113] ACA: C 2339: 129r-v; C 2177: 72v–73r (1404/2/7); C 2208: 141r-v (1409/12/7). Queen
María, however, had herself caused the aljama to enlarge its public debt. On 13 March 1402 she
permitted it to sell an annuity of 137 sous 6 diners to Joan de Cabrera, an official of her household,
for 150 florins (C 2339: 1r). The aljama needed the 150 florins for paying a "large annual pension" of 1,200 sous to Joan Robiols, a resident of Morvedre, and for rendering 50 florins to Andreas
de Aguiló, the queen's servant. The aljama raised the 50 florins for the queen in *gratuito animo.*

[114] ACA: C 2335: 88r (1398/5/18); C 2339: 109r-v (1403/12/6).

[115] ACA: C 2335: 89v–90r (1398/5/18).

ed on Jews in 1400 and 1401. It initially helped the inquisitors that they had
the king's blessing and the cooperation of lay officials. Yet their actions against
Jews did not involve examining the Talmud for heresies and blasphemies or
even trying Jews for encouraging converso backsliding. Instead they imprisoned several Jews on spurious charges of having received baptism in 1391 and
then abandoning the Catholic faith. Given the considerable confusion and
anxiety about religious allegiance, such charges were easy enough to make. All
the prisoners were women. Apparently the inquisitors' plan was to terrorize or
starve these women into submission, in the hope that their demoralized kin
would either follow them into the church or simply flee the kingdom. Gaçó
had experimented with such tactics in 1394, when he managed to precipitate
the flight of conversos from Borriana by jailing women, "both the innocent and
the guilty," and forcing their families to ransom them.[116]

These tactics unfortunately caused the death of the wife of Saçon Najari, a
Jew of Teruel, in 1401. Commissioned by the inquisition, Gil Sanchis Munyós, a canon of the see of Valencia, had proceeded against, and presumably imprisoned, her and her son Isaac. King Martí expressed outrage and surprise that
Sanchis would have damaged his "treasure" in this manner, and commanded
him to desist from vexing the Jews.[117]

Sanchis, it seems, was more obedient than his chief, the inquisitor Gaçó,
who was busy in Morvedre. The object of Gaçó's attention was a Jewish woman
named Mira, whom he accused of returning to Judaism after having received
baptism from a certain chaplain in the home of En Vallariola in 1391. The inquisitor rounded up witnesses to testify against Mira, but the witnesses afterward confessed that they had lied. Undeterred, Gaçó twice imprisoned Mira
for three days at a time, shackling and starving her. On hearing of this "inhu-
mane" treatment of Mira, Queen María had her own agents look into the affair and demanded that Gaçó send her a transcript of the "trial." Satisfied that
the case against Mira was a tissue of lies, she ordered the inquisitor, on 30 September 1401, to cease all action against her.[118] However, two months later and
after two more letters from the queen, Gaçó still held Mira in chains. King
Martí therefore intervened and informed Gaçó that if he did not immediately
release Mira he would be banished from Crown lands within eight days, and
if found there he would "keenly feel the wrath of our most cruel enmity."[119] If
the queen's anger had not fazed him, the king's certainly did.

Thus disciplined, the inquisitor shifted his attention to Jews who influenced
conversos to Judaize, the criminals King Martí had originally wanted him to

---

[116] ACA: C 1861: 34r-v (1394/4/7) [Hinojosa Montalvo 1993a, no. 219].

[117] ACA: C 2175: 18r (1401/8/5). C 2340: 35v–36r (1404/12/3) shows that Saçon later converted and took the name Gabriel de Najari (Nagera). For more on this family, see chap. 6.

[118] ACA: C 2338: 1v (1401/9/30).

[119] ACA: C 2174: 26r-v (1401/11/20–21), two letters [Baer 1929–36, 1: no. 474].

prosecute. Martí, however, was by now so disgusted by the inquisition's abuses that he reconsidered the question of inquisitorial jurisdiction in any cases involving Jews. Still pondering the matter, in December 1401 he significantly ordered only lay officials to investigate the allegations that Jaume de Lorde, a converso of Morvedre, had been "continually consorting" with Jews and "turning to [their] customs, rites, and observances."[120]

The following year the king reached a decision, which he related to Gaçó in August. The inquisitor was at the moment prosecuting Samuel Najari, son of the aforementioned Saçon Najari of Teruel, for having induced his son's conversa nursemaid to practice Judaism. Samuel had probably perpetrated the crime while residing in Valencia; perhaps he was still there.[121] In any case, King Martí rejected Gaçó's argument for inquisitorial jurisdiction over Jews in such cases, which the inquisitor based on the letters of Popes Nicholas IV and Boniface VIII.[122] Martí asserted that since the Jews were not members of the church, they could not fall under the jurisdiction of the inquisition. Furthermore, since the church tolerated the Jews despite their doctrinal errors, all punishment of the Jews pertained to kings and princes. The inquisitor, Martí concluded, was violating royal jurisdiction.[123]

The inquisition was quiescent for a time, but it resumed its offensive against the kingdom's Jews in the summer of 1404 and persisted in prosecuting Jews during the remainder of Martí's reign. In July the king expressed concern that inquisitorial activity might lead to the depopulation of the Jewish quarter of Castelló. There the inquisitor had jailed Samuel Abenafrit "for less than just causes, as is said." When Samuel fled town after being released on bail, the inquisitor attempted to punish his six Jewish guarantors. Again the king claimed jurisdiction over the Jews in matters temporal and spiritual.[124]

The inquisitors' remarkable perseverance in the face of royal opposition was attributable in no small part to the consistent support they received from the bishop of Valencia, Hug de Llupià.[125] The bishop and his agents actually did more than voice approval of the inquisition; they collaborated with it. Thus, when rising to the defense of the Jews of Morvedre in 1405, Queen María discovered that she now had more than one opponent.

---

[120] ACA: C 2233: 76v–77r (1401/12/9): "intendens ad mores et ritus ac observancias judeorum."

[121] ACA: C 2173: 7r-v (1399/8/12) is a royal license to Samuel to "stare et morari ac etiam . . . hospitari cum tuis familiis in quibuscumque domibus tam illorum qui non diu est conversi fuerunt ad fidem catholicam quam aliorum christianorum de natura" for as long as Samuel sees fit.

[122] Simonsohn 1991, 347–348; Grayzel 1989, 174–175, 209.

[123] ACA: C 2174: 105r-v (1402/8/5) [Baer 1929–36, 1: no. 476].

[124] ACA: C 2140: 174r-v (1404/7/15): "ex causis minus juste, ut dicitur";129r (1404/6/2) is Martí's similar response to complaints regarding the initiatives of inquisitors against Jews in Tortosa.

[125] Cárcel Ortí 1998.

First she contended with the inquisition. Realizing that her husband's trumpeting of the plenitude of royal power over Jews had not sufficiently impressed the inquisitors, she took a more pragmatic approach and effected a compromise with them as to their "mode of investigating" and "duly punishing" Jews in Morvedre. If the queen was willing to admit that perhaps some Jews deserved punishment, then presumably some Jews had been conniving in the Judaizing of conversos. Nevertheless, by May 1405 the queen was unhappy, alleging that the inquisitors had violated the agreement and were proceeding "incessantly" against some of her Jews.[126]

María seems to have persuaded the inquisitors to honor the compromise, but in July episcopal officials replaced the ministers of the inquisition as the Jews' tormentors. Much to her dismay, the local bailiff was not willing to prevent the bishop's men from entering the jueria; he probably feared being excommunicated.[127] The queen then proposed to the bishop that they each choose representatives to work jointly on the case that so interested him.[128] Bishop Hug, however, refused her offer, as the matter was of such great import to "the Holy Catholic Faith." It involved not Jews who led conversos astray but Jews who had been baptized and were now living publicly as Jews. The bishop therefore assigned the case to his Official, two masters in theology, and one Johan Carbonell.

The bishop's response evoked unsettling memories of the inquisition's horrible treatment of Mira four years earlier. Worse still, the Jews—more specifically Jewish women—whom episcopal agents meant to try were not ordinary women. One was Jamila, the daughter and heir of the wealthy and powerful Jew of Valencia Jahudà Alatzar (d. 1377). Her husband was Samuel Suxen, scion of the affluent Suxen family of Xàtiva and once adelantat of the aljama of Valencia. The other two women were Jamila's aunt Astruga, the affluent widow of Salamó Abenmarvez of Valencia, and Jamila's daughter, also named Astruga. Were these women condemned, the queen's treasury would sustain significant losses.

A bit of probing by the queen's men revealed that the main charges were against Astruga, Jamila's daughter, and that they had been made by her paternal uncle, the converso Manuel Salvador, formerly Mahir Suxen of Xàtiva. Salvador was apparently claiming that Astruga had returned to Judaism after baptism and that her mother and great-aunt had induced her to commit this grave crime against the Catholic faith. Salvador's intention, the queen maintained, was to have Astruga baptized so that she could then marry his converso brother-

[126] ACA: C 2340: 97v (1405/5/19).
[127] ACA: C 2340: 111v (1405/7/27). The queen also pointed out that King Martí had written to the justice of Morvedre instructing him to arrest the bishop's men if they did not cease acting against the Jews.
[128] ACA: C 2340: 111r-v (1405/7/27).

in-law, the husband of his (and Samuel Suxen's) deceased sister. Salvador had even brought the widowed brother-in-law from Monzón for the purpose. Salvador and his brother-in-law must have had designs on the large dowry that Astruga would bring to the marriage. As a consequence of Salvador's scheming, the bishop imprisoned the three women at the end of June and had all of Jamila's considerable assets inventoried.

The discovery that Johan Carbonell, the one layman assigned to the case, was an advocate of Manuel Salvador increased Queen María's suspicions about the whole affair. By September the bishop still had not conducted a proper trial, though he had managed to extract some confession from the young Astruga. The bishop seems to have believed Salvador's charges, or perhaps he was seizing the opportunity to coerce another Jew into the church and confiscate some of Jamila's wealth in the bargain. The queen, in any case, demanded that the bishop cease this unjust harassment of her vassals and forbid Carbonell's participation in the trial. She suggested that if there really was a crime against the faith, then she and her officials would be pleased to assist in the proceedings in accordance with the agreement she had reached with the inquisition. She then commanded the viceroy to free the women from the bishop's prison and to arrest Salvador if the bishop did not comply with her orders.[129] The bishop must have obeyed, for the women were soon back in Morvedre. Seven years later Astruga, Jamila's daughter, married a Jew of Calatayud, Mossé Constantin.[130]

Queen María's death at the end of 1406 deprived the Jews of Morvedre of their staunchest defender. No longer bound by their compromise with the queen, the inquisitors, and their allies in the episcopal palace, resumed the prosecution of Jews. Their charges against the Jews are obscure, though complicity in the heresy of conversos probably was the main crime alleged. Whatever the substance of the accusations, inquisitorial and episcopal officials were determined to profit from them. Hence they tried Jews and, whether innocent or guilty, granted them "sentences of absolution" for a price. The inquisitors devoted special attention to some of Morvedre's most prominent Jewish families, such as the Legems.[131] Nor had they and the bishop forgotten about the family of Jamila, the daughter of Jahudà Alatzar, and its significant wealth. In the fall of 1407 the inquisition indicted Jamila, her husband Samuel Suxen, and her aunt Astruga, most likely for consorting with conversos. There seems to have been something to the charges against them, for in November the king wrote to his governor about the money the Crown would collect from "the monetary settlements to be made by Samuel Suxen, Jamila, and Astruga, and

---

[129] ACA: C 2340: 121v–122r, 122v (both 1405/9/9).

[130] ACA: C 2360: 16v–17r (1412/8/19).

[131] ACA: C 2150: 137r (1407/2/4). Samuel Legem was arraigned before the inquisitorial tribunal "with other Jews . . . and Christians," undoubtedly conversos.

others before the inquisitor."[132] Martí would not have permitted the inquisition to penalize these Jews on the basis of frivolous charges.

The inquisitors and the bishop, however, were not finished with Jamila,
Samuel, and Astruga, and tried them the following year. This time, it seems,
they were falsely accused of being relapsed converts. By September a panel of
canon and civil lawyers had ruled in favor of Jamila and Samuel, granting them
a "sentence of absolution" and imposing "perpetual silence" on the prosecutor of the court of the episcopal Official. The prosecutor nonetheless appealed
the sentence and in the meantime continued to harass Jamila and Samuel.
King Martí ordered the bishop and the inquisition to reject such malicious appeals and to desist from molesting the couple and other Jews of Morvedre "for
it would only be to destroy and lose that [aljama]."[133]

Aunt Astruga, however, had not been acquitted and she still sat in the
bishop's jail. The king commanded that she be released on bail because "she
is very old and could very easily, due to the arduousness of the said jail, end
her days in it."[134] He was almost right: Astruga died at home shortly after her
release. Grief-stricken and outraged, Jamila desired that her aunt "though
dead, be preserved from all infamy," and thus obtained a sentence absolving
her of any guilt. As the heir of Astruga's property, which royal officials had already inventoried, Jamila had an obvious material interest in clearing her
aunt's name.[135] But it was also a matter of her family's honor, which, in the
eyes of other Jews, slander about Astruga's baptism would stain.

It was not just in Morvedre that the inquisitor, the bishop, and their minions
pursued this campaign of intimidation and despoliation. In the capital they
were disrupting commercial relations with North Africa by having the local
criminal justice remit Jewish, converso, and Muslim merchants to the bishop's
court on dubious grounds.[136] They also ransacked converso homes and inventoried the goods therein while merely alleging that the inhabitants were Judaizers. They showed less and less respect for due process of law, canon and
civil. Provoked by so much inquisitorial action against the conversos, local Old
Christians were calling them "circumcised dogs" and otherwise insulting
them. To escape such treatment, some conversos were fleeing the city and even

[132] ACA: C 2236: 52v (1407/11/23).
[133] ACA: C 2156: 186v (1408/9/12); C 2186: 104r-v (9/16): "no enquieten los dits juheus ne
altres de la dita aliama, car no seria sino destrouir e perdre aquella."
[134] ACA: C 2186: 104r-v: "es molt vella e fort facilment, per la greujament de la dita preso,
poria finir sos dies en aquella."
[135] ACA: C 2163: 82v (1409/6/2). ARV: B 1219: 69r-v (1409/12/23): Samuel Suxen promises,
before the lieutenant bailiff general, to pay what he, Jamila, his daughter Astrugueta, and the deceased Astruga owe to Jacme Vilarzell, a notary of Valencia, for his services during their encounters with the inquisitor and the bishop.
[136] ACA: C 2163: 1v–2r (1409/2/11) concerns Isaac Almalhe, a North African Jew ; C 2237:
86r (3/12) addresses the general problem.

emigrating to Muslim lands to return to Judaism. These excesses, the monkish king remarked, burdened his conscience greatly and damaged his patrimony.[137] He insisted that they cease.

Nevertheless, it is clear that after María's death, King Martí less effectively limited inquisitorial and episcopal abuse of Jews and conversos in the kingdom of Valencia. However extensive the Judaizing of conversos and however great the complicity of professing Jews in their heresies, the modus operandi of the inquisition and the bishop had become increasingly irregular, if not illegal. While filling their own coffers, the inquisitors and the bishop worked to impoverish conversos and Jews, and to drive them either out of the kingdom or irrevocably into the church. Even though the king tried to put an end to the worst abuses, it was often too little too late.

The Christian inhabitants of Morvedre were of course witnesses to the parade of royal, inquisitorial, and episcopal officials descending on the local Jewish quarter, or on Jewish and converso homes outside it, between 1393 and 1410. Their reaction to all this anti-Jewish activity is largely uncertain because the sources are remarkably silent about it. Doubtless some were inspired to inform royal or ecclesiastical authorities about the Jewish observances of a converso neighbor in the company of local Jews or were subpoenaed to testify before the tribunal of the inquisition. Yet the notion, propagated by the inquisition and sometimes by the Crown, that Judaism was now a kind of infection, transmissible to Christians via baptized Jews, did not resonate much in Morvedre. Local Christians did not regard the advent of papal inquisitors as a signal or a justification for rising up to rid their town of its growing Jewish population. Although relations between Jews and Christians in Morvedre were not by any means free of difficulties, the origins and limited extent of local troubles are revealing.

In July 1391, as has been seen, the Christians of Morvedre gave a mixed reception to the mob arriving from Valencia to destroy the Jewish community. Leading families and municipal officials defended the Jews. Other Christians joined the Valencian mob and continued to conspire against the Jews throughout the rest of the year. But by the winter of 1392 most Jews felt safe enough to leave the local castle and return to the jueria. This was a consequence of King Joan's encouraging words and orders, and of the efforts of vigilant royal and municipal officials.

It was therefore ironic that in 1393–94 the actions of royal officials inspired the Jews' local enemies to make trouble for them. The Crown's prosecution of Jacob Façan and David el Rau for having sent their baptized sons to North Africa gave "certain" individuals the idea of denouncing other Jews falsely for the same crime. Although Christian residents of a coastal town exposed to the raids of Maghriban corsairs might well have taken up arms against Jews sus-

[137] ACA: C 2163: 23r (1409/3/8).

pected of maintaining contacts with the "Barbary Saracens," the Jews complained not of threatened violence but of being "exhausted" by unnecessary judicial expenses. Few local Christians seem to have indulged in King Joan's fantasies of Jewish-Muslim conspiracies or Jewish satanic magic.[138]

Yet when local Christians actually did perpetrate violence, it left the Jews quite shaken. Just before dawn, on 10 December 1394, a Jewish widow, Meora, and her maidservant were robbed and murdered. Consequently, King Joan reported, the "aljama and its members stand in great fear, and not without reason, considering that not too long ago there occurred riots against the Jews of the kingdom." Lest an unpunished attack on Jews set in motion an unfortunate train of events, the king enjoined the governor, municipal officials, and local knights to apprehend and rigorously punish the murderers.[139] Despite royal and Jewish anxieties, this isolated homicide was not a prelude to mob violence. In fact, consistent with the pattern of violence in 1391, the Jews of Morvedre were subsequently mistreated less by local Christians than by citizens of the capital.

The governors of Valencia had neither sought nor engineered the destruction of their city's huge Jewish community, but once it was a fait accompli there was, as far as they were concerned, no turning back. The removal of the Jews was, after all, convenient, for it fit with the image of the city as a Christian republic that they self-consciously cultivated.[140] Hence they sacralized the 1391 violence with miracle stories and endeavored to prevent the reappearance of a Jewish blemish on the city's façade. Municipal officials did not approve of King Joan's plans to reestablish an aljama and so worked to isolate and humiliate the remaining Jews, forcing them in 1394 to wear special badges.[141] Obtaining in 1397 the royal "privilege" prohibiting the revival of a Jewish community was a great victory.[142]

The Jews of Morvedre unfortunately still needed to travel to Valencia for business purposes. The citizens of the now Jew-free capital looked none too kindly on the Jewish visitors, and "under the veil of the [royal] privilege . . . very often molest, injure, and offend [them] by word and by deed." The Jews were, as a result, too frightened to enter the city, which was just what the citizens wanted. King Martí, in contrast, desired Jewish freedom of movement in the interest of the kingdom's commerce and the royal treasury.[143]

---

[138] ACA: C 1908: 75v–76r (1394/3/1) [Hinojosa Montalvo 1993a, no. 211].

[139] ACA: C 1862: 157v–158r, 158r-v, 158v–159r (1395/2/25) [Hinojosa Montalvo 1993a, nos. 240–242].

[140] Rubio Vela 1981; Narbona Vizcaíno 1992a, 79–121, and 1994.

[141] ACA: C 1927: 164r–165r (1394/4/3); C 2030: 136v–137r (9/3), 137v (9/15) [Hinojosa Montalvo 1993a, nos. 218, 231, 235], from which it is clear that they were forcing the Jews to wear badges against the wishes of the king and queen.

[142] ACA: C 2209: 149r–150r.

[143] ACA: C 2114: 40v–41r (1397/7/11).

The jurats of Valencia, however, were not persuaded by the Crown's economic arguments. Royal and inquisitorial investigations were making plain the
extent of converso backsliding. A city full of Judaizing heretics, the jurats rea-
soned, was not much better than a city full of Jews. They were intent on shield-
ing the conversos from Jewish influences. Thus, in the spring of 1400, they ordered the criminal justice to arrest and jail Jewish merchants and lenders
visiting from Morvedre.[144] If the letters of the king and queen convinced the
jurats to release the Jews from jail, they did not divert them from their larger
goal. The jurats wrote to King Martí in June, pointing to the Jews of Morvedre
as a special danger.[145] In September they beseeched the king to issue an order
prohibiting all Jews from entering Valencia; the Jews, they suggested, could
employ Christian agents to take care of their affairs.[146] The issue, in which the
Morvedre Jews had a fair amount at stake, was not settled until the Corts of
1403.

The first Corts held by Martí in the kingdom of Valencia, it enacted legislation intended to shield the capital's huge converso community further from
excessive exposure to Jews and Judaism.[147] Jewish residents of the kingdom
were the main object of the legislation, since they were most likely to have baptized relatives in Valencia and therefore most likely to attempt to seduce them
from the church. When visiting Valencia on business they could not be lodged
in the three converso parishes — Sant Thomàs, Sant Andreu, and Sant
Esteve — or in any converso home elsewhere in the city. Nor could they stay
in the city for more than ten days, although the bailiff general could license
them to remain for as long as four months. While in Valencia, they were required to wear a large red and yellow badge on their outer garments. Violators
of these regulations would pay a fine of 50 morabatíns or be whipped through
the city. In the interest of commerce, however, the legislation did not apply to
foreign (non-Valencian) Jews. In fact, the bailiff sometimes permitted them
to be lodged in converso homes.[148] Yet even the foreign Jews were forbidden
to slaughter meat or bake matzah in Valencia, and they had to leave town during any Jewish holiday. This legislation could not have wholly satisfied the municipality, but it suited the Jews' purposes.

However, one element of the 1403 legislation, rather like King Martí's privilege to the city of Valencia in 1397, had the potential to legitimize the anti-

---

[144] ACA: C 2337: 138r-v (1400/4/7). ARV: JC 50: M. 4, 23r–24v (1400) shows that the justice
arrested and interrogated at least two Jews from Morvedre, Salamó Alolaig and Jahudà Corquoz.

[145] AMV: LM g3–7: 1r-v (1400/6/9) [Epistolari, 1: no. 105].

[146] AMV: LM g3–7: M. 2, n.f. (1400/9/18) [Hinojosa Montalvo 1993a, no. 262].

[147] ACA: C 2322: 43r (1403/9/28); ARV: C 630: 350r-v [Hinojosa Montalvo 1993a, no. 270].

[148] ARV: B 1219: 68v (1409/12/20): license to Astruc Abenjarin, from Lorca, Castile, to "posar
en casa d'en Francesch Castellar, convers sartre de Valencia" for two months; 108v (1410/7/14):
license to Isaac Frances of Toledo to be lodged in the house of either Johan Palomar or Lop Rodríguez, both conversos.

Jewish behavior of Christians so inclined. This was the provision demanding
that all Jews wear a badge half red and half yellow in color so that they could
be more easily distinguished from Christians, New and Old. For the Jews of
Morvedre, the problem with this badge was that it was larger and, with its yellow half, more noticeable than the red badge Joan I had ordered them to wear
in 1396. The Jews feared that the new badge would incite Christians to deride
and harass them and would thus make life more difficult for them than it already was. The jurats of Morvedre wasted little time: the following year they
were importuning the local bailiff to force the Jews to wear the more humiliating badge. Queen María then intervened on behalf of *her* Jews, asking the
jurats to refrain from further action until she could consult with them a few
days hence in Morvedre.[149]

Having decided not to enforce the specifics of her husband's legislation, and
indeed to countermand it, María convinced the jurats that the small red badge
was more than sufficient. Later that year, since the Jews of Morvedre traded so
much in Onda, she asked the master of the Order of Montesa not to enforce
the legislation.[150] All officials in any place where the queen possessed "certain
titles" received a command to this effect.[151]

The desire of the jurats of Morvedre to have the Jews wear the new badge
did not stem from a concern to inhibit their fraternizing with conversos. Even
though the inquisitors had made their presence felt in Morvedre, they were not
behind the scenes directing the jurats. The jurats' motives in attempting to humiliate the Jews further were jurisdictional and fiscal rather than religious.
They were lashing out at the Jews in frustration, because they could neither
tax the Jews as they wished nor exercise any authority over them.

Relations between the municipality and the aljama had begun to sour in
1398, just when the aljama—but not the municipality—was attached to the
treasury of Queen María. Whereas in July 1397 the king had lauded municipal officials for "maintaining and defending" the Jews,[152] between 1398 and
1404 he and the queen reprimanded them several times for annoying the Jews.
Municipal officials resented the Jews' new and separate status as special wards
of the queen. Before 1398 municipality and aljama, the two corporations comprising the town, had always been answerable to the same higher authority.
Now, however, Queen María and her own officials were interposed between
municipality and aljama; they upset the status quo. The officers of the munic-

[149] ACA: C 2339: 116r (1404/5/15).
[150] ACA: C 2340: 38r (1404/12/8) [Chabret Fraga 1979, 2: 342 n. 1].
[151] ACA: C 2340: 38r-v (1404/12/8). C 2339: 188v–189r (10/16) is a similar command to the
jurats of Sogorb with regard to the Jews who "stan e habiten" there, and who "se dubten que no
sostinguen molts scarniments e vituperacions" should they "aporten roda o senyal inordonat e pas-
sant mesura." Jews of Morvedre were frequent visitors to Sogorb.
[152] ACA: C 2114: 40v (1397/7/11).

ipality viewed the new situation both as a blow to their own authority as the governors of the town and as an opportunity to profit at the expense of the Jews.

The municipal justice made the first move. Reacting to the efforts of the queen's men to inhibit him from adjudicating civil litigation between Christians and Jews, and thus from collecting any resultant judicial fines,[153] in 1398 and 1399 the justice aggressively and defiantly interfered in cases involving Jews.[154] The next year it was the turn of the jurats and prohomens. They began by unilaterally modifying the agreement of 1370 prescribing Jewish liability for municipal sales taxes; presumably they increased either the rates paid by Jews or the number of taxable items. Then, in 1402–3, they threatened to collect the peita from the Jews for the property they held inside the Jewish quarter[155] and to force the Jews to pay higher peita rates for the houses they owned outside the quarter.[156] The promulgation in 1403 of the new badge law was therefore timely in that it provided municipal officials with another means of forcing their will on the Jews. When Queen María appeared in Morvedre in late May 1404 to cow the jurats into forgetting about the larger badge, she probably also resolved outstanding fiscal issues between them and their counterparts in the aljama. After this, municipal officials were, with regard to Jewish affairs, relatively docile.[157]

Given the tension between aljama and municipality, it is surprising that the officials of the latter did not stoop to turning to the inquisition to bring pressure on the Jews or to appropriating inquisitorial propaganda about "Judaizing heresies" for their own purposes. The jurats must have realized that there was no point in risking the destruction of a community they hoped to tax more heavily.

The web of financial interdependence in which Jews and Christians had

[153] Although the local bailiff, as the representative of the king, had always possessed, and still possessed, supreme jurisdiction over the Jews, the local justice, as the town's main judge, had often adjudicated civil suits between Christians and Jews — e.g., ACA: C 1857: 30v (1393/6/3) [Hinojosa Montalvo 1993a, no. 172]. That things changed under the queen's regime can be seen in ACA: C 2341: 139v (1404/7/13), regarding the plea of Anthoni Cabestany against David el Rau, which the queen's chancery court adjudicated.

[154] ACA: C 2116: 15v–16r (1398/3/1); C 2311: 57v–58r (1399/8/4), 62r-v (10/16); C 2337: 98v–99r (11/4), which is the last instance of such interference. See also Meyerson 2004c.

[155] ACA: C 2311: 80v (1400/9/3); C 2337: 171v (9/18); C 2126: 126r (12/13); C 2311: 85r-v, 85v–86r (1401/1/19); C 2341: 44r (1/20).

[156] ACA: C 2338: 88v–89r (1402/5/20); C 2174: 109r (8/18); C 2339: 8v (1403/5/9). See Meyerson 2004c for details.

[157] Hence they remained unruffled and indifferent when the Jew Maymó Vidal tried to get his Jewish enemy, Jucef Legem, into deep trouble by falsely accusing him of pimping and sleeping with Christian women (ACA: C 2205: 19r-v [1407/7/5]). A Jew living in an ambience of palpable Christian hostility would not have resorted to mudslinging of this sort, for it might endanger not just his enemy but the entire community. Even though the accusation was false, Jucef still had to pay the Crown 70 florins for a "pardon."

been enmeshed was not torn beyond repair in 1391. The events of that year, the repercussions of which compelled the aljama to sell many censals, actually increased the number of Christians with a stake in the Jewish community's survival.[158] Also, when aljama officials periodically farmed out the wide range of sales taxes they levied internally, Christians were most likely among the tax farmers.[159]

Just as Christian farming of Jewish cises and investment in the aljama's communal debt indicate a normalization of the economic relations between the two communities within a decade of 1391, so does Jewish leasing of the Crown's fiscal revenues in Morvedre. The Jews, however, although they had played a prominent role in local tax farming prior to 1391, largely abandoned this activity between 1391 and 1400. Deeming it unwise to antagonize Christians unnecessarily by being implicated in the collection of taxes from them, Jews leased only some of the minor utilities, the wax press and the dyeworks. But by 1400 the Jews' confidence had returned: from this year through 1414 Jews were leasing some of the more important and lucrative utilities, like the royal mills and ovens, and farming a variety of agricultural tithes. In some cases, moreover, Jewish tax farmers pooled their resources with Christian partners.[160] In other words, it was, for the most part, business as usual in Morvedre.

Fernando I

And so it might have remained had not King Martí died an untimely death, leaving no heirs. The dispute over the succession and the resultant Compromise of Caspe, in June 1412, brought a new dynasty to the Crown of Aragon, the Trastámaras of Castile. The triumph of the first Trastámara, Fernando I (1412–16), owed much to the support of the Aragonese pope Benedict XIII

---

[158] E.g., ACA: C 2339: 1r (1403/3/18) concerns the annuity sold by the aljama to Johan Robiols of Morvedre; 14r-v (6/7), the queen's license to the aljama to redeem a censal it had sold to Bernat Palomar of Morvedre for 2,000 sous (it carried an annual pension of 166 sous 8 diners). The local clergy also had an interest in the Jews' presence. The benefice of Santa Ana in the main church, held in 1404 by the priest Francesc Otger, was partially endowed with rents from houses leased to Jews in the jueria (C 2340: 32v [Hinojosa Montalvo 1993a, no. 276]).

[159] ARV: MR 39: 5v, 155v show that Christians farmed the cisa levied on kasher wine in 1419 and 1420; they probably did so in earlier years. ACA: C 2339: 109r-v (1403/12/6), the royal license to the aljama to institute its system of cises, indicates that Jews could sell kasher wine (more likely must) and meat to Christians and Muslims; so does the Crown's lease to Samuel Legem of two butchering tables located at the entrance to the jueria (C 2340: 27v [Hinojosa Montalvo 1993a, no. 275]). Assis 1997, 226–227, regards the Jews' sale of kasher meat to Christians as a source of Christian disgruntlement, itself an indication of how Jewish-Christian relations "deteriorated" in the later thirteenth and early fourteenth centuries. That such sales could occur in the fifteenth century — with royal approval — shows that the deterioration of relations was not irreversible.

[160] Meyerson 1998, 69–71.

and of the Valencian Dominican Vicent Ferrer. Their continued influence on the new king and their own missionary activities had catastrophic consequences for the Jews of the Crown of Aragon.

Intent on converting the Jews, Ferrer preached to captive Jewish audiences throughout Castile and the Crown of Aragon. Even though he had criticized the violence and forced baptisms of 1391, his inflammatory preaching, which attracted large crowds of Christians, caused attacks on Jews. Some demoralized and terrorized Jews converted. Ferrer was also very anxious about the ill effects of contact with Jews on Christians, especially conversos, and therefore called for the complete separation of Jews from Christians. He even demanded the excommunication of Christians who continued to mingle with Jews. Ferrer's ideas inspired the oppressive laws promulgated in Castile in 1412. The aim of these laws, which, if fully enforced, would have reduced the Jews to impoverished pariahs, was to pressure the Jews to convert.

One of Ferrer's converts, Jerónimo de Santa Fé, formerly Joshua Halorki, convinced Pope Benedict to stage a disputation at his court in Tortosa. The pope required each Jewish community in the Crown of Aragon to send from two to four scholars to debate with the Christian spokesman, Jerónimo. The length of the Disputation of Tortosa, which went on from January 1413 to December 1414, and the disadvantageous position of the Jewish disputants, exhausted the Jews and added to their despair. Many more throughout Crown lands sought baptism. In 1415 the pope and King Fernando issued anti-Jewish legislation modeled on the Castilian laws of 1412.[161]

Like all Jews of the Crown of Aragon, the Jews of Morvedre were deeply affected by these traumatic happenings. Special circumstances, however, left them more vulnerable to injury than most Jewish communities. First of all, the municipality of Morvedre developed a close, symbiotic relationship with the new monarch and was disposed to do his bidding. During the interregnum extending from Martí's death to the decision at Caspe the kingdom of Valencia had been divided between supporters of the Castilian Fernando and those of the rival candidate, Jaume, count of Urgell, the great-grandson of Alfons III, Martí's grandfather. Jaume's adherents were headed by the noble faction of the Vilaragut and included the governor and the city of Valencia. Another noble faction, the Centelles, captained Fernando's backers. Moved by their longstanding grievances against the capital, the political elite of Morvedre, and the nobles of its terme, sided with the Centelles. On 27 February 1412 the decisive battle between the two parties was fought outside Morvedre, where the Centelleses' forces had gathered. Fernando's supporters triumphed. Only one week after being publicly declared king, on 5 July 1412, Fernando rewarded Morvedre by restoring autonomy to the town.[162] Valencia immediately ap-

[161] Baer 1961, 2: 166–243; Kriegel 1979, 181–226; Vendrell 1950, 1953 and 1960.
[162] Chabret Fraga 1979, 1: 299–311.

pealed the king's decision and his successor, Alfonso IV, would later rescind it. In the meantime, the people of Morvedre cooperated enthusiastically with their new king.

Second, Vicent Ferrer visited Morvedre on at least two occasions. Local Christians could not have been unmoved by his passionate orations, for when preaching on his home turf and in his native tongue, the Valencian friar was at his best. Ferrer, "with all his honest company," came to Morvedre sometime in June 1410 "to preach and to celebrate masses."[163] He returned there in the fall, in the company of Bishop Hug, in order to calm the mounting hostility between the townspeople and the government in the capital. Morvedre had been refusing entry to the governor, and only Ferrer, a great peacemaker, could persuade the jurats to recognize, temporarily, the governor's authority. The town, however, soon enough joined the Centelles and embraced Fernando's cause.[164]

Whether Ferrer preached to the Jews on these occasions, or spoke about the Jews in his sermons to Christians, is unknown. Given that Morvedre had the largest number of Jews in the kingdom, it is hard to see how he could have resisted the temptation to confront the Jews or at least to admonish Christians to keep a distance from them. If he ignored Jewish affairs for the moment, it was only because political issues during the interregnum were more pressing.

Ferrer appeared again in Morvedre in late November 1412, with his "society" of male and female followers.[165] This time Jewish conversion and segregation were almost certainly on his agenda. Such objectives would have been consistent with his preaching campaigns among the Jews of Castile and Aragon the previous two years and the new Castilian Jewish laws, promulgated at his instance.

They also would have been consonant with the measures that the municipality of Valencia took against converso Judaizing in early 1413, in response to Ferrer's preaching and counsel. In December 1412 the inquisitor, Francesc Sala, had demonstrated to the jurats that Judaism still had many adherents among the city's conversos.[166] Among other things, conversos were washing and rubbing the baptismal chrism off their infants, circumcising their male

---

[163] Chabret Fraga 1979, 1: 301, citing the now lost registers of the municipal council of Morvedre. AMV: LM g3–10: 12r–13v, 19r-v (1410/6/17–22) treat Ferrer's coming to Valencia.

[164] Chabret Fraga 1979, 1: 303–305.

[165] AMV: LM g3–11: 136r (1412/11/26).

[166] On 9 November 1412 the jurats wrote to Pope Benedict XIII asking that he restrain Sala, who had allegedly been unduly vexing local conversos (AMV: LM g3–11: 128r-v). One month later, however, they asked the pope not to intervene, since Sala had appeared before them with records of his *processus* against the neophytes. A law professor, Guillem Çaera, was about to examine them so that it could be determined "quid per justiciam sit agendum" (AMV: LM g3–11: 144v–145r [12/9]). Judging by the letters issued by the jurats in 1413, it seems that Sala had convinced them that there was indeed a lot of converso Judaizing. See also Meyerson 2003a.

children, not receiving extreme unction at time of death, and performing Jewish rituals.[167] In April 1413 the jurats and the city council decided on a plan of action. "Moved by the holy teachings of the reverend Master Vicent Ferrer touching this matter," the council decreed that all the New Christians must live among the Old Christians; those still residing in the area of the former jueria had to vacate it within fifty days. This would facilitate the full assimilation and Christianization of the converso population.[168]

Almost every place Ferrer preached about the dangers of Jews and Judaism to Christians and of the need to isolate the Jews who still refused baptism, he incited local Christians to maltreat the Jews in some way. During the year following his visit to Morvedre, some Christians were molesting the Jews "in divers manners," prompting King Fernando to admonish municipal officials to protect the Jews from all "oppression and violence."[169] As the king did not issue these instructions until 4 November, almost a full year after the Dominican preached in Morvedre, news from the papal court at Tortosa, where Judaism was then being put on trial, must also have spurred Christians to harm the Jews. The combination of Ferrer's fiery sermonizing and Pope Benedict's assault on Judaism was almost too much provocation for any Christian to withstand.

It was also too much for some Jews to bear. Whether as a result of Ferrer's harangues, the abuse of Christians, or the distressing news from Tortosa, at least four Jews in Morvedre sought baptism. They were Samuel Legem and his son Abraham, who took the Christian names of Joan de Sant Feliu and Francesc Suau, respectively; David, the grandson of the deceased David el Rau, who became Pere de Pomar; and a converso named Gabriel Andreu. There were probably others.[170]

Fernando I's efforts to proselytize the Jews, at the instance and through the agency of Vicent Ferrer and Benedict XIII, thus bore fruit in Morvedre. Still, Fernando wanted to protect the remaining professing Jews. They formed part of his patrimony, and assaults on them constituted an affront to royal authority. On the same day that he urged the jurats of Morvedre to defend the Jews,

[167] AMV: LM g3–11: 191r (1413/3/13).

[168] AMV: LM g3–11: 204r-v (1413/4/17), 205r-v (4/19): the jurats inform the king of their intentions. AMV: MC A-25: 179r–180v (4/12) [partially transcribed in Hinojosa Montalvo 1993a, no. 288] is the actual legislation of the Consell. MC A-25: 197r (7/15), 248v (7/26) show that enforcement of the legislation was delayed until September 1413.

[169] ACA: C 2384: 81v (1413/11/4).

[170] For the Legems, see below. ACA: C 2375: 173r-v (1415/8/23) concerns Pere de Pomar. ARV: MR 3992: 24r (1413) notes the collection of 6 sous from Gabriel Andreu, converso, due to Bernat Matzen's charge against him. ACA: C 2388: 67r (1415/1/10) refers to "alguns conversos" in Morvedre. See also chap. 6. As for the impact of the Disputation of Tortosa on the Jews of Morvedre, neither Pacios López 1957, 1: 51–58, nor Riera i Sans 1974 gives any evidence of a representative of the aljama of Morvedre at the disputation. This does not mean that a Jew or Jews from Morvedre were not present. In any case, news from Tortosa would have reached Morvedre quickly enough.

he also licensed the aljama to levy internal sales taxes for another five years.[171] This, however, was not a prelude to heavy taxation. Indeed, aside from ordinary taxes, he demanded only minor extraordinary subsidies from the aljama during the rest of his short reign.[172]

Balancing the desire to convert the Jews with the duty to preserve the royal patrimony proved difficult for the king. After the success of the Disputation of Tortosa, which caused many Jews in his realms to seek baptism, proselytizing Jews and seeing to the needs of the neophytes emerged more clearly as priorities.[173] In Morvedre he devoted more attention to the recent converts than he did to the Jews.

Fernando took considerable interest in the affairs of the family of the convert Samuel Legem, or Joan de Sant Feliu. A prominent member of the Jewish community, Legem had been an adelantat, tax farmer, and lessee of the Jewish abattoir. The king understood that the Crown's treatment of this converso's family and its fortunes after his baptism would be noticed by other Jews and would perhaps sway some to consider baptism more seriously. First the king had to help Samuel persuade his wife, Bonafilla, and their children to join him in the church. To this end, he permitted Samuel to continue living with his family in the jueria; in such close quarters he could hopefully wear down their resistance.[174] He also sweetened the deal by offering to free Samuel and Bonafilla for ten years from all their debt obligations to other Jews and the aljama. The grant of this *guiatge*, however, was conditional on Bonafilla's conversion.[175] Neither this bribe nor other royal expressions of goodwill, like the protection of her dowry from her husband's creditors, succeeded in drawing Bonafilla away from the synagogue.[176]

Still, one adult son, Abraham, followed his father's example. Paternal persuasion alone had not changed Abraham's mind; the Crown had dangled before him the prospect of a bright financial future. King Fernando licensed both father and son to become brokers. He also allowed Abraham, now Francesc

[171] ACA: C 2384: 81v (1413/11/4).

[172] ARV: MR 3992 (1412–18) for ordinary revenues. Extraordinary taxes included 440 sous for the coronation of King Fernando, collected in 1413 (ACA: CR Fernando I, caixa 28, no. 3569; ARV: MR 34: 63r-v [Hinojosa Montalvo 1993a, no. 286]); 275 sous for the coronation of Queen Elionor, and the same quantity for expenses related to Sardinia, both collected in 1414, and 330 sous for the marriage of Prince Alfonso to María of Castile, collected in 1415 (ARV: MR 35: 71v; MR 36: 31v, 88v, 91v, 93r [Hinojosa Montalvo 1993a, no. 291]).

[173] Vendrell 1950; Baer 1961, 2: 210–243.

[174] ACA: C 2394: 83v–84r (1415/6/22). Fragmentary evidence shows that Samuel Legem had been adelantat in at least 1397 (ACA: C 2114: 40r-v), 1401 (ARV: P 1446, B. de la Mata: n.f. [8/29]), and 1404 (ACA: C 2339: 160r–161r).

[175] ACA: C 2388: 132v–133r (1415/6/20).

[176] ACA: C 2375: 134r-v (1415/7/12). ARV: B 318: M. 2, 29v (1422–23) shows that Bonafilla was still Jewish in November 1423.

Suau, to stay in his house in the Jewish quarter.[177] The king hoped that other Jews contemplating the success of this young converso broker would be impressed by the material advantages of baptism.

The king's show of favor to neophytes does not seem to have induced many other Jews to abandon their faith. Much of the damage had already been done by Vicent Ferrer, Pope Benedict, and Jerónimo de Santa Fé. Furthermore, the behavior of some of the neophytes toward their former coreligionists was not likely to have caused the latter to look more favorably on Christians and Christianity. The converts of 1413–14 were a different breed than those who had opted for baptism in 1391 in an atmosphere of absolute terror. Ferrer and his flagellant followers were frightening and the reports from Tortosa disturbing, but the Jews who sought baptism in 1413–14 did so after careful deliberation and rationalizing. Unlike the converts of 1391, who had immediately regretted their decision and returned to performing Jewish rituals with other Jews, this second group of apostates endeavored to justify to themselves and to Old Christians their abandonment of Judaism. Hence, instead of returning to Judaism, they openly denigrated it; and instead of gently entreating Jews to join them in the church, they viciously turned on them in manifest denial of their own origins. By 1415 it was primarily neophytes, not Old Christians incited by Ferrer, who, along with some "other subjects," were conspiring to cause Jews in Morvedre to be "mistreated and to come to some inconvenience."[178]

King Fernando ordered his officials to put a stop to such activities. Yet he himself was soon "inconveniencing" the Jews much more than the conversos were. Pope Benedict was eager to finish the work he had started with the Tortosa disputation. Many Jews had converted; through applying the right kind of pressure the others, already demoralized, would follow. Thus in a papal bull of 11 May 1415 he called for a series of restrictive measures against the Jews. On 23 July Fernando ratified the pope's provisions and ordered that they be enforced throughout the Crown of Aragon. Copies of the Talmud, the cause of the Jews' "blindness," were to be confiscated; Jews were to attend the sermons of Christian preachers three times each year; among other economic activities, Jewish usury and tax farming were prohibited; Jews were to wear a red and yellow badge; and Jews were to reside in separate areas.[179]

King Fernando was dead within nine months of issuing this order, but there was time enough for at least some of the measures to be put into effect in Morvedre. The Jews ceased farming the Crown's fiscal revenues, and, though the king permitted the Jews to collect the debts that had been contracted be-

[177] ACA: C 2374: 190r-v (1415/7/15). Apparently Abraham had converted just a few weeks earlier, for ACA: C 2375: 113v–114r (1415/6/22) still refers to him as Abraham Legem, the son of Joan de Sant Feliu and Bonafilla.
[178] ACA: C 2388: 67r (1415/1/10).
[179] Vendrell 1960.

fore 23 July, they probably did not make any new loans.[180] At the urging of
Jerónimo de Santa Fé himself, municipal officials took steps to delimit and enclose the Jewish quarter. First they precisely designated the boundaries of the
quarter and then they instructed the Jews themselves to close it off by the end
of September. By late December, however, the Jews still had not acted. True,
the local bailiff, Bernat Çaydia, had granted them an extension, but even that
had expired. The king thus reprimanded the bailiff, who then forced the Jews
to enclose the undoubtedly smaller Jewish quarter.[181] In 1420 King Alfonso IV
would observe that the place is "so confined" and conditions so crowded that
the Jews could "hardly cohabit in it decently."[182]

Even though they were crowded and economically disadvantaged, the Jews
of Morvedre did not endure the same kinds of abuse that Christians inflicted
on their brethren in some Aragonese and Catalan towns.[183] For whatever reason, Christians in Morvedre did not take advantage of the king's orders to molest local Jews inordinately. If the nine months leading up to King Fernando's
death were not as long as they might have been, the changes brought about by
his successor were no less dramatic.

[180] Meyerson 1998, 71; ACA: CR Fernando I, caixa 16, no. 1941 (n.d.).
[181] ACA: C 2391: 61v–62r (1415/12/20).
[182] ARV: C 393: 22v–23r (1420/3/4).
[183] E.g., Baer 1929–36, 1: no. 495, on Huesca.

Chapter Two

REVIVAL IN THE SHADOW OF VALENCIA

AFTER THE DEATH of Fernando I in April 1416, the atmosphere of fear, despair, and persecution that had frequently pervaded the Jewish quarter of Morvedre since the summer of 1391 slowly but surely dissipated. In its place an ambience of security and optimism arose. The reigns of Fernando's successors, Alfonso IV (1416–58) and Juan II (1458–79), constituted an era of recovery and prosperity for the Jews of Morvedre. Compared to the ups and downs the Jews had experienced since 1348, or even since 1283, these six decades were remarkably placid.

The most obvious sign of the well-being of the aljama of Morvedre was its demographic growth. In 1492 the community numbered seven hundred; it had nearly tripled in size since 1390.[1] Morvedre became more Jewish than ever before as the town's Christian population plummeted. The Jewish community's expansion resulted partly from the rearrangement of the kingdom's socioreligious landscape and the displacement of Jews from the capital and other towns to Morvedre in and after 1391. Yet the desire of Jewish immigrants to remain in Morvedre and the ability of new as well as established Jews to survive and thrive there were attributable, more positively, to several interrelated factors. First and foremost was the monarchy's return to a favorable Jewish policy. Apart from the royal personalities involved, this was made possible in part by the development of the monarchical state. Its more efficient fiscal machinery and growing reliance on new credit mechanisms, which had already been changing the Jews' position in the kingdom's credit markets, allowed for a relaxation of intense fiscal pressure on the Jews and thus broke the vicious cycle that had linked Jewish moneylending and debt collection to royal taxation and that had injected much hostility into Jewish-Christian relations. Almost as crucial was the role of Morvedre's town fathers; they usually welcomed the Jews and, because of the Jews' demographic weight and importance to the local economy,

---

[1] Hinojosa Montalvo 1995, 281–282, and 1983, 112, 119. Yet ARV: C 138: 39r-v (1496/2/9) notes 120 Jewish households, "in which there were more than five hundred souls." In order to explain the discrepancy, I would suggest that this figure refers to those Jewish families who had a fixed, permanent domicile in Morvedre, whereas seven hundred includes Jews who were members of the community, and were thus counted as such at the moment of embarkation in 1492, but who, as itinerant merchants or lenders, or as farmers, had domiciles in other regional towns and villages. Such a dispersed residential pattern of the "Jews of Morvedre" would be consistent with their geographically wide-ranging economic activities.

increasingly depended on them. At the same time, the mutually beneficial relations between the Jews and the Christians of the town and its environs broadened and deepened. Even the governors of the city of Valencia, under whose
jurisdiction Morvedre remained, became well-disposed toward the Jews of
Morvedre who traded in their city and contributed to the regional economy.
For them, there was nothing incongruous about their city without Jews lording it over a town full of them just up the coast.

Royal Policy

A great Renaissance prince, Alfonso IV, the Magnanimous, pursued dynastic
ambitions in Italy more assiduously than he administered his territories in the
Crown of Aragon. He spent very little time in the kingdom of Valencia; after
1432 he never returned to his Iberian realms from Italy, where he ruled from
1443 as the king of Naples. Such royal absenteeism was not without its benefits for the Jews of Morvedre and other Crown aljamas, for after the excessive
attention of Fernando I, they could stand a bit of benign neglect. Yet Alfonso's
Jewish policy was not merely passive. Early in his reign, before fully immers-
ing himself in Italian affairs, he took decisive steps that markedly improved the
status of the Crown's Jewish communities, including Morvedre. In doing so,
he laid the foundations of a Jewish policy that was consistently followed by his
brother Juan, whether functioning as lieutenant general of the kingdom of Valencia or as king.
   Even as a prince acting in his father's stead in the kingdom of Aragon, Alfonso had shown himself to be a less than enthusiastic supporter of the anti-
Jewish initiatives of Vicent Ferrer and Pope Benedict XIII. Whether on hu-
manitarian and legal grounds or at the urging of influential converso officials
from the Cavallería clan, he intervened on behalf of Aragonese aljamas subjected to the harassment of municipal officials inspired by Ferrer's preaching
and his own father's statements. Alfonso also opposed the anti-Jewish ordinances of Benedict XIII subsequently sanctioned by his father's pragmatica.
When the Council of Constance, in its effort to heal the Schism, called on all
three popes to renounce their claims to the papacy, Alfonso took a harder line
against Benedict than his father, who reluctantly abandoned the Aragonese
pope in January 1416. The election of a new pope, Martin V, in November
1417, enabled Alfonso to seek the annulment of Pope Benedict's anti-Jewish
bull and to revoke his father's pragmatica.[2]
   Alfonso and Pope Martin did not act immediately, however. Not until February 1419 did the pope, at Alfonso's request, nullify Benedict XIII's ordi-

---

[2] Ryder 1990, 29–31, 37–43, 57–59; Jiménez Jiménez 1959, 254–255; Baer 1961, 2: 244–
245; Riera i Sans 1993b, 76–77.

nances.[3] Then, on 21 March, heeding the remonstrations of the aljamas that his father's anti-Jewish legislation had taken them to the brink of "destruction and depopulation," Alfonso agreed to rescind the laws.[4] His order of rescission addressed the Jews' concerns point by point. Talmudic texts would be returned to the Jews once a board of theologians, including one converso, expunged all heresies and statements against the Catholic faith and the New Testament. Jews would no longer be compelled to leave their quarter to hear the sermons of Christian preachers; instead, the preachers would be allowed to enter the Jewish quarter along with some Christians whose number a royal official would limit. Jews could practice medicine and function as brokers and tax farmers, as long as the latter task did not entail their exercising jurisdiction over Christians. Jews could own stores in Christian neighborhoods and keep them open during daylight hours as long as their homes were in the Jewish quarter. Jews could establish all sorts of notarized contracts and *instrumenta* with Christians as long as they were not usurious.[5] Jews could dispose of their property in wills, and if they died intestate their heirs could still inherit in accordance with Jewish law. However, if any of the heirs were Christian, they too would receive their legitimate portion. Finally, in order to obviate any danger to Jewish travelers, Jews would be allowed to travel outside their hometown without wearing the Jewish badge.[6]

There was nothing revolutionary in all of this. What had been truly extraordinary was the conjunction of a Vicent Ferrer, a Pope Benedict XIII, and a king, Fernando I, willing to follow their lead. Alfonso's revocation of his father's ordinances signified a return to tradition, for unlike that trio, he did not contemplate or push for realms devoid of Jewish and Muslim subjects. His view of the Jews' place in Christian society was rather Augustinian. A few years later, on learning that some Christians in Borriana were threatening to inflict violence on the local Jews, Alfonso enjoined municipal officials to protect them, pointing out that "divine wisdom" permitted the "perfidious and stubborn" Jews to live in memory of the penalty they suffered for having "inhumanly crucified" Christ. He also reminded the officials that the Jews "are part of our royal treasure."[7] Indeed, more than theology, what guided Alfonso in his treatment and defense of the Jews was "a strictly patrimonial view of his office," a concern to preserve "the powers, properties, and attributes of his crown."[8]

[3] ARV: C 630: 235r–237r (1419/3/21) [Hinojosa Montalvo 1993a, no. 304].
[4] ARV: C 630: 235r–237r; Jiménez Jiménez 1959, 259–262; ACA: C 2590: 170r–172r (1419/6/28) [Hinojosa Montalvo 1993a, no. 306].
[5] ACA: C 2590: 173r-v (1419/6/28) [Hinojosa Montalvo 1993a, no. 308].
[6] ACA: C 2590: 182r-v (1419/7/12) [Hinojosa Montalvo 1993a, no. 309].
[7] ARV: C 39: 11v–12r (1427/3/4).
[8] Ryder 1990, 360; cf. Riera i Sans 1993b, 78. Thus when Alfonso learned from aljama officials that some Jews had moved from Morvedre to seigneurial lands, he declared that the Jews, as the royal treasure, did not have the right to settle in seigneurial villages without his permission, and

Once the oppressive legislation of 1415 was repealed, Alfonso could take more positive steps to promote patrimonial interests in Morvedre. Working on the principle that "the greater the number [of Jews] the more useful it will be for us and for them [the Jews of the aljama]," he called in 1420 for an end to the confinement of the Jewish community and for the physical expansion of the Jewish quarter. Overcrowding had probably made the community more vulnerable to the plague that struck in 1417 and reduced its population. The king hoped that his measure would alleviate the discomfort of the current Jewish inhabitants, still sizable in number, and attract new ones.[9] A year later the community numbered sixty households, a noticeable increase on the fifty-three counted in 1409.[10] Some of the sixty may well have moved to Morvedre from lordships in the vicinity immediately after the renovation of the jueria. In any case, in 1424 the king encouraged the commercial activities of these sixty householders with a safe-conduct protecting their persons and goods wherever they might travel.[11] While fostering his Jewish communities, in Castelló and Borriana as well as in Morvedre, Alfonso also endeavored to draw Muslims from seigneurial lands to royal towns. During his reign a Muslim aljama reemerged in Castelló; efforts to increase the population of the recently constructed *moreria* of Morvedre continued.[12] This certainly was not the sort of urban landscape Vicent Ferrer had envisioned for his native land.

King Alfonso's early, personal efforts on behalf of the Jews of Morvedre and other aljamas did not come to naught as a result of his long absence from the Crown of Aragon. On the contrary, owing to the absenteeism of Alfonso and his successor, Juan II, who spent much of his reign fighting a civil war in Catalonia, a larger and more effective royal bureaucracy perforce developed. In the kingdom of Valencia the lieutenant general, the king's alter ego, was a key official, but most important for Jewish affairs was the bailiff general, the guardian of the royal patrimony. Members of the Mercader family, a veritable dynasty, occupied this office through much of the fifteenth century.[13] They faithfully and vigorously pursued the Jewish policy initiated by King Alfonso.

Self-interest, not simply a sense of duty, motivated the bailiffs general and the local bailiffs to safeguard Jewish interests and administer Jewish affairs ef-

he commanded the bailiff to take all necessary actions to ensure that "our royal rights and prerogatives are preserved" (ACA: C 2458: 131v–132v [1416/10/4]).

[9] ARV: C 393: 22v–23r (1420/3/4); MR 41: 294v–295v (1422/5/28) [Hinojosa Montalvo 1993a, no. 322] noting the impact of the 1417 plague.

[10] Hinojosa Montalvo 1995, 278.

[11] ARV: C 32: 51r (1424/3/3) [Hinojosa Montalvo 1993a, no. 333].

[12] Doñate Sebastià and Magdalena Nom de Déu 1990, 46–50, 177–178; Díaz de Rábago 1994, 37–38. *Aureum opus*, 197r (1428), for Alfonso's legislation encouraging the transfer of Muslims to royal towns. King Martí had initiated this policy early in the century, but not until 1413 was a new Muslim quarter established in Morvedre; it had fourteen households (ARV: MR 3992: 23v). Meyerson 1991, 18–33.

[13] Furió 1995, 176–182; Belenguer Cebrià 1989, 351–373; Piles Ros 1970.

fectively. Damage to Jewish persons and property, restrictions on the movement of Jewish traders, and the undue interference of municipal or seigneurial officials in Jewish concerns challenged the bailiffs' authority and eroded one of their sources of revenue. The bailiffs general, moreover, were all jurists with a precise understanding of the royal laws and privileges that regulated Jewish life and defined their own jurisdiction over the Jews. Not only did they enforce the king's laws, but they drew on their legal arsenal to admonish those who dared to violate them. After the bailiff of Alcalà de Xivert arrested a Jew visiting from Castelló for not wearing the Jewish badge, he received a cautionary letter from the bailiff general to which was appended a copy of King Alfonso's Latin privilege, issued twenty years earlier, permitting Jews to travel incognito.[14] Municipal justices most frequently encroached on the bailiffs' jurisdiction over the Jews. When the lieutenant justice of Morvedre, Francesc Scrivà, overstepped his authority, the bailiff general bombarded him with copies of nine royal letters detailing the prerogatives of the office of bailiff.[15] In a kingdom with a mushrooming bureaucracy whose inhabitants increasingly turned to the courts to settle their disputes, the Jews were fortunate to have on their side royal officials skilled at wielding the law. It helped, too, that the most recent laws relative to Jews were the very favorable ones King Alfonso had promulgated.

The transition from the reign of Alfonso IV to that of Juan II could not have been smoother for the Jews of Morvedre. In 1459 King Juan readily confirmed the privileges which his predecessors, including Alfonso, had vouchsafed them. The 500 sous the aljama had rendered on the occasion of his succession encouraged his benevolence, but it was hardly a princely sum.[16] Like his brother, Juan protected his Jewish and Muslim subjects and promoted the development of their communities in royal towns. As a matter of course he ordered the indemnification of two Jews of Morvedre unjustly fined for riding on the road to the capital without their badges on display, and reprimanded officials hindering the commerce of Jews in the Vall d'Uixó.[17] The Jewish community in Morvedre as a whole, however, did not require any special royal initiatives.[18] By Juan's reign it was already vibrant and populous. From 1462, when King Juan became fully occupied with the Catalan civil war, Valencian Jews were left in the capable hands of the bailiff general.[19] In the long term

---

[14] ARV: B 1148: 542r-v (1439) [Hinojosa Montalvo 1993a, no. 458].

[15] ARV: B 1150: 80r–83v, 90r (1447/4/15) [Hinojosa Montalvo 1993a, no. 487].

[16] ARV: C 281: 78r (1459/2/5) [Hinojosa Montalvo 1993a, no. 580].

[17] ARV: C 280: 141r–142r (1459/7/20); C 90: 59r-v (1461/7/28) [Hinojosa Montalvo 1993a, no. 605].

[18] But that in Xàtiva did: King Juan offered current and future Jewish inhabitants a five-year moratorium on the payment of debts, and licensed them to fix the royal coat of arms over the door of the synagogue as a symbol of the king's protection (ARV: C 287: 103r–104r [1462/2/26]).

[19] After February 1462 there is a striking dearth of specifically royal letters treating Valencian Jewry until the reign of Fernando II.

the extended absences of Alfonso IV and Juan II probably worked in the Jews' favor, inasmuch as the monarchs were not around to tamper with policies that had proven fundamental to their recovery.

The persisting religious and social problem of the conversos had surprisingly minimal impact on how Alfonso IV and Juan II treated their Jewish subjects. Early in the reign Alfonso evinced concern about converso Judaizing in the city of Valencia. On 12 April 1419 he ordered the dissolution of the converso confraternity of Sant Cristòfol. He believed that separate converso confraternities and cemeteries served only to perpetuate division and "rancor" between Old and New Christians. Furthermore, he had been informed that the confreres engaged in ceremonies "deviating from good Christian practice." Although the king changed his mind a few months later, after having been persuaded that some of the suspicions about the confraternity's activities were unfounded, he still would not permit the confraternity to enlarge its cemetery, a symbol of converso segregation. He also threatened the brothers with severe punishment if they performed Jewish rituals.[20]

Crown officials and churchmen continued to regard excessive contact with Jews, especially Jewish relatives and friends, as a factor inhibiting Valencia's conversos from fully assimilating into Christian society. Still, they recognized, as King Martí had, that the commerce of Valencian and foreign Jews could not flourish if they were denied access to the capital. Joan Mercader, the bailiff general, was not about to propose anything that would severely hamper Jewish trade. After conferring with the bishop of Valencia, Alfons de Borja (or perhaps his deputy, the Franciscan Nicolau Martorell), and the royal counselor and Carthusian Francisco de Aranda, Mercader decided in 1433 that the most that could be done to "avoid the enormous abominations resulting from the comradeship and participation of Jews with the neophytes of that city" would be to enforce more vigilantly the restrictive legislation enacted in the Corts of 1403. He therefore had public criers make proclamations to that effect throughout Valencia. Prince Juan, Alfonso's lieutenant general, approved Mercader's measures and ordered officials throughout the kingdom to announce and execute the laws. Such restrictions would not have prevented — and indeed did not prevent — conversos committed to Judaism from observing Jewish holy days, but they might have furthered the gradual assimilation of Valencia's converso population by limiting its exposure to the sights and sounds of the Jewish festive year. Jews were also prohibited from working as artisans in the city or its suburbs.[21]

Though more rigorous enforcement of the laws perhaps inconvenienced Jewish traders from Morvedre and other Valencian towns, it did not cause any

---

[20] ARV: B 1145: 211r-v (1419/4/12). Castillo Sainz 1993, 197–198, 201–202.

[21] ARV: C 398: 113v–114r (1433/11/13); C 630: 323v [Hinojosa Montalvo 1993a, no. 473]. See chap. 1 for the 1403 legislation.

real hardship. Throughout the reigns of Alfonso IV and Juan II the kingdom's Jews were hardly bothered by measures stemming from royal and ecclesiastical anxieties about converso Judaizing. The monarchs' anxieties were in any case not terribly high. Alfonso, who had expressed concern in 1419 about the alleged Jewish rituals of the converso confraternity of Sant Cristòfol, in 1426 licensed Cresques Nasci of Morvedre and his entire family to reside in any parish of the capital for four years.[22] Licenses of this sort, which violated the restrictions of 1403 and perhaps prompted the bailiff general to reiterate them a few years later, made it easier for any interested confrere of Sant Cristòfol to learn more about Judaism and to participate in Jewish rituals. By 1453 King Alfonso was so out of touch with the affairs of Valencian conversos that he permitted the confraternity to expand its cemetery and thereby accentuate the ethnic particularity of its members.[23] Juan II, who had seconded Joan Mercader's efforts twenty-five years before his accession, did little that affected Valencian conversos other than appointing them to posts in his own government.[24]

Consistent with their benevolent and protective Jewish policies, King Alfonso and King Juan kept the Dominican inquisitors at a healthy distance from the Jews.[25] The Jews' experience under these monarchs thus differed markedly from that of the 1391–1416 period, when the inquisitors prosecuted and at times persecuted Jews in the course of their campaigns against Judaizing conversos. The inquisition, however, was not inactive in Valencia. During the 1460s it tried fifteen conversos, several of Castilian and Portuguese origin, for Judaizing. These families attracted the attention of the inquisitors because they were attempting to travel to the East, where they intended to return to Judaism and await the Messiah. The fall of Constantinople to the Ottoman Turks in 1453 had sparked messianic hopes and movements among converso communities in Valencia and other Iberian towns.[26] Had the inquisitors at this point conducted investigations as thorough as those the Spanish Inquisition would pursue in the 1480s, they would have uncovered considerable evidence of conversos leading a Jewish ritual life and of Jews from Morvedre assisting them in their endeavor.[27] The rather desultory efforts of the papal inquisition in the Crown of Aragon during the reigns of Alfonso and Juan afforded the Jews and most conversos a lengthy reprieve.

In Valencia, moreover, the economic success and sociopolitical ascent of a good number of conversos did not generate the heated controversies and political violence that plagued converso life in contemporary Castilian towns. Va-

[22] ARV: C 394: 100v (1426/8/3).

[23] Castillo Sainz 1993, 197–198.

[24] Garcia 1987, 68–69.

[25] This is obvious from the silence of the Valencian documentation; also Riera i Sans 1993b, 77.

[26] Baer 1961, 2: 292–295; García Cárcel 1976a, 38; Carrete Parrondo 1992, 47.

[27] See chap. 6.

lencian conversos were important merchants; they entered the professions and government offices largely unimpeded by the discriminatory legislation the conversos of some Catalan and Aragonese towns faced.[28] Only at the end of Juan II's reign, in 1477–78, did the jurats of Valencia attempt to ban conversos from holding posts in the municipal government. The jurats and their allies opposed the conversos because they regarded them as agents of a monarchy then tightening its grip on the city. This political maneuvering, however, did not bring violence in its wake; nor did it seriously hamstring the conversos.[29] Relative calm reigned in Valencia, a factor of great significance for the Jews of Morvedre who traded and visited converso friends and relatives there.

Taxation and Migration

The monarchy's return to a more traditional Jewish policy and relief from inquisitorial oppression were fundamental to the revival of the Jewish community in Morvedre. The Jews benefited as well from the fiscal regime that had emerged in the last third of the fourteenth century and was consolidated in the fifteenth. In the era of reconstruction following the Castilian invasion the Jews had scarcely had time to enjoy the relative financial stability the new regime afforded them before the catastrophic events of 1391 threw Jewish life into disarray. King Joan and especially King Martí had then worked energetically to hold the Morvedre community together and to keep its finances reasonably healthy, but persistent inquisitors and the triumvirate of Vicent Ferrer, Benedict XIII, and Fernando I threatened and nearly ruined whatever stability and progress had been achieved. The fairly peaceful years under Alfonso IV and

---

[28] Guiral 1975; Garcia 1987, 66–76. See Meyerson 1995a, 106–110, for a comparison of the circumstances of conversos in Castile and in the Crown of Aragon. Although I would qualify my comments in light of Riera i Sans 1993b, 86–89, I believe that my larger points are still valid. For Catalan and Aragonese discriminatory legislation, Riera i Sans 1993b. A general plea by Catalan and Valencian conversos to Pope Eugenius IV, dated 31 January 1437, regarding the efforts of Old Christians to deny them access to public office is the only evidence of attempted discriminatory measures in Valencia (Beltrán de Heredia 1961, 37–38). If there were such measures in Valencia, they did not last long and had minimal effect. The only town in the kingdom of Valencia that saw anticonverso violence like that which erupted in Castile was Oriola in the south (Hinojosa Montalvo 1993a, 276–277). This was, I believe, because Oriola had a political culture much like that of Castilian towns.

[29] Garcia 1987, 77–82; Belenguer Cebrià 1976, 73–81; Cruselles 1992, 132–135. Rubio Vela 1998, 87–90, suggests, however, that some Old Christian members of the municipal oligarchy harbored resentment for conversos that was bitter enough to have led to violence. Still, violence did not erupt. Old Christian action against conversos occurred earlier in Catalonia (Riera i Sans 1993b, 86–89) because opposition to the Trastámara monarchy arose sooner there and was, during the civil war (1462–72), considerably more violent. In contrast, Valencians consistently cooperated with Alfonso IV and Juan II.

Juan II permitted the Jews to feel fully the effects of integration into the state's new fiscal apparatus.

For the Jews the main virtues of the fifteenth-century fiscal regime were its regularity, predictability, and moderateness. The Jews were no longer subjected to the dramatic and demoralizing raids of kings and royal tax collectors on their resources. They no longer had to deal with the sort of direct extraordinary taxation that, until the 1360s, had left their aljamas scrambling and scraping to come up with the huge subsidies frequently and sometimes perversely demanded by the king. Of course, in the larger scheme of things, after 1416 the monarchs did not really view the significantly smaller and poorer Jewish population of the Crown of Aragon as their "treasure," except as a matter of patrimonial principle.[30] At the regional level, though, an official like the bailiff general of the kingdom of Valencia might well label the flourishing Jewish community in Morvedre as the "king's treasure" without the slightest bit of irony.[31]

Still, however worthy of exploitation the monarchs regarded their Jewish aljamas individually or in the aggregate, they did not need to dwell on the matter because the new fiscal machinery, especially that operating in the kingdom of Valencia, enabled them to exploit the resources of their subjects — Jewish, Christian, and Muslim — in a different and more efficient manner. The politically pliant and economically vibrant kingdom of Valencia furnished both Alfonso IV and Juan II with substantial sums for their various enterprises, like the conquest of Naples and the Catalan civil war. It provided far more than either Catalonia or the kingdom of Aragon.[32] Indirect sales taxes, duties on commerce and production levied by the Valencian Corts to pay royal subsidies, and recourse to credit, in the form of censals, by the Corts and the municipalities in order to finance their subventions and loans to the monarchy — these were the key elements of the fiscal system. Liability to the wide array of taxes and contributing to the annuity payments of their respective municipalities and aljamas proved burdensome for individual taxpayers of all faiths, but for the Jews this system, in its regularity and predictability, was less distressing than the sudden fleecings to which their forebears had been subjected.[33]

Throughout the fifteenth century the peita that the Crown collected from the aljama of Morvedre annually remained fixed at 2,000 sous. To this was added a standardized "right of protection" tax of 150 sous.[34] The aljama also contributed to the "salary" of the local bailiff with annual payments ranging from 900 to 1,850 sous.[35] The size of the payment was based, presumably, on

[30] Riera i Sans 1993b, 78–79; Meyerson 2004a for the pre-1360 period.

[31] Cf. Küchler 1968, 234–236, 241–243.

[32] Sevillano Colom 1951; Küchler 1997.

[33] Furió 1997b; Garcia Oliver 1997a.

[34] ARV: MR 3998–4024 (1398–1492).

[35] Records of the sums the Jews paid the bailiff are spotty: ARV: MR 45: 88v–89r (1424–25):

the number of services the bailiff had performed on the Jews' behalf the previous year. Given the bailiff's crucial role in Jewish affairs, it was money well
spent. All these sums — peita, protection tax, and bailiff's salary — the aljama
rendered every year without fail.

The Jewish householders on whom peita payments were incumbent actually rendered significantly more than the portion of the 2,000-sous "royal peita"
for which aljama officials assessed them. They also paid the "communal (or aljama) peita," which was based on a valuation of their assets, especially real estate. The aljama retained the majority of its peita income to defray communal
expenses, which included disbursing annuities to its many creditors.[36] Hence,
when individual Jews grumbled about the amount of their contribution to the
peita, they were referring less to their share of the royal peita than to their share
of the communal peita. Furthermore, by virtue of the agreement of 1370, Jews
also paid the peita to the municipal government for the property they held outside the Jewish quarter. They therefore contributed to the peita that the Crown
received from the municipality.[37] However anomalous it might have been for
Jews to pay the peita to both municipality and aljama, the latter body could not
have met its responsibilities to its constituent families, much less to its creditors and the king, without receiving such revenue.

Another key source of revenue for the aljama was the series of taxes (*cises*) it
levied on the sale of foodstuffs, especially kasher meat and wine, and other
items between Jews, both locals and visitors. The aljama had benefited from
some such system of indirect taxation since 1327.[38] In the fifteenth century,
however, because the royal peita had become a fixed quantity, the Crown
began to draw on the substantial sums aljama officials annually received when
they farmed out the cises to Jewish and Christian investors. From as early as
1416 the Crown received one-fifth of the cisa revenue collected by the aljama.
The sums deposited in royal coffers could be substantial: 1,120 (of 5,600) sous
in 1416; 1,004 (of 5,020) sous in 1419; and 1,022 (of 5,110) sous in 1420.[39]

King Alfonso viewed his fifth of aljama sales taxes as discretionary funds he
might employ to assist the aljama when it fell on hard times. In January 1418,
on account of a recent outbreak of plague, which left the aljama "diminished

---

1,500 sous for 1424, 1,000 sous for 1425; MR 48: 96v (1429): 900 sous; MR 49: 97v (1430): 1,000
sous; MR 50: 94r-v (1431): 1,850 sous in two payments; MR 57: 100r (1442): 1,440 sous; and MR
96: 72r (1487): 1,699 sous 6 diners.

[36] I am assuming that aljama fiscal organization paralleled that of the Christian municipalities
(cf. Baer 1961, 2: 35–73; Assis 1997, 67–109), on which see Viciano Navarro 1990, 645–647, and
1992, 513–517; Furió 1997b, 515–516; Mira Jódar 1997, 538–539.

[37] See introduction; also Doñate Sebastià and Magdalena Nom de Déu 1990, 66–90, 278–
281.

[38] Meyerson 2004a.

[39] ACA: C 2384: 81r-v (1413/11/4): royal license to the aljama to institute internal cises for a
five-year period. ARV: MR 39: 85r-v [Hinojosa Montalvo 1993a, nos. 299, 301] for 1416; 155v for
1419; MR 40: 46r-v for 1420.

and very oppressed [by debt]," he empowered the *maestre racional*, the Crown's fiscal auditor, to remit one-half of the royal fifth to the aljama. It used the funds to liquidate censals owed to specific creditors.[40] Cisa revenues were affected throughout the 1420s and into the 1430s by recurrent plague and famine.[41] The aljama thus took advantage of the king's assistance and received further remissions from the maestre racional in 1421, 1422, 1423, and 1427.[42] In 1430, because of another famine, the aljama abolished the cises with royal consent, otherwise already dear basic foodstuffs would have been priced out of the reach of the poor.[43]

Apparently the aljama did not receive or even request another license to levy cises until 1450.[44] Because of the economic uncertainty caused by more famine and other natural catastrophes, attracting prospective tax farmers willing to put their money at risk had become too difficult and bothersome for aljama officials.[45] There was also the danger of antagonizing poorer Jewish families by reimposing sales taxes. In November 1438 the adelantats complained that a recent outbreak of plague as well as other "adversities of the aljama and its members" had caused such "depopulation" in the Jewish quarter that they doubted whether the aljama could even pay the royal peita. As it happened, the Crown did collect the peita.[46] The community, in fact, had not sustained losses such as to deter King Alfonso from exacting 3,300 sous from it little more than a year later to subsidize his conquest of Naples.[47]

As a result of nature's afflictions, to which the northern half of the kingdom in particular was subjected, the Christian population in Morvedre, which had

[40] ARV: MR 41: 294v–295v [Hinojosa Montalvo 1993a, no. 322]. King Alfonso was, from the beginning of his reign, quite scrupulous with regard to taxation of the Jews. Thus in 1416, when aljama officials asserted that the aljama had not previously been liable for the *cena de presencia* Alfonso was then demanding, Alfonso personally examined "the book of cenas" documenting King Martí's seven visits to Morvedre. He discovered that Martí had never collected the cena from the Jews and decided to follow Martí's example (ACA: C 2456: 181r-v [10/30]).

[41] Iradiel 1989, 270–272; Piles Ros 1969, 115–119.

[42] ARV: MR 41: 294v–295v (1421); MR 42: 311v–312r (1422); MR 44: 74r-v, 306r-v (1423) [Hinojosa Montalvo 1993a, nos. 322, 325, 328–329]; MR 46: 97r, 139v (1427). It is striking that in 1423 the total cisa revenues collected by the aljama — 1,958 sous 6 diners — amounted to less than half of the sum the aljama received in 1420. In 1423 and 1425 the Crown did not receive any cisa revenue from the aljama due to its "great poverty" (MR 43: 62v [1423]; MR 45: 88v–90r [1425] [Hinojosa Montalvo 1993a, nos. 324, 345]).

[43] ARV: B 1147: 301v–302r (1431/10/4). García Marsilla and Sáiz Serrano 1997, 315–320.

[44] ARV: B 1151: 100r-v (1450/8/28) [Hinojosa Montalvo 1993a, no. 510].

[45] Jews of Morvedre had themselves ceased farming municipal taxes between 1415 and 1445 — Meyerson 1998, 71–72.

[46] ARV: B 1148: 468r (1438/11/22) [Hinojosa Montalvo 1993a, no. 457]; MR 4000: 5r, 27r.

[47] ARV: B 1149: 6v–7r (1440/1/29) [Hinojosa Montalvo 1993a, no. 463]. This was part of the 10,000-florin subvention the king was collecting from all his Muslim and Jewish aljamas (Küchler 1968, 231, 233–234, 241). The aljama of Morvedre did not cry poverty to the king; it merely sought permission to borrow money in order to pay him quickly.

already diminished from 1,297 hearths in 1379 to 878 in 1421, shrank to only 768 households in 1445. Not all had succumbed to plague or famine; some had emigrated to the capital to replenish its population. The Jewish population descended from sixty to fifty-two households between 1421 and 1445.[48] The Jews, however, could not have moved to Valencia, though there were other royal towns or even seigneurial villages where they might have migrated.

By 1450, when the bailiff general granted the aljama the cisa license, the Jewish community had already entered a phase of unmitigated demographic and economic expansion that continued until the expulsion. Recognizing the vitality of the community, the bailiff general reissued the license in 1452 with the added stipulation that the aljama must render annually 770 sous for the royal fifth.[49] Although at this juncture in the community's history 770 sous represented significantly less than one-fifth of cisa revenues, the frequency of substantial lags between the farming out of cises and the aljama's actual receipt of revenue from the tax farmers made it more sensible for the bailiff to demand a quantity the aljama could easily hand over in timely fashion.[50]

Understanding that the collection of the cises was, for the tax farmers, a slow process, Juan II simply remitted to the aljama the royal fifth of cisa revenues when he renewed its cisa license for another twenty years in 1459.[51] The king was not displaying unusual generosity here; rather he was adopting a strategy for the more efficient and rapid fiscal exploitation of the aljama. The aljama could now use all its cisa revenues to pay the annuities it would sell to creditors in order to finance the subsidies the king required. Thus, at the same time, Juan also granted the aljama permission to sell censals valuing 4,000 sous so that it could immediately render 1,000 sous to him and the queen on the occasion of their succession and in return for his confirmation of its privileges.[52]

King Juan, however, did not tax the Jews of Morvedre too heavily. After all, compared to the sums he could and did receive from the city of Valencia, or even from the kingdom's Muslim communities, Jewish revenue was small potatoes.[53] Like his predecessor, he required the Jews of Morvedre to pay small

---

[48] Hinojosa Montalvo 1995, 280; Iradiel 1989, 268; Piles Ros 1978. The 1445 data is problematic, however, as it comes from a list of Jews paying the peita with the aljama of Morvedre. By virtue of the accord reached between the kingdom's aljamas in 1437 (see below), Jews who had since then come from other towns to Morvedre would still have paid the peita with their aljama of origin, and vice versa.

[49] ARV: B 1151: 568v–570r (1452/7/31) [Hinojosa Montalvo 1993a, no. 529]. This was the same quantity stipulated by the Crown in the short-lived cisa license issued in 1428 — ARV: C 256: 11v–12r (8/12) [Hinojosa Montalvo 1993a, nos. 365–366].

[50] Cf. Küchler 1997, 134–135.

[51] ARV: C 281: 78v–79r (1459/2/5) [Hinojosa Montalvo 1993a, no. 581].

[52] ARV: C 280: 58v–59v. In this permit the king reminded aljama officials that the remitted royal fifth of cisa revenues would help them finance the aljama's public debt. Cf. Mira Jódar and Viciano 1996, 141–146; García Marsilla and Sáiz Serrano 1997, 325–327; Furió 1997b, 509–510, 524–525.

[53] Sevillano Colom 1951; Küchler 1997, 433–467, and 1968, 234–236, 240–241.

quantities to subsidize royal coronations or the marriages of members of the royal family.[54] Juan demanded some larger sums as well. For instance, in 1461, when political tensions with Castile prompted him to borrow 110,000 sous from Valencia, he also exacted 2,500 sous from the aljama of Morvedre. He promised the Jews that he would not seek such subventions or even loans for the next five years.[55] The king honored his promise.[56]

Fernando II (1479–1516) exacted extraordinary subsidies from the aljama of Morvedre more frequently than his father had.[57] Royal licenses to the aljama to sell censals came in tandem with these demands.[58] The burden of censals carried by the aljama therefore grew, though from 1482 the bailiff general insisted in each license that the aljama liquidate its debts to the purchaser of the censal within four years.[59] The bailiff inserted this condition in the licenses to prevent the aljama's public debt from spiraling out of control.[60] Thus the aljama's experience would not likely have paralleled that of the municipality of Valencia, which royal taxation and a mounting public debt brought to the point of financial crisis in the early sixteenth century.[61]

More importantly, the extraordinary fiscal demands that King Fernando made of the Jews of Morvedre were, like those made by his father and uncle, moderate. After 1438, when nature had treated the community severely, aljama officials did not express any doubts about their ability to provide the funds the Crown required; they did not complain about institutional poverty. Royal

---

[54] Küchler 1968, 235. The Jews of Morvedre paid the following to Juan II: 550 sous in 1461 for Juan's coronation (ARV: MR 71: 233r); 275 sous for the coronation of Queen Juana (MR 71: 237v); 220 sous in 1473 for the marriage of Princess Juana (MR 94: 191v–192r); 123 sous 4 diners for the marriage of Juan's illegitimate daughter Leonor (MR 94: 198r) [Hinojosa Montalvo 1993a, nos. 606, 717, 723].

[55] ARV: C 287: 51r-v (1461/9/14); Küchler 1997, 436–437.

[56] Hence not until 1466 was the aljama asked to pay the salaries of Christians of Morvedre serving the king in Catalonia (ARV: B 1153: 725v–726r [Hinojosa Montalvo 1993a, no. 661]). Regarding additional subsidies, sometime prior to October 1475 nineteen members of the aljama jointly sold an annuity to Francesca, the wife of Luis Erau, for the purpose of gathering funds for a "donation" of at least 1,000 sous to the king (B 1155: 517r-v [Hinojosa Montalvo 1993a, no. 751]). Just one month before King Juan's death the aljama paid him a small fee of 500 sous for the renewal of its cisa license (ARV: C 396: 133r-v [1478/12/20]).

[57] ARV: C 303: 80v–82r (1479/10/10). Fernando's confirmation of the cisa license granted by his father in 1478 (see n. 56) is indicative of the new king's intention to impose a heavier tax burden — he demanded a fee of twice the size.

[58] APPV: P 17861, L. Miralles (1479/10/13): the aljama sells an annuity of 120 sous to a local notable, Joan Castellnou, for 1,600 sous, to raise funds for a royal subvention of 2,000 sous.

[59] ARV: B 1157: 156v–157r (1482/1/7) [Hinojosa Montalvo 1993a, no. 795]. This censal was sold to help finance a royal subsidy of 2,000 sous. ARV: B 218: 63r-v (1485/3/18); B 219: 24r-v (1488/2/21) are later licenses linked to royal subsidies of 2,000 and 3,000 sous, respectively.

[60] The aljama still had to pay off debts outstanding from censals incurred decades earlier. ARV: B 217: 661v–662r (1483/12/17) for the censal sold to Jaume Munyós in 1388 and now the property of Joan de Sant Feliu; 663v–664r (1484/1/26) for the censal sold to Francesc Berenguer in 1406. All three were members of notable Christian families of Morvedre.

[61] Belenguer Cebrià 1976; García Cárcel 1981, 39–90.

taxation neither dampened nor thoroughly exploited the community's prosperity in the half century preceding the expulsion. The size and frequency of
the king's extraordinary taxes did not keep pace with the demographic and economic expansion of the community. Jewish industry and commerce were of
course taxed by the growing number of fees and duties, but this distressed Jews
no more than it did Christians or Muslims. The Jews no longer occupied a special place in the calculations of the king's treasurers; they had perforce ceded
the limelight to municipalities like Valencia. Being indispensable had benefited the Jews, but so did the loosening of the Crown's fiscal vise.

Despite the relative moderateness and regularity of the fiscal regime during
the fifteenth century, the Jews of the kingdom did wrangle over questions of
taxation. The disputes erupted more frequently between aljamas than within
them. They were usually sparked by the movement of a Jewish family from one
community to another, as each aljama claimed the family's tax payments for
its own coffers. In contrast to earlier centuries, when interaljama quarrels had
been timed in accordance with the Crown's frequent though irregular fiscal
demands, now, under a more moderate and predictable fiscal regime, the particular economic and political strategies of Jewish families determined the tim-
ing of conflict between aljamas.

For the smaller aljamas more was at stake in these contests than revenue;
there was also the issue of their autonomy vis-à-vis the chief aljama of Morvedre. Each time the smaller communities lost a tax-paying household, their ability to function as autonomous, self-sustaining entities diminished. Yet as the
century progressed the issue of autonomy became less explosive. As a result of
exogamous marriage and migration in pursuit of defined economic strategies,
many Jewish families established branches in two or three towns. The communities increasingly intertwined. The smaller aljamas remained autonomous, but many of their constituent families were embedded in economic and
kinship networks the lines of which led to Morvedre.

The first skirmish between the aljamas concerned especially the question of
their relative power and status. After emerging from the dark years of 1391–
1416, the other aljamas had trouble adjusting to the Morvedre community's
predominance among Valencian Jewry. That the aljama of Morvedre had indeed assumed the position once held by the aljama in the capital was nonetheless evident to King Alfonso and the bailiff general. Over the course of 1418
and 1419 they therefore issued instructions to Bernat Çaydia, the bailiff of
Morvedre, to compel all Jews in the kingdom of Valencia — really those living
in the northern half of the kingdom — to contribute to the peita rendered annually by the aljama of Morvedre. Çaydia was supposed to tax Jews resident in
towns and seigneurial villages without established aljamas as well as Jews who
were members of the aljamas of Castelló, Borriana, and Vila-real. As long as
Çaydia could locate them, taxing the former was easier. Most would have had
ties with the aljama of Morvedre.

The bailiff met with greater resistance when he approached the other aljamas. Though unhappy, the Jews in more distant Castelló agreed to pay the aljama of Morvedre 100 sous each year. They made a formal complaint only when Çaydia attempted to collect the sum retroactively.[62] The Jews in Borriana, the town closest to Morvedre, objected more strenuously to the apparent derogation of their aljama; they could not bear being placed under the thumb of the Jews in nearby Morvedre. They threatened to abandon Borriana, and told the bailiff "that they preferred to pay the lord king whatever quantity he wanted than to be called, for any reason, *peyters* or tributaries of the Jews of Morvedre, and that they would rather endure being sold than to have such a reputation." Royal officials devised a face-saving solution for the proud Jews of Borriana: they would pay 200 sous annually to the office of the maestre racional, who then, "without the said Jews of Borriana knowing anything," would convey 150 sous to the aljama of Morvedre.[63]

Despite the bluster, the Jews in Borriana could not easily resist the attraction of Morvedre, whose large Jewish community offered more security and new opportunities. During the 1420s at least some of Borriana's Jews felt a need for both. Until May 1428 the Christian population troubled them with physical threats, illicit taxation, and limitations on their ability to obtain and sell meat and other foodstuffs.[64] Litigation between the two aljamas ensued on the migration of Jews like Gento and Vidal Ardit to Morvedre. They battled in the court of the bailiff general over the proper destination of the immigrants' tax payments.[65]

At the end of the 1420s, however, Jewish families began to leave Morvedre for Borriana and Castelló. In Castelló problems attendant to the establishment of a new Jewish quarter were resolved in 1429, while in Borriana the Christians were obeying King Alfonso's admonitions and behaving themselves. In the jueria of Morvedre, in contrast, social tensions and economic difficulties prompted some families to try their luck elsewhere.[66] Gento Ardit, after no more than ten years in Morvedre, moved again to Castelló.[67] Encouraged by the more settled conditions in Castelló and Borriana, some of Morvedre's more established families began playing the old game of holding sizable assets in

[62] ARV: B 1145: n.f. (1418/12/12), 218v (1419/5/18), 244r-v (1419/7/5). ACA: C 2458: 131v–132v (1416/10/4) refers to Jews from Morvedre on seigneurial lands.

[63] ARV: MR 40: 51r (1420) [Piles Ros 1990, 393–394, no. 2]; Piles Ros 1990, 142–146.

[64] ARV: C 39: 11v–12r (1427/3/4); C 37: 171v–172r (1427/9/12); C 41: 48v–49r (9/13); C 42: 138r-v (1428/5/4); Doñate Sebastià and Magdalena Nom de Déu 1990, 238–241, nos. 89–90.

[65] ARV: B 1146: 75v (1424/5/24), 92v–93r (7/3), 233v (1425/5/30), 283r–v (8/22); B 1147: 138v (1430/4/26) [Hinojosa Montalvo 1993a, nos. 338, 339, 349–351, 379]. The latter document also treats the case of the immigrant Naçan Lobell. See also Piles Ros 1990, 161–163.

[66] Doñate Sebastià and Magdalena Nom de Déu 1990, 46–50. The silence of the documents after May 1428 suggests that problems in Borriana had ended, at least for a while. For Morvedre, see above and chap. 5.

[67] ARV: B 1147: 544r (1433/11/4) [Hinojosa Montalvo 1993a, no. 405].

Morvedre and environs while setting up their official residence elsewhere. In 1430 Abraham Legem, a member of the highly mobile and ambitious Legem clan, transferred to Borriana from Morvedre, where he left relatives and a house. Abraham naturally objected the following year when the bailiff of Morvedre confiscated the house toward his payment of the peita with the local aljama, since he was at the moment responsible to the aljama of Borriana. But not for long: by the time his plea reached the bailiff general he had joined the aljama of Castelló.[68]

All this movement to and fro was maddening for officials but especially for those in Morvedre, whose aljama during the 1430s was losing more members than it was attracting.[69] Maintaining fiscal jurisdiction over emigrant families for as long as possible was crucial for the aljamas, since they used most of the peita collected from Jewish householders to handle communal expenses. At the insistence of the aljama of Morvedre, representatives of the three aljamas finally met in August 1437 and hammered out an agreement about peita obligations.[70] They decided that the Jewish householder who transferred to another aljama should continue to pay to his aljama of origin the part of the peita he had been accustomed to pay before he moved. This clearly benefited Morvedre. Although the accord smoothed the feathers of the representatives from Borriana and Castelló by stipulating that the aljamas not "be subjected to one another," they recognized that their communities were in Morvedre's orbit and that their newer members still kept one foot in Morvedre.[71]

After 1438, when pestilence afflicted Morvedre,[72] the population of its Jewish community began to rise steadily, owing in part to a shift in the migratory current, which now flowed from the smaller communities *to* Morvedre. The aljama of Borriana felt the loss of householders most keenly.[73] Disputes over

---

[68] ARV: B 1147: 160r (1430/6/27); sixth quire, letter K, n.f. (1431/2/19); B 1148: 305v (1436/12/24) [Hinojosa Montalvo 1993a, nos. 380, 386, 449]; B 1148: 329r (1437/3/5). Abraham Huisqui was another Jew who left Morvedre, for Alzira (B 1147: 654r [1434/8/18]), and finally Borriana (see n. 74). See Meyerson 2004a on the Jews' strategic changes of residence prior to 1391.

[69] Some Jews, however, moved *to* Morvedre in the early 1430s, e.g., Profet Crespi, from Borriana — ARV: B 1147: 553r (1433/12/9); C 264: 140v (1434/6/30). Profet had clashed with his brothers-in-law, Ruben and David Bonet of Borriana, over his wife's dowry.

[70] Since they were acquiring more families than they were losing, the aljamas of Borriana and Castelló avoided attending a meeting as long as they could: ARV: B 1148: 133r (1435/10/5), 137v (10/21), 182r (1436/2/10),185r (2/17) [Hinojosa Montalvo 1993a, nos. 435–436, 439, 446–447]. The accord: ARV: C 266: 156v–157v (1437/8/20) [Piles Ros 1990, no. 1]; C 68: 106r-v (1438/4/7) [Hinojosa Montalvo 1993a, no. 452].

[71] Piles Ros 1990, 144–145. Even though the aljamas of Borriana and Castelló saved face by ensuring that their portion of the 2,000-sous royal peita would be paid directly to the maestre racional (not to the aljama of Morvedre), their representatives acknowledged Morvedre's sway and the tenuousness of their own communities when they raised the issue of what would happen if their aljamas could not pay the royal peita because of their "diminution."

[72] The plague drove some Jews from Morvedre to more salubrious rural villages and perhaps to other royal towns — ARV: B 1148: 468r (1438/11/22) [Hinojosa Montalvo 1993a, no. 457].

[73] ARV: B 1149: 428r (1445/1/20, 29) [Hinojosa Montalvo 1993a, nos. 475–476].

the fiscal responsibilities of the immigrants from Borriana erupted intermittently during the next two decades.[74] By 1465 so many Jews had left Borriana for Morvedre that Vidal Comte, originally from Borriana but now envoy of the aljama of Morvedre, informed the bailiff general that it was time to end the fiction of the separate peita payment of the aljama of Borriana. The aljama of Morvedre would pay Borriana's portion and the adelantats of what remained of the Borriana community need not bother assessing its erstwhile members for the tax.[75] One of the Jews left in Borriana, David Bonet, could see the handwriting on the wall. In his will, probably redacted in 1473, he left half of his property to the synagogue of Borriana and the other half to the synagogue of Morvedre. The executors of the will, Isaac and Mossé Bonet, lived in Morvedre.[76] The process of absorption was completed in 1486: the one or two Jewish households remaining in Borriana conveyed the Torah scrolls and ornaments of the local synagogue to Morvedre for safekeeping.[77]

The aljamas of Castelló and Vila-real did not decline as dramatically as that of Borriana. They resisted the pull of the aljama of Morvedre more successfully because they were more distant from it. Even so, they too saw some members depart for Morvedre and thus occasionally clashed with its aljama over fiscal issues.[78] On the eve of the expulsion the Castelló community consisted of some twenty households; the community in Vila-real was smaller.[79]

The Jews of Borriana, Castelló, and Vila-real who decided to relocate in Morvedre abandoned towns whose Christian populations were dwindling as a consequence of natural calamities and emigration. The demographic descent

---

[74] According to the 1437 accord, the immigrants should have been sending their peita payments back to Borriana. Samuel Façan was, but in 1442 the aljama of Morvedre taxed him anyway (ARV: B 1149: 151r [Hinojosa Montalvo 1993a, no. 468]). The main problem was the refusal of Jewish inhabitants of Borriana to render their due to the local adelantats. Their resistance was probably a reaction to the violation of the 1437 accord by some Jews who had emigrated to Morvedre. To set things right, in November 1445 the bailiff general ordered the collection of the peita from *all* Jews resident in Borriana (B 1150: 33v [Hinojosa Montalvo 1993a, no. 480]). However, Abraham Huisqui, who had immigrated to Borriana from Morvedre in the 1430s, complained in 1451 that the aljama of Borriana was taxing him even though he already paid his peita to the aljama of Morvedre (B 1151: 239r [Hinojosa Montalvo 1993a, no. 517]). Abraham of course was observing the 1437 accord. In 1456 the bailiff general ruled that Jews who had emigrated from Borriana to Morvedre still must pay the peita to their former aljama (ARV: B 1152: 1236r [Hinojosa Montalvo 1993a, no. 555]), a ruling that affected at least eight Jewish householders: Salamó, Vidal, and Abraham Comte; Samuel Façan; Gento and Pastor Ardit; Orbona, the widow of Abraham Cabelmale; and Morquada, the widow of Isaac Morcat (listed in B 1152: 1235v).

[75] ARV: B 1153: 623v–624r (1465/7/16) [Hinojosa Montalvo 1993a, no. 654].

[76] ARV: B 1155: 166r (1474/6/27) [Hinojosa Montalvo 1993a, no. 727].

[77] ARV: B 1158: 213v–214r (1486/4/17) [Hinojosa Montalvo 1993a, no. 813]; Piles Ros 1990, 385–388.

[78] ARV: B 1152: 1507v–1508r (1458/9/27); B 1154: 361v (1469/4/10), 479r (12/7) [Hinojosa Montalvo 1993a, nos. 576, 689, 695]; Doñate Sebastià and Magdalena Nom de Déu 1990, 85–86, 100, 145.

[79] Magdalena Nom de Déu 1974, 274; Doñate Sebastià and Magdalena Nom de Déu 1990, 59–62, 275–281.

was most striking in Borriana: it had some 592 hearths in 1418; 214 in 1451; 166 in 1469; and only 108 in 1487. The population of Castelló declined from 1,100 hearths in 1418 to only 479 in 1493, and that of Vila-real from 598 to 350 between the same years.[80]

The mere experience of living in "depopulated" towns with "uncultivated" termes was not the only factor prompting Jews to pack their bags for Morvedre.[81] The reactions of the municipalities and of local Christians to their more straitened circumstances also influenced the Jews' decisions. Faced with huge public debts and fewer taxpayers, municipal governments increased the tax rates of all town residents. The Jews of Castelló griped about this to the bailiff general and were told that if the Christians were enduring the same tax hike, they should just grit their teeth and bear it. Like many Christians and Jews in Borriana, not all were prepared to do so.[82]

Growing fiscal pressure and economic hardship stimulated Christian nastiness toward the Jews in particular. In Borriana the rector of the local church laid criminal charges against the Jewish aljama in 1448, claiming that he had direct lordship over the synagogue and that the Jews therefore owed him an annual rent. The Jews countered that their "house of prayer neither can nor ought to be subject to the said rector," and that, besides, "he has not shown nor can he show any title to it." Still, the rector's agitation, which must have provoked his parishioners, caused the flight of Jews to Morvedre.[83] At around the same time in Castelló municipal officials were removing headstones from the Jewish cemetery and preventing the Jews from ritually slaughtering their meat and importing kasher wine. Their actions, which persisted until 1452, drove many Jews out of town; the community quickly revived, however.[84] Christian hostility flared up again in the 1470s: Jews in Castelló complained about Holy Week violence, while their coreligionists in Vila-real maintained that local Christians were mistreating them with impunity.[85] In 1488 the municipal council of Castelló prohibited Jews from working as brokers, a function the Jews had long been licensed to perform in the town. The council asserted that Jewish brokerage was not only against divine law but damaging to the public good,

[80] Iradiel 1989, 268.

[81] ARV: B 1155: 25r (1473/2/8) [Hinojosa Montalvo 1993a, no. 711], regarding Vila-real. The same description would have fit Borriana and, to a lesser degree, Castelló.

[82] ARV: B 1149: 434r (1445/2/13) [Hinojosa Montalvo 1993a, no. 477]; Viciano Navarro 1992, 519–528.

[83] ARV: B 1150: 270r-v (1448/5/30): "per causa del dit proces . . . sen anats certes casades [of Jews] a Murvedre, dient encara los dits juheus que la lur sinagoga es casa de oracio e no pot ne deu esser suffragania del dit rector e menys feu lo dit cens, e lo dit rector no'n mostra ni'n pot mostrar titol algu." Also, B 1150: 270v (6/5) [Hinojosa Montalvo 1993a, no. 496]; Piles Ros 1990, 386.

[84] ARV: B 1150: 428r (1449/6/25) [Hinojosa Montalvo 1993a, no. 506]; Hinojosa Montalvo 1993a, 129–130, 242; Doñate Sebastià and Magdalena Nom de Déu 1990, 50–51.

[85] Doñate Sebastià and Magdalena Nom de Déu 1990, 52, 266.

since the Jews—all of a sudden—acted improperly and fraudulently.[86] In the eyes of the Christians of Borriana, Castelló, and Vila-real the shrinking Jewish populations in their towns were, if not quite expendable, hardly indispensable. Fortunately the Jews of these towns always had the burgeoning Jewish quarter of Morvedre as an optional place of residence.

JEW-FREE VALENCIA AND JEWISH MORVEDRE

That Morvedre would remain through much of the fifteenth century the destination of choice for Jews elsewhere in the kingdom was probably not what the town's Jews and Christians expected at the outset of Alfonso IV's reign. Morvedre, after all, stood practically in the shadow of Valencia, and King Alfonso's rulings of May 1417 and September 1419, which put Morvedre back under the capital's jurisdiction, ensured that it stayed that way, juridically as well as geographically.[87] Alfonso seems not to have noticed that subjecting Morvedre to Valencia did not quite correspond with his efforts to revive and protect the Jewish community in Morvedre, for Valencia, in all its fifteenth-century splendor, was officially not very friendly to Jews.

Prior to Alfonso's reign, the governors of the capital had adjusted smoothly to the destruction of the Jewish quarter and the baptism of most of its inhabitants. The conversions had fulfilled some of the millenarian dreams of the Franciscan Francesc Eiximenis (d. 1409), the main ideologue of the municipality, and even if a new age had not been ushered in, the city had been made more Christian.[88] By obtaining from King Martí the "privilege" of 1397, municipal officials had then made sure that a Jewish population at least would never again besmirch the city's image. Anxious about the religious leanings of the large converso population, they had also moved Martí to enact the legislation of 1403 that severely limited the entry of Jews into Valencia.[89]

Despite King Alfonso's favorable Jewish policy, the capital did not open its gates wide to the Jews. On the contrary, in 1419 public criers ordered all Jews to leave the city within eight days.[90] Jews nonetheless continued to visit Valencia, sometimes for lengthy stays, with the permission of the king or of the bailiff general who resided there. In 1423 a concentration of some thirty Jews attracted attention. The maestre racional observed that "their stay in the said city was very odious to the people," who perhaps feared the reemergence of a

---

[86] Doñate Sebastià and Magdalena Nom de Déu 1990, 160, no. 75. Yet the municipal justice had licensed a Jew, Abraham Rodrich, to work as a broker as recently as January 1488 (100 n. 107).

[87] *Aureum opus*, ff. 175r–176r, 180v–181v; Chabret Fraga 1979, 1: 313–315; Cueves Granero 1959, 453–454; ARV: C 29: 33v–34r (1420/5/3).

[88] Sanchis Guarner 1980, 665; Viera 1985, 205–207, and 1992, 249–253.

[89] See chap. 1.

[90] ARV: MR 39: 273r [Hinojosa Montalvo 1993a, no. 303].

Jewish community in their midst.[91] If so, their fears were unfounded. A more persistent and realistic concern of Valencia's governors was the influence of Jewish visitors on converso citizens. The bailiff general's public reiteration of the 1403 legislation assuaged their anxiety somewhat on this score.

After 1423 municipal officials did not banish Jews from the city, nor did the citizens find the visits of Jews repugnant. Only in 1455, when a Christian mob sacked the Muslim quarter and put any non-Christian at risk, did Jews from Morvedre encounter serious difficulties.[92] Economic interest dampened the hostility of Valencia's governors and created an opening for Jews in the capital. In Valencia there was a perpetual tension between religious and economic motivations, for even as Vicent Ferrer thundered against merchants as usurers and frauds, Eiximenis praised them as most beneficial for the public good.[93] Out of a desire to promote the city's commercial prosperity, the jurats had, in 1403, welcomed penitent renegade conversos back from North Africa. Throughout the fifteenth century they permitted Jewish merchants from North Africa, Portugal, and Castile to trade and lodge in Valencia.[94] Sometimes these traders even stayed in the homes of conversos.

Jews from Morvedre, too, were frequent visitors to the capital, often lodging in the Muslim quarter and sometimes with conversos.[95] Jewish retail merchants from Morvedre played a key role in distributing the commodities of international trade and the products of Valencia's industries to the towns and villages in the region extending from Valencia to Castelló. Their main commercial partners were conversos.[96] The jurats of Valencia did not hesitate to act on behalf of Jews from Morvedre who furthered their city's trade. In 1438 they wrote to the king of Castile requesting the release of four Jewish merchants from Morvedre whom a Castilian galley had captured at sea. The Jews had been en route to North Africa on a ship whose patron was Miquel Bonet, a citizen of Valencia.[97] In 1485 the jurats rebuked the procurator of the viscount of Biota and the castellan of Mançanera for having perpetrated the "insult" of taking 350 sheep from Salamó Çaporta, the most active and affluent Jewish businessman in Morvedre. The jurats remarked that Salamó, as promised, had paid the *herbatge* for grazing his sheep in Mançanera, whereas the addressees did not act in a manner befitting "men who keep their word." The jurats demanded that they return all the sheep to "En Çaporta, for you know what a

[91] ARV: MR 43: 118r-v [Hinojosa Montalvo 1993a, no. 327].

[92] ARV: C 280: 141r–142r (1459/7/20), referring to events in 1455, later addressed by Juan II (see at n. 17).

[93] Maravall 1969; Rubio Vela 1981, 24–28; Sanchis Guarner 1980, 668–670; Narbona Vizcaíno 1992a, 94–95; Llop Català 1995, 121–201.

[94] AMV: LM g3–8: 23v–24r (1403/8/22) [*Epistolari*, 1: no. 109]; Piles Ros 1984.

[95] See chap. 6.

[96] Guiral 1986, 353; Meyerson 1998, 80–81; chap. 3.

[97] AMV: LM g3–19: second quire, n.f. (1438/8/12) [Hinojosa Montalvo 1993a, no. 453].

good *contractador* he is and that he pays well to whomever he is obliged." Seven
years before the expulsion and just three years before Salamó Çaporta was exiled by Crown and inquisition for abetting converso Judaizing, the jurats of Valencia could not conceal their respect for this successful Jewish entrepreneur.[98] What mattered most to them was that Çaporta kept his word, and that
his ventures contributed much to the prosperity of Morvedre and therefore of
Valencia. Jews from Morvedre were increasingly welcome in the capital as
long as their homes were in Morvedre's Jewish quarter.

Access to the capital was absolutely essential for the Jews of the flourishing
Morvedre community. It enabled them to profit from and contribute to the
commerce and industry of this great urban center, which, as the century progressed, consolidated its hegemony over the rest of the kingdom. Visiting the
capital also allowed the Jews of Morvedre to maintain their ties to converso
families in Valencia and to offer assistance to those conversos still adhering to
Judaism. Through providing such help some Jews derived a sense of mission
and spiritual enrichment.[99] For the Jews of Morvedre the relationship with Valencia was not without its risks but was on the whole fruitful.

The governors of Valencia could easily have lived without a Jewish community in Morvedre, but they had no problems living with it. Their acceptance
of an increasingly Jewish town under their jurisdiction was not simply compliance with the wishes of the king and his watchdog, the bailiff general. It was
also attributable to their recognition that the Jews were crucial to Morvedre's
economic life and that the town would suffer without them. The location of
an expansive and prosperous Jewish community in Morvedre was wonderfully
convenient for the municipality of Valencia. Because the Jews did not live *in*
Valencia, the city's Jew-free image could not be sullied; because the Jews were
in a town under the city's jurisdiction, it could profit from them. The Jews of
Morvedre were just near enough to and far enough from Valencia to satisfy
everyone.

ALJAMA AND MUNICIPALITY

Morvedre's political elites were more than content with the arrangement.
Fiercely jealous as ever of the town's limited autonomy and their own prerogatives, they would not have seconded any initiatives taken against local Jews by
the government or citizens of Valencia.[100] Their perception of the Jewish com-

---

[98] AMV: LM g3–31: 95r-v (1485/10/6): "[E]n Çaporta, lo qual sabeu quant es bon contractador e que pagua be al que es obligat." See chaps. 3, 6.

[99] See chaps. 3, 6.

[100] Relations continued to be tense in the fifteenth century. In 1440 the townspeople almost
rose in armed rebellion against Valencia over fiscal issues. See Chabret Fraga 1979, 1: 319–323.

munity was primarily shaped by compelling demographic and economic realities. Like their counterparts in Borriana, Castelló, and Vila-real, the town fathers of Morvedre witnessed the erosion of the Christian population: from 1,297 households in 1379 to only some 550 by 1492.[101] But unlike them they also beheld, particularly in the latter half of the century, demographic growth in the Jewish quarter tantamount to a population explosion. If the Jewish population snowballed, through a combination of natural increase and immigration, to reach a total of some 700 by 1492, it was partly because the town fathers allowed it to happen, because they did not subject the Jews to the same sorts of harassment that drove Jews out of other towns. By the 1460s the Jewish population in Morvedre had reached such a critical mass that only officials intent on ruining the town's economy would have desired its departure. One year after the expulsion, the jurats and prohomens would plaintively and pathetically inform their "most Christian king" that "due to the vicissitudes of time and to the general expulsion of the Jews . . . the town stands depopulated and is left in the greatest need."[102]

Local officials considering the Jews' importance to the life of the town thought not just about the Jews' role in commerce and industry but also about their contributions to the municipal treasury. The agreement of 1370, in which the aljama and its members had consented to pay municipal as well as royal taxes, assumed ever more significance for the municipality as the fifteenth century progressed and the Christian population dwindled. Though still a separate corporation, the aljama became more of a partner to the municipality. Municipal officials perceived it less as a body of "the king's Jews" imposed on the town and paying taxes only to the Crown. In terms of their fiscal responsibilities to the municipality, Jewish householders and Christian citizens were, more than in previous centuries, on the same footing. The municipality's financial health depended on the Jews' presence more than ever before. Whereas the jurats of towns like Borriana and Castelló regarded the departure of the few local Jews with insouciance or delight, the sight of a jueria emptied of taxpayers filled the jurats of Morvedre with despair.

The liability of the Jews to municipal levies entailed periodic clashes between aljama and municipality over fiscal questions. The combination of a growing public debt and a shrinking Christian population, which was characteristic of several other towns, also forced Morvedre's officials to increase the tax rates of all inhabitants and to squeeze the Jews as much as was feasible. They could hardly have resisted the temptation, given the size of the Jewish

---

[101] Hinojosa Montalvo 1995, 280–282; Chabret Fraga 1979, 1: 326–327; García Cárcel 1976b, 176.

[102] ARV: C 309: 189v–191r (1493/12/6): "axi per la concurencia del temps com encara per lo general desterro dels jueus per vostra altesa novament fet, com a christianissimo rey, de sos regnes, la dita vila sta depopulada e constituida en grandissima necessitat."

community and the wealth of some of its members, like Abraham Legem, in the walls of whose house two Christian laborers found 1,400 or 1,800 florins "according to what is said and rumored in the said town."[103] Yet precisely because the aljama was so large, it could better combat the municipality, usually with the firm support of the bailiff general in nearby Valencia. Municipal officials, on the other hand, dared not torment the Jews too much, lest they provoke Jewish flight. The small Jewish communities in other Valencian towns, however, found it more difficult to withstand the pressure of local officials who did not deem Jewish emigration a distressing prospect. For both Crown and municipality, the stakes were higher in Morvedre.

The armed intervention of King Alfonso in Castile, in 1429–30, on behalf of his relations, the Infantes of Aragon, brought about the first conflict between the aljama and municipality of Morvedre. In 1431, in order to help defray the cost of the troops the king had sent to Castile, the bailiff general exacted a subvention from the municipality. He exempted the aljama since it rendered other taxes to the Crown. The jurats protested, arguing that a precedent for the aljama's contributions to the Crown's military efforts had been set during Pere III's war with Castile. Impatient with the ensuing lengthy lawsuit, the jurats attempted in 1434 to force the aljama to contribute retroactively to the subvention and confiscated the property of Jews as security for the sums allegedly owed. After the bailiff general cautioned the jurats to halt their procedures and to produce the required fourteenth-century evidence,[104] Prince Juan, the lieutenant general, summoned fifty-one Jewish householders of Morvedre before his court to answer the charges of the municipality's attorney. The Jews probably paid something to satisfy the municipality; in return their property was restored to them.[105]

This flare-up had occurred when the population of the Jewish community was at best stagnant. Small surprise, then, that municipal officials endeavored to tax the community more heavily once it entered a phase of vigorous demographic expansion. During the 1450s there was a running debate between aljama and municipal officials over the fee the Jews paid to the municipality for milling bread grain. Prior to 1451 both Christian and Jewish residents had rendered a tax of 4 sous per *cafís* (199.44 liters) of grain milled. That year, however, the jurats reduced the rate paid by Christian households while com-

---

[103] ARV: B 1148: 313r (1436/12/12), 305v (12/17) [Hinojosa Montalvo 1993a, no. 449].

[104] ARV: B 1147: 634v–635r (1434/6/2), 639r-v (6/9). In 1366 the municipality of Morvedre helped subsidize the salaries of crossbowmen in the service of the Crown. That same year Queen Elionor criticized municipal officials for taxing the local Jews immoderately and forcing them to contribute to castle repairs and other necessities (ACA: C 1574: 116v). It is not wholly clear from this letter whether the jurats taxed the Jews licitly in 1366 nor whether the sums collected from the Jews were used for the salaries of the crossbowmen.

[105] ARV: C 264: 16v–17r (1434/6/16); B 1147: 682r (1434/11/22) [Hinojosa Montalvo 1993a, no. 424].

pelling the Jews to pay the former and higher cisa rate. The aljama naturally objected, and the bailiff general insisted that the local bailiff ensure that the jurats taxed Jews and Christians equally.[106]

Their creative fiscal reforms frustrated, the jurats retaliated by attempting to shame the Jews. When the Jews came to reveal to the collector of the cisa the amount of flour they had milled, the jurats were forcing them to take the humiliating "oath of the Maledictions" in their presence in addition to swearing on the Decalogue. The bailiff general again intervened on the Jews' behalf, but not before one Jew, Samuel Façan, was especially antagonized.[107]

Façan did not forget the humiliation he had endured at the hands of the jurats. Four years later, when the municipality was weighed down by outstanding censals and feeling fiscally the effects of disease and poor harvests, the jurats, acting in good faith, gave all inhabitants the choice of paying either the tax of 4 sous per cafís of grain milled or the less burdensome head tax (per eater) they had levied on the Christian population in 1451. But Façan, through his "many words," so insulted and alienated the collectors of the cisa that the latter did not reach any agreement with the Jews. The collectors simply demanded that the Jews pay the standard per cafís fee. Inflamed by Façan, the Jews then refused to inform the collectors how much grain they had milled. The jurats felt that they had no choice but to enter the Jewish quarter and register, for purposes of taxation, the sacks of flour milled by its residents.[108] Some weeks later, as a means of further dissuading the Jews from challenging their authority overtly, the jurats threatened to make them wear the Jewish badge inside the jueria and when traveling out of town.[109] Imposing, or threatening to impose, humiliating oaths and symbols was the jurats' method of keeping the Jews in line.

The problem of the milling cisa simply would not go away, primarily because the jurats could not leave well enough alone. In 1457 they resolved to abolish the per cafís fee and to collect instead the head tax from all the town's

---

[106] ARV: B 1151: 271v (1451/7/29) [Hinojosa Montalvo 1993a, no. 518]. In an effort to provide some relief to poorer Christian families, the jurats decided to levy a head tax of 4 sous 6 diners on the Christian population — literally on each "eater" (*menjador*) of bread. This head tax was less burdensome for households than the tax levied on each cafís of milled grain for which the Jews were still liable. To compensate for the resultant shortfall in revenue garnered from the Christian population for this cisa, the jurats increased the peita rate paid by all town residents. The Jews were thus left paying both higher cisa and higher peita rates. There can be no doubt that the Jews made frequent use of the local mills. In 1496 Jaume de Sant Feliu, who had leased the local *molins fariners* from the Crown in 1492, complained about the loss of clientele caused by the expulsion of the Jews (ARV: C 138: 39r-v).

[107] ARV: B 1151: 301r (1451/9/3) [Hinojosa Montalvo 1993a, no. 520].

[108] ARV: B 1152: 1055v (1455/8/5),1055v–1056r (8/6) [Hinojosa Montalvo 1993a, nos. 548–549]. ARV: C 58: 72v–74r (1455/4/30) treats the municipality's financial difficulties in the wake of "mortalitats . . . grans sterilitats."

[109] ARV: B 1152: 1160r–1161v (1455/10/14).

inhabitants. The jurats, however, imposed a heavier head tax on the Jews. Perhaps they hoped that the Jews would not notice the discrepancy. The Jews did and informed the bailiff general, who in August sent the jurats a letter full of the usual dire warnings. The jurats nonetheless continued to inventory the Jews' property and to penalize them when they resisted paying the higher capitation. Samuel and Mossé Façan led the Jews in this tussle with the jurats.[110] Though Samuel's knowledge of the wiles of the jurats helped, only repeated commands from the new king, Juan II, finally convinced them to back down. The jurats had either to tax the Jews as they had done fifteen or twenty years ago or to accept a lump sum of 500 sous from the aljama for the milling cisa.[111]

During this decade of skirmishing over taxation between the aljama and the municipality, aljama officials sensibly took steps to inhibit Jews, particularly Jewish women, from flaunting their wealth. In 1456 they issued sumptuary legislation limiting the ornateness of their clothing and the amount of jewelry they could wear.[112] The bailiff general approved this legislation, no doubt recognizing, as did aljama officials, that the jurats might be less intent on obtaining more fiscal revenue from the Jews if the wealth of upper-class Jews was less on display. Some of the women did not see matters in quite the same light and had to be reminded in 1459 to observe the laws. The bailiff general, however, permitted the women to adorn themselves as they wished for the festivities to be held for the entry of the new king, Juan II.[113]

The more modest dress of Jewish women, before or after the parties, did not fool municipal officials. Even if Jewish women wore sackcloth, the fact that the Jewish community was flourishing and the Christian one diminishing could not be ignored. It nagged at the jurats and the councillors. They believed that the Jews had to be persuaded to contribute more to the expenses of the struggling municipality, which owed the Crown 135,000 sous.[114] Pointing out that the "jueria has augmented," the town fathers beseeched the bailiff general in 1476 to prevail on the Jews to pay a new and higher tax rate so that the town could better bear its burdens. They had already broached the matter with the adelantats, but the latter, citing earlier agreements and custom, showed no signs of cooperating. The bailiff general realized that, for the good of the town and of the relationship between its Jewish and Christian communities, established fiscal arrangements would have to be adjusted to fit demographic reality. He advised the adelantats to compromise with municipal officials. If this proved too difficult, he assured the adelantats, he would intervene to effect a

---

[110] ARV: B 1152: 1486r (1458/8/17), 1485r (8/30) [Hinojosa Montalvo 1993a, no. 575].

[111] ARV: C 280: 152v (1459/8/8). After this letter, there is no evidence of additional problems relative to this particular tax.

[112] ARV: B 1152: 1259r (1456/6/1) [Hinojosa Montalvo 1993a, no. 559]; cf. Orfali Levi 1993, 83–85; Hughes 1986, 26–27.

[113] ARV: B 1152: 1595v (1459/1/23).

[114] Chabret Fraga 1979, 2: 350 n. 1.

just compromise, one that would enable the aljama to coexist well with the municipality. An arrangement satisfactory to both corporations was evidently achieved; conflict between them did not erupt subsequently.[115] The new arrangement, however, did not solve all the municipality's financial difficulties, particularly its debt to the Crown. To handle it, the jurats borrowed money from local Jews in October 1479, leaving them as pledges "a plate from the silver of Santa Agueda, the parish cross, and some chalices."[116]

Litigation over the military subsidy of 1431 or even the tactics of the jurats in the battle over the milling cisa in the 1450s did not elicit great shudders from the Jews of Morvedre. They were not menaced by violence or systematic abuse; their food supply was not cut off. The jurats' persistent efforts to tax the Jews more heavily in the 1450s were in fact a function of the Jews' growing number and prosperity; they were more a sign of Jewish strength than of Jewish weakness. The final attempt of the jurats and town council to persuade the Jews to put more into the municipal coffers involved not threats or subterfuge but earnest negotiation. The jurats, almost with hats in hand, approached the adelantats. And the adelantats did not then turn to the bailiff general with complaints about the jurats' scheming; rather it was the jurats who looked to the bailiff to use his influence with the Jews on the municipality's behalf. Though the scene in Morvedre on the eve of the succession of Fernando the Catholic was not ideal, the idea of expelling the local Jewish community was the furthest thing from the minds of municipal officials.

JEWS AND CHRISTIANS

The Jews' relationship with local Christian elites involved much more than squabbling with the jurats over taxation. Leading Jewish families, like the Legems, Façans, and Çaportas, and influential Christian families, like the Sant Felius, Munyós, and Dezpertas, in certain respects shared a bourgeois outlook that manifested itself in specific economic strategies. Jewish and Christian elites both invested in tax farms, the leasing of public utilities, and urban and rural real estate.[117] They did not simply proceed along parallel economic paths, however. Their paths frequently crisscrossed to form a dense web of economic interdependence. Most importantly, through their investments Christian elites came to have a real stake in the Jewish community and its survival.

---

[115] ARV: B 1155: 567r-v (1476/1/10) [Hinojosa Montalvo 1993a, no. 755]. There was one minor problem in April when the town mustaçaff, the market inspector, penalized a Jew for some infraction. The official was allowed to fine Jews only for using false weights and measures (B 1155: 629v [Hinojosa Montalvo 1993a, no. 761]).

[116] Chabret Fraga 1979, 2: 350 n. 1.

[117] For the Jews, chap. 3. On Christian elites, Viciano Navarro 1989, 99–114; 1995; and 1997; Narbona Vizcaíno 1992b and 1995b.

Some local notables leased property to Jews. Gento Avincanes, for example, held land by enfiteutic contract from Francesc Llopis Doteyta, a member of a knightly family whose relative Joan received annuities from the aljama.[118] Indeed, the censal, more than anything else, structured the economic relationship between Christian elites and the Jewish community, and gave the former a vested interest in the growth and prosperity of the latter. The knights, merchants, and lawyers of Morvedre were overwhelmingly the predominant investors in the public debt of the local aljama.[119] The receipt of annuities from the aljama was integral to their lifestyle as noble or patrician rentiers.[120] For some of these notable families, like the Munyós and the Sant Felius, the censal only strengthened the bonds their ancestors had forged with the Jewish

[118] APPV: P 17865, L. Miralles: n.f. (1473/3/4). Avincanes purchased the land from the farmer Barthomeu Roda; like Roda, he then owed an annual rent of 4 sous 6 diners to Llopis. P 17861, L. Miralles: n.f. (1479/9/7) records the payment of the 75-sous pension to Joan; it was due on 27 July each year. There are many other examples. At the time of his death in 1476, the gentleman (*domicellus*) Thomàs Rubau had been receiving annual rents of 7 sous and 5 sous from Vidal Astori and "Mazalto, alias Bonaventura," the widow of Samuel Chifalla, respectively. Rubau's widow sold her rights to the Jews' rents to the Centelles family (P 17867, L. Miralles: n.f. [1476/3/29]), a lineage of lawyers and notaries who had purchased censals from the aljama as early as 1422 (ARV: MR 41: 294v–295v [Hinojosa Montalvo 1993a, no. 322]). The knightly Francesc Arnau Esparça sold land to Mossé Asseyo (APPV: P 17880, L. Miralles: n.f. [1482/5/29]). The land, "quoddam troceum vinee malolli cum guarrofferis," was allodial and sold for 1,400 sous. On the enfiteutic contract, see chap. 3 at n. 12.

[119] Although Valencia's censalistas dominated the kingdom's credit market and invested in censals sold by municipalities and seigneuries everywhere (Furió 1993a, 519–520, 533–534; Viciano Navarro 1997, 619), they seem to have invested little in the corporate debt of the aljama of Morvedre. As for the aljama's creditors, of the ten censalistas recorded in the registers of the notary Lleonard Miralles (housed in the APPV) between 1471 and 1492 all were residents of Morvedre. The Miralles registers, which cover 1469 to 1492 and offer a reasonably full picture for those years, are unfortunately the only extant registers of a notary who worked consistently in Morvedre in the medieval period. Scattered evidence from earlier in the century is nonetheless consistent with this pattern. Still, there were some creditors from Valencia early in the fifteenth century. ARV: P 1446, B. de la Mata: n.f. (1401/8/29): the aljama owes 300 sous per year "de violario ad vitam" to Joan Roïs de Corella. ARV: B 318: second quire (for 1421), 48r-v (9/10), refers to the censal sold by Samuel Legem to Maria Ferrández, the widow of the *donzell* Joan de Natera, in 1398. By 1421 Legem had converted to Christianity; the censal, however, was incumbent on his still Jewish wife, Bonafilla. Salamó Caxo also sold a censal to dona Maria in 1398; he died in 1431 and his house was then sold toward liquidation of the censal (B 319: 142r-v).

[120] The knight Francesc Arnau Esparça purchased a censal from several Jews who were raising money to buy houses from a coreligionist, Jahudà Jabba (APPV: P 17880, L. Miralles: n.f. [1482/4/26]). The Jewish vendors were Mossé Rodrich and his wife, Or; Mossé Asseyo; Abraham Soriano; Menahem, the son of Mossé Gallego; Jahudà Barbut; Samuel Adzoni "minor"; Duenya, the widow of rabbi Cahas Soriano; and Salamó Levi and his wife, Sol. The censal was secured on the homes of Rodrich and Levi. P 17871, L. Miralles: n.f. (1485/4/15) records Pere Esparça ceding his rights to a censal, owed by members of the Jewish Bonet and Legem families, to Yolanta, the wife of Pere Eximeneç of Sogorb. Eyego Esparça, domicellus and uncle of Pere, had originally purchased the annuity in 1419 from a member of the Bonet family.

community in the fourteenth century.[121] It was thus well worth it for the Jews to pay interest on the sums they borrowed from Christian notables through selling them censals, for the money extended to them was also a form of social credit. The censal, the linchpin of the fifteenth-century fiscal regime, perpetuated and broadened a system of Jewish clientage to powerful Christian patrons crucial to Jewish endurance in Morvedre.[122]

The fostering of ties with lords in the countryside continued to be fundamental to the Jews' economic success. That some of the aforementioned members of Morvedre's upper crust possessed small lordships in the terme of the town of course helped. But the Jews of Morvedre wandered farther afield and cultivated their connections with more potent seigneurs like the Pròixidas of Almenara and the commanders of the Order of Montesa in the more northerly town of Onda. Without the continuation of mutually beneficial relations between the Jews and the seigneurs, the mobility integral to their way of life would not have been possible.

Itinerant Jewish merchants, artisans, and tax farmers did not just halt briefly in a village, sell a few articles, and then move on. Through the cooperation of seigneurs and local authorities, a number of them possessed residences outside Morvedre. These homes away from home enhanced the Jews' mobility and enabled them to concentrate on particular regions, using one town or village as a base from which to do business in other places nearby. As aljama and royal officials sometimes discovered to their frustration, the additional residences also facilitated the concealment of taxable assets or worse. Pursuing Jews enjoying the patronage of powerful lords proved difficult.

Jews from Morvedre had long frequented the lands of the Pròixida family, the lords of Almenara. Moneylenders in particular had done a healthy business in Almenara in the fourteenth century; the fifteenth century opened with various tenants and vassals of Olf de Pròixida and the knight Gilabert de Cen-

---

[121] On the Munyós and the Sant Felius in the fourteenth century, Meyerson 2004a. ARV: B 1153: 363r (1462/9/1) [Hinojosa Montalvo 1993a, no. 630]: Joan Munyós demands execution on the home of Mossé Beor for an outstanding annuity. APPV: P 12213, L. Miralles: n.f. (1492/4/30): Mossé Alateffi, his father, Abraham, Mossé Asseyo, and his wife, Dolçina, liquidate a censal they had sold to Jaume Munyós in 1475. P 17864, L. Miralles: n.f. (1471/9/27): the aljama pays the second half of an annuity of 418 sous 6 diners to Ysabel, the wife of Joan de Sant Feliu. There are also records of these payments for the years 1472–77. Other leading families who received annuities from the aljama or individual Jews include: Castellnou (APPV: P 17859, L. Miralles [1477/12/15]; P 17861, L. Miralles [1479/10/13]); Berenguer (ARV: MR 46: n.f. [1427]; B 217: 661v–662r [1483/12/17]; APPV: P 17873, L. Miralles [1487/6/15]; ARV: MR 103: 208v [1492/6/19]); Erau, alias Folch (ARV: P 2785, J. de Campos Jr. [1474/7/6]); Malonda (ARV: B 1157: 156v–157r [1482/1/6] [Hinojosa Montalvo 1993a, no. 795]); and Sabata (ARV: B 323: 206r [1479/2/5] regarding a censal originally sold in 1442).

[122] Viciano Navarro 1997, 620–621, observes that the development of the state's fiscal apparatus reinforced the economic power and hegemony of seigneurs and urban oligarchs by facilitating their profitable investment in tax farms and in the public debt of municipalities.

telles indebted to David el Rau.[123] The Pròixidas familiarized themselves with
the Jews who visited Almenara and came to favor some Jewish families and factions over others. In 1469, when the royal prosecutor, acting for the plaintiffs
Mossé Sermati and Na Perla, denounced Jucef Quatorze and Salamó Arroti,
don Joan de Pròixida intervened on behalf of the latter. He obtained for Quatorze and Arroti a safe-conduct enabling them to appear in the bailiff general's
court to answer the charges.[124] A few years later, in September 1475, the same
Jucef Quatorze witnessed in Almenara a formal arbitration between the enemies Isaac, the son of Mossé Xamblell, and Astruc Rodrich. Dona Elionor, the
wife of Nicolau de Pròixida, and Pere Esparça, a knight of Morvedre, acted as
the arbitrators. This act, however, did not end the grudge the Xamblells harbored against the Rodrichs and their in-laws, the Comtes. Less than two weeks
afterward one of the Xamblells assaulted Vidal Comte, the father-in-law of Pastor Rodrich, in the jueria of Morvedre and took refuge in Almenara, "where
he is accustomed to be and reside." From Almenara Xamblell and some local
Christians then swooped down and robbed Pastor Rodrich on the royal
road.[125]

Onda, a town under the lordship of the Order of Montesa, continued to be
a hub for the Jews of Morvedre. In 1450 there were so many Jewish silversmiths
and tailors living and working around a particular suburban square that one of
the town's jurats attempted to have them transferred to the Muslim quarter,
where they could be segregated from the Christian population.[126] Some of
Onda's part-time Jewish residents came from Borriana, Castelló, and Vila-real,
but many were from Morvedre. Members of the Xamblell, Comte, Rodrich,
Levi, Vinaig, and Tarfon families were active in and around Onda in the latter half of the fifteenth century.[127] The Comtes, for example, used Onda as a

[123] ACA: C 2340: 30r (1404/12/1). The debtors were obliged to the heirs of the now deceased
David "in aliquibus peccunie quantitatibus et aliis rebus nonnullis." In this case Centelles and
Pròixida were not cooperating but instead were seizing the money and property in question for
themselves.

[124] ARV: B 1154: 359r (1469/4/10) [Hinojosa Montalvo 1993a, no. 688].

[125] APPV: P 25226, J. Argenti: n.f. (1475/9/25); ARV: B 1155: 498v–499v (1475/10/7) [Hino-
josa Montalvo 1993a, no. 750]. Jucef Quatorze had himself robbed Vidal Comte in 1471 (ARV:
MR 81: 174v [Hinojosa Montalvo 1993a, no. 701]). In 1477 dona Yolant, the widow of Joan de
Pròixida, the son of Nicolau and Elionor, sold a mule to Vidal Astori, one of the witnesses to the
failed arbitration (APPV: P 11380, M. Esparça: n.f. [1477/9/1]; ARV: B 323: 216r-v [1479/3/18]).
The barony of Nules, just up the road from Almenara, also saw a fair amount of Jewish traffic from
Morvedre. E.g., ARV: B 1150: 161r (1447/11/13) [Hinojosa Montalvo 1993a, no. 492]; APPV: P
13415, J. Calaforra: n.f. (1477/8/23); ARV: B 323: 534r (1482/2/9); B 1158: 46v–47r, 61v–62r
[Hinojosa Montalvo 1993a, nos. 807, 809].

[126] ARV: B 1151: 69r (1450/5/4) [Hinojosa Montalvo 1993a, no. 508]. On earlier contacts with
Onda, Meyerson 2004a; on the Order and the Crown, Guinot Rodríguez 1986.

[127] ARV: B 1152: 1175v–1176r (1455/11/18), 1180v (11/13), 1180v–1181r (11/23) concern a
suit between Abraham Xamblell of Onda and Isaac Xamblell of Morvedre and most recently of
Onda; B 1154: 350r (1469/4/28) concerns the confiscation of securities from the house of Haim

base from which to do business with the Muslims of nearby Artesa, Tales, and
Suera, whose lord was Francesc Sanchis Munyós.[128]

The Jews of Morvedre were not always able to move about the kingdom with
such facility. Not all lords were as welcoming or as conniving as the Pròixidas
of Almenara. Some seigneurs in the fifteenth century had to contend with a
shortage of tenants, declining revenues, and mounting debts, usually in the
form of censals, burdening themselves and their tenants.[129] They were therefore reluctant, at certain critical junctures, to allow their tenants to become indebted to Jews, whether through purchasing goods on credit from them or
through borrowing small sums of money from them. The financial difficulties
of the seigneury might worsen if peasant families assumed unmanageable burdens of debt.

Such concerns perhaps moved Felip Boïl, the lord of Massamagrell, to forbid Jews "to stay, reside, or do any work of their office" in the village. Boïl's decision, taken in 1447, was sudden, a "novelty." The bailiff general urged Boïl
to permit the Jews of Morvedre to stay and do business in Massamagrell "as
they have been accustomed in times past." Boïl's attorney counseled him that
the bailiff could not "force" him to allow Jews to stay there for more than three
days at a time. Thus Boïl's wife fined Çaçon Arroti 60 sous for remaining
longer. The Jew objected, pointing out to Boïl that he had never been advised
of this new rule. The lord returned the 60 sous to Arroti but then ordered him
and another Jew, Abraham Levi, to leave Massamagrell.[130]

Tensions between the Jews and the Boïls eventually abated. Members of the
the Toledano family at least earned the lords' favor. Their purchase of land in
Massamagrell, which they then held in enfiteusis, may well have pacified the
Boïls, who, like most other lords, were always on the lookout for new tenants.[131] In the 1470s Abraham and Mossé Toledano were busy there investing

---

Vinaig in Onda because Vinaig trespassed into the garden of a Christian of Onda; B 1158: 46v–
47r (1485/6/27) [Hinojosa Montalvo 1993a, nos. 687, 807] treats the 970 sous Mossé Levi owed
Pere Romeu of Onda for wheat purchased; ARV: C 135: 45v–46r (1488/4/13) treats the sale of
cloth by Onofre Falcó of Onda to Gento Tarfon of Morvedre when the latter was in Onda.

[128] ARV: B 1152: 933r (1454/11/7) for Artesa; 988r (1455/3/20) for Tales. ARV: P 2785, J. de
Campos Jr.: n.f. (1474/3/16): Vidal Comte appoints his brother Abraham as his procurator to collect debts owed by the lord and Muslim tenants of Suera. An ally of the Comtes, Jacob Rodrich,
visited Ayódar, another seigneury belonging to Sanchis; he was fined for sleeping with a Christian
woman there (ARV: C 261: 56r–57r [1443/10/11]).

[129] Furió 1997a, 137–141, 144–151; Garcia Oliver 1991, 67–94.

[130] ARV: B 1150: 87r-v (1447/5/8–24).

[131] ARV: P 442, J. de Campos Jr.: n.f. (1475/5/10) regarding land purchased by Abraham
Toledano in 1471; B 324: 280r-v (1491/7/12) regarding the "casa e heretat" of the deceased Mossé
Toledano in Massamagrell. The local justice refers to him as "quondam juheu terratinent nostre."
A significant upturn in the financial fortunes of the Boïl family may have influenced their view of
the Jews as well. Berenguer Vives de Boïl (d. 1477) received an annual revenue of 50,000 sous
from censals—see Furió 1997a, 146.

in livestock and in provisioning the village butcher shop; in 1492 various members of the family farmed the ecclesiastical tithes of Massamagrell and El Puig.[132]

The mobile Jews of Morvedre were sometimes caught in the crossfire between antagonistic lords and townsfolk. Hostility simmered in the later fifteenth century — and would boil over in the early sixteenth century — as municipal magistrates sought to extend their judicial authority over seigneurial vassals resident in villages in the municipal district and to exact whatever taxes they could from them.[133] Reluctant to see townspeople, of whatever faith, profit at their vassals' expense, "some knights" possessing lordships in the terme of Morvedre in 1474 prohibited their vassals from doing business with the town's Jews.[134] This measure, however, was taken partly in retaliation for the attempt of the jurats of Morvedre the previous year to prohibit the Jews from dealing with the Muslim tenants of the nearby seigneury of Petrés and thereby to deprive the Muslims of the Jews' needed services.[135] In this urban-rural struggle, powers on both sides saw the curtailment of Jewish activity as an effective tactic. For the lords, boycotting the Jews meant damaging Morvedre's economy; for the jurats, restricting the Jews meant inflicting hardship on the lords' tenants. The bailiff general quickly removed all such obstacles to the Jews' progress.

Most lords who caused problems for the Jews of Morvedre were more intent on gaining larger, illegitimate profits from Jewish trade than on denying the Jews access to their estates. The seigneurs' efforts to augment their revenue at the Jews' expense increased in the later fifteenth century, when a demographic boom in the jueria of Morvedre resulted in more Jewish traffic on their lands. In 1461 Joan de Torrella, the *procurador general* in the Vall d'Uixó for the sixteen-year-old Prince Enrique, nephew of Juan II and new lord of the valley, thought it a good idea to compel all Jews working in the valley's villages to conduct their business in one place. Torrella aimed to control Jewish trade as a means of more effectively taxing it. But when he arrested and fined Jews who refused to cooperate, King Juan intervened to prevent him from going any further with his plan.[136]

---

[132] ARV: P 3148: n.f. (1474/2/28); P 2092, B. Sans: n.f. (1474/11/25); B 1160: 439v–440r (1492/5/7) [Hinojosa Montalvo 1993a, no. 841].

[133] Furió 1997a, 124–125, and 1997b, 523–524; Garcia Oliver 1991, 73–75, 87–91; Barrio-Barrio 1993; Meyerson 1991, 21–25, 33–36, 89–90; García Cárcel 1981, 39–90; E. Duran 1982, 143–205.

[134] ARV: B 1155: 338r–339r (1474/11/21) [Hinojosa Montalvo 1993a, no. 738].

[135] ARV: B 1155: 150v (1473/11/22), 150r (11/23) [Hinojosa Montalvo 1993a, nos. 725–726]. Jews subsequently did business in Petrés. E.g., ARV: B 1220: M. 3, 9r (1485/12/9) treats the debt of Yuceff Matoti, a Muslim of Petrés, to Abraham Adzoni, Jew of Morvedre, for cloth purchased.

[136] ARV: C 287: 38v–39v; C 90: 59r-v (1461/7/28) [Hinojosa Montalvo 1993a, no. 605]. Also Llorens 1967, 57–60; López Elum 1974. ARV: B Procesos, Letra P, 2618: 73r (1430/8/16) indicates how well established some Jews of Morvedre were in the Vall d'Uixó. Here, Joan Ganer, the

Torrella was not the only seigneur, or seigneurial official, who regarded the
busy Jewish artisans and merchants as tempting targets. When the aljama of
Morvedre asked the new king, Fernando II, to renew its privileges in 1479, it
also beseeched him to correct certain alleged seigneurial abuses. In violation
of the Crown's jurisdiction over the Jews, some lords had been trying Jews in
seigneurial courts, sometimes on spurious charges, and extorting fines from
them. Other lords had been engaging in a kind of economic blackmail, refusing the Jews entry to their estates unless the Jews agreed to render them a certain monetary settlement.[137] Whether and how rapidly the new king rectified
these problems is difficult to know. Even though Fernando II was not one to
tolerate such infringements of the Crown's domain, there were practical limitations to what he and his bailiff general could do. Some Jews probably had to
pay the lords a little in order, they hoped, to earn a lot. It was part of the give-
and-take between enterprising Jews and often hard-pressed seigneurs.

The self-interested patronage and protection offered by Christian elites un-
derlay Jewish revival in fifteenth-century Morvedre. The few incidents in
which powerful Christians employed questionable methods to exploit the Jews
who inhabited their town or visited their estates did not impede the progress of
a community that hit its stride by midcentury. The elites' largely beneficent
treatment of the Jews, however, was by itself no guarantee of calm and comfort. The rest of the Christian population in Morvedre and environs had its own
views and experience of the Jews. If nonelite Christians for the most part in-
teracted benignly and nonviolently with the Jews, it was not just because they
were following the lead of their social betters. Indeed, with regard to the Jews,
they often acted of their own accord or took their signals from the church.

No other group influenced popular opinion of the Jews more than the
clergy. As ever, Catholic liturgy, parish life, and preaching accentuated the differences between the two religious communities and carried the kind of charge
that could explode into anti-Jewish violence. Yet in contrast to earlier times,
when the clergy had encouraged Christian laypeople to use religious ritual to
bludgeon the Jews into an inferior position, when bishops and their underlings
had aggressively campaigned against Jewish usury, and when Vicent Ferrer and
his mendicant predecessors had preached passionately to and venomously
about the Jews, after 1419 the clergy did little to stoke the flames of Christian
hostility toward the Jews. The coexistence of church and synagogue in Morvedre was less troubled than ever before.

The Christians of Morvedre had neither ceased to venerate the body of

---

royal castellan in the valley, testifies on behalf of Salamó Tarfon. According to Ganer, Tarfon, "que
usava de offici d'argenteria" in the valley, was regarded by the people of the place as a "home simple, benigne, no bregos, no escandalos, mas hom reposat e de bona fama." Tarfon's nephew, Mossé
Maymó, also had a silver smithy there (44v). See at n. 141; Meyerson 2003b.

[137] ARV: C 303: 80v–82r (1479/10/10).

Christ nor forgotten their membership in it. They still participated in the cathartic rituals of Holy Week, when they vented their anti-Jewish spleen and reaffirmed the Jews' role in Christian past, present, and eschatological future. Each year the Jews paid the king 150 sous for the "tax of protection" and the local justice 100 sous for guarding the Jewish quarter during Holy Week.[138] Yet these sums were taxes, their payment as indicative of bureaucratic routine as they were of a persistent physical threat to the Jewish community. The Jews of Morvedre did not once complain about Holy Week violence during the fifteenth century. True, youths, encouraged by the clergy, probably threw stones and shouted insults, but they did not mount the kind of assaults or manifest the sort of animosity that worried the Jews or exercised the justice and his guards, if they were even needed. The Jews had become accustomed to this annoying routine.

The salient point is that during the fifteenth century Holy Week rituals, and other religious rituals, seem never to have transcended the routine. They did not because the Christians of Morvedre no longer felt that they had something to prove, either to the Jews or to themselves. In the later thirteenth and early fourteenth centuries, when the clergy for the first time actively encouraged Valencians to adore the Corpus Christi, Christians had employed Holy Week rituals and eucharistic processions to humiliate and even terrorize Jews, to put the Jews in their place. These violent religious demonstrations had been integral to the process through which the Jews were disempowered and the Christians fully empowered. The process did not need to be reenacted in the fifteenth century, no matter how numerous and affluent the inhabitants of the Jewish quarter were. No Jew had the power or authority of the Jewish bailiffs of yore, and the Jews were absent from the city of Valencia, the seat of royal and episcopal power. After 1391, when Jewish survival was a more pressing concern than Jewish power, no Christian felt a compulsion to break into Jewish homes on Good Friday to remind the Jews where they stood.

Christians, however, were sensitive to perceived Jewish slights to their religion or coreligionists. Local officials thus took care to penalize Jews whose rowdiness might disrupt the solemnity of Christian holy days or whose negligence suggested disrespect for the Catholic faith. The bailiff fined Mossé Levi 60 sous for using arms "in a brawl he had with Jahudà Abenardut, alias Leó, during Holy Week."[139] Many years later a member of the Toledano family incurred a penalty for having disobeyed the proclamation of the mustaçaff that "every businessman should sweep the streets [in front of his shops and rental proper-

---

[138] See Meyerson 2004a for Christian attitudes and actions in the pre-1391 period. ARV: MR 3992–4024 (1413–92) for the "protection" payments to the Crown; and MR 7057: 42 (1432) [Hinojosa Montalvo 1993a, no. 391]; MR 7058: 8r (1438); MR 7059: 24v (1439); MR 7060: 3r (1446) for the payments to the local justice.

[139] ARV: MR 3992: 108r (1417).

ties] through which the body of Jesus Christ must pass" on Corpus Christi day.[140] Of course, Toledano was not just any businessman, he was a Jewish businessman. Even so, Toledano's laziness did not outrage many Christians, no more than had Mossé Levi's violence. If Christians had fingered Toledano and Levi, the penalization of the Jews satisfied them. In any case, these infractions were few and far between, and only indirectly offensive to Christianity. Jews were careful not to insult the Catholic faith, especially at sacred moments. Toledano did not throw garbage at the Corpus Christi procession, and if he neglected to sweep before his "houses" located along the procession route, it was probably owing less to laziness or malice than to his desire to be well away from it.

Had Mossé Levi attacked a Christian instead of another Jew during Holy Week, the potential for a Christian backlash against the Jewish community would have been quite high. At any time of year, bloodshed accentuated the boundaries between communities, forcing the members of each one to focus on their religious identity and communal allegiance, and hence to desire vengeance for a murdered or wounded coreligionist. Jewish violence against Christians was especially dangerous, since it made the fairly vulnerable Jewish community the target for Christian retaliation.

After Mossé Maymó, a Jew of Morvedre, ambushed and killed the Christian Pau de Sant Martí on the road to the capital, the local bailiff reported that "there was much murmuring in this town, [the Christians] saying that a Jew has killed a Christian." In order to quiet the hubbub, the bailiff arrested and delivered into the custody of an officer of the bailiff general Salamó Tarfon, an uncle of Maymó who had allegedly sent his teenaged son to the Vall d'Uixó to instruct his nephew, then residing in the valley, to pursue Sant Martí. As it turned out, the victim, Sant Martí, was not an Old Christian but a converso, one of several casualties in a feud between competing factions of Jews and conversos from Morvedre and Valencia. Furthermore, five Old Christians were willing to testify on Tarfon's behalf. Pelegrina, tavern-keeper and wife of Goçalbo de Vitoria, was an old acquaintance of Tarfon and, like many people (*moltes gents*), deemed him "a good man and a good Jew, and of good reputation." Another acquaintance of the Tarfon family, the widow Jacmeta, remembered that Salamó had passed by her door on the day of the murder and asked, "Na Jacmeta, have you seen my son?"[141] Other Christians, however, did not know Salamó Tarfon, his son, or the victim, Sant Martí. They only heard that a Jew had murdered a Christian. That was enough to spur the local bailiff to arrest Tarfon quickly and get him out of town until the facts of the case could be uncovered and publicized.

---

[140] ARV: MR 11764: 6v–7r (1471–72).

[141] ARV: B 1147: 219v (1430/7/17) [Hinojosa Montalvo 1993a, no. 378]. ARV: B Procesos, Letra P, 2618: 79v–80r (8/28), 85r–86v (9/1) for the testimonies of Jacmeta and Pelegrina, respectively. See also n. 136; chap. 6; Meyerson 2003b.

The Jews, too, understood that Christians would require retribution in such cases and might resort to vigilante-style justice to get it. Twenty-eight years after the demise of Pau de Sant Martí, a North African Jewish immigrant, Abraham Chilicori, and some Jewish accomplices wounded a Christian of Morvedre. When a local posse set out "to apprehend the Jews who wounded the Christian," the Jews of the town promised a reward to Joan Ferrer, a member of the posse, probably so that Ferrer would prevent the posse from taking extrajudicial revenge.[142]

These two cases, and that of another Jew arrested in 1464 on the suspicion of having wounded a Christian, did not add up to a terribly high Christian body count.[143] The number of Jews of Morvedre killed or wounded by Christians was not any higher.[144] Intercommunal violence in Morvedre, then, was hardly a social problem. Yet the memory and the fear of Christian violence lingered at the back of the Jews' minds and came to the forefront every time they visited Valencia's former jueria, every time they rendered the symbolic protection payments, every time one of their brethren did something as rash as to lash out at a Christian. Thus they kept in close contact with the bailiff general, requited the local bailiff for services rendered, and assiduously cultivated connections with the patricians, knights, and nobles of the region. They also greatly prized King Alfonso's privilege exempting them from wearing the Jewish badge when traveling outside Morvedre, where they were more vulnerable to the abuse of Christians unacquainted with them. The Jews had much less to fear from Christians who knew them and whom they knew.

Knowledge of Christians, generally and individually, was indeed a powerful tool. Due to their hard-earned knowledge of the Catholic liturgical year and its effect on the mood of the Christian population, Jews avoided being in the wrong place at the wrong time. Owing to their knowledge of individual Christians and of Christian social mores, Jews could pull the right strings, grease the right palms, and even yank the rug out from underneath their Christian enemies.

Gento Quatorze strikingly displayed such survival skills in 1472, when the innkeeper Salvador Martí, alias Sorribes, accused the Jew of having committed theft when he lodged at his inn on the road linking Morvedre to the capital. According to Sorribes, Gento had stolen clothing and other items worth 100 sous, which he bundled up and tossed out the window to his older brother

---

[142] ARV: B 1152: 1457r (1458/4/29), 1458v (5/7), 1469r (5/30) [Hinojosa Montalvo 1993a, nos. 572–573].

[143] ARV: B 1153: 552v (1464/6/19) [Hinojosa Montalvo 1993a, no. 647].

[144] For the post-1419 period, I have encountered only one possible case of the killing of a Jew of Morvedre by Christians: the murder and robbery of the wife of Salamó Fanduix (ARV: C 36: 10v [1426/3/26]). Oddly, King Alfonso asked the local bailiff to inform him "de vita et moribus dictorum judei et judee," as if an evaluation of their character would help him determine how severely to punish the still unknown murderers. There may have been other cases. Still, it is clear that the Jews of Morvedre were not frequently the objects of violent attack by Christians.

Jucef waiting in the street below. The plaintiff's charges, however, carried not a hint of anti-Judaism and ended with a defamation of the Quatorze brothers in religiously neutral terms: "the said Cuberets [the nickname of the Quatorzes] are great, public and famous thieves, and are persons infamous for many thefts . . . and as such are held, regarded, and reputed among those who know them."[145]

Gento's defense and countercharges, presented by his attorney, the notary Joan Colivella, had two aspects. On one hand, like Sorribes, he played on notions of morality and character shared by Christians and Jews. He defended his own character, stating first that he was a "good young man (*bon jove*)," and only then "a good Jewish youth (*bon jove juheu*)." He was accordingly "honest, without vice . . . of good reputation, life, and conduct."[146] Sorribes, in contrast, was a dishonest man who had abandoned his wife — she still lived in the terme of the capital on the Morvedre road — and was living "publicly with a *dona* he keeps in the inn."[147] Gento also compared himself, "a good worker, a silversmith working at his craft and living from it," to Sorribes, a farmer who avoided laboring on his lands and who "lives reposed and without work," subsisting on the profits earned from running an inn with his mistress.[148] Here Gento was not simply emphasizing his own honest labor, a trait much esteemed by Christians, especially those who were not rentiers, but, for the purpose of defaming Sorribes, cleverly inverting a calumny sometimes hurled at Jews.

On the other hand, Gento suggested that Sorribes's charge was not unbiased and that Sorribes had targeted him precisely because he was Jewish. Gento claimed that Sorribes and his companion, aside from stealing from their guests, "have already charged Muslims and *other guests* who come to lodge in the said inn, saying that they have stolen and taken things." Sorribes would then extort money from the guests who preferred to pay up rather than "be detained or mistreated."[149] Gento did not need to mention Jews in this countercharge to make his point; indeed, it was better that he did not. Gento understood that no

---

[145] ARV: B Procesos, Letra P, 52: 6r (1472/8/12): "los dits Cuberets . . . son grans ladres publichs e famosos e son persones diffamades de molts furts . . . E. per tals son hauts, tenguts e reputats per e entre los conexents aquells." There was something to the charges of Sorribes, for the older brother, Jucef Quatorze, was not exactly an upright citizen (see nn. 124–125). ARV: B 1157: 156v–157r (1482/1/7) [Hinojosa Montalvo 1993a, no. 794] treats accusations against Jucef for somehow tampering with the royal coinage. B 1155: 62r (1473/5/28), 73v–74r (7/3) [Hinojosa Montalvo 1993a, nos. 720–721] suggest that one of the Quatorzes—"hun juheu apellat Cuberet"—ran off to the seigneury of Borriol with the wife of a rabbi, Jucef Abenmuça.

[146] ARV: B Procesos, Letra P, 52: 19v (8/22).

[147] ARV: B Procesos, Letra P, 52: 17v.

[148] ARV: B Procesos, Letra P, 52: 17v, 19v: "bon treballador, argenter treballent en son offici e vivint de aquell." Gento also alleged that pimps and other riffraff frequented the inn of Sorribes.

[149] ARV: B Procesos, Letra P, 52: 17v: "sens esser se fet ne perpetrat furt algu en lo dit hostal, altres veguades han ja impetrat moros e altres hostes que venien a posar en lo dit hostal de furts, dientque havien furtat e preses coses del dit hostal . . . extortint ne peccunies per no esser detenguts o mal tractats per aquells."

court would disqualify a plaintiff because he or she was bigoted against Jews and Muslims. Gento took such prejudice as a given among Christians of all classes. He knew that the presiding judge, the bailiff general, did too and would thus find his description of Sorribes's extortion racket plausible. The bailiff and his assessors would not criticize or penalize any Christian for holding biases they themselves shared, but nor would they readily accept the charges of unsavory characters against religious minorities merely because the latter were Jewish or Muslim. Gento, then, knew Christians, knew Sorribes, and knew how to operate in the legal system.[150]

The confidence and competence of a Gento Quatorze to manipulate Christian values and prejudices in a Christian court in order to neutralize a Christian opponent grew out of social experience, the experience of living in a town and region where the multiplicity of economic and social ties between Jews and Christians nuanced and qualified all religious stereotypes. And the intricacy of these ties only increased — becoming a veritable tangle — over the fifteenth century as the Jewish population and the range of its interaction with Christians expanded. The character of the individual, and his or her position in overlapping networks of association and obligation mattered more and more; his or her Jewish or Christian identity was a less compelling factor. Thus Sorribes did not label the Quatorze brothers as "thieving Jews" but as "thieves" to all Christians, Jews, and Muslims "knowing them." Likewise, Gento rated himself and Sorribes on a scale of values common to members of all three faiths before alluding to his own Jewish identity or hinting at Sorribes's bigotry.

The Christian clerics of Morvedre were just as entangled as laypersons in the web of relations with local Jews, and so were not easily carried away by fantasies of the archetypal Jew of their theological education. The secular clergy at least stood to lose a great deal were they to agitate against the Jews or orchestrate destructive Holy Week violence against them. In the late 1460s and 1470s, for which significant notarial evidence survives, the Jews Jahudà Jabba and Mossé Bonet farmed the tithes and firstfruits pertaining to the church of Morvedre.[151] In 1471, one of Bonet's partners was the priest Joan Ferriols.[152] During these years, the archdeacon of Morvedre, the official responsible for leasing ecclesiastical revenues, was Gil Munyós, member of a local family long

---

[150] In the royal and municipal courts of the kingdom there was a remarkable respect for due process of law, which benefited the religious minorities and even slaves, especially once they learned to manipulate the legal system to their own advantage. See Meyerson 1991, 209–216, and 1996, 340–342; Blumenthal 2000. As for the result of the case of Sorribes vs. Gento Quatorze, the extant file is incomplete. The file ends with Salamó Zamero, Mossé Asseyo, and Samuel Quatorze posting bail for Gento on 25 August 1472 (B Procesos, Letra P, 52: 22v).

[151] APPV: P 17863, L. Miralles: n.f. (1469/11/29); three more entries (1470/5/14). Miralles was not the sole notary who worked in Morvedre, but only his registers survive and only for certain years. There is no reason to think that the Jews' farming of ecclesiastical taxes was anything new ca. 1470. See also chap. 3.

[152] APPV: P 17864, L. Miralles: n.f. (1471/4/24). P 17871: n.f. (1485/3/9) finds Ferriols selling to the Jew Jacob Toledano his rights to a censal owed him by Christian peasants.

linked to the Jewish community.[153] At the same time, no fewer than seven priests holding benefices in the local church were partially supported by the rents they received from Jews for rural properties or even houses in the Jewish quarter. One of these priests was Joan Ferriols; another was Ferran Malonda, member of a prominent local family who received annuities from the al-jama.[154] Hence local clerical and lay elites, themselves intertwined through kinship, both depended on the Jews to some degree.[155]

When Mossé Bonet and Joan Ferriols pooled their resources to lease or farm the ecclesiastical firstfruits, they had a third partner, the Christian Matheu Guallen, a local farmer. The three actually sublet the firstfruits from Joan Gil, the principal lessee and a citizen of Valencia. In almost all the other cases in which Jews farmed church taxes, they had local Christian partners, either Guallen or Berthomeu Camarelles Jr., or both.[156] Guallen and Ca-marelles also teamed up with Jews and other Christians to farm royal taxes in 1462.[157] After 1445, when members of the expansive Jewish community in-vested increasingly in farming the Crown's fiscal revenues, they frequently formed partnerships, or companies, with local Christians for this purpose. The Christian partners represented a fairly broad spectrum of local society, though all were reasonably well-off. On the lower end of the scale were pros-perous farmers like Matheu Guallen, and on the upper end were knights like

[153] See nn. 121, 151–152.

[154] The evidence is again fragmentary and is culled from the sales of real estate recorded by Miralles after 1470. It is indicative of a much larger phenomenon of Jews leasing rural and urban real estate from the church, usually by enfiteutic contract. APPV: P 17864: n.f. (1471/9/6): Gento Avincanes purchases land held under the direct lordship of a beneficed priest G. Berbegual for an annual rent of 3 sous; P 17862: n.f. (1472/2/20): Avincanes again purchases land for which he will owe an annual rent of 18 sous 4 diners to the priest F. Rubiols; P 17865: n.f. (1473/8/16): Samuel Agí purchases land to be held in enfiteusis from J. Ferriols, who holds the benefice of S. Vicent in the *ecclesia majori* of Morvedre, with an annual rent of 3 sous; P 17868: n.f. (1483/1/29): Salamó Çaporta sells a sheepfold, which he had held under the direct lordship of the benefice of Corpus Christi in the *ecclesia majori*, currently held by the priest J. Ros; P 17875: n.f. (1490/2/16): Samuel Agí buys land to be held in enfiteusis from the benefice of the Evangels, then held by the priest G. Simó de Capatoso, with an annual rent of 3 sous; P 12213: n.f. (1492/1/9): Bonadona, the widow of Gento Avincanes, holds houses in the Jewish quarter and land — carrying rents of 3 sous and 4 sous 4 diners, respectively — under the direct lordship of the benefice of Corpus Christi, then held by the priest Ferran Malonda. In 1482 the aljama sold an annuity to Francesc Malonda (ARV: B 1157: 156v–157r); one member of the family had been a jurat in 1476 (B 1155: 567r-v) [Hinojosa Montalvo 1993a, nos. 795, 755]. Doñate Sebastià and Magdalena Nom de Déu 1990, 91–94, for parallels in Castelló.

[155] The bishop in Valencia could not complain too strenuously about this state of affairs, since the almonry of the see received from Abraham Toledano alone 12 sous annually for the rent of a vineyard (APPV: P 17858, L. Miralles: n.f. [1475/1/2]).

[156] See nn. 151–153; Meyerson 1998, 74–75; chap. 3.

[157] ARV: MR 4009: 4r. The partnership consisted of the Christians Camarelles, Guallen, Joan de Sant Feliu, and Berthomeu Benet, and the Jews Mossé Benalrabi, Abraham Comte, and "oth-ers." They leased the *terç de delme* on bread, wine, and oil for 8,000 sous.

Joan de Sant Feliu and Baltasar Olives.[158] Yet another aspect of the economic interdependence of the two communities, these tax-farming partnerships probably had the additional, though unintended, benefit of reducing the resentment of Christian taxpayers toward Jews, whom they could less easily equate with tax collectors.

The Jews' farming of ecclesiastical and royal taxes was mirrored by the Christians' farming of the aljama's internal sales taxes. Potential Christian lessees had to bid for cises in the synagogue. There the adelantats auctioned them to the highest bidders, Jewish or Christian, just like the royal bailiff auctioning the king's taxes in the town's main plaza. Not all Jews appreciated the competition, as Miquel Cardona discovered when Jahudà Legem pulled a dagger on him in the synagogue. The unflappable Cardona nonetheless leased the cisa on kasher wine in 1418–19.[159] Some Christians purposely sought Jewish partners or backers to facilitate their investment in Jewish taxes and utilities. In 1483, when Miquel Aguilar leased the Jewish butcher shop, Abraham Legem acted as his principal guarantor.[160] In a town with a large Jewish community, a brisk trade in kasher wine and meat could translate into significant income for some Christians.[161]

Annuities, tax farms, and the leasing of rural and urban properties most clearly defined the mutual interests of Jews and Christians, giving each community a stake in the other's prosperity. Less obvious and less recorded were the myriad transactions that fostered familiarity and inspired trust between Jews and Christians. Trust freed Jews and Christians to designate an adherent of the other faith as a procurator, their legal agent for carrying out essential business. Abraham Alateffi thus empowered a local farmer, Pere Get, to collect all debts owed him, while Laurenç Cetina, also a farmer of Morvedre, appointed Jacob Toledano to demand the 75 sous a Christian of Puçol owed him from the purchase of livestock.[162] Such acts were hardly extraordinary; Christians and Jews needed to cooperate to get things done. Rather more unusual was the employment of a Christian procurator, Anthoni de Beses, by a Jewish woman named Mira for the purpose of recovering her dowry from her husband, Mossé Pelig. Mira felt compelled to take this step because she had fled her husband's household and retreated with her father's family to Xèrica three years earlier. Mossé had since taken a second wife but now lay ill. It was difficult and distasteful for Mira or her relatives to return to Morvedre and demand,

---

[158] ARV: MR 4006–4012 record Jewish-Christian tax-farming partnerships in 1455, 1461–64, and 1468. See also Meyerson 1998, 69–74.

[159] ARV: MR 3992: 129v (1418); MR 3993: 5v (1419); MR 39: 155v (1419).

[160] APPV: P 17868, L. Miralles: n.f. (1483/10/21).

[161] Municipal officials in Morvedre thus had little interest in emulating their counterparts in Castelló and Borriana who periodically obstructed the Jews' acquisition of these foodstuffs (nn. 64, 84).

[162] APPV: P 17863, L. Miralles: n.f. (1470/2/23); P 17862, L. Miralles: n.f. (1472/5/8).

as de Beses did, an inventory of Mossé's goods for the purpose of securing the dowry.[163]

Despite the extenuating circumstances, such Christian involvement in the intimate affairs of Jewish families troubled aljama officials. It seemed to threaten Jewish autonomy and give Christians too much knowledge of, if not a vested interest in, the Jewish community's internal affairs and disputes. Hence in 1454 the aljama sought renewal of an earlier communal ordinance prohibiting Jews engaged in lawsuits against coreligionists to designate Christians as their guarantors. Aside from infringing Jewish autonomy, Christian backing of one or another Jewish family or faction might complicate relations and unintentionally produce friction between the two communities. Cognizant that some Jews were willing to run that risk, the bailiff general was prepared to hear their objections before sanctioning the renewal of the ordinance.[164] Some Jews did protest in 1480 after the adelantats singled out the notary Pau Camporrelles in a communal ordinance that forbade members of the aljama to employ him as procurator in their suits against Jews. They deemed the ordinance a violation of their right to choose whichever procurator they saw fit. Camporrelles also complained, since he would lose clientele. The expertise in Jewish concerns that made Camporrelles an effective advocate for some Jews disquieted the adelantats. The bailiff general nonetheless called for the repeal of the ordinance.[165] Camporrelles would continue to serve his Jewish clients.

Economic transactions between Jews and Christians, however, were not all about bonding and strengthening mutual confidence. They could lead to litigation and tension, though between individuals, not between the Jewish and Christian communities. The missives of the bailiff general or, less frequently, of the king, which addressed the appeals of Jewish and Christian plaintiffs, do not evince patterns of economic conflict or special problem areas. If they show anything, it is that Jews were more frequently the targets of lawsuits initiated by Christian creditors or landlords. Anthoni Guerau, for example, sued to eject a Jewish tenant from the house he had recently purchased in the Jewish quarter.[166] Joan Ferrer, a dyer of Valencia, demanded that Profet Rodrich, or his guarantor Samuel Legem, pay him the 40 sous owed from the purchase of dyes.[167]

---

[163] ARV: B 1146: 42r (1424/4/3), 133r-v (10/26), 134r-v (10/30) [Hinojosa Montalvo 1993a, nos. 334, 340, 343], 331r (1426/7/1).

[164] ARV: B 1152: 881v (June 1454).

[165] ARV: B 1156: 709v–710r (1480/1/28) [Hinojosa Montalvo 1993a, no. 786].

[166] ARV: B 1152: 1331r (1457/3/30) [Hinojosa Montalvo 1993a, no. 568].

[167] ARV: B 1155: 303v (1474/9/19) [Hinojosa Montalvo 1993a, no. 737]. AMC: Justicia: n.f. (1481/7/5) and ARV: B Procesos, Letra P, 69 (7/6) treat the suit of Pere Abat, a carpenter of Morvedre, against the Jew Jacob Rodrich, who skipped town when payment was due on the 406-sous worth of textiles and clothing he had bought from Abat.

The bailiff general was especially interested in Christian claims against Jews that resulted in the confiscation and auctioning of the Jewish debtor's house in the jueria, and consequently had implications for the affairs of the Jewish community.[168] An especially perplexing and legally significant suit pitted a local Christian creditor against Mossé Gallego, and potentially against the aljama. In 1451, when the Christian asked the municipal justice to place a lien on a house belonging to the insolvent Mossé, he met unexpected opposition from another Jew, Jacob Vinaig, to whom Mossé had already mortgaged the property five or six years earlier in exchange for a loan of 400 sous. When Jacob displayed copies of the mortgage agreement that a rabbi, acting in a notarial capacity, had authorized, the Christian asserted that only charters redacted by Christian notaries were valid. The adelantats immediately dispatched a letter to the bailiff general warning that acceptance of the Christian's argument would put at risk a wide range of contracts affirmed between Jews without the intervention of a Christian notary. They cited nuptial agreements and dowry arrangements in particular, noting that the dowries and marriage gifts of Jewish women could not be protected against the claims of their husbands' creditors. The bailiff general must have concurred with the weighty legal arguments of the adelantats.[169] Mossé Gallego still would have had to requite his creditor, though by some other means.

The suits filed by Jews against individual Christians were not especially frequent, nor were they the source of intercommunal animosity.[170] Noticeably and significantly few were legal actions taken by Jewish creditors against Christian debtors. A revealing case of this sort, adjudicated in the governor's court in 1491, pitted Mira, the plaintiff and widow of Salamó Çaporta, against Jacme Serra, a farmer of Morvedre. Jacme, the designated executor of the will of his relative (probably brother) Pere, had for almost four years neglected to fulfill one of its clauses of interest to Mira. In the clause Pere expressed his wish that the Çaportas be repaid the 330 sous he had borrowed from Salamó to buy two horses.[171]

---

[168] E.g., ARV: B 1151: 20v (1450/2/3) [Hinojosa Montalvo 1993a, no. 507], regarding the local bailiff's auctioning of a house owned by Jucef Cerfati to two other Jews so that a debt allegedly owed by Jucef to the Christian Pere Berenguer could be satisfied.

[169] ARV: B 1151: 202r-v, 202v–203r (1451/5/17–18) [Hinojosa Montalvo 1993a, nos. 514–515]. There is no indication that the validity of contracts established between Jews and authorized by rabbis and communal officials was ever seriously in doubt. See Assis 1997, 132–135; Burns 1996.

[170] A typically mundane suit was that filed by Mossé Ardit of Morvedre against a Christian of Sogorb named Gaçó. Mossé sought to recover from Gaçó the ass he had rented to him in Borriana so that Gaçó could carry the baggage of an Augustinian friar to Valencia. Gaçó had subsequently sold the animal to Abdalla Moni, a Muslim of Sogorb (ARV: B 1151: 520v–521r [1452/5/10]).

[171] ARV: G 2392: 41r, 324r–326v, 336r-v (1491/3/3–4/12). The governor decided in favor of Mira.

In the gamut of Jewish-Christian interchange over the course of the fifteenth century, Salamó Çaporta's loan to Pere Serra was hardly unique. Serra's testamentary request that his Jewish creditor be repaid may not have been either. Even if unique, such an expression of good intentions toward a Jewish lender was consistent with the remarkable lack of Christian complaint and protest about Jewish usury in the decades following Alfonso IV's succession to the throne. These largely tranquil decades stood in dramatic contrast to the thirteenth and fourteenth centuries, when Jewish moneylending had frequently evoked Christian resentment and grievance and occasionally sparked violence.

Together with the changing structure of the kingdom's credit networks, which it both reflected and effected, a modification of official and contractual discourse defused what had once been an explosive issue. Royal Jewish policy and the new fiscal regime established the framework for the changed discursive and financial practices.

Fernando I had taken the decisive step in 1415 by confirming the legislation of Pope Benedict XIII that, among other things, prohibited Jewish usury and forbade notaries to redact contracts between Jews and Christians in which usury might be hidden. When Alfonso IV revoked the restrictive laws and authorized notaries to redact "all and whatever contracts, instruments, and public writings . . . between Christian and Jew," he nonetheless insisted that the contracts be "nonusurious." Royal officials and notaries took this to heart. In response to the demand of Jamila, the widow of Samuel Suxen, that the heirs of Abducalem Allahuen and other Muslims of the Serra d'Eslida repay her the 1,000 sous she had lent them, the bailiff general instructed the *amīn* of Eslida to force the debtors to requite Jamila — but "without any usury." The bailiff further enjoined: "you should neither allow nor permit the Muslims of the said Serra to borrow [on interest] or make such [usurious] contracts."[172]

If the bailiff general admonished Muslims thus, he and his colleagues were undoubtedly exacting with Christian borrowers and notaries. Consequently, the notary Lleonard Miralles, who worked in Morvedre in the latter half of the century, always wrote in the instruments he redacted that the Jew was lending the money to the Christian (or Muslim) borrower *gratiose*, that is, without charging interest.[173] Likewise, when Christians appeared before the court of the justice of Castelló (whose records are extant) to acknowledge their liability to repay Jews from whom they had borrowed money, they almost always stated that the loan was "gratuitous" and never mentioned any interest charged.

Yet the same municipal justice also took oaths from Jewish lenders in which

---

[172] ARV: B 1146: 211v (1425/5/10): "sens usura alguna. E no consintes ni permetes que los moros de la dita serra manleven ni facen tals contractes."

[173] APPV: P 17864 (1471), 17862 (1472), 17858 (1475), 17859 (1477), 17861 (1479), 17880 (1482), 17868 (1483), 17871 (1485), 17873 (1487), and 12213 (1492) are the registers of Miralles in which Jewish loans are recorded.

they swore not to charge interest of more than 4 sous per pound, in essence, not to charge interest beyond the old royal rate.[174] There was, in other words, a disjunction between what Christian debtors said the Jews did — or did not do — in their formal statements of obligation before the justice's court and what the Jews actually did and were permitted to do. Notaries like Miralles merely disguised the interest charged in the "gratuitous" loan contracts they drew up. Kings and bailiffs general took the fiction one step further. In their letters describing and promoting the economic activities of Jews in rural villages — precisely where they did the most lending — they noted Jews engaged in industry, commerce, tax farming, and, ambiguously, the work of "their office," but they never mentioned Jewish moneylending.[175]

Christian borrowers, of course, still agreed to pay interest to the Jewish lenders. Some may well have resented it. But there was no longer an official discourse to stir up, articulate, and channel their resentment at Jewish usurers. Kings and their officials, and even the clergy had decided not to make an issue of Jewish usury. The bishops of Valencia, who acquiesced in the proliferation of the censal, did not view the minor lending operations of Jews as a significant problem.[176] Priests in Morvedre acted as witnesses when Jews loaned money to Christians *gratiose*.[177] After 1398 no royal investigations were conducted into Jewish usury *ultra cotum*. After 1415 there was not supposed to be any cotum, any official rate of interest, at all. The "guilt" of Jewish usurers was no longer presumed as much as ignored. Christian borrowers accepted the fiction of the gratuitous loan with its disguised interest because they needed money to tide them over through the lean months, and because they had always borrowed it from the Jews. Since the authorities were content to perpetuate the fiction, the borrowers did not, or could not, complain. The fiction did not shock and outrage borrowers because it merely sanctioned long-established usage.

Lay and ecclesiastical authorities did not give much attention to Jewish moneylending because the Jews were now minor players in the kingdom's credit market. The dominant figures were the Christian censalistas, who, through the purchase of censals, extended loans to the Crown, to municipali-

[174] Magdalena Nom de Déu 1988, 84–86. The registers of the justice's court recorded 214 cases of monetary loans between 1416 and 1492. Three Jews — Abraham and Jahudà Legem, and Samuel Azarilla — took the oath between 1441 and 1455. See also Mira Jódar 1993, 108–125.

[175] E.g., the documents cited in nn. 130, 134–135. Motis Dolader 1997a, 88–89, indicates similar changes in the Jews' purveying of credit in Aragon proper but makes no suggestions as to the possible significance of these changes for Jewish-Christian relations.

[176] Because it yielded relatively low rates of interest, the censal had been tolerated by the church in the fourteenth century. In 1425 Pope Martin V explicitly legitimized the censal. See Schnapper 1965, 976–983; Ferrer Micó 1997, 648–655.

[177] E.g., APPV: P 17873, L. Miralles: n.f. (1487/1/31) where the priest Miquel Corbera is recorded as a witness to Abraham Legem's loan of 200 sous to Bernat Oliver, a Morvedre innkeeper.

ties, to the church, to seigneurs and their villages, and even to Jewish aljamas. The Jews made only small loans to farmers and artisans. To the degree that the credit market structured relations of power and consolidated the position of elites in the kingdom, the Jews were no longer engaged in the kinds of credit operations that seemed to put them on top, that seemed to give them inordinate power. In the thirteenth and fourteenth centuries the extension of credit to the Crown had enabled some Jews to acquire royal bailiates and Jews like Jahudà Alatzar to exercise enormous influence in the city and kingdom of Valencia. The importance of Jewish taxes to the royal treasury had also necessitated and perpetuated widespread Jewish lending and debt collection, the latter with royal complicity and a kind of insistence that gave the idea or myth of Jewish power a longer life than it deserved. Through their wielding of financial power, Christian censalistas put that myth to rest in the fifteenth century. In Morvedre the aljama and individual Jews were most often in debt to them. Screaming about Jewish usury was difficult when almost everyone, including the Jews, were in thrall to the censalistas.

On the eve of the expulsion bonds of mutual interest firmly tied the Jews of Morvedre to local elites, to the lords of the region, and even to the clergy of the local church. The Jews were still "useful" to many in the town and region but were no longer deemed threatening. Christians saw Jews neither as too powerful nor as usurious exploiters of the Christian poor. A much changed fiscal regime and credit market freed both Jews and Christians from the yoke of "Jewish usury." The institutions of a more powerful state created the conditions for a promising era of Jewish-Christian coexistence in post-1419 Morvedre.[178] Unfortunately, the Spanish Inquisition, an institution established by the state for religious reasons, would bring this era of amelioration to an untimely end.

[178] See also Meyerson 1991 and 1995a; c.f., e.g., Motis Dolader 1997b.

Chapter Three

WINE, MONEY, AND MOBILITY

In the later fifteenth century the Jewish community in Morvedre was large and prosperous. The Jews benefited from the protection of the monarchy and vigilant royal bailiffs, and from a more moderate fiscal regime. Their relations with the Christian population were benign and free of serious conflict; their ties with members of the Christian elite, local and regional, were particularly solid. The Jews had established a safe place for themselves in the town on the lower Palancia, a place of their own. Comprising roughly one-quarter of Morvedre's total population, they were an important, nearly indispensable component of its economic and social fabric. The Jews enjoyed a level of influence unseen in the town since the late thirteenth century, when Jewish bailiffs held the keys to the local castle. Although Jews were not conspicuous authority figures like some of their thirteenth-century forebears, their community's demographic weight and economic clout were impressive.

The community's ascent to this zenith of prosperity, however, was not simply a result of more Jews doing the same things the Jews of the town had always done. The Jews of Morvedre had perforce adjusted to the new economic, social, and legal realities brought about by the violence of 1391 and subsequent royal policies. The extinction of the Jewish aljama of Valencia and the rise in its place of a large, vibrant, and highly entrepreneurial converso community presented the Jews of Morvedre with new challenges — particularly of a religious nature — but also offered them new economic opportunities. Collaboration with conversos became essential and profitable for Jews involved in wine production, trade, and the textile industry. The rearrangement of the kingdom's socioreligious geography, moreover, brought both Jewish bodies and Jewish capital to Morvedre. This Jewish migration broadened the agricultural and industrial sectors of the Morvedre community while augmenting the resources available to local Jews for investment. At the same time, the Crown's prohibition of Jewish usury and the growing use of new credit mechanisms by its subjects compelled well-to-do Jews to modify their investment strategies.

Still, there was a great deal of continuity with the economic patterns prevailing prior to 1391. The wide region extending from Valencia in the south to Castelló in the north remained the stomping ground of the Jews of Morvedre, and mobility continued to be crucial for their success. As ever, individual Jews often engaged in a number of pursuits simultaneously. Few Jews were just wine producers, moneylenders, tax farmers, artisans, or merchants; instead, they might be found practicing any two or three of these occupations. This and their diversified investment of capital enhanced their ability to adapt to structural changes. When necessary, they could privilege one activity over another or abandon a particular activity altogether. Economic diversification was a means of success as well as of survival.[1]

Brimming confidence and optimism characterized the Jews of Morvedre from the 1430s. Secure in their relations with monarchy, Christian elites, and the bulk of the Christian and Muslim populations, the Jews moved about the region boldly and unhesitatingly, as a royal letter of 1461 vividly describes:

> the greater part of the Jews of the said aljama [Morvedre] are merchants, silk-weavers, shoemakers, and artisans . . . [who] were and are accustomed, in almost any week and for the greater part of the time, to travel outside the said town through the valleys and villages near it and through other places, whether of Christians or of Muslims, and to stop in them to sell their handicrafts and their goods — for example, silverware, silk, and other items — and to farm some taxes, and this [they do] pacifically and tranquilly, and without molestation, vexation, and contradiction of any kind, just as they please and as the law [fur] provides for.[2]

Even this documentary snapshot does not fully capture the wide-ranging activity and energy of the Morvedre Jews during their final decades. Ready and able to seize opportunities, some of them were branching out into new areas. Their prospects appeared bright.

AGRICULTURE

The Jews of Morvedre remained close to the soil. They were as active as ever in the regional land market.[3] Between 1471 and 1492 just one notary, Lleonard

[1] The loss of the records of the municipality of Morvedre and of almost all the notaries who worked there prevents a quantitative analysis of the Jews' economic activities after 1391. Still, the fragmentary evidence culled from the letters of kings and royal bailiffs, combined with that contained in the relatively few extant notarial contracts and in the terse accounts of local bailiffs, does permit a reasonably detailed qualitative treatment, one that clarifies the differences between the Jews' pre- and post-1391 economic life.

[2] ARV: C 287: 38v–39v (1461/7/28): "Quod cum pro maiori parte judei dicte aljame sint mercatores, siricarii, sutores et mecanici ut . . . consueti fuerunt et sint quasi in qualibet septimana et pro maiori parte temporis extra dictam villam per valles et loca illi coniutiva et alia, tam cristianorum quam sarracenorum, incedere et ad eas et ea declinare ad vendendas operas et res suas, ut puta argenti, sirici et alias mercancias, item et ad emendas merces nonnullas, et hoc pascifice et quiete et absque cuiusquam molestia, vexatione et contradictione juxta mentem et dispositionem fori." The fur in question was issued by Pere II and provided for freedom of commerce throughout the kingdom.

[3] For instance, a letter from 1369 describes the Morvedre Jews as holding "lands and other possessions" in places under the jurisdiction of "great lords, nobles, knights, and others" (ACA: C 1577: 32v–33r). Others, from 1366, treat the bona sedentia et moventia possessed by Jucef Çer-

Miralles, recorded ten sales of land located within the town's terme to Jews—
nine by Christians and one by a Jewish widow—and five to Christians by Jews.[4]
Outside the terme, Abraham Toledano, for example, purchased 13 *fanecades*
of cereal land in the seigneury of Massamagrell.[5]

The kinds of land possessed by Jews varied, though higher-quality irrigated
parcels, located in the municipal district and on seigneuries, were more common than parcels located in dry farming areas.[6] Jews owned irrigated land in
several *alqueries* of the terme, like Montiber, Ponera, Almarda, Almudaffer,
Gausa, and Benuera.[7] As for the crops cultivated on these lands, there is sparse
evidence of cereal grains or of fig and carob trees.[8] Evidence of Jews milling
and marketing grain is more substantial, but most of this grain was obtained
through lending operations and tax farming, not from the crops harvested on
their own properties.[9] Vineyards by far predominated among the lands held by
the Jews of Morvedre, who were still producing and marketing wine on a large
scale.[10]

Though some Jews of Morvedre owned allodial parcels, most of their land
was leased from other landlords.[11] Jews leased their land according to enfiteutic contract—that is, having usufruct of the land and in return paying an an-

ruch and Jacob Avenrodrich, Jews of Morvedre, in the district of Borriana (ACA: 729: 121r-v; C
731: 21r).

[4] The sales to Jews are APPV: P 17864: n.f. (1471/9/6); P 17862: n.f. (1472/2/20); P 17865: n.f.
(1473/3/4, 8/16); P 17866: n.f. (1474/4/2); P 17858: n.f. (1475/1/21); P 17867: n.f. (1476/3/2); P
17880: n.f. (1482/3/27, 5/29); P 17875: n.f. (1490/2/16). The sales to Christians are P 17862: n.f.
(1472/1/10) [the sale originally took place 1462/1/14]; P 17880: n.f. (1482/2/18); P 12213: n.f.
(1492/7/13, 7/16, 10/14). The July sales were made by the Jewish owners themselves just before
they departed Iberia. Hirles Abros, a Christian procurator acting on behalf of the expelled Salamó
Tarfon, made the final sale.

[5] ARV: P 442, J. de Campos Jr.: n.f. (1475/5/10). Abraham bought the land for 400 sous from
Barthomeu Almuder of Albalat. Abraham held the land in enfiteusis from the local lord and was
obliged to pay an annual rent in kind of 2 *almuts* (1 *almut* = 4.18 liters) of wheat and "other *almuts*" of barley for each *cafissada* (= 6 *fanecades*).

[6] Garcia Oliver 1994, 255.

[7] APPV: P 17862: n.f. (1472/1/10, 2/20): Montiber; P 17867: n.f. (1476/3/21): Ponera; P
17880: n.f. (1482/2/18): Almarda; (3/27): Almudaffer; (5/29): "l'alqueria d'en Guayta"; P 12213:
n.f. (1492/1/9): Gausa. Meyerson 2004a for the pre-1391 period.

[8] See n. 5 for cereals. APPV: P 17867, L. Miralles: n.f. (1476/2/19) and P 17880, L. Miralles:
n.f. (1482/5/29) for carob. Archivo Municipal de Alcoy: P, Pere Benavent: n.f. (1492/7/13) [Hi-
nojosa Montalvo 1993a, no. 861] for figs. Many of the documents mentioning Jewish ownership
of land make only general references to Jewish *hereditates* or *terra*.

[9] E.g., ARV: MR 7056: 5v (1375); B 1152: 1055v–1056r (1455/8/6) [Hinojosa Montalvo 1993a,
no. 549]; APPV: P 17873, L. Miralles: n.f. (1487/5/13).

[10] See below. Jews living in communities that were not involved in major wine production also
owned vineyards from which they manufactured small amounts of wine for their own consumption: Motis Dolader 1985, 362–375; Magdalena Nom de Déu 1974, 276.

[11] An example of an allod is APPV: P 17867, L. Miralles: n.f. (1476/3/21), recording Mossé
Alateffi's purchase of a *troceum vinee francum* from a local farmer, Vicent Ramon.

nual rent, usually in cash but sometimes in kind to the landlord. While the
landlord retained eminent domain over the land, the Jewish lessee was, for all
intents and purposes, its real owner; provided he paid the rent, he could pass
the land on to his heirs.[12] The Jews rented from various landlords: the Crown,
seigneurs outside the terme, local knights and clergy, and the see of Valencia.[13]

Whether full owners of the land or lessees, the Jews did not necessarily cultivate the land themselves. In some cases they probably leased or sublet the
land to Muslim or Christian tenant farmers. In others, however, Jews performed the labor, especially the viticultural labor. As the Jewish community expanded in the fifteenth century, more Jews, particularly lower-class Jews,
worked in the vineyards.[14]

The manufacture of kasher wine was far more than a minor or subsidiary occupation for the Jews of Morvedre; geared to supplying external markets, it had
long been one of the mainstays of the community's economy. Due to the scale
of production, the Jews customarily had recourse to Gentile labor for crushing
the grapes. In the cisa ordinances of 1403 and 1452, communal authorities explicitly acknowledged Gentile involvement in the production process. They
required the collection of the cisa from Christians or Muslims "making Jewish
wine" and from Jews "making Jewish wine in the power of Christians of the
said town" or buying "Jewish wine" from the Christians. The Jewish wine in
question was not the finished product but the must, which could be treaded in
vats owned by local Christians.[15]

Before 1391 the Jews in Valencia had constituted the largest and most reliable group of customers for the kasher winemakers of Morvedre. Numbering
more than two thousand in the later fourteenth century, they had depended
on Morvedre's kasher vintage, for, as they asserted in 1375, "they neither have
nor possess vineyards from which they might gather [grapes to manufacture]
wine for their sustenance or for resale."[16] The destruction of the Jewish community in the capital forced the Jewish winemakers of Morvedre to orient their
production more toward satisfying the needs of Jews outside the kingdom.

---

[12] Furió 1982, 106–119; Císcar Pallarés 1977, 76–77.

[13] ARV: MR 3992: 107v (1417): the Crown; APPV: P 17865, L. Miralles: n.f. (1473/3/4): the
knight Francesc Llopis Doteyta; (8/16): the priest Joan Ferriols; P 17858, L. Miralles: n.f. (1475/
1/2): the see of Valencia. Also, n. 5.

[14] Meyerson 2004a for pre-1391 patterns; see below.

[15] ACA: C 2339: 109r-v (1403/12/6): "vinum judahicum in posse quorumvis cristianorum dicte
ville"; ARV: B 1151: 568v–570r (1452/7/31) [Hinojosa Montalvo 1993a, no. 529]. Soloveitchik
1978, 172–173, 178, 187; Toaff 1996, 74–83; Meyerson 2004a.

[16] ACA: C 781: 152v–153r (1375/9/1). The Jews made this assertion in the course of a successful plea to Pere III that the jurats of Valencia not be allowed to apply to the Jewish community
their protectionist laws, which were designed to protect local Christian winemakers and vintners
from external competition . C 734: 33v (1368/1/10) is a similar plea. For earlier laws, see, e.g.,
AMV: MC A9: 14r (1349/7/23), 98v–99r (1350/7/29); for later ones, García Marsilla 1993, 50,
53, 60, 109–110.

Even if the Old Christians, or Muslims, of Valencia occasionally bought their wine, it was no compensation for the loss of thousands of Jewish consumers.[17] Observant Valencian conversos seeking kasher wine for ritual purposes probably gave Morvedre's Jewish winegrowers some business, but, in order to evade the inspection of royal and municipal officials, their purchases would have been clandestine and in small quantities. In any case, the ritual consumption by a segment of the converso population hardly matched the daily or frequent consumption by Valencia's entire Jewish community.[18]

The flight of Iberian Jews and forced converts to North Africa, however, considerably increased the demand for kasher wine in the enlarged Maghriban Jewish communities. Several factors helped the Jews of Morvedre at least partially meet it. First of all, the Morvedre Jews' efforts to export kasher wine in greater volume took place during Valencia's great age of commercial expansion, when it superseded Barcelona as the Crown of Aragon's most important port. There was no direct relationship between the kasher wine trade and Valencia's rise, but the growing traffic of merchants from all over the Mediterranean, and even the Atlantic, created conditions more conducive to it.[19] Limitations on the length of time that Jews of the kingdom might stay in the capital did not inconvenience the Jews of Morvedre much or hamper their negotiations with foreign merchants and Valencian exporters.[20]

Second and most important, Valencian conversos were heavily involved in the city's export commerce and therefore could function as intermediaries between Morvedre's Jewish winegrowers and North Africa's Jewish consumers.[21] They dealt, in fact, not just in kasher wine but in "ordinary" wine from Morve-

---

[17] ARV: P 519, D. Català: 3r-v (1470/1/6): Samuel Agí of Morvedre is paid the rest of the 120 sous for the wine he sold to Domènec Carbonell, a plowman of Valencia. A *responsum* of R. Simon ben Ẓemaḥ Duran (*She'elot u-teshuvot*, 3: no. 88) refers to a Jew of Morvedre, Aaron Pelos, who sold wine to Muslims from his tavern in Meliana, a village in the terme of Valencia. See Gutwirth 1985, 204.

[18] Although I have not encountered for Valencia explicit legislation forbidding the sale of kasher wine to New and Old Christians, such as that enacted in Mallorca in 1400 and in Lleida in 1410 (Riera i Sans 1988, 304), according to the legislation passed in the Corts of Valencia in 1403, Jews conducting commerce in the city of Valencia were obliged to appear in the court of the bailiff general with a detailed inventory of all their merchandise (ARV: C 630: 350r-v [Hinojosa Montalvo 1993a, no. 270]). In ARV: B 1219: 131r-v (1410/9/22) Simó Valleriola, a converso silkweaver, asks the bailiff general to place a lien on the "money or wine" that a city gatekeeper had confiscated from Samuel Najari, a Jew from Morvedre. Perhaps Valleriola knew that Samuel sold wine to local conversos and was thus ready to file suit when the gatekeeper caught him.

[19] Guiral 1986; Hinojosa Montalvo 1976. Garcia Oliver 1997b, 45; Iradiel 1989, 278, for the agrarian context.

[20] Hinojosa Montalvo 1979, 24–25, shows that thirty-three Morvedre Jews came to Valencia for commercial purposes between 1391 and 1433. Given the limitations of Hinojosa Montalvo's sources, however, the entry of many Jews would not have been recorded. Furthermore, officials did not note the place of origin of 255 Jews whose entry they did record.

[21] Guiral 1975, 88.

dre, which they exported to Flanders and Normandy.[22] Still, their familial and (secret) religious ties to Iberian Jews transplanted to North Africa made them the ideal purveyors of Morvedre's kasher wine. Valencian conversos often acted in association with Mallorcan conversos and shipped the wine to the Maghrib through the port of Mallorca, which functioned as a center of distribution for Valencian wine. Some Mallorcan converso merchants came to the kingdom of Valencia and purchased kasher wine directly from Jews of Morvedre. When questions arose as to the *kashrut* of wine sent by one such merchant to the Jews of Ténès, Rabbi Simon ben Ẓemaḥ Duran accepted his assurances that it was indeed kasher wine from Morvedre. The rabbi, an immigrant to Algiers from Mallorca, declared, "this wine surely was not produced by the Mallorcan convert, since, as everyone knows, it has the appearance and taste of wine from the kingdom of Valencia."[23] Jews with discriminating palates obviously appreciated the wine of Morvedre.

Rabbi Isaac ben Sheshet Perfet, however, was not always inclined to believe that the wine converso merchants sold was kasher wine from Morvedre, or elsewhere, uncorrupted by the touch of Gentiles.[24] The traffic in kasher wine from Morvedre to North Africa nonetheless continued unabated. Morvedre's winegrowers doubtless made sure that their product was transported in sealed casks and accompanied by a certificate of kashrut.[25] The Valencian converso Guillem Ramon Splugues, who had moved to the capital from Morvedre after his baptism in 1463 at the age of thirty-five, obviously knew how Morvedre's Jewish winegrowers manufactured and traded in kasher wine and had no doubt that there was still a healthy market for it in the Maghrib. Thus, as he confessed to the Spanish Inquisition, he determined, in 1476 or 1477, to export more than ten thousand liters of kasher wine to Tunisian Jews in the following manner:

> in the town of Nules . . . he [Splugues] bought the 1,000 *cànters* [1 *cànter* = 10.77 liters] of wine [i.e., must] exiting from the vat and had three Jews make it [the wine] kasher with full Jewish ceremony inside the house of the said En [Johan or Pere] Verdejo. The three Jews were the oldest son of Bendito, who is named Mossé Bendito and today lives in Morvedre, and is the son-in-law of Aluex, once Jew of

---

[22] Guiral 1975, 84–86; and 1986, 86–87, 233–234.

[23] S. Duran, *She'elot u-teshuvot*, 2: no. 60. See also Gutwirth 1985, 203–205; Abulafia 1994, 223–226; Epstein 1968, 30–31, 48. Orfali Levi 1982, 26–29, 31 (on the opinions of Duran's son), 56; and Netanyahu 1973, 35, 42–43, offer further, and somewhat contrasting, discussions of Duran's views.

[24] Perfet, *She'elot u-teshuvot*, no. 12, where in response to a query from a rabbi in Oran about the kashrut of wine sent by Mallorcan conversos, who had asserted that it was kasher wine from Morvedre, Perfet maintained that conversos could not ensure that the wine they sent had not been touched by Christians. See also Magdalena Nom de Déu 1988–89, 193–194; Hershman 1943, 70–71; Orfali Levi 1982, 25–26, 55; Netanyahu 1973, 27.

[25] This was the case of the wine approved by Rabbi Simon ben Ẓemaḥ Duran above, as noted by Epstein 1968, 48 n. 27; Hershman 1943, 71 n. 21. Also, Netanyahu 1973, 48–49.

Nules; the other Morcat, or Mossé Morcat of Borriana; and the other Gento Tarfon, silversmith of Morvedre who was then in Nules and is uncle of the confessant. The confessant paid them their wages. And the confessant intended to transport the said kasher wine to Tunis, in Muslim lands, in order to sell it to Jews.
[But] after a few days the said wine turned bitter and the confessant threw it out
and it was not shipped for sale.[26]

However much some North African rabbis questioned the kashrut of wine
handled by converso merchants, Jewish winemakers in Morvedre were not
wholly, or perhaps not even primarily, dependent on the services of the latter.
Throughout the fifteenth century North African Jewish merchants visited the
port of Valencia. Little is known about the goods with which they returned
home, but they must have departed with cargoes of kasher wine. Usually the
local factors and partners of these Maghriban Jews were Valencian conversos
who could easily have arranged for their acquisition of Morvedre wine.[27] The
Maghribans, however, did not have to rely on converso middlemen. The "Barbary Jew" David Cohen, for instance, stayed in Morvedre for a time himself
and then sailed for Mallorca on business. He may well have been shipping
Morvedre wine to North Africa through Mallorca.[28]

Occasionally Morvedre Jews themselves voyaged to North Africa to market
their wine, though, given the activities of converso and Maghriban merchants,
such trips were not crucial for their business. In 1456–57 Samuel Ardutell set
out for Oran carrying wine, textiles, and sugar.[29] Morvedre's Jewish merchants
also traveled to Almería in the sultanate of Granada, which housed a Jewish

---

[26] AHN: Inq., leg. 538, caja 2, no. 27: 37v (1491/1/31): "Ço es que pot haver quatorze o quinze
anys poch mes o menys que . . . en la villa de Nules . . . ell compra los dits mil quanters de vi ra-
jant de cub y hague tres juheus que'l feren caçer ab tota la cerimonia judayca dins la dita casa
del dit en Verdejo, e los dits juheus eren lo hu fil major de Bendito, e huy se nomena Mosse Bendito e esta en Murvedre y es gendre de Aluex, juheu de Nules quondam, y lo altre Morcat o Mosse
Morcat de Burriana y lo altre Gento Tarffon, argenter de Murvedre, qui esta lavors en Nules y es
oncle del confessant, als quals ell confessant los paga lurs jornals. E tenia ell confessant deliberat
de aportar lo dit vi caçer en Tuniz, terra de moros, pera vendre aquell a juheus. E apres a cap
de dies lo dit vi se torna agre e ell confessant lança lo dit vi e no'l sen porta a vendre." See also
chap. 6.

[27] Piles Ros 1984, esp. 221–222; Guiral 1974, 107–110. Piles (225), Guiral (117), and Hinojosa Montalvo 1979, 27, all emphasize that the extant sources reveal almost nothing about goods
exported, unless they were prohibited items (coses vedades) requiring a special export license from
the bailiff general.

[28] ARV: B 1151: 469r-v (1452/3/4) [Hinojosa Montalvo 1993a, no. 528]. It is of interest, too,
that a Jew of Morvedre, Salamó Zamero, and his wife traveled to Algiers in 1480 to claim an inheritance (ARV: B 1156: 729r-v [Hinojosa Montalvo 1993a, no. 788]). They either had immigrated
to Morvedre from North Africa or maintained ties with their family in Algiers. In either case, such
connections facilitated the trade in kasher wine from Morvedre inasmuch as they enabled
Maghriban Jews to know more about the wine's manufacture.

[29] Hinojosa Montalvo 1979, 34. Jacob Ardutell, a relative of Samuel, went on a Galician ves-
sel to Oran to "mercadejar" in 1428 (ARV: B 264: 92r [Hinojosa Montalvo 1993a, no. 364]).

community. Samuel Chifalla, who was definitely involved in the wine trade, and his son Jacob were frequent visitors there in the 1460s and 1470s.[30] A Mediterranean Jewish community outside Islamdom, that of Cagliari, Sardinia, was also paid a visit by a wine merchant from Morvedre, Jucef Agí.[31]

Increasingly important as a nexus between the Mediterranean and Atlantic worlds, Valencia saw the passage of numerous Portuguese and Vizcayan merchants. The Portuguese became "lovers of the wine of Morvedre," usually loading their ships with it, in either Valencia or Morvedre itself, for the voyage home.[32] The Portuguese Jews who came to Valencia on these ships no doubt added kasher wine to their cargoes.[33] One Jewish family of Morvedre, the Astoris, had by the 1480s established a branch in Portugal for commercial purposes. While importing black African slaves to Valencia, they probably exported wine, kasher and "ordinary," to Portugal.[34]

Some Jews in fact became involved in the commerce of "ordinary" wine through farming the royal tax on bread, wine, and oil, which was often paid in kind by residents of Morvedre's terme. Once the wine was rendered to them, Jewish tax farmers like Salamó Çaporta then sold it to export merchants in Valencia.[35]

For Morvedre's manufacturers of kasher wine the overland trade with Aragonese Jewish communities was perhaps as vital as the maritime trade. The Jews of Teruel in particular frequently purchased wine in Morvedre.[36] From

[30] Ruzafa García 1988, 350, 362, 365–368; Hinojosa Montalvo 1979, 34. The travel licenses issued to the Chifallas state only that they carried "merchandise." A letter sent by the bailiff general in 1473, however, shows that Samuel Chifalla engaged in wine production. In it the bailiff orders Johan de Bellvis of Guerau to deliver to Chifalla "dotze gerres olieres plenes de vi [i.e., must]." Bellvis was supposed to have made the delivery "a les veremes [vintage] del any LXX proppassat" (ARV: B 321: 54r [2/4]).

[31] Hinojosa Montalvo 1979, 34.

[32] Guiral 1986, 416–417. ARV: B 1147: 27v (1429/4/8) concerns Portuguese and Vizcayan ships "anades al port e carregador de la mar de aqueixa vila [Morvedre] per carregar vi e portar aquell en lo dit Regne de Portogal e de Vizcaya." Another indication of the fame of Morvedre's wine comes from 1488, when King Fernando II had ships stop there to load up with wine "por nos servir y provehir nostre real huste que agora . . . metemos en el dicho Reyno de Granada" (B 1159: 58r).

[33] Guiral 1986, 417. ARV: MR 68: 289v (1457/4/21) concerns procedure against "certs juheus mercaders portugueses" who went to Morvedre from Valencia without paying the proper duties on their imports. They were probably in a hurry to purchase wine for the return voyage.

[34] ARV: B 217: 691v (1484/8/30) concerns the sale of a slave by Jahudà Astori, "juheu del realme de Portogal." Jahudà was the son of Vidal and the brother of Samuel, both Jews of Morvedre. Earlier in the century, another Astori, Salamó, was involved in the export of kasher wine from Morvedre to Teruel (ARV: MR 3997: 15r [1430–31]).

[35] ARV: B 1220: M. 3, 4v (1485/12/1). G 2392: 41r, 324r–326v, 336r-v (1491/3/3–4/12) shows that Çaporta had hired a local peasant, Pere Serra, to transport wine for him.

[36] E.g., ARV: MR 3997: 15r (1430–31) recording the fine paid by Salamó Astori for having sent 36 *carregues* of wine to Teruel without paying the transit duty. Astori had been acting as procurator for the Jew Almorori of Teruel. Cf. Iborra Lerma 1981, 145–147.

Teruel, they may well have distributed it to other Aragonese aljamas. Because the Jews of Teruel depended so much on the wine from Morvedre, they complained to Fernando II in 1481 when the aljama of Morvedre levied a sales tax of three diners per cànter of wine sold. A cisa on wine was nothing new, but in the past it had been paid by the vendor; now the buyers were being required to pay it. Pointing out that "wine is bought continually all year in the said Jewish quarter [of Morvedre] . . . by many strange and foreign Jews, and especially by those of the said city of Teruel," representatives of this Aragonese aljama argued that the Jews of Morvedre were taking advantage of their monopoly of the kasher wine trade. The sales tax was bad enough, but the Jews of Morvedre had also passed a new ordinance stipulating that "foreign" Jews had to purchase their wine from the local vendors whom aljama officials would choose by lot. The intention of communal officials in Morvedre, where so many Jews were involved in wine production, was to give all local winegrowers an opportunity to sell their product and to inhibit a price war, which would ultimately hurt all of them. The Jews of Teruel, of course, feared that this ordinance would result in unduly high prices. After much deliberation, King Fernando finally decided in 1483 that the aljama of Morvedre could collect the cisa from the buyers, and that it could also regulate the wine market in this fashion, provided that the vendors thus designated sold wine of good quality and at a reasonable market price.[37]

One factor responsible for the increased production and export of kasher wine by the Morvedre community after 1391 was its demographic expansion. There were, simply stated, more Jews around to manufacture wine. Poorer Jews in particular derived a good part of their income from making and selling wine. In 1431 some Jews of the community appeared before the bailiff general to protest the aljama's abolition of all internal sales taxes except that levied on kasher wine, which was still to be collected from the vintners at a rate of two diners per cànter. The complainants asserted that maintaining this one cisa was prejudicial to lower-class Jews, who "for the most part support themselves and live from the wines which they scoop up [from the treading tubs] and make," and, of course, sell. Wealthier Jews, whose investments were diversified and who did "not care to sell or trade in the said wines," would not be burdened by the tax.[38]

---

[37] ARV: C 130: 16r-v (1481/6/13): "por muchos strangeros e foranos judios, e senyaladamente por los de la aliama de la dicha ciudat de Teruel, todo el anyo continuamente se compre vino en la dicha juderia." *Foranos* were Jews of Teruel and other Jews of the Crown of Aragon; *strangeros* were Jews from outside the Crown of Aragon, such as the Maghriban and Portuguese Jews. C 129: 178r-v (1481/12/10); C 305: 219r-v (1483/5/20) also address the case. King Fernando initially ordered the aljama of Morvedre to revoke both the new cisa and the new system of market control, but, after hearing the arguments of representatives from Morvedre, he reconsidered and allowed the new ordinances to stand.

[38] ARV: B 1147: 301v–302r (1431/10/4): "juheus de menor ma . . . los quals per maiori parte

The complainants probably received a sympathetic hearing from the bailiff general, for in later years, when the aljama instituted internal cises, the usual wide range of transactions was taxed; the winegrowers were not singled out.[39] The sales tax on wine nonetheless remained a drain on the income of the wine manufacturers, especially the poorer ones. The number of these increased as the Morvedre community experienced its population explosion in the latter half of the fifteenth century. The communal legislation of 1481, to which the Jews of Teruel strenuously objected, was in all likelihood aimed at alleviating their material difficulties. Instead of Morvedre's winegrowers rendering the cisa, the aljama would now collect it from "foreign" Jewish buyers. All the winegrowers, moreover, would be given a fair chance to sell their product, or at least they would all have to rely on the luck of the draw.

Lower-class Jews, however, were not the only ones involved in wine production. Most, if not all, of the Jews whose purchases of vineyards the notary Lleonard Miralles recorded were upper- or middle-class Jews. Gento Avincanes, who between 1471 and 1474 bought four parcels of land, at least three of which were planted with grapevines, also invested in urban real estate, loaned substantial sums, farmed taxes, and sold cloth. He served as adelantat in 1468, and 1471–72.[40] Another example, Samuel Agí, was a silversmith and treasurer of the aljama in 1476.[41]

Well-to-do Jews like Gento Avincanes likely had a role in organizing the production and sale of wine: renting or subletting their land to Jewish, Christian, or Muslim tenants, perhaps according to some sort of sharecropping arrangement; and then, like the converso Splugues, hiring poorer Jewish laborers to convert the vintage or must into kasher wine. Such Jews, not just those from the lower class, also would have favored the abolition of the sales tax or its collection from the buyers, though the tax obviously would have burdened them less. On the other hand, the interest of more affluent Jews in wine production may have ended with their purchase and leasing of vineyards. Knowing how

---

se sostenen e viven dels vins que cullen e fan. E los maiors e pus richs, qui . . . no curen vendre ne mercadejar dels dits vins, son exempts de la dita sisa." The result of this protest is unrecorded.

[39] E.g., the cises of 1452 (ARV: B 1151: 568v–570r [Hinojosa Montalvo 1993a, no. 529]).

[40] APPV: P 17864: n.f. (1471/9/6); P 17862: n.f. (1472/2/20); P 17865: n.f. (1473/3/4); P 17866: n.f. (1474/4/2): land purchases. P 17862: n.f. (1472/4/6): purchase of a workshop in the town's main plaza. P 17858: n.f. (1475/6/13): loan of 562 sous 10 diners to Ysabel, the wife of the prominent Joan de Sant Feliu. P 17859: n.f. (1477/8/19): sale of cloth. ARV: MR 70: 98r (1460) [Hinojosa Montalvo 1993a, no. 596]: tax farming in the terme of Borriana. He appears as adelantat in ARV: MR 78: 261r (1468/5/13); APPV: P 17864: n.f. (1471/9/27); P 17862: n.f. (1472/11/18).

[41] APPV: P 17865: n.f. (1473/8/16); P 17875: n.f. (1490/2/16): purchases of vineyards. He appears as clavari in P 17859: n.f. (1477/3/28), referring to 1476. Other examples of prominent Jews purchasing vineyards are the tax farmer Abraham Toledano (P 17858: n.f. [1475/1/21]), who was elected adelantat the same year (P 17858: n.f. [6/27]); and the moneylender Mossé Alateffi (P 17867: n.f. [1476/3/21]), who served as adelantat in 1481 (ARV: B 1157: 54r–55r).

many Jews were involved in the manufacture of wine, they may have been content simply to collect rents from the Jewish winegrowers who needed the land, or at most to sell the vintage harvested by the tenants on their land to the wine manufacturers. These affluent Jews, even if they were somewhat involved in the manufacture and sale of wine, also invested their capital in various other enterprises. Substantial artisans like Samuel Agí probably only supplemented their income with profits from the wine trade. Unlike the poorer Jews, upper- and middle-class Jews did not depend on the manufacture and sale of wine for their subsistence.

Moneylending and Tax Farming

The Jews of Morvedre practicing moneylending on a large scale in the pre-1391 era mostly belonged to the plutocratic families with the necessary disposable income and assets that made them major taxpayers and wielders of political influence.[42] Because moneylending was such risky business, especially during the two decades following the Black Death, when the aljama lurched from one disaster to another, most of these lenders did not employ all their capital in credit operations, but invested it as well in real estate, livestock, commerce, and tax farming.

Toward the end of the fourteenth century some of the wealthier Jews of Morvedre began to invest more of their capital in tax farming. This shift in investment strategy had less to do with the risks inherent to lending than with significant changes in the kingdom's credit market brought about by the introduction and spread of the censal. As the diversified and growing group of Christian censalistas purchased annuities from cash-poor kings, municipalities, lords, villages, and aljamas, Jewish lenders perforce assumed a lesser role.[43] The change was gradual but it accelerated after 1415, when King Fernando I legislated against Jewish usury to Christians, a prohibition that his successors kept in place.[44]

By the 1380s at least one Jew, Jahudà Legem, had decided to invest the bulk of his considerable resources in tax farming instead of moneylending.[45] In that decade Jahudà emerged as the preeminent tax farmer in Morvedre.[46] With the exception of one year, 1385, between 1382 and 1386 he farmed all of the royal taxes collected in the municipal district, offering huge bids that ranged from 21,000 to 29,000 sous. In 1385 Jahudà was outbid by Joan Suau Jr. and Miquel

[42] Meyerson 2004a. Cf. Emery 1959, 27–29; Furió 1993b, 140; Lourie 1989, 62 n. 64.
[43] Furió 1993a, 504–515, and 1993b, 155, 160; Garcia Oliver 1997a, 153–154.
[44] See chaps. 1, 2.
[45] ACA: C 1828: 110v (1387/11/4) shows that another Jew of Morvedre, Vidal Sibili, had been farming taxes in Castelló with "alios consocios."
[46] For more on Jahudà and his family, Meyerson 2004a.

Tapujada, two merchants from Valencia, the locus of most of the kingdom's big money.[47] This, however, was merely a temporary setback; he farmed Crown rents again in 1386 and 1390, and probably in the intervening years.[48] Not surprisingly, Jahudà was an influential figure in the aljama, which he served as treasurer in 1386.[49]

Still, other important Jewish families, such as the Façans and the el Raus, continued to dedicate much of their time and money to credit operations, before and after 1391.[50] The violence of 1391, then, did not bring a halt to the usurious activities of the Jews of Morvedre, although it did hamper debt collection in the short term.[51] The flight of Jews to Morvedre from the devastated Jewish quarter of Valencia actually injected some new old money into the Morvedre community and increased the number of families engaged in moneylending. Three wealthy immigrants in particular continued to be heavily involved in credit operations: Jamila, daughter of the fabulously rich Jahudà Alatzar (d.); her husband, Samuel Suxen; and Astruga, the widow of Salamó Abenmarvez and aunt of Jamila. According to the register of just one notary, Barthomeu de la Mata, between early June and November 1401 Jamila was party to eleven different credit transactions amounting to 2,293 sous. Her aunt's twelve loans during the same period totaled 2,550 sous, while her husband made six loans valuing 725 sous altogether. The borrowers were for the most part residents of villages located in a region extending from the terme of Alzira to the terme of Morvedre: Guadassuar, Torrent, Almussafes, Alcaicia, Russafa, Mislata, Quart, Albalat, Benifaió, and Benifairó de les Valls. A few were artisans and fishermen from the capital.[52] The widowed Jamila was still extending loans to Muslim villagers as late as 1426.[53]

The upheavals of 1391 had a greater impact on Jewish participation in tax farming in Morvedre. Since renting and collecting royal taxes was a public activity that required a good measure of confidence and security as well as capi-

[47] ARV: MR 3985: M. 1, 1r-v (1382); M. 2, 1r-v (1383); M. 3, 1r-v (1384); M. 4, 1r-v (1385); M. 5, 1r-v (1386). Records for the rest of the decade are not extant.

[48] ACA: C 1849: 3r-v (1390/11/30) concerns a suit between Jahudà and David el Rau "occasione arrendamenti facti certo precio per dictum supplicantem [Jahudà] de redditibus regiis ville predicte."

[49] ARV: P 2810, B. de la Mata: n.f. (1386/9/20).

[50] Archivo Histórico Municipal de Segorbe: Varia, no. 240 (1377/3/22) records the debt of 692 sous 6 diners owed by a Christian couple of Castellnou to Jacob Façan. ACA: C 1855: 85v (1393/5/15) [Hinojosa Montalvo 1993a, no. 166]; C 2330: 131v–132r (1397/2/23); C 2339: 110v–111r (1404/3/17) treat his lending in the environs of Sogorb. In December 1391 David el Rau was asked to consider rescheduling the debt payments of the "poor and miserable" Bernat Stepa and his wife (ACA: C 1879: 93v); in 1404 David's heirs laid claim to the debts owed him by the tenants of the nobles Olf de Pròixida and Gilabert de Centelles (ACA: C 2340: 30r).

[51] See chap. 1.

[52] ARV: P 1446, B. de la Mata (1401). A few of the loans were actually contracted in the 1390s. The figures I have given nonetheless provide a good sense of the scope of their credit operations.

[53] ARV: C 37: 11r-v (1426/8/9).

tal, Jews were understandably reluctant to engage in it during the unsettled years that followed. None did until the second half of the decade, and even then they only leased royal utilities, like the dyeworks and the wax press. In this way Jahudà Legem kept a hand in the public domain, but he and other Jews still shied away from the potentially inflammatory farming and indirect collection of taxes.

By 1400, however, the Jews' confidence returned: from 1400 through 1414 Jews were leasing some of the more important and lucrative utilities, like the royal mills and ovens, and farming a variety of the *terços de delme* (the "thirds" of the ecclesiastical tithes that the papacy had granted Jaume I the right to collect in all territories under direct royal lordship), ranging from the most lucrative terç on bread, wine, and oil, which was auctioned off for a price as high as 5,650 sous in 1413, to some of the less valuable terços, such as those collected on garden crops (for 400 sous in 1413), from fish vendors (for 837 sous in 1412), and from the inhabitants of the villages of Algar and Carcel (for 470 sous in 1409).

During these fourteen years the bailiff rented out fiscal revenues in piecemeal fashion, and no single Jew was able, or perhaps even desired, to farm all royal taxes as Jahudà Legem had once done. To the extent that Jews farmed taxes in Morvedre, only three prosperous individuals did so consistently: Samuel Legem, carrying on in the tradition of his relative (probably father) Jahudà; Jahudà Çerruch; and Isaac Xamblell, an immigrant from Valencia. While each was capable of farming taxes on his own — especially Legem, who seems to have been the wealthiest of the three — they occasionally pooled their resources for this purpose.[54] Besides their involvement in tax farming, Legem, Çerruch, and Xamblell shared other characteristics. Both Legem and Xamblell were lenders,[55] and all three served in aljama government.[56] Legem's illustrious career in Jewish circles ended abruptly in 1415 with his baptism, from which he earned the goodwill of Fernando I.[57]

The tax-farming partnerships these Jews sometimes formed with Christians attest to a normalization of Jewish economic relations with Christians within

[54] For the preceding material on tax farming, Meyerson 1998, 69–70 nn. 10–19.

[55] ARV: P 1445, B. de la Mata: 164v (1399/6/16); P 1446, B. de la Mata: n.f. (1401/9/23) for loans of 180 sous and 60 sous, respectively, by Xamblell to Christians of "la puenta Albuferie Valencie" and Albalat d'en Codinachs; P 1446: n.f. (1401/11/9) for a loan of 660 sous by Legem to a Christian couple of Torrent.

[56] ACA: C 2339: 160r–161r (1404/8/28) for Çerruch as councillor; APPV: P 13900, M. Arbucies: n.f. (1412/11/19) for Xamblell as adelantat. For Legem as adelantat, see chap. 1, n. 174. It should be kept in mind that the evidence on holders of aljama office is quite fragmentary.

[57] See chap. 1. However, he had also been favored by King Joan, who in 1394 granted him the right to lease in perpetuity two stalls in the town abattoir designated for Jewish use (ACA: C 1906: 218v–219v; C 2340: 27v–28r for the renewal in 1404 [Hinojosa Montalvo 1993a, nos. 220, 275]). ACA: MR 395: 41v (May 1394) shows that Samuel rendered the Crown a rent of 110 sous b. for the stalls.

a decade of 1391. Such partnerships may have had the side benefit of reducing the hostility of Christians who would not have been rendering fees or taxes
to Jews alone. Moreover, in always farming the terç of Algar and Carcel, whenever they farmed the terç of a specific collectory within the terme, Çerruch and
Legem perhaps hoped that the resultant familiarity with the villagers would
make tax collection smoother and less conflictive. In any case, Christian and
Muslim inhabitants of the municipal district could hardly have seen tax farming as a particularly Jewish occupation;[58] on the whole Christians (occasionally conversos), both locals and investors from Valencia, dominated the field.[59]

The Jews of Morvedre ceased farming royal taxes between 1415 and 1445,
initially on account of the anti-Jewish legislation enacted by Pope Benedict
XIII and King Fernando I. After 1419, however, there were no obvious political or social obstacles to Jewish tax farming. King Alfonso IV pursued a Jewish
policy favorable to the Jews and tensions between Jews and local Christians
did not escalate. The chain of natural disasters that afflicted the region in the
1420s, 1430s, and 1440s seems to have discouraged Jews from investing their
funds in this way.[60] Epidemic disease, drought, flood, and poor harvests
made the farming of largely agricultural tithes a more uncertain and unwise
investment.

As long as the system of aljama sales taxes was in place, Jews continued to
farm them. Until 1421 the cises brought in substantial revenue. Most of the
Jews involved — Jahudà Legem, Mossé Levi, Cresques Nasci, Salamó Fanduix,
Salamó Bonet, Abraham Gallego, and Mossé Alateffi — were, like the farmers
of the king's taxes, members of families linked to aljama government in some
way.[61] Yet in the 1420s, as has been seen, agrarian difficulties and demographic

---

[58] Meyerson 1998, 70–71 nn. 19–24. Only twice, in 1412 and 1413, did Jews farm more than
one terç or lease more than one utility, and only once did Jews alone farm the most lucrative and
far-reaching terç, on bread, wine, and oil.

[59] ARV: MR 3988–3992. In 1408 Nicholau de Valldaura and Pere de Campos, conversos of
Valencia, farmed the terç on bread, wine, and oil for 5,600 sous (MR 3991: 7r).

[60] See chap. 2.

[61] Documentation on the farming of internal cises is very limited and is extant only for 1417,
1419, and 1420 (ARV: MR 39: 85r [Hinojosa Montalvo 1993a, no. 299]; MR 39: 155v; MR 40:
46r-v). In 1417 Legem farmed the cisa on kasher meat for 1,600 sous; in 1419 Bonet, Gallego, and
Fanduix for 1,500 sous; in 1420 Arroti for 1,600 sous. In 1417 Levi farmed the one on kasher wine
for 1,200 sous; in 1420 Alateffi for 1,400 sous. In 1419 Nasci, Isaac Alborgi, and Salamó Arroti
farmed the cisa on commercial transactions (mercaderies, braçatges e logers) for 2,080 sous; in 1420
Nasci farmed it alone for 2,110 sous. In 1430–31 Levi acted as messenger and sindic of the aljama
(ARV: B 1147: 138v; sixth quire, letter K [Hinojosa Montalvo 1993a, nos. 379, 386]). Nasci rendered aljama taxes to the Crown in 1419 and 1424, a task of considerable importance (ARV: MR
39: 85r; MR 44: 233v [Hinojosa Montalvo 1993a, nos. 299, 332]). Bonet was lieutenant adelantat
in 1423 (MR 42: 311v–312r [Hinojosa Montalvo 1993a, no. 325]). Gallego was clavari in 1401
(ARV: P 1446, B. de la Mata: n.f. [8/29]). Alateffi was clavari in 1429 (MR 48: 263r). Fanduix was
clavari in 1427 (MR 46: 111r) and adelantat in 1430 (ARV: B 1147: 160r [Hinojosa Montalvo
1993a, no. 379]). In addition to farming the cisa on meat, Fanduix and Gallego — in this case

stagnation caused cisa revenues to decline to such a degree that between 1431 and 1450 Jewish communal officials, finding it difficult to attract bidders, opted to do without the internal levies.[62] Yet, given the small number of Jews who farmed taxes, royal or communal, the Jews' long-term withdrawal from this sphere was not necessarily symptomatic of a general economic crisis among the Jews of Morvedre. The families migrating to and from Morvedre were seeking, and sometimes finding, new opportunities.

One indication of the economic revitalization of the Morvedre community in the mid-1440s was the Jews' return to farming the Crown's fiscal revenues; their consistent pursuit of this activity until the expulsion reflected the community's unabated growth. Still, as in the years 1400–1414, the Jews did not monopolize tax farming in the district of Morvedre. Up until 1482, Jews farmed more than one terç in only three years — 1464, 1467, and 1470.[63] In 1482, however, Salamó Çaporta emerged as the dominant player in the field and farmed nearly all of them for the next eight years.[64]

During the years 1445–82 there were notable changes in the pattern of Jewish tax farming within the terme of Morvedre. First, reflecting the growing population and prosperity of the community, the number of Jews involved increased: instead of the triumvirate of Legem, Çerruch, and Xamblell, there were at least twenty-five individuals from eighteen different families. The number may well have been larger, for the bailiff sometimes recorded multiple Jewish partners without listing them by name, as, for instance, "Cresques Façan and other Jews." Of the families comprising the earlier triumvirate, only the Legems remained active in the field.

Second, tax-farming partnerships were more common, at least for the most valuable terç on bread, wine, oil, and (from 1465) sugar. Jews were among the lessees of this tax on twelve different occasions; in eight of the twelve, there were *companyies* or partnerships consisting of as many as ten partners. In six cases, moreover, the partnerships included Christians. The partnership served two purposes: it provided a broader base of capital and simultaneously distributed the risk over a greater number of investors. This latter was an important consideration. Tax farming entailed some financial risk, especially since most of the taxes were levied on a variety of agricultural products. Poor harvests were not the only danger; since the terços were often collected in kind, there were considerable risks and costs involved in collecting and marketing the perishable produce. Some tax farmers found themselves in debt to the Crown, un-

---

Menahem — were involved in provisioning the Jewish butchery as well. On 15 November 1418 they purchased sheep valuing 1,130 sous from Joan Pereç, a shepherd of Altura (APPV: P 25970, P. Castellar: n.f.).

[62] See chap. 2.
[63] Meyerson 1998, 72 n. 29.
[64] See below.

able to render the sums they had originally bid in timely fashion.[65] Because of the risk, few, if any, Jews of Morvedre regarded tax farming as their primary economic activity. Even those Jews affluent enough to bid for tax farms did not do so with great frequency. Only rarely did Jews farm taxes in consecutive years, and some did so just once or twice.[66] Diversity and wide geographic range characterized the investments of many tax-farming families.

Due to previous and ongoing Jewish migration between Morvedre, Borriana, Castelló, and Vila-real, and the resultant kinship connections, Jews from Morvedre were able to farm taxes in these other royal towns as well. The Legem clan, for example, maintained branches in Morvedre and Castelló.[67] Still a force to be reckoned with, despite the baptism of Samuel and his son Abraham in 1415, it was active farming taxes,[68] lending money,[69] and selling agricultural products[70] in both towns, as well as farming the rents of the Order of Mon-

[65] E.g., when Samuel Façan died in 1465 he still owed between 1,500 and 1,600 sous to the Crown from his farming of royal rents. King Juan gave his son Mossé five years to pay off his father's debts (ARV: B 1153: 689r-v [Hinojosa Montalvo 1993a, no. 658]).

[66] Meyerson 1998, 72–73, nn. 32–38, 40.

[67] From the 1420s Jacob headed the family branch in Morvedre. In 1425 he served as clavari of the aljama (ARV: MR 242r); in 1429 he was lieutenant adelantat while his younger kinsman Jacob "pus jove" was adelantat (MR 48: 263r). In 1434 a Jacob Legem was referred to as "rabino" (ARV: C 264: 16v–17r); in 1450 he was adelantat (MR 65: 257v). Abraham headed the Castelló branch; on his career there, see Mira Jódar 1993. He moved back and forth between the towns, however, as is evident from his election as adelantat of the Morvedre aljama in 1442 (ARV: B 1221, M. 1: 27v) and his long absences from Castelló (Magdalena Nom de Déu 1988, nos. 336–486).

[68] ARV: MR 57: 100r–101r (1442) [Hinojosa Montalvo 1993a, no. 466] for Castelló in 1439; Meyerson 1998, 72, for Morvedre.

[69] E.g., in 1439 Abraham Legem sued Johan Bernat, an inkeeper in Castelló, who allegedly owed him 160 sous (ARV: G 2268: M. 1, 24r-v; M. 6, 16r–17r); see Mira Jódar 1993 for more on his operations. APPV: P 17871, L. Miralles: n.f. (1485/11/11): his son Samuel lends 215 sous to the Benet family of Morvedre. AMC: Justicia: n.f. records loans made by Jacob Legem — kinsman of Samuel and brother to another Abraham Legem — to various Christians of Castelló: 465 sous (1483/1/31); 150 sous (2/12); 120 sous (9/25); 50 sous (10/6). The same source records procedures against various debtors in Castelló at the instance either of Abraham Legem of Morvedre, acting as procurator of Jacob Legem of Castelló, or of Jacob, acting as agent of Abraham (1486/8/14–17); procedure against the Museros family of Castelló for its debts to Abraham Legem of Morvedre (1490/2/8); and procedure against Johan de Loscos of Morvedre, at the instance of Abraham, acting as guardian of the children and heirs of the deceased Jacob (1491/12/22). APPV: P 12213, L. Miralles: n.f. (1492/7/15): Abraham acknowledges receipt of 220 sous from Guillem Munt and the clavari Miquel Johan of Castelló, part of a larger sum they had borrowed from Jacob "per obs de la dita vila." Johan, however, retained 40 sous from this quantity because Jacob had owed it to the Crown from his tax farms in Castelló.

[70] E.g., APPV: P 17873, L. Miralles: n.f. (1487/5/13) for Abraham Legem's sale of more than 7 cafíçes of wheat to the Alos family of Canet for 146 sous; P 12213, L. Miralles: n.f. (1492/7/15) for the payment of 330 sous by Joan Jorda of Torres-Torres for the 16 cafíçes of barley he had bought from Abraham on 16 February 1491. This is not the same Abraham discussed in n. 67 and in Mira Jódar 1993 but either his or Jacob's descendant.

tesa in Borriana.[71] The Façans, another leading family, farmed royal revenues in all three towns; they also labored as silversmiths.[72] Other families, like the Toledanos, specialized more in the farming of ecclesiastical and seigneurial tithes and rents.[73] The farming of taxes and tithes enabled such families to become dealers in agricultural produce on a fairly large scale.[74] Through their contacts in various towns and villages they kept apprised of related investment options, like village butcher shops.[75]

[71] ARV: B 1150: 235r (1448/4/11) [Hinojosa Montalvo 1993a, no. 497], 320v–321r (11/22). The bailiff general was granting Abraham safe-conducts to travel to Borriana because among the rents collected by the Order in the town, and hence by Abraham as tax farmer, was the royal peita the Order transferred to the Crown. The master of Montesa believed that Abraham feared he would be jailed in Borriana on account of debts outstanding from the tax farm.

[72] ARV: MR 57: 100r–101r [Hinojosa Montalvo 1993a, no. 466] for Samuel's farming of taxes in Castelló in 1440; B 1150: 92r (1447/5/24) for his suit against a truant Muslim taxpayer of Castelló in his capacity as agent, and probably partner, of the Valencian merchant and tax farmer Daniel Barceló. Meyerson 1998, 72–73, for tax farms in Morvedre. For the tax farms of Samuel and Mossé in Borriana, as well as their resultant debts to the Crown, B 1152: 1415v (1458/1/2); MR 69: 98v; B 1152: 1721r-v (1459/12/12); MR 70: 97r; MR 71: 96v [Hinojosa Montalvo 1993a, nos. 599, 604]). MR 89: 96r (1479) [Hinojosa Montalvo 1993a, no. 783], which identifies Pere Gençor of Valencia as the farmer of royal rents in Borriana, records Mossé paying royal officials on his behalf. Mossé was probably Gençor's partner, as his father had been the partner of the Valencian Daniel Barceló. In both cases the Façans would have been the active partners, doing the bidding and collecting on site, while the Valencians would have been the passive partners providing most of the capital.

[73] ARV: B 1160: 439v–440r (1492/5/7) [Hinojosa Montalvo 1993a, no. 841] for their farming of the tithes on bread and wine collected by the Valencian church in El Puig and Massamagrell; B 324: 280r-v (1491/7/12) concerns Mossé's farming of the tithes in Pobla de Farnals. Mossé died just before the redaction of the latter document. It suggests that a Valencian Christian merchant, Lorenç Vich, was his partner. One of the Toledanos and Abraham Comte had also been farming ecclesiastical taxes in the diocese of Tortosa (B 1154: 408v–409r [1469/7/10]). For their farming of royal tax farms in Morvedre, see MR 4012: 4v (1468), 25v (1470). For other Jews of Morvedre farming church tithes, see chap. 2.

[74] E.g., Mossé Toledano sold 15.5 cafíçes of barley to a Christian farmer of El Puig (ARV: P 439, J. de Campos Jr.: n.f. [1472/10/15]), and 7 cafíçes of seed grain to the village council of Massalfassar (P 444, J. de Campos Jr.: n.f. [1483/11/27]). After Abraham Toledano's death in 1469, Vidal Andaix, the procurator of his heirs, demanded the restitution of 2.5 cafíçes of oats, which were "dels fruyts" of a royal tax farm and which somehow had come into the possession of Astruga, the wife of Mossé Façan. The bailiff was ordered to sell the oats on the local grain exchange and to use the proceeds for paying whatever Abraham had owed the Crown from the tax farm (ARV: B 1154: 414v [Hinojosa Montalvo 1993a, no. 690]). Just prior to going into exile, Jacob Toledano unloaded some 3,780 liters of oil on a Valencian merchant, Galceran Adret, for the price of 1,890 sous (APPV: P 6054, J. Casanova: n.f. [1492/4/26]).

[75] In 1474 (ARV: P 2092, B. Sans: n.f. [11/25]) Mossé Toledano became the financial backer of Francesc Jaffer, a farmer of Massamagrell and lessee of the local butcher shop. Jaffer, Mossé, and two other investors agreed to pay 8 diners for every pound of meat slaughtered to Francesc Jener, a citizen of Valencia who was provisioning the butcher shop with livestock; they were to divide among themselves the profits from the sale of meat and hides. At the same time, Mossé and

However impressive the mobility and enterprise of the Legems, the Façans, and the Toledanos (and they were not alone), none quite matched Salamó Çaporta, whose fortunes peaked just as Fernando II and the Spanish Inquisition snuffed out the multifaceted activity of Morvedre's Jewish entrepreneurs. A licensed physician, Salamó's father, Astruc, laid the foundations for his son's more illustrious career through lending money and farming taxes, on one occasion in the district of Borriana in collaboration with Gento Avincanes.[76] Astruc also took part in international commerce, selling cloth in the Granadan ports of Almería and Málaga. Salamó acted as his father's agent in one of these ports.[77]

Like his father, Salamó engaged in some moneylending, extending credit to Christians, Muslims, and Jews.[78] Before his major tax-farming ventures, however, commerce, both domestic and foreign, consumed most of his energies. In Morvedre itself Salamó owned a shop where woolens were sold; he was also the partner of Jacob Toledano in a retail business that mainly serviced a local clientele.[79] His interest in woolens led him to invest heavily in sheep and other livestock. He owned substantial flocks; on one occasion he sold animals valuing nearly 4,000 sous to a butcher in Xàtiva.[80]

Abraham Toledano jointly owned a flock of sheep with Pere Dasió, a local farmer (ARV: P 3148: n.f. [1474/2/28]).

[76] An Astruc Çaporta appears in the morabatí list of 1409 (ARV: MR 11800), but he must have been a great-uncle of Salamó, not his father. The Astruc I presume to have been Salamó's father appears as a creditor of Muslims in the Vall d'Almonesir in 1434 (ARV: B 1147: 608r-v), and as a tax farmer in 1460 (MR 70: 98r [Hinojosa Montalvo 1993a, no. 596]). Astruc raised funds for tax farming and other ventures by selling annuities — B 1153: 16r-v (1460/1/25) [Hinojosa Montalvo 1993a, no. 600]. ARV: C 274: 18r-v (1453/7/6) is a license to Astruc to practice medicine and surgery in the kingdoms of Valencia and Aragon.

[77] ARV: C 705: 322v–323r (1462): Astruc is licensed to travel on a Venetian galley to these ports with cloth valuing 4,400 sous and to "fer venir dos fills seus que te en les dites parts." I presume that one of these sons was Salamó. The identity of the other son is unknown. The deceased Astruc Çaporta of Tortosa, for whose heirs Salamó acted as guardian in 1474–75, must have been a cousin or an uncle, for Astruc's sister Durona, to whom reference is made in one document, was not Salamó's sister (ARV: B 1296: 38r; P 1995: third quire, 14r-v [Hinojosa Montalvo 1993a, nos. 734, 752]).

[78] ARV: P 1999, J. Salvador: n.f. (1479/4/1) — Çaat Mayna, Muslim of Beselga; G 2392: 324r–326v, 336r-v (1491/3/3–4/12) — Pere Serra, Christian of Morvedre; B 217: 479r–481v (1482/2/27) — Jucef Quatorze, Jew of Morvedre.

[79] ARV: B 1158: 111r-v (1485/11/11) [Hinojosa Montalvo 1993a, no. 811], 123r-v, and 127r treat the complaints of Salamó and another cloth merchant, Mossé Ardit, regarding new regulations imposed by the local market inspector. Salamó's arrangements with the Valencian dyer Joan Bonjoch (ARV: P 1995, J. Salvador: 132v–133r [1475/5/23]) and the broker Gabriel Pertusa (P 1999, J. Salvador: n.f. [1479/3/23]) probably concerned his cloth business. B 1431: n.f. (1491/3/16) [Hinojosa Montalvo 1993a, no. 832] treats the partnership with Toledano and provides a list of the clients and the sums owed; it does not state what items were sold.

[80] ARV: C 148: 29r-v (June 1492). AMV: LM g3–31: 95r-v (1485/10/6), where Salamó is herding a flock of 350 sheep.

On the Iberian peninsula his commercial network encompassed the kingdoms of Aragon, Murcia, and Castile;[81] it extended overseas to Italy as well.
The cloth trade was Salamó's area of expertise. In fact, in 1479 he was commissioned to purchase on behalf of the king Venetian silks worth more than
3,000 sous.[82] He had clearly estabished a reputation as a *bon contractador*, the
label given him by the jurats of Valencia.[83]

By 1481 Salamó had become something of a royal favorite. At the very least
King Fernando regarded him as a businessman he could trust. Thus when
Salamó obtained the farm of practically all the royal terços in Morvedre for a
five-year term, he did not have to bid for it in the usual manner. Salamó's well-
placed request and royal fiat were enough. In December 1481 the king informed Francesc de Sant Feliu, the bailiff of Morvedre: "Bailiff, we have decided irrevocably to lease, and in fact we have leased, to Salamó Çaporta, Jew
of Morvedre, all the terç de delme of Morvedre for a period of five years."[84]
Considering that in 1479 the terç on bread, wine, oil, and sugar alone had been
auctioned off for 8,430 sous, the terms of the lease, which required Salamó to
render 5,000 sous annually, left him with a significant profit margin.[85]

Since Salamó made the annual payments in timely fashion, Fernando did
not hesitate to renew the farm in 1487 for another three years.[86] Even when
Salamó was being tried by the inquisitors for promoting "Judaizing," the king
did not lose faith in the skills of his Jewish servant. He advised the bailiff general not to re-lease Crown revenues in Morvedre while Salamó's case was pend-
ing.[87] Remarkably, after the inquisitors condemned Salamó in May 1488 to
two years of exile, the king still insisted that Salamó's three-year farm of the
taxes of Morvedre be allowed to run its course until the end of 1489. Having
protected his investment and his family, Salamó went into exile, where he later
died. His friend Salamó Cavaller made the 1489 payment in his stead.[88]

---

[81] See at n. 132.

[82] ARV: MR 90: 286r (1479/10/20). At the same time Salamó may have exported some of his
own wool to Venice on the Venetian galleys that visited the port of Valencia regularly. See Igual
Luis 1994, 188–199, on imports and exports.

[83] See chap. 2.

[84] ACA: C 3563: 72v (1481/12/5): "deliberat arrendar e de fet havem arrendat an Salamo Çaporta, juheu de Morvedre, tot lo terç de delme de Morvedre per temps de cinch anys." The same
letter was sent to the governor of the kingdom, Luis de Cabanyelles. Also, ARV: MR 4017: 3r
(1483). The accounts for 1481–82 are not extant.

[85] ARV: MR 4016: 3v (1479). The lessees were Jucef Tarfon and other unnamed Jews.

[86] ARV: B 122: 659v (1486/11/14); C 308: 116r (1488/12/18) [Hinojosa Montalvo 1993a, no.
823].

[87] ACA: C 3665: 51v (1487/3/5).

[88] AHN: Inq., leg. 536, caja 2, no. 19. Samuel was sentenced on 12 May 1488. His exile was
supposed to begin on 1 June 1488. That it did not is clear enough from the king's letter of 18 December (ARV: C 308: 116r [Hinojosa Montalvo 1993a, no. 823]). ARV: MR 99: 106r (1489)
records Cavaller's payment. See also chaps. 6, 7.

Most of the families involved in tax farming during the fifteenth century also, as has been seen, practiced some moneylending. Both activities required disposable capital and both were integral to the broader economic strategies of these families. Not all of the lenders, however, invested in tax farming; some doubled as merchants or artisans.[89]

In areas where there still were Jews, Christian and Muslim farmers and artisans continued to find Jewish lenders useful. The size of the loans extended by Jews and the reasons for which they were contracted, by Christians or Muslims, had not changed appreciably since 1415. The great majority of the loans were for less than 100 sous, the small amounts borrowers needed to purchase seed, tools, materials, or foodstuffs to tide them over during lean months.[90] What had changed was the extent to which individual Jewish families, and the Jewish community as a whole, depended on lending. For both it loomed less largely. A rough sense of the diminished importance of moneylending in the economy of the Morvedre community can be gained from comparing mid-fourteenth- and late fifteenth-century data. Of the forty-five households indemnified in 1352 after the attack of the Union, eighteen (from eleven distinct lineages), or 40 percent, belonged to lineages known to have lent money.[91] Between 1440 and 1492, when the community came to have more than one hundred households, only twenty-one householders (from fifteen different lineages) — perhaps 20 percent in any given year — are known to have engaged in credit operations.[92]

Most importantly, no Jewish family in Morvedre after 1415 seems to have regarded moneylending as its primary means of subsistence, as some families

[89] The lenders Abraham Alateffi and his son Mossé were involved in the wool trade. Some of their loans were recorded by the notary Lleonard Miralles. E.g., APPV: P 17864: n.f. (1471/4/18): Abraham lends 260 sous to four Christians of Morvedre for their purchase of a fishing net. ARV: B 1160: 641v (1493/3/19) treats the collection of 1,600 sous from families in Morvedre and Xilxes by officials of the Crown, to which all debts owed Mossé had been conceded. Another example is the lender/silversmith Astruc Rodrich, who seems to have had a largely Muslim clientele. E.g., ARV: B 322: 107r (1475/3/14) treats a 100-sous loan to a Muslim of Argelita; P 442, J. de Campos Jr.: n.f. (1475/4/4) records loans of 320 sous to Muslims of Aín and the Serra d'Eslida.

[90] Mira Jódar 1993, 120, regarding the loans of Abraham and Samuel Legem recorded in the registers of the justice of Castelló between 1422 and 1492 (Magdalena Nom de Déu 1988). Borrowers of small sums normally swore before local justices to repay their creditors the recorded sums at a specific time, making recourse to notaries unnecessary. Thus, although the average loan recorded in the registers of Lleonard Miralles was 278 sous (Meyerson 1998, 77), lenders like the Alateffis only bothered seeking a notary for their larger loans. Were the records of the court of the justice of Morvedre extant, they would in all likelihood reveal a pattern very similar to that of Castelló. For earlier practices, Meyerson 2004a.

[91] Meyerson 2004a; Chabret Fraga 1979, 2: 429–433.

[92] The twenty-one householders are Abraham, Jacob, and Samuel Legem; Naçan Lobell; Mossé and Abraham Toledano; Astruc and Mossé Azar; Jucef Quatorze; Astruc Rodrich; Abraham Agí; Astruc and Salamó Çaporta; Mossé and Abraham Alateffi; Gento Avincanes; Mossé Asseyo; Mossé Façan; Vidal Comte; Gento Carser; and Salamó Tarfon.

undoubtedly had prior to 1415. Competition from Christian censalistas especially, the new fiscal regime, and antiusury legislation — even if honored in the
breach — forced and allowed the Jews to diversify. The big money in the kingdom was in the hands of Christian censalistas; a good number of Morvedre's
Jewish tax farmers, lenders, and successful merchants sold annuities to them
in order to obtain funds for their own ventures.[93] In the hierarchy of creditors,
Christian notables now stood over the Jews.

Even though they were no longer the main purveyors of credit in the kingdom and credit operations figured less prominently in their varied economic
activities, Jewish families like the Façans, Çaportas, and Toledanos still pros-
pered. Their investment strategies in many ways paralleled those of successful
Christian bourgeois families, and, like their Christian counterparts, they dominated communal government. For instance, of the nineteen Jewish families
farming taxes in the terme of Morvedre between 1445 and 1492, all but four
held an official post in the aljama.[94] The jurats of Valencia could thus see a bit
of themselves in the bon contractador Salamó Çaporta. The leading Jewish
families in Morvedre had bounced back from the calamities of 1391 to 1416,
and had managed it in a manner that irritated Christians much less.

INDUSTRY AND COMMERCE

Artisans formed the silent majority of Morvedre's Jewish community.[95] Unlike
the tax farmers and lenders, whose activities concerned kings and bailiffs, their
commonplace labors rarely merited a mention in the letters issued by the royal
chancery. In the fifteenth century, as a function of the Jewish community's demographic growth, both absolutely and in proportion to Morvedre's total population, the number of crafts Jews practiced, especially in the sphere of cloth
production, increased. Due to the decline of the town's Christian population
and its need for productive inhabitants, there was no opposition to Jews moving into newer areas of industry.

From the early fourteenth century until 1492 the silversmiths were the most
prominent Jewish artisans in Morvedre. They were organized into a guild with
its system of apprenticeship and quality controls. Before setting up shop on
their own, apprentices learned and labored in the homes of master silversmiths
for two years. In return, they received, besides the secrets of the trade, a salary

---

[93] E.g., ARV: B 323: 206r (1479/2/5) regarding the censal originally sold in 1442 by the tax
farmer Abraham Adzoni to dona Ysabel Sabata; B 323: 596r (1481/3/16) regarding the debts of
the tax farmers Jahudà and Mossé Jabba to the doctor of law Baltasar de Gallach; P 445, J. de Campos Jr.: n.f. (1486/10/23) on the debt of 150 gold ducats of Vidal Astori, silversmith and merchant,
to Cristófol de Basurto, citizen of Valencia. See also n. 76.

[94] On the Christian families, see chap. 2; on aljama government, chap. 5.

[95] See at n. 2.

and articles of clothing. The silversmiths of Morvedre had by the end of the fourteenth century established such a reputation that Jewish youths came from other towns to train with them.[96] Though they earned this reputation through craftsmanship, the destruction of the Jewish community of Valencia with its many artisans contributed to their preeminence.[97] In 1442 the Morvedre silversmiths did not hesitate to impose regulations on all Jewish silversmiths in the kingdom, demanding, on pain of a 50-florin fine, that they work with silver valuing 12 sous per ounce.[98] In 1465 the silversmiths even arrogated the right to legislate for all Jewish artisans in Morvedre, but the protests of the silkweavers and other artisans forced them to back down.[99]

The presumption of the silversmiths stemmed partly from the fact that their guild included some of the most affluent and influential Jews in the community: Jahudà Çerruch, one of the tax-farming triumvirate between 1400 and 1414; Cresques and Mossé from the ambitious Façan family; and Vidal Astori, silversmith and envoy of King Fernando II and international merchant.[100] In order to afford the materials with which they worked, most silversmiths had to be of at least middle-class status. Such was the case of families like the Agís, Maymós, Tarfons, Crespis, and Ardits.[101]

Some silverworking families, like the Astoris and the Agís, evinced their professional pride through practicing the craft over the course of generations.[102]

[96] ARV: P 1445, B. de la Mata: 34r (1399/1/20): Mossé Agí of Morvedre, the son of Isaac Agí of Borriana, affirms a contract of apprenticeship with Jahudà Çerruch, silversmith of Morvedre; P 440, J. de Campos Jr.: 62r-v (1478/1/30): Isaac Ardit of Teruel does the same with Isaac Crespi of Morvedre. In the latter a salary of 200 sous as well as two shirts, stockings, and shoes were specified. ARV: B 1151: 640v (1453/1/16) treats an unsuccessful apprenticeship. After Abraham Rodrich placed Abraham, the son of Jucef Toledano, as an apprentice in the household of the silversmith Jacob Vinaig, Jacob, for an unknown reason, threw Abraham out before completion of the contract.

[97] Hinojosa Montalvo 1985, 1559–1560, on Valencia prior to 1391.

[98] ARV: B 1149: 150v (1442/1/30) [Hinojosa Montalvo 1993a, no. 467]. ARV: MR 11764: 38v–39r (1473–74) lists some fines collected by the local market inspector from Jewish silversmiths for having silver that was not properly certified.

[99] ARV: B 1153: 662v (1465/10/15) [Hinojosa Montalvo 1993a, no. 657].

[100] On Çerruch, see n. 96. In ARV: P 2785, J. de Campos Jr.: n.f. (1473/10/23) the silversmith Isaac Crespi makes Mossé Façan, also a silversmith, his procurator. APPV: P 17861, L. Miralles: n.f. (1479/12/14) records a debt of "Creixques Façan argenter" to a church vicar. On Vidal Astori, e.g., ARV: B 1156: 768r-v (1480/4/30), a letter of Fernando II to the bailiff general referring to Vidal as "argenter nostre" and noting that Vidal was "en Castilla per servey nostre."

[101] My evaluation of their status is based on the fact that they were not otherwise prominent as tax farmers and financiers. It is a rough guideline, but it seems to have separated them from the likes of the Façans and the Astoris. The claim of the silversmith Mossé Levi that he was a "poor person" was disingenuous, meant to halt the appropriation of his land by Martí Esparça, a local knight (ARV: C 82: 36v [1440/11/12]).

[102] See n. 96 for Mossé Agí in 1399, and ARV: B 1150: 161r (1447/11/13) [Hinojosa Montalvo 1993a, no. 492] for his descendant Abraham. The Astoris can be traced from one Jahudà (B 319: 142r-v [1431/4/21]) to Vidal and his two sons, both described as silversmiths in 1489 (B 1159: 185v–186r [Hinojosa Montalvo 1993a, no. 827]).

The membership in the guild of brothers, fathers, uncles, and grandfathers from the same family enhanced the guild's solidarity, at least vis-à-vis other kinds of artisans. Within the guild, however, that same familial solidarity might translate into particularly intense professional competition. In the 1430s a bloody feud erupted between factions captained by the brothers Abraham and Samuel Agí, on one hand, and the brothers Mossé and Jahudà Maymó, and their maternal uncle Salamó Tarfon on the other. All were silversmiths.[103]

The fame of Morvedre's silversmiths resulted in part from their assiduous self-promotion. As mobile as the moneylenders and tax farmers, they were frequently on the road selling their manufactures. Some of them owned or rented workshops in other towns and villages such as Onda and Uixó.[104] This helped them familiarize themselves with potential customers and produce wares that accorded with their tastes.

Though not as illustrious as the silversmiths, the cobblers and tailors were also itinerant, marketing their shoes and garments in other towns and villages as well as in Morvedre. The tailor Jucef Mardahay, for instance, consigned a sack of hoods, sleeves, and cuffs to a widow of Sogorb, María Sánchez, for sale.[105] Some families of tailors were fairly well-to-do. When they were not farming taxes or buying land and livestock, the Toledanos — Mossé, Abraham, Gento, and Jacob — were busy sewing and selling garments and cloth to farmers in places like El Puig and Canet.[106] Among the tailors and shoemakers, however, the success of these families was unusual.[107]

---

[103] Meyerson 2003b.

[104] ARV: B 1151: 69r (1450/5/4) [Hinojosa Montalvo 1993a, no. 508] for the silversmithies in Onda; Meyerson 2003b for those owned by Salamó Tarfon and Mossé Maymo in the Vall d'Uixó. See also above at n. 2 and below for commerce.

[105] ACA: C 2338: 73v (1402/4/24). Jucef accused María of stealing the sack he had "comenada" to her. The queen ordered the justice of Sogorb to investigate the matter, "attesa la art de que lo dit juheu usa." Later in the century, Gento Gallego, presumably a tailor, sold some cowls or hoods (*capuchos*) to a fisherman in Sueca (ARV: B 1156: 404v [1479/3/11]). See also n. 2.

[106] ARV: P 442, J. de Campos Jr.: n.f. (1475/5/10): Jaume Requart of El Puig owes 200 sous to Abraham Toledano for *panni*. APPV: P 17867, L. Miralles: n.f. (1476/1/25): Gento Toledano sells black cloth valuing 107 sous to Pere Romeu, a local merchant, for the funeral of his father-in-law. P 17868, L. Miralles: n.f. (1483/2/4) records Gento's sales of garments to two farmers of Canet for 40 and 87 sous. The same year his kinsman Jacob sold cloth to an inhabitant of Canet (P 17868 [11/19]). At the same time Mossé Toledano, also a tailor, was in debt to Bernat Guimerà, a merchant of Valencia, for 540 sous, the price of "tres draps pebrets," obviously for his own workshop (ARV: B 323: 679r). On the eve of the expulsion Gento was in debt to Ramon Berbegual, *apuntatori pannorum* of Valencia, for *certo panno* he had purchased (ARV: P 2009, J. Salvador: 357v–358r [1492/7/12]). Members of another family, the Ardits, performed complementary tasks in the clothing business: Gento was a tailor (APPV: P 17862, L. Miralles: n.f. [1472/2/26]) while Mossé ran a textile shop (ARV: B 1158: 111r-v [Hinojosa Montalvo 1993a, no. 811]) for which he purchased cloth in Valencia (B 323: 242r-v [1479/5/11]).

[107] With the exception of the indebted Mossé Levi (ARV: B 323: 661r-v [1482/12/5]), I have not come across any other tailors, and only one cobbler, Gento Jacoti, who bought leather in 1478 and 1483 from Jaume Caldes, a tanner of Valencia, for 240 sous and 160 sous, respectively (APPV:

The production of cloth, including silk, was a growing concern of Morvedre's Jewish artisans and investors. Presumably some Jews had always been involved in cloth manufacturing, but in the fifteenth century, especially the latter half, the numbers increased as a result of the dramatic development of the industry in the city and kingdom of Valencia, and the demographic expansion of Morvedre's Jewish community.[108] Economic diversification both fueled and was necessitated by the rapid growth of the Jewish population. Lower- and middle-class Jews were attracted to promising and relatively new areas of industry, while affluent Jews sought new areas of investment outside the credit market.

In attempting to repopulate Morvedre's Jewish quarter in 1493 with Christian wool-dressers, municipal officials and the bailiff general were probably taking advantage of abandoned workshops, looms, and dyeworks.[109] Eighteen years before the expulsion, the weaver Jucef Arueti, Gento Gallego, and the cobbler Gento Jacoti, and their wives purchased "two looms with all the apparatus for weaving" from Jaume Moriella, a local Christian weaver.[110] In addition to weavers, and weaving shoemakers, there were also Jewish dyers,[111] some of whom leased or purchased dyeworks from the Crown.[112]

The number of Jews in Morvedre involved in the silk industry gradually increased over the fifteenth century, consonant with the remarkable "take-off" of the industry in the capital.[113] There, a silkweavers' guild, comprising many conversos, was established in 1465; silkweavers of Genoese origin were largely responsible for the foundation of another body, the Art de Velluters, in 1479. By the end of the century, some one thousand artisans were employed in Valencia's silk industry.[114] Manufacturing for local consumers and for those in-

---

P 17868, L. Miralles: n.f. [1483/3/27]). In 1483 Gento and his wife, Clara, still had not requited Caldes for the 1478 purchase.

[108] Iradiel 1989, 314–318; Navarro 1992.

[109] ARV: C 596: 133 bis r-134r (1493/9/3) [Hinojosa Montalvo 1993a, no. 879]; C 309: 189v–191r (1493/12/6); Piles Ros 1957, 369–370, 373.

[110] APPV: P 17866, L. Miralles: n.f. (1474/7/12): "duo telaria cum omnibus aparatibus textuendi."

[111] ARV: B 1155: 303v (1474/9/19) [Hinojosa Montalvo 1993a, no. 737]: Profet (or Jacob) Rodrich owes 60 sous to Joan Ferrer, dyer of Valencia, for *tintes* purchased. APPV: P 17858, L. Miralles: n.f. (1475/6/23): Jacob and his wife Regina purchase woolen cloth valuing 110 sous from Jaume Ramó of Morvedre. AMC: Justícia: n.f. (1484/3/3) concerns the confiscation of unfinished cloth from Jacob, then residing in Nules, because of his debts to a Christian of Castelló.

[112] ARV: MR 3988: 2r (1398): Haim Barzilay; 5r (1399): Salamó Barzilay. In 1405 (MR 3989: 13v) Haim purchased a royal *tintoreria*. MR 3988: 9r (1400): Jahudà Coffe and Jucef Abencabal. In 1412 (MR 3992: 5r) Salamó and Jucef Abencabal also purchased a *tintoreria*.

[113] The silkweaver Astruc Rodrich led the "Jewish silkweavers and other artisans" (ARV: C 287: 38v–39v) in their protest against the pretensions of the silversmiths (at n. 99). Despite the obvious importance of the silkweavers as a group, I have specifically identified only one other silkweaver, Mossé Asseyo (B 217: 479r–481v [1482/2/27]).

[114] Navarro 1992, 43–85; Iradiel and Navarro 1996.

habiting towns and villages to the north and west, the Jewish silkweavers of Morvedre avoided competing with silkweavers in the capital whose hands were full satisfying local and international demand.

The participation of Morvedre's Jews in the silk industry in the later fifteenth century was symptomatic of their economic vitality and adaptability, but it was also a matter of continuity. Since the 1380s Jews, and after 1391, conversos had been key players in the silk trade in Valencia and Barcelona. There were early links with Morvedre. The Valencian merchant Jahudà Coffe, who was associated with silk merchants from Barcelona in 1381, moved to Morvedre after 1391. His leasing of the local dyeworks in 1400, and his relative Samuel's later dealings with a Valencian velvet weaver, may well have been related to silk production.[115] In 1410 a Valencian broker, Pere Dezclausells, had business with Samuel Agí, a Jewish silkweaver of Borriana. The Agí family had a branch in Morvedre.[116]

In the 1460s the Çaportas of Morvedre emerged as pivotal figures, having one hand in the international silk trade and the other in Morvedre's textile trade. Valencia's established position as the main center for the redistribution of unworked Granadan silk to Italian silk industries facilitated the commerce conducted by Astruc and sons in the Granadan ports of Almería and Málaga, and Salamó's later acquisition of Venetian silks for the king.[117] The Çaportas were also closely connected with the converso silkweavers of Valencia for reasons economic and religious.[118] The development of a noticeable body of Jewish silkweavers in Morvedre no doubt owed something to the Jews' continuous contacts with conversos in the capital.[119]

Jewish "merchant-entrepreneurs" like Salamó Çaporta probably played an important role in promoting and organizing the production of textiles, both woolens and silks, by Jewish artisans in Morvedre. In Christian Valencia it was increasingly common for artisans to rely on the services of merchants, who supplied them with working capital through credit on supplies and advance payment on sales, and sometimes organized the entire process of production. The artisans, in essence, came to work for the merchants.[120] Jewish artisans may well have had a similar relationship with Salamó. With his commercial connections and investments in sheep, Salamó could advance them the raw silk and wool easily enough; with his textile shop in Morvedre, Salamó could sell what they produced.

---

[115] See n. 112 for the dyeworks; ARV: B 1219: 150r (1410/11/18) for Samuel Coffe's transactions with "Na Clara . . . texidora de vels."

[116] Navarro 1992, 36. On Barcelona, Mardurell 1965; Voltes Bou 1968.

[117] Navarro 1992, 37–38; above at nn. 77–82.

[118] ARV: P 2001, J. Salvador: n.f. (1482/5/10) records Salamó paying a pension de censal to an affluent converso silkweaver, Lluís Boïl; Navarro 1992, 59. P 1999, J. Salvador: n.f. (1479/3/23) concerns a transaction between Salamó and Joan Celma, a silkweaver of Valencia acting on behalf of the broker Gabriel Pertusa. See chap. 6 for religious contacts.

[119] See chap. 6.

[120] Iradiel 1989, 317, on the *mercader-empresari*; in general, Thrupp 1981.

Mossé Xamblell and his stepson Jucef Gracia formed a "company" with similar objectives in mind. They purchased a large quantity of unfinished cloth that they planned to have artisans full and weave; they would then market it. A falling-out of the two partners put an unfortunate end to the enterprise before it had progressed very far.[121] Gento Avincanes, a wealthy owner of vineyards who leased them out to poorer Jewish winegrowers, seems to have assumed an analogous role in the sphere of cloth production. He purchased workshops, which he leased to textile workers, and then sold the cloth they produced.[122] After all, Gento was no more likely to have woven cloth than to have pruned grapevines and crushed grapes.

The artisans, their entrepreneurial bosses, and the winegrowers were all, as has been seen, involved in commerce, in the sale of their own handiwork or in that of the producers in whose labor they had invested. Artisans traveled about the region manufacturing and vending their wares, or retailers did it for them. Moneylenders and tax farmers also traded in agrarian products like grain, oil, and wool, all of which they acquired when borrowers and taxpayers paid them in kind. To a greater or lesser extent, this had been the case since the late thirteenth century. Very few, if any, Jews in Morvedre ever dedicated all their labor and capital to commerce alone; yet rare was the Jew who did not engage in trade at some point in his career.

The century following 1391 saw much continuity with past practices but new developments as well. The Jews of Morvedre continued to play a crucial role circulating foodstuffs, materials, and manufactures throughout the region extending from the capital to Castelló. Municipal officials in Morvedre and regional lords thus occasionally used the Jews' commerce as a weapon in their disputes with one other, restricting or boycotting it.[123] Such tactics reflected the vitality of the Jews' commerce and only temporarily hampered it.

The importance of the Jews of Morvedre in regional trade actually grew during the fifteenth century, especially after the accession of Alfonso IV.[124] This was not simply a function of the community's demographic expansion. Rather, with the destruction of the aljama of Valencia, the Jews of Morvedre assumed more fully a role they had previously played to some extent, that of intermediaries between the capital, with its international commerce and industry, and the towns and villages of the northern half of the kingdom. Morvedre's mid-

---

[121] ARV: B 1153: 552v (1464/5/18), 557r (6/22), 558r (6/27) [Hinojosa Montalvo 1993a, nos. 646, 648, 649].

[122] APPV: P 17862, L. Miralles: n.f. (1472/4/6) records Gento's purchase of a workshop for 420 sous. P 17859: n.f. (1477/8/19) and P 17868: n.f. (1483/4/16) record sales of cloth to farmers of Canet and a local "honored citizen" M. Aguilar, respectively.

[123] See chap. 2.

[124] In 1424 King Alfonso granted the Jews of Morvedre in particular a royal safe-conduct protecting them and their "rebus, bonis et mercibus" wherever they might travel in his realms. ARV: C 32: 51r (3/3) [Hinojosa Montalvo 1993a, no. 333]; B 1146: 33r.

dlemen bought a variety of goods from Valencia's wholesalers, artisans, and merchant-entrepreneurs for resale.[125] A good number of their commercial contacts in Valencia were conversos who had risen rapidly into the ranks of the city's mercantile elite.[126] Valencia was also the home of converso brokers from Morvedre who had moved to the capital after their baptism. Possessing an intimate knowledge of the operations of Morvedre's Jewish retailers and of Valencia's market, they facilitated the bulk purchases of the former in the capital.[127] Jews of the kingdom visiting Valencia could stay there for several days at a time; some Morvedre families leased or owned domiciles in the Muslim quarter for business purposes.[128]

The involvement of the Morvedre Jews in international trade, overland and overseas, increased in the fifteenth century. In the previous century Castilian and Aragonese Jews had been frequent visitors to Valencia, carrying back Valencian manufactures and Mediterranean imports to their home kingdoms. The Jews of Valencia had been their main associates and had themselves sometimes journeyed to Castile and Aragon for commerce.[129] After the destruction of Valencia's Jewish community, Valencian conversos filled the role its merchants had played in the trade with Castilian and Aragonese Jews. Notwithstanding the predominance of the conversos, some Jews of Morvedre took ad-

[125] In 1418 Aaron Benaron and Ayon Benabrafim of Morvedre bought goods valuing 1,840 sous from the Valencian merchant Pere Climent (ARV: B 1145: 226v). B 1221: M. 2, 15r (1441/11/7); M. 1, 18r (1442/3/15) concern the transactions of the Valencian spice merchant Rafael Peligri with the Jewish retailers Jucef Façi and Salamó and Jucef Frances. APPV: P 444, J. de Campos Jr.: n.f. (1484/11/17) records the 280-sous debt of Samuel Adzoni to the merchant Bernat Ribes for cloth purchased; Samuel's son Abraham later sold the cloth to a Muslim of Petrés (ARV: B 1220: M. 3, 9r [1485/12/9]). Morvedre's Jewish peddlers might even buy their packmules in Valencia. Jucef Azen, "mercatori judeo," purchased three mules for 760 sous from Fernando Lópiz, a Castilian merchant resident in Valencia (APPV: P 21593, Joan de Carci: n.f. [1476/1/18]). I emphasize the northern half of the kingdom because one rarely encounters these individuals operating south of the capital. One exception is ARV: B 1151: n.f. (1450/1/15), concerning the complaint of Salamó Sorfati of Morvedre, from whom officials in Alzira confiscated cloth that, presumably, Salamó was selling.

[126] Guiral 1986, 353.

[127] Two prominent converts in 1415, Samuel and Abraham Legem, were both licensed as brokers prior to their transfer to Valencia. Another convert from later in the century, Guillem Ramon Splugues, a member of the Jewish Castillo family of Morvedre, also became a broker and moved to Valencia. See chaps. 1, 6.

[128] ARV: B 1147: seventh quire, letter G, between 264v and 265r (1430/2/9) [Hinojosa Montalvo 1993a, no. 374] concerns Jews of Morvedre "que stan e habiten en la ciutat de Valencia" and who must return to Morvedre for fiscal purposes. ARV: B Procesos, Letra P, 52 (1470/8/12–1472/8/25) shows that one of the Façans of Morvedre owned a house in the moreria where Quatorze, Crespi, and other Jews lodged. ARV: P 2785, J. de Campos Jr.: n.f. (1474/1/19) notes that Isaac Crespi was temporarily residing in the moreria. This document records Crespi making the Christians N. Torell and J. Segura his procuratores for collecting from Galceran Martí the 120 sous Martí owed him from the purchase of a horse.

[129] Ferrer Navarro 1980; Hinojosa Montalvo 1985, 1554–1559.

vantage of the changed circumstances to participate more vigorously in the
commerce with Aragon and Castile. In 1400 Salamó Aluleix exported arms,
metal implements, and lead to Murcia and Castile proper.[130] Jacob Façan imported merchandise from Teruel, in Aragon.[131] By the 1460s Salamó Çaporta
had become a major player in the commerce with Aragon and Castile. He exported goods to Murcia and various Aragonese towns. He employed several
Jewish agents, some from Morvedre, to pursue his interests in these places. He
also formed partnerships with the Jew Nicem Benvenist from Almansa, Castile,
and with Secon Siltori of Zaragoza, who consigned him merchandise for resale in Valencia.[132]

As has been seen in regard to the wine trade, both the conversos and visiting North African Jewish merchants created a framework for the increased participation of Morvedre's Jews in Mediterranean commerce. Besides exporting
wine, Jews like Samuel Ardutell, Samuel and Jacob Chifalla, and Astruc and
Salamó Çaporta exported sugar, woolen textiles, and silk to North African and
Granadan ports. Although in some instances they traveled abroad themselves,
usually they were sedentary partners.[133]

In the latter half of the century some farsighted Jews of Morvedre began to
look toward trade with Portugal and the opening Atlantic world. Initially they
conducted trade with Portugal through the Portuguese Jewish merchants who
frequently came to Valencia. In the 1480s, however, the royal silversmith and
merchant Vidal Astori, who had visited Castile and Portugal in the king's service, established his son Jahudà as his agent in Portugal. His other son, Samuel,
acted as the family agent in Valencia. The Astoris presumably exported Morvedre wine and Valencian manufactures to Portugal. They imported black slaves
acquired by the Portuguese in west Africa. Between September 1484 and October 1485 the Astoris sold nineteen black African slaves to Valencian customers for a total sum of 10,575 sous.[134] The Astoris' participation in the prof-

---

[130] ARV: MR 19: 60v (1400).

[131] ACA: C 2281: 93r (1401/7/5). Façan resisted the efforts of officials of the aljama of Teruel
to collect a sales tax from him.

[132] ARV: P 1995: third quire, 5v (1468/7/21) [Hinojosa Montalvo 1993a, no. 741]: Salamó em-
powers various Jews of Calatayud and Ariza, his agents, to show officials the royal letter exempting him and his goods from all commercial tariffs. In P 1999, J. Salvador: n.f. (1479/7/14) he em-
powers Jewish agents from Murcia and Morvedre to do the same. Litigation between Salamó and
Benvenist, on one hand, and various "personas, corpora, collegia et universitates," on the other,
indicates commerce with Castile (ARV: C 135: 71v [1488/6/3]), as do the sums paid by Salamó
in 1471–72 for melting down Castilian silver coins he obtained through commerce (ARV: MR 81:
175r, 177v; MR 82: 175r [Hinojosa Montalvo 1993a, nos. 703–705]). The sums were not, as the
editor suggests, penalties, but fees collected by the Crown for the royal share. B 1154: 265v (1468/
7/21) concerns the suit between Siltori and the Çaportas over "mercaderies e robes per aquell [Sil-
tori] les son stades acomanades."

[133] Hinojosa Montalvo 1979, 21–36; and above at nn. 29–30.

[134] ARV: B 217: 691v (1484/8/30), 694r-v (9/2); B 218: 38r–39r (1485/2/16), 45v, 46r, 46v–

itable African slave trade ended abruptly in 1486 when the bailiff general issued a decree forbidding Jews or Muslims to purchase black slaves from "Guinea" lest their Christianization be impeded.[135] As in the case of Salamó Çaporta, the monarch's anxieties about the Christian faith of his subjects, even enslaved subjects, curtailed a remarkable career.

Valencian silk, black African slaves, the beckoning Atlantic world: here lay the future of Valencia and of Spain. The bon contractador Salamó Çaporta and the ambitious silversmith Vidal Astori made themselves part of that future from the town on the Palancia River. They and the other Jews of Morvedre had rebuilt on the rubble of 1391 a remarkably vital and economically successful community. The region between the Turia and Millars rivers had become their domain. By the end of the century they were looking toward more distant horizons. The Jews of Morvedre had every reason to believe that they had built something lasting. Even when exiled by the inquisitors for two years, Salamó Çaporta expected to return home. He died in 1490, hopeful, saved from the pain of knowing that Morvedre could never be home again.

47v, 48r (2/21), 49r, 50v (2/22), 52v–53v, 54r–55r (2/23), 58r–59r (2/28), 59v–61r (3/4), 62r (3/15), 126v–127r (8/25).

[135] ARV: B 1220: M. 3, 5v–6r (1486/8/29); 15r–16r (9/19) more explicitly relates the order to official anxieties over converso Judaizing in Valencia.

Figure 1. Entrance to the Jewish quarter of Morvedre. Photo courtesy of Robert Shechter.

Figure 2. A street in the Jewish quarter of Morvedre ascending toward the castle walls. Photo courtesy of Robert Shechter.

Figure 3. Another entrance to the Jewish quarter of Morvedre. Photo courtesy of Robert Shechter.

Figure 4. A view of the castle of Morvedre from the road skirting the top of the Roman amphitheater. Photo courtesy of Robert Shechter.

Figure 5. Another view of the castle from the town below. Photo courtesy of Robert Shechter.

Figure 6. An overview of Morvedre (present-day Sagunto) from the castle. The church of Santa Maria and the roofs of houses in the adjacent Jewish quarter are in view. Photo courtesy of Robert Shechter.

Chapter Four

JEWS AND MUSLIMS

THE RELATIONSHIP of the Jews of Morvedre to the Muslim population of the region was less crucial to their fifteenth-century revival than their relationship with the Christian majority. It was of course the latter whose attitudes, actions, and policies created the conditions for the flowering of Jewish life and who, finally, brought about the Jews' expulsion. Interaction with the Muslims was nonetheless of considerable consequence for the life and livelihood of the Jews. In the region stretching from Valencia to Castelló, many towns and villages, especially those located on seigneurial domains, housed substantial Muslim communities. The Jews frequently conducted business and socialized with the Muslims. Such activities had been integral to the lifestyle of Valencian Jewry since the early days of colonization.

Although important changes had taken place since the thirteenth century, when Jewish bailiffs and Jewish estate-owners joined their Christian counterparts in lording it over the conquered Muslims, there was much continuity in the pattern of relations among the three religious communities. The Jews' perception of their own position and potential in fifteenth-century Valencian society was shaped in part by their understanding of the history of Jewish association with the kingdom's two other communities. The Jews still saw themselves as the allies of Valencian Christians and as somehow occupying a higher rung on the kingdom's social ladder than the Muslims. This Jewish perspective was not clearly enunciated but manifested itself in economic and social action.

The distinct relationships that the religious minorities maintained with Christian authority were a legacy of thirteenth-century conquest and colonization. Although they no longer rebelled against Christian rule, the loyalties of Valencian Muslims remained divided. Political obedience to their Christian overlords did not inhibit the Mudejars from continuing their contacts with coreligionists in Granada and North Africa for commercial, familial, religious, and even political purposes. At the end of the fifteenth century Valencian Muslims were still capable of correspondence with the Ottoman Turks on behalf of the beleaguered sultanate of Granada.[1] Although no longer royal bailiffs and cogs in the Christian monarchy's colonial machinery, the Jews necessarily continued to focus their political energies on gaining the favor and protection of the monarchs and on strengthening their ties with local Christian patrons. If

---

[1] Meyerson 1991, 64–68.

the numerous and restive Muslims continued to constitute, to some degree, a potentially subversive state within the state, the Jews remained, as ever, a prop of the state.

Less than four years before Fernando and Isabel completed the conquest of the sultanate of Granada and expelled the Jews, Valencian Muslims and Jews evinced their divergent readings of political circumstances. After the forces of the Catholic Monarchs captured Málaga, a key city of the Nasrid sultanate, and enslaved its Muslim population, hundreds of Malagan captives flooded Valencia's slave market. Valencian Muslims, who had often in the past expressed their allegiance to the wider Muslim world by ransoming or otherwise assisting captive foreign Muslims, now mobilized their resources as never before. Muslim aljamas from throughout the kingdom, but especially its northern half, ransomed, or purchased with the intention of ransoming, many enslaved Malagans.[2] Even if Valencian Jews did not, like Castilian Jews, serve as Arabic interpreters for the conquering Catholic Monarchs, and even if they were not especially cheered by the monarchs' progress against the Nasrids, they were nonetheless ready to reap the benefits of their firm allegiance to the monarchy and to profit from its subjugation of Muslim enemies.[3] Astruc Rodrich of Morvedre purchased at least six Malagan captives, four from the Crown and two from a merchant, probably with the intention of reselling them at a profit.[4] Though both Jews and Muslims had recently been prohibited from buying animist black African slaves, lest they impede their Christianization, Jews could still own Muslims.[5]

Captive foreign Muslims were not the only Muslims whom Jews could own. Jews sometimes, though not frequently, purchased Valencian Mudejar slaves as well.[6] The Mudejars' continuing vulnerability to enslavement inhered in their origins as conquered Muslim enemies. The Christian authorities, ever anxious about possible Mudejar sedition, enslaved Mudejars for various infractions, which they conceived as acts of political disobedience, as violations of the surrender agreements of long ago. Originally the allies of the Christian conquerors of Valencia, the Jews were not enslaved by Christians; rather, they continued to share with Christians the power to own criminal and defiant Mudejars. Even in the fifteenth century, institutionalized Mudejar slavery vi-

[2] Meyerson 1996, 318–321.

[3] Gutwirth 1989b, 244, for the interpreters. King Fernando perhaps used the horse trappings with gold filigree decorations that Vidal Astori, a Jewish silversmith of Morvedre, had presented to him in 1467–68, when he was still a prince. See Ainaud de Lasarte 1972, 219.

[4] ARV: B 219: n.f. (1488/9/30, 10/1); P 2169, F. Soler: 56r-v (1488).

[5] ARV: B 1220: M. 5, 5v–6r (1486/8/29): Meyerson 1996, 332 n. 156.

[6] ARV: B 1220: M. 1, 49r (1485/11/4): Salamó Cavaller, Jew of Morvedre, promises to pay 96 sous to the bailiff general as part of the price of the enslaved Mudejar Açen who had been sold to a notary named Toda. It is not clear from this who ultimately would be the owner of the slave, Cavaller or Toda. Perhaps it was a joint venture and the Jew and the Christian intended to resell the Muslim at a higher price.

talized memories of the thirteenth-century conquest and of the postconquest regime in which Christians and Jews had joined forces to control and colonize formerly Muslim territories.[7] Despite all that had transpired since 1283, the memories of conquest and colonialism continued to haunt the relations of Jews and Muslims and, perceptibly, to affect their behaviors.

Beyond merely being susceptible to penal servitude in a way that Jews were not, Valencian Muslims had become so inured to the possibility of enslavement that they at times voluntarily accepted debt servitude to creditors, usually Christians, or pledged their children to creditors as securities for outstanding debts.[8] The postconquest regime had not conditioned Jews, no matter how poor, to act thus. Even if Muslims only rarely placed themselves or their children in the hands of Jews, the fact that they did so powerfully reflected the relative political status of each minority community.[9] Though largely disempowered, Jews were still somehow associated with the conquering group.

Just the same, it was highly unusual, and distasteful, for Muslims to give themselves over to Jews in this way. In June 1487 Nexme, the wife of Çahat Pereta, a Muslim barber of Xàtiva, agreed to become the slave of Vidal Astori, a Morvedre Jew then in Xàtiva, "and to do the things of servitude for him by day and by night, [provided they are] licit and honest, for a period of four years." Nexme took this course of action in order to raise the 300 sous she owed the knight Lope Ferrández, the master of her husband, Çahat, who had been enslaved for some crime. Ferrández had released Çahat into the hands of Nexme and some Muslims from Valencia who were hoping to raise money for Çahat's ransom. Çahat's flight had left Nexme and her friends responsible for reimbursing Ferrández the 1,000 sous for the price of Çahat. The arrangement between Nexme and Astori, however, did not last long—only one month. Nexme apparently could not bear being the slave of a Jew; thus "she wished to become a Christian and she could not serve Vidal Astori, Jew."[10]

In Morvedre and its terme the distribution of economic and social power

[7] Meyerson 1995b.

[8] Meyerson 1995b, 169.

[9] ARV: B 1156: 459v (1479/6/1) [Hinojosa Montalvo 1993a, no. 782] is the case of a Muslim from Pedrola, Aragon, who pledges his seven-year-old son to a Jewish tailor of Xàtiva as security for the 1,000 sous he owes the Jew.

[10] ARV: B 1220: M. 8, 3r–4r (1487/6/22): "se met e afferma ella dita Nexme ab lo dit Vidal Astori, juheu present e acceptant, a servir aquell e fer coses de servitut de aquell licites e honestes, axi de dia com de nit, per temps de quatre anys comptadors." B 1220: M. 5, 41r (1486/12/11) is the original agreement between Lope Ferrández and the Muslims from Valencia. B 1220: M. 8, 14v (1487/7/20): "ella se vol fer crestiana e no poria servir a Vidal Astori, juheu." APPV: P 25214, J. Argent: n.f. (1470/11/5) is another example, in which the Jew Salamó Zalmati of Xàtiva purchases a Mudejar slave, Abrahim Gogori, from the wife of the nobleman Nicolau de Pròixida. Zalmati, or Zalmari, was by 1474 a resident of Morvedre [Hinojosa Montalvo 1993a, no. 735]. The Pròixidas, the lords of Almenara, had close and long-standing ties with several Jews of Morvedre (see chap. 2).

was reminiscent of the postconquest decades. Often joined through economic
interest and patronage, Christians and Jews still dominated the scene. In the
town proper, the Muslim community, which had died out in the early fourteenth century, revived, with royal encouragement, in 1413. But it was a small
community. Beginning with fourteen households, its population peaked at
twenty-six households in 1423. Afterward — and in marked contrast to the Jewish community — it declined steadily: thirteen households in 1438, eight in
1448, five in 1468, and none in 1474. Fostered by Fernando II, the Muslim aljama recovered to include ten households by 1492.[11] The Muslim and Jewish
aljamas coexisted with minimal conflict. The one recorded dispute typically
involved taxation, ensuing when the Jewish and Christian tax farmers of the
cisa on meat unjustly attempted to collect it from the Muslims for the sheep
they had slaughtered for the Feast of the Sacrifice (commemorating Abraham's
sacrifice of the ram).[12]

Compared to the Jews, the Muslims of Morvedre, both the householders in
the moreria and the visitors from outlying villages, had the appearance of an
underclass. Muslim laborers and artisans received small salaries from the local
bailiff for repairing royal utilities, like ovens and mills, and for hauling sand
and stone to town for this purpose. Muslim prostitutes frequently plied their
trade in Morvedre.[13] Local Jews, who did not keep Muslim concubines in this
period, may well have made use of the prostitutes' services. In 1462, a Muslim
woman, probably an enslaved prostitute, was found hiding in the Jewish quarter from her Christian master or pimp.[14] Even if the woman viewed the Jews
as possible rescuers, other Muslims would have regarded her presence among
Jews as shameful. Valencian Muslims strictly guarded the sexuality of their
women and deemed extramarital intercourse, with other Muslims and especially with non-Muslims, as dishonorable. The Jewish males' use of Muslim
prostitutes was evocative of the alignment of political and sexual power in pre-

---

[11] ARV: MR 3992–4024 (1412–92); Meyerson 1991, 32.

[12] ARV: B 1153: 459r-v (1463/9/12). On 457r (8/31) it is established that the Muslims cannot
be forced to pay the cisa for the meat slaughtered on this festival. In Morvedre Jews and Muslims
had their own separate butcheries (MR 3992–4024). The sale of meat did not excite the sorts of
controversies between Jews and Muslims noted in other towns by Nirenberg 1996, 169–172. The
license granted to the Jewish aljama of Morvedre to levy sales taxes indicates the possibility of Muslims and Christians buying kasher meat from Jews (B 1151: 568v–570r [Hinojosa Montalvo 1993a,
no. 529]).

[13] ARV: MR 3992–4024 (1412–92) record the payment of the Muslims' salaries, and the receipt of licensing fees from Muslim prostitutes. Also, Meyerson 1991, 159.

[14] ARV: B 1153: 365v (1462/9/13) [Hinojosa Montalvo 1993a, no. 631]. Here the bailiff general was seeking information on whether the woman was a *cativa del senyor rey*. Many Muslim
women made slaves of the Crown were sold to Christians who then put them to work as prostitutes (Meyerson 1988). Although I have not encountered cases of it in Morvedre, Jewish ownership of Muslim concubines was not uncommon in the thirteenth and fourteenth centuries. See
Nirenberg 1996, 182–188; Assis 1988, 36–40.

vious centuries, when Christian and even Jewish men had had greater access to and control over the bodies of Muslim women. While there may well have been a few Jewish prostitutes in Morvedre, it was the richly adorned Jewish matrons who stood out, in conspicuous contrast to the Muslim prostitutes.[15]

Jewish interaction with the Muslim villagers of the town's terme was much more extensive than that which took place inside the town's walls; it was also, owing to the tensions between the Muslims' seigneurs and the municipality, more complex. When Jews worked as farmers and collectors of municipal taxes, the seigneurs and their Muslim tenants could easily view them as the collaborators of municipal officials endeavoring to tax and otherwise control the villages. In 1474 some lords of the terme interpreted even Jewish commerce and moneylending in this light and thus forbade their vassals to do business with Jews from the town.[16]

Yet boycotting Jewish business was an unusual tactic for the lords engaged in fiscal and jurisdictional struggles with the municipality. Seigneurs and their Muslim tenants most often welcomed Jewish businessmen, a pattern of behavior replicated outside the municipal district in the lordships dotting the countryside between the capital and Castelló. Long-term Jewish clientage to local knightly families facilitated Jewish activity within the terme; the careful cultivation of connections with lords and the discreet payment of "entry fees" accomplished the same on seigneurial estates farther afield.

Christian lords and Muslim tenants did not view the Jews in quite the same way, particularly when Jews farmed the lord's taxes and had at their disposal the lord's coercive power. When a Jew like Vidal Comte, who farmed the taxes of Suera in the Serra d'Eslida, confiscated securities from Muslims whose taxes were in arrears, he obviously needed the support of the lord and his officials.[17] It was no different if the seigneur was the king, as when Samuel Façan, acting as the agent of Daniel Barceló, merchant of Valencia and farmer of royal rents in Castelló, had royal officers jail Mahomat Mugib for outstanding taxes.[18] In such circumstances, the Muslims could hardly have avoided seeing the Jewish tax farmer as an adjunct of a demanding and at times oppressive seigneurial regime.

Of course, it was not their farming of seigneurial revenues that made the Jewish visitors from Morvedre useful, if not vital to Muslim peasants. The Muslims relied on itinerant Jewish artisans and merchants "selling their work and

---

[15] Meyerson 1991, 248–251; Assis 1988, 44–45; Hinojosa Montalvo 1993b, 53–54; Peris 1990, 195 n. 45.

[16] See chap. 2.

[17] ARV: B 1155: 171r (1474/2/5) [Hinojosa Montalvo 1993a, no. 728] does not state explicitly that Comte was farming the taxes of Suera, but, in ordering Comte to settle accounts with a certain Munyós, apparently the local castellan, and with the Muslims, it strongly implies it.

[18] ARV: B 1150: 92r (1447/5/24); 110r-v (6/22) [Hinojosa Montalvo 1993a, no. 488].

merchandise" to bring them needed or desired manufactures, such as cloth and jewelry.[19] Due to their investments in the agricultural sector, Jews from Morvedre were also in a position to provide the Muslims with grain and live-stock. Vidal Comte, for example, sold ninety-nine sheep to Muslim and Chris-tian peasants in Benifairó de les Valls for 772 sous, which the peasants were obliged to pay within eighteen months.[20] As in this case, the Jews often sold goods to Muslim peasants on credit.

The Muslim inhabitants of the villages frequented by Jews from Morvedre depended on the Jews to provide them with small loans to tide them over dur-ing the lean winter months. Occasionally the loans were made in kind, in the form of bread grain, but usually they were made in coin.[21] Not all the loans were small, however. Indeed, many of the loans that generated litigation — and the extant correspondence of royal bailiffs — exceeded 100 sous and were sometimes as large as 1,000 sous.[22] Muslims borrowed such large sums most likely for the purpose of purchasing new land, livestock, or tools. Many Mus-lims were mobile and enterprising; Jewish capital enabled them to embark on new agrarian, industrial, and commercial ventures.[23]

Jewish lenders charged interest to Muslim borrowers, probably in accor-dance with the old royal rate to which Muslim borrowers had long been ac-customed. Alfonso IV's orders of 1419 forbidding Jews to make usurious loans to Christians did not apply to the kingdom's Muslims, but the bailiff general and the notaries acted as if they did. Notaries thus recorded Jewish loans to Muslims as having been made *gratiose*.[24] In a kingdom with such a large Mus-lim population, it made little sense for notaries to redact two sorts of loan con-tracts — one for Christians, the other for Muslims — especially since in both cases interest was really being charged.

[19] E.g., ARV: B 1220: M. 3, 9r (1485/12/9): Yuceff Matoti, Muslim hemp-sandal maker of Petrés, acknowledges a debt of 16 sous to the Jew Abraham Adzoni for cloth purchased; APPV: P 17862, L. Miralles (1471/12/31): Mahomat Xuart of Xilet purchases gold jewelry from the Jew Salamó Tarfon for 70 sous. ARV: C 90: 59r-v (1461/7/28), which treats the Jews' activities in the Vall d'Uixó, contains the phrase "venrre obres e mercaderies sues."

[20] APPV: P 24680, B. Roca: n.f. (1459/10/1).

[21] An example of a loan in kind is ARV: P 1445, B. de la Mata: 302r (1399/11/6), in which a Muslim family of Perenxisa acknowledges a debt of 99 sous to the Jew Samuel Suxen for wheat purchased, or, in effect borrowed. Some examples of small monetary loans are P 1446, B. de la Mata: n.f. (1401/6/22): 77 sous from Samuel Suxen to two Muslim families residing in Mislata; MR 3995: 12v (1424): 48 sous 2 diners from Salamó Fanduix to Maymó Vellet, Muslim of Petrés; B 1152: 1626r (1459/3/18) [Hinojosa Montalvo, no. 584]: 50 sous from Gento Carser to Abdalla Serra of the Vall d'Uixó.

[22] E.g., ARV: MR 3994: 11v–12r (1423) regarding the 250 sous owed by Abducalem Allahuen of Eslida to Levi Almarori; B 1146: 211v (1425/5/10) regarding the 1,000 sous owed by the heirs of the same Muslim to Jamila, the widow of Samuel Suxen; B 1220: M. 2, 48v–49r (1487/11/7) regarding the 586 sous owed by "Chiqual" of Valencia to Astruc Rodrich.

[23] Meyerson 1991, 114–142.

[24] See chap. 2.

The Jews' changed position in the kingdom's credit market, which in the fifteenth century modified the Christians' image of and actual relations with Jews, affected the interaction of Jews and Muslims minimally. The sorts of transactions conducted between Jews and Muslims did not differ markedly from those of previous centuries. The predominant relationship reflected in the public discourse was still that of Jewish creditor to Muslim debtor.[25] Although Muslims needed the loans Jews provided and the goods Jews sold them on credit, and despite the fact that Muslims normally repaid Jews without a hitch, this one-sided relationship had a deleterious impact on the attitudes of at least some Muslims toward the Jews.

Jewish creditors from Morvedre efficiently enlisted royal bailiffs to pursue and pressure Muslim debtors, even on seigneurial lands. Sometimes the bailiff of Morvedre, or more usually the municipal justice, would force Muslim inhabitants of villages nearby to pay their debts as well as the *pena del quart*.[26] With regard to insolvent Muslims of more distant villages, the bailiff general, at the behest of Jewish creditors, often called on local Muslim officials to take action. They usually cooperated. After the bailiff general wrote to the amīn of Argelita about the debt owed by a local Muslim to Astruc Rodrich, the amīn responded in an Arabic missive that when he saw the Muslim in question, he advised him either to requite the Jew or to appear before the court of the bailiff general to explain himself.[27] A confident Jew like Astruc Çaporta might approach Muslim officials directly about proceeding against recalcitrant debtors. At the instance of Astruc, the *qāḍī* of the Vall d'Almonesir condemned several local Muslims to pay the Jew the 340 sous remaining from a larger quantity. Only after the debtors chose to ignore the Muslim judge's sentence did Astruc turn to the bailiff general, who then sent the necessary instructions to the local amīn.[28]

[25] One rarely encounters cases of Jews in debt to Muslims. One example is APPV: P 17858, L. Miralles: n.f. (1475/8/7), recording the 320-sous debt of Abraham Agí, Jew of Morvedre, to Hamet Ayup, Muslim of Fanzara, for the price of a black mule. Cf. Gutwirth 1989b, 256–257; Hinojosa Montalvo 1993b, 62–63; Nirenberg 1996, 174–177.

[26] Normally the municipal justice was responsible for proceeding against such insolvent debtors (Magdalena Nom de Déu 1988, 39–67); unfortunately, there are not any extant registers from the court of Morvedre's justice. Occasionally the royal bailiff intervened in these cases. E.g., ARV: MR 3993: 11v (1419), 41r (1420); MR 3994: 11v–12r (1423); MR 3995: 12v (1424), which all record sums exacted from Muslims of Petrés indebted to Jews of Morvedre.

[27] ARV: B 322: 107r (1475/3/14) [Barceló Torres 1984, no. 56]. The debtor, however, did not heed his advice, which moved the bailiff general to order the amīn to confiscate property of the debtor toward the payment of the debt. That same year Rodrich empowered his brother Pastor and a Christian notary, Pere Alfons, to collect the 320 sous owed him by three Muslims of Aín in the Serra d'Eslida (ARV: P 442, J. de Campos Jr.: n.f. [4/4]). The Muslims responded by depositing with the qāḍī general, the chief Muslim judge in the kingdom, a load of wax, the proceeds from the sale of which would be used to reimburse Rodrich (B 1155: 462v [5/23]; B 1296: 125r-v [Hinojosa Montalvo 1993a, no. 753]).

[28] ARV: B 1147: 608r-v (1434/4/7).

Such pressure from Jewish creditors kindled the resentment of some Muslim debtors and their relations, leaving them with the impression that Jews were bent on exploiting them. Loppo, a blind Muslim of Mascarell, a village in the barony of Nules, seems to have been guided by such a notion when fashioning his accusations against Abraham Agí, a Jewish silversmith from Morvedre. Loppo assumed, moreover, that others would regard his accusations as plausible. By Loppo's account, a dream had revealed to him that there was a sack of money underneath a stone in the floor of his abode. Sure enough, when he lifted up the stone the sack was there. Just then, Abraham Agí happened by. He entered Loppo's house and offered to change the money for him. According to Loppo, Abraham lied to him about the true value of the money and, taking advantage of his blindness, cheated him. When Loppo told the story to a baronial official, a certain Torroella, the latter took the unusual step of ordering the adelantats of Morvedre's aljama to compel members of the community, while in the synagogue, to come forth with any information relevant to the case. Abraham, who had since left Mascarell, where there was an order for his arrest, maintained that he did not even know the blind Muslim, much less rob him. He then headed straight for the court of the bailiff general to make his case.[29]

Little came of Loppo's accusations, which the adelantats described as a "fantasy." Yet other Muslims had such fantasies of Jews as wealthy and exploitative, but instead of laying charges against them in court, they attacked and robbed them in rural villages or on the kingdom's roads. Muslim violence against Jews, in fact, exceeded that of Christians against Jews, undoubtedly because Muslims were still, much more than Christians, under the thumb of Jewish creditors.

In 1421, for example, Jucef Bonet, a Jew of Morvedre, filed suit against a Muslim couple of Bétera, Mahomat Ubequer and Hebo, asserting that when he entered their house on some business, they seized him and forcibly extorted money from him.[30] Later in the century, Samuel Agí claimed that while he was traveling through the Vall de Sego en route to Canet, a Muslim of the valley, named Garri, accosted him, whacked him over the head twice, and stole his cloak and doublet.[31] Bonet and Agí were more fortunate than some Jews in their encounters with Muslim assailants. Two Jews were robbed and murdered near Eslida by Mahomat Çuleymen and his accomplice.[32] Three Muslims robbed and almost killed Abraham Huisqui on the royal road. Representatives of the Jewish aljamas of Morvedre and Borriana expressed their

---

[29] ARV: B 1150: 161r (1447/11/13), 161v (11/14) [Hinojosa Montalvo 1993a, nos. 491–492].
[30] ARV: MR 41: 109r (1421): the Muslim couple had to pay a settlement of 220 sous.
[31] ARV: B 1220: M. 2, 28v (1486/6/13).
[32] ARV: B 1151: 576r (1452/8/12).

concerns to the bailiff general about Abraham's case.[33] If the kingdom's roads were unsafe, Jews could not travel about on business.

The Jews of Morvedre felt vulnerable. Since the livelihood of many of them depended on business with Muslims throughout the region, they took care to avoid any questionable practices that might anger the Muslims. When traveling through the mountains, valleys, and villages outside Morvedre, they were, they knew, at the Muslims' mercy. Thus when the Jewish silversmiths of Morvedre learned that some of their fellows were selling silverware of inferior quality in Muslim villages, they immediately obtained the support of the bailiff general for legislating quality controls, not just for the silversmiths resident in Morvedre but also for those living in Castelló and Borriana. In his letter to the bailiff of Morvedre ordering the enforcement of the new legislation, the bailiff general pointed out why the silversmiths wanted it: so that they would not be "maltreated by the [Muslim] aljamas of those [places] for reason of the said sales."[34]

Yet in acting so decisively the Jewish silversmiths of Morvedre were merely ensuring that they would be able to carry on with the Muslims the kind of business they had safely conducted for many decades. The silversmiths' quality controls apparently had their intended effect. Muslims did not grumble about Jews selling them shoddy silverwork, nor did Jews worry further about Muslim anger on this score. True, the silversmiths' anxiety was rooted in real vulnerability, to which the handful of recorded attacks of Muslims on Jews attest, but in light of the incessant activity of Jewish artisans, lenders, and merchants in villages heavily or wholly populated by Muslims, these same attacks appear atypical. Even if during the fifteenth century the reverberations of conquest and colonialism still affected the relationship of Jews to Muslims, the relationship was for the most part noncontentious and nonviolent.

Despite the very occasional purchase of a Muslim slave by a Jew or the Jews' skill at ingratiating themselves with Christian nobles, after 1391 Valencian Muslims could not have harbored too many illusions of "Jewish power." In an era when the great Jewish community in the capital was but a memory and most other Jewish communities were diminished, Muslim communal authorities no longer needed to concern themselves with what had been in the fourteenth century troubling social phenomena: Jewish ownership of Muslim slaves and keeping of Muslim concubines, and the conversion of Muslims to the religion of the often wealthier and more influential Jews.[35] If, in terms of demography and power, Jewish fortunes in the kingdom of Valencia largely

---

[33] ARV: B 1149: 444r (1445/3/8) [Hinojosa Montalvo 1993a, no. 479]. Huisqui, once an inhabitant of Morvedre, had recently moved to Borriana.

[34] ARV: B 1149: 150v (1442/1/30) [Hinojosa Montalvo 1993a, no. 467].

[35] Boswell 1977, 379–380; Nirenberg 1996, 183–188.

waned after 1391, those of the Muslims in many ways waxed. The Muslims did
not constitute an immobilized mass of peasants subject to the terror and exploitation of Christian lords and their entrepreneurial Jewish clients. Labor
shortages increased the bargaining power and mobility of many Muslim peasants, both of which were enhanced by the monarchy's persistent efforts to create and expand the Muslim quarters of royal towns at the expense of the
seigneurs. Bringing new land under cultivation and embarking on new industrial and commercial enterprises, many Muslims improved their economic position. Although a Christian mob sacked the moreria of Valencia in 1455, the
effects of the violence were limited. The relationship between Muslims and
Christians was, on the whole, stable and less upset than in earlier centuries by
the Crown of Aragon's clashes with Muslim polities. Like the Jews of Morvedre, the Muslims in many towns and villages adapted successfully to fifteenth-
century conditions.[36]

But the Jewish community in Morvedre was, after all, an anomaly, its growth
and prosperity by no means indicative of the Jews' situation elsewhere in the
kingdom. Nor were there other towns where Jews appeared to be so wealthy
and powerful in comparison with the Muslims. In later fifteenth-century
Castelló, for example, the Jewish community stagnated demographically and
economically while the Muslim community flourished.[37]

Furthermore, the Muslims' borrowing of money or purchasing of goods on
credit from Jews did not necessarily entail Jewish economic domination of the
Muslims. The relationship of Jewish creditor to Muslim debtor attested to so
frequently in the records had less to do with relative prosperity than with historical economic function. The town-dwelling Jews had long had greater access to capital than the Muslims and continued to pursue forms of livelihood
requiring the investment of capital, like moneylending, tax farming, and retail
merchandising. The Jews remained useful to the Muslims as purveyors of
capital, since usury among Muslims was prohibited. The far more numerous
Muslims still lived mainly in rural areas for ideological as well as economic
reasons.[38] While many of them received consumption loans from Jews, others
borrowed Jewish and Christian capital to finance their own agrarian, industrial, and commercial ventures. Still others purchased luxury items, like gold
and silverware, from Jews on credit. If the Muslims had less disposable capital
to reimburse the Jews immediately in coin, they usually were able to repay
the Jews on schedule once they marketed their own crops and manufactures.
Muslim borrowers often left gold jewelry with Jewish lenders as collateral; they
were cash-poor, not materially poor.[39] The resort to Jewish credit was a tem-

[36] Meyerson 1991; Ruzafa García 1990.
[37] Magdalena Nom de Déu 1972, 346–352; Díaz de Rábago 1994, 57–102.
[38] Meyerson 1991, 259–260.
[39] E.g., ARV: B 1154: 447r-v (1469/10/5); B 1156: 880v (1480/10/30) [Hinojosa Montalvo
1993a, nos. 692, 792].

porary and necessary expedient, one to which the Muslims had grown accustomed after the dust of conquest settled. It was not usually a sign of Muslim poverty.

Even when Muslim debtors could not come up with the wherewithal to requite their Jewish creditors, the latter sometimes forgave them the debt or extended the term of repayment indefinitely. Familiarity with at least one of the four Muslim families of Benifairó de les Valls borrowing 330 sous from him allowed the Jew Abraham Alateffi, in March 1472, to negotiate with the Muslims a loan contract containing lenient and unusual terms. Although Abraham did not proffer the loan "gratuitously," as the notarized contract asserts, he did give the Muslims two full years in which to reimburse him. In return, one of the Muslims, Yayell Adnagar, alias "the *faqīh*" (jurist), promised to give Abraham the use of a room "in one of [his] houses" during the two-year payment period and for one additional year. There Abraham could store oil and other agricultural products. Abraham never collected the debt from Yayell and friends. His heir Mossé did, but not until 6 July 1492, just before he departed Morvedre for good. Abraham and Mossé had been content to let the debt linger indefinitely and, presumably, to utilize Yayell's storeroom all the while.[40]

Among the creditors of Muslim peasants, the true tormentors were not the Jews, who loaned them only small sums for the most part, but the Christian censalistas, who purchased annuities from the Muslims' cash-strapped lords or, at their lords' insistence, from the Muslims' aljamas. The burden of censals borne by Muslim aljamas grew steadily over the century. Since the fiscal revenues accruing from and, as a last resort, the property belonging to Muslim peasants were mortgaged to secure the censals, Muslim communities increasingly found themselves being hounded by censalistas demanding their pensions. By the end of the century the desperate flight of Muslim families from their lords' creditors was not uncommon.[41] Muslim families did not pack their bags at the approach of Jewish creditors from Morvedre.

In the Muslim villages where Jews from Morvedre conducted business, the Jews were in some cases more than frequent visitors; they were part-time residents. Jews owned or rented domiciles and workshops in places like the Vall d'Uixó, which enhanced their mobility and facilitated their cultivation of a local clientele. Jews even possessed domiciles in the capital's Muslim quarter, whence they could deal with local merchants and communicate with converso friends and family. The Jews' setting up of shop and household in Muslim vil-

---

[40] APPV: P 17862, L. Miralles: n.f. (1472/3/12). In an earlier example, the Jewish widow Jamila (Suxen) forgave the Muslim Çalema Malull most of the 53-florin debt he owed her (ARV: P 1446, B. de la Mata: n.f. [1401/6/6]). Çalema resided in Valencia, Jamila's home until 1392. Jamila, however, was not always so forgiving — e.g., her suit against Muslim debtors in the village of Quartell (ARV: C 37: 11r-v [1426/8/9]).

[41] Meyerson 1991, 179–183; Garcia Oliver 1991, 120–126; and 1997a, 158–173; Pastor Zapata 1984.

lages and neighborhoods presupposed a reasonably friendly reception from the Muslim inhabitants.

In such circumstances Jews and Muslims became rather well acquainted, well enough to get involved in one another's feuds. When Mossé Maymó of Morvedre set out from the Vall d'Uixó, where he had a silversmithy and domicile, to waylay a converso enemy, he was accompanied by three local Muslims he had quickly recruited.[42] The dozen or so Muslims from various villages in the Palancia River valley who mortally wounded Mahomat Royo while attacking him and his friends on the royal road had two Jews from Morvedre in their armed band.[43]

Jews and Muslims also teamed up for less bloody business. In 1473 Salamó Zalmari, resident of Xàtiva and Morvedre, formed a partnership with Açen Catim, a Muslim of Betxí, to hunt for treasure in the villages of Pobla Tornesa and Benicàssim near Castelló.[44] Prior to departing Iberia in 1492, Jacob Toledano and Mossé Façan of Morvedre amicably dissolved the commercial partnership they had formed with the Muslims Azmen Robayti of Onda and Amet Xaxo of Betxí. Perhaps the Muslims had been functioning as the agents or vendors for the Jews in these places.[45]

There may well have been considerable contact and cooperation between Jews and Muslims in the related fields of medicine, alchemy, and magic. In the fifteenth century Jews from Morvedre were still being licensed by the Christian authorities to practice as physicians and surgeons.[46] Muslims, who had been for the most part marginalized from the world of official, scholastic medicine, only rarely received such licenses, but they continued to practice as empirics and even among Christians maintained a reputation for being effective practitioners of medicine and therapeutic magic. Notwithstanding the reluctance of Christian authorities to sanction their activities, the medical knowledge of some of these Muslim healers was probably acquired from the study of classical Arabic medical texts as well as from the oral advice and example of

[42] ARV: B Procesos, Letra P, 2618: 9r (1430/7/14); Meyerson 2003b.

[43] ARV: G 2324: M. 2, 25r-v (1468/3/7). The Muslim assailants—Hubaydal Hamira; Yucef, Mahomat, and Ali Galip; and eight to ten others—were residents of Albalat, Petrés, and Sot. The Jews are not identified beyond "dos juheus de la vila de Morvedre."

[44] ARV: B 1155: 54v–55r (1473/5/7); B 1296: 41v–42r (1474/8/29) [Hinojosa Montalvo 1993a, nos. 716, 735]. Treasure-hunting required a license from the Crown, which received a share of the find.

[45] Archivo Municipal de Alcoy: P, Pere Benavent: n.f. (1492/7/8) [Hinojosa Montalvo 1993a, no. 855]. Although the agreement does not explicitly mention a partnership, the fact that the Muslims and Jews were arriving at a "componum . . . in et super omnibus mercibus, rebus, pecuniis, etc.," indicates as much.

[46] E.g., ARV: C 274: 18r-v (1453/7/6) is a license to Astruc Çaporta to practice "artibus fisice videlicet et cirurgice" after being examined by "fisici et cirurgici domus nostre [Prince Juan] magistri Johanni de Bordalna"; C 148: 24v (1492/6/23), which mentions Samuel Cavaller, Jewish physician of Morvedre.

successful empirics.[47] Though less than in earlier centuries, it was not unusual for erudite Jews in the Crown of Aragon to learn Arabic for the purpose of scientific and medical studies.[48] Learned Jewish physicians from Morvedre who frequented Muslim villages and who could therefore probably speak some Arabic may well have read Arabic medical texts too. A shared interest in the Arabic medical tradition would naturally have brought Jewish and Muslim practitioners together. Jahudà Toledano, a licensed Jewish physician from Morvedre, worked with or employed Mahomat Burgi, a Muslim barber-surgeon from nearby Petrés.[49]

Samuel "of Granada," a licensed Jewish physician and alchemist of uncertain origins who lived and practiced in the city of Valencia from 1414 to 1416, consulted both Muslim practitioners and Arabic texts. Fluent in Arabic, Samuel engaged in alchemical experiments in Valencia with two Muslim assistants, and he discussed alchemy with other Muslims. When a local Christian approached him about curing his impotence, allegedly the result of sorcery, Samuel told him, "Sir, I need to go outside [the city] for a while [to see] a Muslim, my great friend, to learn about your bewitchment."[50] After his daughter fell ill, Jacob Façan of Morvedre called in practitioners of all three faiths to attend to her. King Joan's purposeful description of them as "sorcerers" should not obscure the fact that Muslims, Jews, and Christians were apt to turn to the experts of other faiths in cases of medical emergency.[51] The services of one "Master Isaac," a physician who circulated between Morvedre and Castelló, were much sought by the inhabitants of the villages near Castelló.[52]

A Jew like Jacob Façan who dealt frequently with Muslims and who saw fit to have Muslim healers treat his sick daughter not surprisingly shipped his forcibly baptized son David to Muslim North Africa to return to Judaism. David Façan was one of many baptized Valencian Jews who sought refuge in North Africa after the violence of 1391.[53] Muslim lands were a natural choice for Valencian Jews who were familiar with Muslims, their customs, and sometimes their language. After the fall of Constantinople to the Ottoman Turks in

[47] García Ballester 1988, 31–45; and 1994, 362–367, esp. 364, regarding the copying of a medical work of Ibn Rushd in Valencia in 1480. For examples of Christian recourse to Muslim empirical practitioners, see *Visitas pastorales*, 124–134.

[48] Gutwirth 1989b, 239–244; cf. García Ballester 1994, 368–369.

[49] ARV: B 1220: M. 1, 13r (1485/6/28). Here Mahomat accuses Jahudà of having given him false coins, which perhaps formed part of his salary. APPV: P 17880, L. Miralles: n.f. (1482/4/25) also describes Jahudà as a *fisicus*.

[50] Meyerson 2003a. ARV: B Procesos, Letra P, 2617: 4v: "'Senyor, yo haure de necesitat anar de fora un poch a un moro, gran amich meu, per saber lo vostre ligament.'"

[51] ACA: C 1906: 64r–66r (1393/5/10); see chap. 1.

[52] Magdalena Nom de Déu 1972, 350 n. 14. The same "Master Isaac," who paid the peita in Castelló in 1433, was listed among the Jews of Morvedre in 1434 (ARV: C 264: 16v–17r).

[53] ACA: C 2330: 131v–132r (1397/2/23) shows that Muslims from Sogorb and nearby lordships were indebted to Façan. See chap. 1 for the refugees.

1453, some conversos in Valencia, thinking more in millenarian than in practical terms, attempted to set sail for Ottoman domains. The Turks' capture of Constantinople did not, however, inspire the Jews of Morvedre or other Valencian towns with the same millenarian dreams.[54] Their circumstances in and after 1453 did not dispose them to applaud the Turks' progress and flee Christian rule. They were content to stay put.

In 1492, when the Jews of Morvedre had no choice but to leave, a few may have decided to emigrate to North Africa for the same reasons some of their ancestors had in 1391: familiarity with the Muslims and their culture, and the existence of established Jewish communities there. Yet the great majority set their sights on Italy, on Christian lands.[55] Consideration of the peace and prosperity they had enjoyed in the Christian kingdom of Valencia for the past several decades weighed heavily in the Jews' decision-making. They cast their lot with Christian princes again because that was what they had been doing since 1248, when they first settled in Morvedre. However much business they did with Muslims, and however much they shared with Muslims the difficulties of living as non-Christians in a Christian realm, most Jews of Morvedre, like most Valencian Jews, could not easily forsake their association with the Christian conquerors. Alliance with the Christians had in bygone days given them power, prestige, and wealth. Even if they had suffered humiliation and demotion at Christian hands, they had never, in their own minds, sunk quite as low as the subjugated Muslim population. The fact that Jews in their very own town had just a few years earlier bought Muslim slaves shipped in from conquered Granadan cities reminded them whence they had come and where, with any luck, they still might go. Until the very end, the memories of conquest and of the exercise of power haunted and inspired the Jews of Morvedre.[56]

---

[54] See chap. 6.

[55] Hinojosa Montalvo 1993a, 291, 295.

[56] I do not assume that the interpretation of Jewish-Muslim relations in the kingdom of Valencia presented here applies to other parts of Christian Spain, such as the kingdom of Aragon (on which see Catlos 2003; Nirenberg 1996, 166–199). I believe that the Jews' particularly prominent role in the administration of Valencian territories immediately after their conquest from the Muslims initiated a distinct dynamic in Jewish-Muslim relations in the kingdom of Valencia. The relationship between Jews and Muslims in Aragon proper was, from the start, more balanced and less burdened by the legacy of conquest and colonialism.

Chapter Five

THE POLITICS OF PLENTY

THE FLOURISHING of the Jews of Morvedre in the fifteenth century, most palpable in their interaction with Christians and Muslims and in their economic activities outside the Jewish quarter, was also manifest in the internal life of the community. Social relations took on an added complexity, owing to the aljama's dramatic growth, and a new kind of politics emerged. The community's good fortune, however, did not translate into political placidity. In an enlarged community the stakes in the contest for power were, if anything, higher. Aggressive status competition had long characterized and structured social and political relations within Valencian Jewish aljamas and continued to do so after 1391. What changed was less the intensity of intracommunal conflict than the class and familial affiliation of the parties involved and the tactics they used to achieve their political goals. Such conflict, however it was pursued, did not threaten the survival of the community. Channeling their social energies inward and performing before a Jewish audience, individuals, families, and factions struggled over prizes that ultimately only the Jewish community could reward.

The more moderate and regular fiscal regime under which the Jews of Morvedre lived from the accession of Alfonso IV until the expulsion modified the nature and conduct of politics in a community where questions of taxation had been central to class relations, institutional reforms, and the political maneuvers of families. During these decades of corporate fiscal solvency and familial enterprise and prosperity the community saw far less class conflict and few, if any, calls for institutional change. Struggles between families of the same social status, however, were vigorous. As rival families increasingly adopted the violent discourse of the feud, Jewish politics came to resemble that practiced by Valencian Christians. This changed political discourse was not the result of Jews aping Christian usage but the effect of royal policies that altered the framework of Jewish political life.

Of course, the monarchy had changed its methods of financing and of taxing Jews before the reign of Alfonso IV — indeed before 1391 — and one effect of this new fiscal regime had been a slight, perceptible diminution of conflict over taxation in the jueria of Morvedre. But the economic and social ramifications of the 1391 violence — namely, a larger public debt for the aljama and the problems associated with integrating refugee families — had lent fiscal issues a greater importance than they might otherwise have had. The persistent harassment of the inquisitors and the proselytizing policies of Fernando I had further limited the beneficial impact of the Crown's reformed fiscal administration on the Jews. The Jewish community thus had to undergo a difficult period of social and institutional adjustment before arriving at new ways of governing itself and sharing power.

OLIGARCHS IN A TIME OF TRANSITION

From 1391 until Alfonso IV's accession in 1416 the community's political life centered on the Façan, el Rau, and Legem families. Relations among the three families and between each family and the rest of the community were at times rocky, even embittered. These families had risen to the top recently, as has been seen, and had clashed along the way.[1] The el Raus and the Legems, for instance, had come to blows in 1380,[2] and a decade later they needed Christian arbitrators to resolve a disagreement stemming from a tax-farming partnership.[3] But by 1391 most controversy revolved around the strong personality of Jacob Façan. Jacob was actually all set to move from Morvedre to the Jewish quarter in the capital when Christian mobs descended on it.[4] He was unhappy in Morvedre. The adelantats adjudicating a lawsuit between himself and Ismael Toledano of Teruel, probably his uncle, had ruled against him. Jacob and the aljama were also litigating over certain unsettled accounts, which likely stemmed from his own term in office as adelantat in 1390.[5] While serving as adelantat Jacob had made enemies. When the Crown prosecuted Jacob for spiriting his forcibly baptized son to North Africa, they took revenge by informing the royal prosecutor of some of the "crimes" he had allegedly committed in office. Apparently Jacob had been a harsh judge of moral transgressors: he had two Jewish men and two Jewish women beaten through the streets of Morvedre, probably for sexual improprieties.[6]

---

[1] See introduction and Meyerson 2004a for pre-1391 politics.

[2] ACA: C 935: 200v (1380/5/27). Here King Pere suspends for six months all judicial procedure against David el Rau and Jahudà Cap "de vulneribus diu est illatis in personas Jucefi Bonet et Samuelis Alatgem [Legem]."

[3] ACA: C 1849: 3r-v, 3v (both 1390/11/30). David el Rau had financially backed Jahudà Legem in his farming of royal revenues. The dispute concerned accounting.

[4] ACA: C 1899: 223v (1391/6/2): a royal license to Jacob and family to change residence.

[5] ACA: C 1847: 100r (1391/1/14); C 1848: 116r (1391/6/2). Two local Christians, Francesc Berenguer and Vicent Dixer, a notary, were to handle Jacob's suit with the aljama with the counsel of a lawyer, and render a decision "de foro, ratione vel lege ebraica." The local bailiff, who seems to have favored the aljama, was removed from the case.

[6] ACA: C 1906: 64r–66r (1393/5/10). If Jacob had indeed taken such stern measures, he would have been acting in accordance with the recommendations of Rabbi Isaac ben Sheshet Perfet, who in a response to the query of Rabbi Isaac Gabriel regarding Mossé Vidal, an unrepentant adulterer of Morvedre, advised that Vidal be whipped through the streets (*She'elot u-teshuvot*, no. 351;

Jacob had also reportedly abused his authority in order to injure his rival David el Rau. He had a communal ban imposed on David's friend Jahudà Cap, though without prior warning, it was said. When the aljama sought from King Joan—and obtained in December 1390—a general pardon for all its members, he secretly deleted the name of David's grandson from the letter of request.[7] After the baptism of David's grandson, perhaps the same grandson, in the summer of 1391, Jacob called him a "renegade . . . in disgrace of the Christian faith" and, of course, of David. Whether Jacob indeed attacked the el Rau family thus, or "with great pride" pulled the beard of a Jew named Maura in the synagogue, or illegally had repairs done to the roof of his house on the Jewish Sabbath is impossible to know.[8] Jacob and David el Rau, however, later battled each other in the kingdom's courts; and Jacob was certainly not universally beloved in the jueria of Morvedre.[9]

But Jacob could not leave town; the violence of 1391 stranded him in Morvedre. Despite their rivalry, both he and David el Rau were convicted and heavily fined for complicity in the clandestine flight of their forcibly baptized sons. Both also sought King Joan's intervention in 1393 because aljama officials were not taking their now reduced assets into account when assessing them for taxes.[10] Yet only Jacob was still in conflict with the aljama over taxation the following year, for David enjoyed a better relationship with the reigning officials. After Jacob failed to win the king's support in this contest through sending him a surreptitious and allegedly fallacious appeal, he transferred to Valencia, where the Jewish community was not yet definitively abolished.[11] Jacob was nonetheless obliged to pay taxes with the aljama of Morvedre for the fiscal year 1394. The animosity of communal officials, who had managed to recruit the bailiff Bonafonat de Sant Feliu to their cause, impeded a quick settlement.[12]

---

also Baer 1961, 2:79; Magdalena Nom de Déu 1988–89, 202–203). In this moral climate accusations of sexual impropriety could be dangerous. In 1387 King Joan learned "quorundam relatione" that one Davi Abraam of Morvedre "habuit rem carnalem cum mulieribus christianis" and demanded investigation (C 1973: 61r); in 1393 he pardoned Sol, the wife of Mossé Alateffi, and her mother, whom Salamó and Maymó Tello falsely "defamed" (C 1905: 80v–81r [Hinojosa Montalvo 1993a, no. 167]). The Morvedre community seems not to have had *berure averot*, special officers dealing with moral violations, but as Assis 1997, 315, points out, in smaller communities the adelantats handled such cases in ad hoc fashion.

[7] ACA: C 1906: 64r–66r; C 1898: 141r-v (1390/12/10).

[8] ACA: C 1906: 64r–66r. The grandson in question was probably Daniel el Rau, who took the Christian name Jaume de Lorde and in 1401 was reportedly still communicating with Jews and practicing Judaism (C 2233: 76v–77r).

[9] ACA: C 1858: 147v (1393/11/17); C 1862: 172r-v [Hinojosa Montalvo 1993a, nos. 193, 243]; C 2330: 56r (1396/11/27), but without detail on the substance of the litigation.

[10] ACA: C 1854: 177v–178r (1393/5/13) [Hinojosa Montalvo 1993a, no. 165].

[11] ACA: C 1861: 26v–27r (1394/4/18); C 1859: 105v–106r (5/21) [Hinojosa Montalvo 1993a, nos. 222, 223].

[12] ACA: C 1861: 48v–49r; C 1859: 106r-v (1394/5/21) [Hinojosa Montalvo 1993a, nos. 225, 224].

Many Jews in Morvedre soon found, however, that they could more easily live with Jacob than live without him. Still feeling the effects of the 1391 riots and the Jewish refugee crisis, they needed Jacob's financial muscle, however weakened. Neither David el Rau nor other families could compensate for the loss his emigration represented. By 1395 some families were abandoning Morvedre, fearing that they could not handle royal taxes without Jacob's help. In February the king ordered his return to Morvedre.[13]

King Joan's death in May 1396 enabled Jacob Façan to strengthen his position in Morvedre. He quickly ingratiated himself with Queen María, to whose treasury the aljama of Morvedre was now attached, and became her Jewish favorite. His access to the queen proved beneficial for the community; indeed, he was instrumental in obtaining for it a series of important royal privileges and provisions. But Jacob was now a much more formidable opponent to his rivals. David el Rau complained that Jacob had been using his "power" and influence to drag him before various Christian tribunals, thus violating the jurisdiction of Jewish courts while exhausting him with needless legal expenses.[14]

Even though Jacob used his influence with Queen María on behalf of the community, aljama officials, at least those serving in 1398, were more resentful than grateful. That year they refused to reimburse Jacob after he paid 3,130 sous to the queen's treasurer in return for her various concessions to the community. Nor would they take his expenditures into account when they assessed him for taxes. On receiving a letter from the queen enjoining them to put their rancor aside and requite Jacob, the aljama officials turned to the lieutenant bailiff, Remiro Remírez, for assistance, shrewdly inflaming his indignation at the special jurisdiction over the Jewish community that Queen María and her underlings claimed. Remírez marched over to the Jewish quarter, disdainfully displayed the queen's letter while impugning her authority in Jewish affairs, and then seized Jacob. He also persuaded the sindic of the aljama, who allegedly needed little persuading, to defy the queen publicly. Jacob Façan found himself at the center of a jurisdictional conflict between Queen María on one hand and the royal bailiff and the municipality on the other. María needed at least another six months to resolve Jacob's difficulties.[15] Events would prove that it was much to the benefit of the Jewish community that the queen did not

[13] ACA: C 1862: 159v (1395/2/25) [Hinojosa Montalvo 1993a, no. 239].

[14] ACA: C 2330: 59r-v (1396/12/2). Here Queen María responded favorably to David's plea, commanding the bailiff to have the suits remitted to Jewish judges if they warranted such adjudication. (Jacob himself made similar appeals to the dominion of Jewish law, informing the queen that the ruling of the local bailiff in his suit with one Maymó Feraig over the ownership of an ass contradicted the legal opinions enunciated by Maimonides in the *Mishneh Torah* [C 2335: 81v–82r (1398/5/18)]). David and Jacob did not resolve their disputes for a long time. In June 1399 Miquel Arbucies, a notary of Valencia who had been appointed as arbitrator, had to postpone yet again the sought-for compromise (ARV: P 25915, G. de Ponte: n.f. [6/20]). By 1403, however, Façan and el Rau were able to work together; see below.

[15] ACA: C 2335: 140r-v [two letters] (1398/11/2), 143r (12/11); C 2336: 62v (1399/4/7), 77r-v (5/23). See chap. 1.

shrink from confrontation, whether defending her favorite Jacob or rescuing his fellows from the oppression of the papal inquisitors.

Jacob Façan was not the only "important individual" in the community whose controversies threatened to damage the public good. In 1397 King Martí commissioned special arbitrators to settle the differences between David el Rau and Samuel Legem, but after learning that Legem was then serving as adelantat and that aljama affairs were therefore implicated, he postponed the arbitration until the next year.[16]

A new problem arose in 1398: more "important individuals" than usual were vying for office and influence in aljama government. With the definitive abolition of the aljama of Valencia in 1397, prominent Jewish refugees from Valencia who had decided to remain permanently in Morvedre recognized that they needed relatives or friends in office to protect or further their interests. Isaac Xamblell had already improved his chances with a strategic marriage to Jacob Façan's daughter Jamila.[17] Still, neither he nor other affluent refugees, like Samuel Suxen and his spouse, Jamila, the daughter of the redoubtable Jahudà Alatzar, could escape making significant fiscal contributions to the struggling aljama. As always, it was a question of degree. This and other issues were hotly disputed, leading to "tumult, sedition, and scandal." The adelantats, clavari, and councillors were prevented from meeting to elect the new officials.

The new permanent residents of Morvedre's jueria naturally objected to an electoral regime that was practically a closed shop and that offered them only a slight possibility of breaking in any time soon. King Martí therefore opened up the elections: instead of just the current officials, "each and every Jew of the said aljama, at least those who comprise or represent the aljama," were to choose by majority vote the adelantats, tercer, and clavari. Martí's definition of the electorate was deliberately vague; those who demanded a voice were given one. The king also made sure that the elections did not degenerate into a brawl: the royal bailiff would preside and the notary of the aljama would record the vote of each Jew "separately and secretly."[18]

Once the adelantats were chosen, Queen María provided for the election of the councillors. Every three years the current adelantats would choose seven councillors, instead of the previous twelve. The seven were to represent the upper, middle, and lower classes, but the queen did not specify how seven should be divided by three. She most likely intended three of the seven councillors to be drawn from the upper class so as to consolidate its control of communal government. After all, the queen was most accustomed to dealing with the Jacob Façans of the Jewish world. In fact, she included in her provisions a clause authorizing the adelantats to keep their friends on the council for an-

---

[16] ACA: C 2114: 40r-v (1397/7/11); C 2112: 186v (1398/7/11), where the king restarts the arbitration. The reasons for the lawsuits are unknown.

[17] ACA: C 1906: 64r–66r (1393/5/10).

[18] ACA: C 2189: 180v–181r (1398/3/1).

other term "if sufficient persons, who might be elected as councillors in the said number, cannot be found in the aljama."[19] As for the election of the adelantats themselves, María presumed that the open elections just held at the urging of her husband were only a temporary measure designed to bring new wealthy residents into aljama government. After this brief opening, the electoral regime dominated by the now expanded group of plutocrats could again be closed.

For many in the community this closed system was unsatisfactory. Tensions mounted. In 1403 the aljama cried out for a change and Queen María listened. Rescinding the provisions of 1398, she agreed that the election of the executive officials — adelantats, tercer, and clavari — should be conducted "in a larger council." María and her Jews had in mind the open electorate King Martí had called for in 1398 — that is, open to Jews sufficiently interested and esteemed by their fellows to merit a political voice. The adelantats and clavari thus elected would then select the seven members of the multiclass advisory council. Elections were to be held every year, for the executives as well as the councillors, which enabled a greater number of families to participate in communal government. As had long been the case, close relatives were not to serve together. This flexible system met the needs of a growing and changing community, furthering oligarchy and stability while making some room for the lower and middle classes, especially their most upwardly mobile members. It functioned, in theory at least, until the reign of Fernando II.[20]

One reason Queen María and the Jewish oligarchy proved amenable to these changes was that some Jews excluded from the electoral system had begun informing. The queen knew that Pere III had given the adelantats considerable latitude to prosecute and severely punish such "*malsins,*" and was indeed surprised that they had been so remiss in proceeding against them.[21] Responsible members of the Jewish elite had concluded, however, that electoral reform rather than harsh punishment would best cure the malady of *malshinut.* The adelantats were nonetheless pleased the following year to receive from the queen full power to deal with Jews who were "quarrelsome and evil

[19] ACA: C 2335: 85r-v (1398/5/18): "cum contigerit ipsos consiliarios eligi dictis adelantatis videbitur non posse inveniri in ipsa aljama sufficientes personas que possint sub dicto numero in consiliarios eligi possint illos . . . vel partem eorum in consiliarios noviter pro triennio tunc venienti eligere."

[20] ACA: C 2339: 73v–74r (1403/11/29): "in consilio ampliori." ARV: B 1150: 356v (1449/1/29) [Hinojosa Montalvo 1993a, no. 502] shows that the electoral system was still functioning in accordance with the 1403 provisions.

[21] ACA: C 2339: 129v–130r (1403/11/28). This letter was issued the day before that detailing the modification of the electoral system. Here the queen encouraged the adelantats to prosecute and punish the informers. She graciously permitted them to keep one-third of all monetary fines exacted for the community almoner; the remaining two-thirds were to go to her treasurer. The same division was to apply to the 200 sous that the adelantats were obliged to render her whenever they passed a death sentence against an informer.

speakers."[22] With inquisitors nosing around, informers had to be combated by all possible means.

No doubt a fair measure of the informing or appealing (the definition was in the eye of the beholder) centered on the perennial issue of tax assessment. True, fiscal politics in the early fifteenth century was not nearly as intense and sordid as it had been in the era preceding the Black Death, but well-to-do families momentarily lacking friends in communal government might receive the unwelcome attention of adelantats striving to reduce the aljama's budget deficit. In 1401 the principal complainants were Samuel Suxen, his wife, Jamila, and her aunt Astruga;[23] in 1403 David el Rau and his grandchildren. David, at least, had not been shirking his responsibilities to the community. Having settled their differences, he and Jacob Façan had raised 2,000 sous for the aljama through the sale of an annuity, the payment of which they guaranteed through mortgaging their homes. David had also permitted aljama officials to use some of his property — a domicile and a piece of land — to secure other loans.[24] Hence the queen initially responded favorably to David's plea, ruling that two Jewish arbiters — one selected by the adelantats, the other by David — should decide on the appropriate rate of taxation. She soon changed her mind, however, fearing that she would be overwhelmed by the appeals of other Jews expecting similar treatment.[25]

Still, there was no avoiding the fact that, due to his great wealth, David el Rau was a special case. The king and queen paid much attention to the complex affairs of his family. In June 1402 Queen María licensed David to take a second wife because his first wife, Regina, was beyond the age of childbearing.[26] David had lost one son to forced baptism and emigration in 1391; his remaining son, Haim, had, together with his wife, Oro, passed away in 1401.[27] He still had a Jewish grandson, David, the son of Haim, but he wanted a son to inherit his wealth.[28] His second wife, Jamila, bore him a son, Davinet, or "little David," but he had little time to enjoy the infant before his own death in July 1404.

---

[22] ACA: C 2340: 35r-v (1404/12/6).

[23] ACA: C 2338: 17v–18r (1401/11/24). In 1415 the widowed Jamila again clashed with aljama officials and consequently considered emigration (C 2375: 164r, 168v [8/20–21]).

[24] ACA: C 2339: 14r-v (1403/6/7). They sold the censal to Bernat Palomar of Morvedre, who was to receive an annual pension of 166 sous 8 diners. Here the queen was licensing the aljama to sell other annuities in order to redeem this one. C 2339: 78v–79r (1404/2/20) treats David's plea for the restoration of his property; communal officials had been delaying.

[25] ACA: C 2339: 8r (1403/5/7), 61r (12/19), 130v–131r (1404/2/7).

[26] ACA: C 2338: 89v (1402/6/6). On Jewish bigamy, Assis 1981 and 1997, 261–264.

[27] On his (unnamed) son's emigration to the Maghrib, see chap. 1. ACA: C 2338: 41r-v (1402/2/1), 53r (3/1) address the suit filed by Alatzar Abenardut of Teruel, brother of Oro and brother-in-law of Haim, against David el Rau for the restitution of his sister's dowry. According to Alatzar, Oro had made to him a "donationem . . . inter vivos . . . per publica instrumenta in ebrayco et in latino facta" of her dowry, which valued 700 gold florins.

[28] On David ben Haim, see chap. 6.

Even before David's widows and heirs could lay claim to his inheritance, aljama officials acted. Just a few days after David's passing, they related to Queen María their fears that the heirs of David, the "biggest taxpayer," would abscond with all his taxable assets, a potential disaster for communal finances. The queen urged the bailiff to move quickly and tax the deceased's property in accordance with the current assessment.[29] David's death inspired communal officials to devise new legislation, for other affluent Jews, like Jacob Façan and Samuel Suxen, were also getting on in years. On 9 August the adelantats and the councillors met in the synagogue and passed an ordinance empowering the local bailiff to place liens on every piece of property owned by Jews who had died in the past ten years or who might die in the future. This property would then be auctioned off until the fiscal obligations of the deceased were fulfilled. Communal officials were to employ the proceeds for liquidating the aljama's corporate debts.[30]

David el Rau's death without adult male heirs eliminated his family as a political force in the community. The Façans and the Legems were still formidable, and in 1407 they crossed swords — literally. Mossé Legem and Jahudà Arrami wounded Mossé, the son of Jacob Façan. King Martí pardoned the assailants in return for a 50-florin compensation payment.[31]

The Legems seem to have been gaining the upper hand on the Façans, partly because they outnumbered them. Compared to the several branches of the Legem clan, Jacob Façan had only his sons, Mossé and Isaac, and his son-in-law, Isaac Xamblell. The Legems, however, had other enemies. Maymó Vidal falsely accused Jucef Legem, the son of Abraham Legem, of pimping for Christian prostitutes. Though innocent, Jucef still had to pay 70 florins for a pardon.[32] Others unsuccessfully challenged Samuel Legem's possession of the Jews' two stalls in the town abattoir.[33] Frequently elected as adelantat and a tax farmer, Samuel was the most influential member of the Legem clan. His holding of the butchery concession was simply another symbol of his local power.

It was not their Jewish rivals but Fernando I and Vicent Ferrer who did the most damage to the Legems. In 1415 Samuel Legem and his son Abraham converted and abandoned Morvedre for the capital. Yet the strength of the Legems in numbers and wealth enabled them to absorb these losses and continue to place family members in aljama government for the next several decades. The Legems sometimes served alongside their old ally Jahudà Arrami. The

[29] ACA: C 2339: 138v (1404/7/17).

[30] ACA: C 2339: 160r–161r (1404/8/28) is the queen's confirmation of the new ordinance.

[31] ACA: C 2236: 2v (1407/6/5); C 2205: 14v–15r (6/28); C 2260: 125r (7/28); C 2236: 15v (8/18). The cause of the violence is not revealed.

[32] ACA: C 2205: 19r-v (1407/7/5); C 2151: 178r (7/21).

[33] ACA: C 2285: 44r (1407/12/1). The claims of Samuel's unidentified opponents that they had rights to the stalls were without foundation. Joan I had conceded the stalls to Samuel in perpetuity in 1394 (C 1906: 218v–219r [Hinojosa Montalvo 1993a, no. 220]).

Façans and their in-laws, the Xamblells, occupied government posts too. The baptism of Samuel and Abraham Legem had not destroyed Legem power but had worked as an equalizer. Thus, with the exception of the el Raus, the community's most important families survived through the hellish years of inquisitorial persecution and the dark reign of Fernando I to lead it in brighter times.

GOVERNMENT, COMMUNITY, AND FACTION

After 1416 antagonism between social classes in the Jewish community lessened markedly. One clear sign of this was the widespread and long-term contentment with the electoral system Queen María had instituted in 1403. Unlike in the past, the lower classes did not agitate for electoral reform and for the alteration of the methods by which property was assessed and taxes collected. The changes to the electoral system that Fernando II would impose in 1481 (see below) were meant to augment the Crown's control over the aljama and were not a response to the entreaties of the disgruntled lower classes.

The monarchy's unpredictable demands for exorbitant, extraordinary subsidies had been mainly responsible for exacerbating class tensions among the Jews. With the lightening of the tax burden, this irritant was nearly eliminated. The far more predictable fiscal requirements of the Crown enabled aljama officials to pursue more rational, long-term financial planning. The officials' recourse to deficit financing, through selling censals, tended to appease the lower classes, since it was the officials themselves or other upper-class Jews who secured the censals through mortgaging their own property. Both the aljama's annual payments of pensions to censalistas and the levying of internal sales taxes that facilitated these payments were regular and expected. Their very predictability helped avert the instantaneous, heated controversies between families and social classes that grasping monarchs had once provoked. Instead of haggling over how contributions to the latest royal subsidy were to be apportioned, members of the community now regularly paid the bulk of their taxes through an array of indirect levies and through the peita, a property tax. Lower-class Jews were thus less preoccupied with the question of what their wealthier fellows were or were not contributing; they were less resentful. The changes in the fiscal regime and in aljama financing deprived lower-class Jews of a major cause to rally around. The solidarity of poor and middle-class Jews pursuing electoral and fiscal reform was largely a thing of the past.

Humble Jews, however, were not politically unconscious. They could mobilize when the oligarchs tampered with the fiscal regime to which they had grown accustomed. In 1431 Jews of the lower class, many of whom were at least part-time winegrowers, protested when communal officials did away with all the sales taxes except that on wine. The lower-class representatives argued that it too should be removed, and further suggested that if abolishing all the cises were necessary, then it would be wise to levy a new graduated income tax to compensate for the resultant shortfall in aljama revenue.[34] Yet this was an isolated protest, an exception to the lower classes' contentment with, or grudging acceptance of, the status quo.

Relations between the poor and the rich in the jueria of Morvedre were characterized less by outright conflict than by dependence of the former on the latter. Poor Jews often labored as servants in the homes of the well-to-do, like Samuel Corquoz and Citi Foyola, the man- and maidservant of Samuel and Jamila Suxen.[35] The employers assumed legal responsibility for the servants living and working under their roof. The wife of Astruc Çaporta paid the mustaçaff the fine of 5 sous that her maidservant (moça) had incurred for washing in an irrigation ditch.[36] Jahudà Jabba rose to the defense of "the two Jewish youths who stay with him" when the bailiff fined them for gambling in a game prohibited by the aljama.[37]

Much like in Christian society, many of the boys and young men working in the households of others would have been learning a trade and earning a salary in the process. Morvedre's Jewish silversmiths had a well-developed system of apprenticeship; for poor boys, entry meant a fairly sure climb up the socioeconomic ladder.[38] The highly esteemed merchant and tax farmer Salamó Çaporta employed one Jucef Serrano, "my youth," and authorized him, along with other Jewish agents, to present to officials copies of royal privileges exempting him from commercial tariffs.[39] Poor Jewish girls did not learn a trade but worked as domestics in the homes of their employers. As in the case of the stepdaughter of Abraham Xuayt, who was sent into the service of Samuel Asdrilla of Castelló, the salaries they received were to be used "in aid of [their] marriage."[40]

The moderate taxation of the aljama by Alfonso IV and Juan II in all likelihood enabled the administrators of its caritative institutions to respond more effectively to the needs of the truly indigent. They were not faced, as they had been in the midfourteenth century, with the members of once well-off families, devastated by a combination of relentless taxation and bad luck, attempting to recover the pious legacies of their dead relatives. The Talmud-Torah so-

[34] ARV: B 1147: 301v–302r (1431/10/4); and chap. 3.
[35] ARV: B 1219: 117v (1410/8/1), a license to the Suxens to visit Valencia with "Samuel Corquoz, macip lur, e Citi Foyola, lur macipa." Another example is B 1152: 1180v (1455/11/13), which mentions "Samuelet, moço del dit Abraam Xambell."
[36] ARV: MR 11764: 32r-v (1431–32).
[37] ARV: B 1150: 379r (1449/4/4) [Hinojosa Montalvo 1993a, no. 504].
[38] E.g., in 1452 Gento Benjacobi sued the silversmith Samuel Agí for the salary allegedly due him "from the time he has served" (ARV: B 1151: 419r [Hinojosa Montalvo 1993a, no. 525]); also, see chap. 3. Cf. Guiral 1986, 378–391; Navarro 1992, 134–146; Iradiel et al. 1995, 148–156; Iradiel 1986, 248–259.
[39] ARV: P 1999, J. Salvador: n.f. (1479/7/14): "Serranum juvenem meum." See also chap. 3.
[40] ARV: B 1151: 20v–20r bis (1450/2/4): "en ajuda de son matrimoni."

ciety, for example, possessed sufficient reserves, after attending to poor students, to pay for the release of an Aragonese Jew from jail in Valencia.[41] Sensitivity to the feelings of the Jewish poor, or at least a desire to avoid arousing their hostility at the material comforts of the affluent, partly motivated aljama officials "in full council" to pass sumptuary legislation limiting the jewelry and luxurious clothing that might be worn by wives and maidens.[42] On the eve of the expulsion communal officials did not hesitate to pay 4,000 sous to the bailiff general on behalf of twenty-four households too poor to render the peita and other levies.[43] These were, of course, extreme circumstances. Still, the consistent provision of relief to the indigent probably helped eliminate serious class conflict through much of the fifteenth century.

Rather than organizing against the oligarchs, lower-class Jews channeled more of their energies — sometimes their violent energies — into competition for prestige within their own class or classes. As a consequence of the dramatic demographic growth of the community after 1445, the number of Jews belonging to the lower and middle classes was much larger. Hence humbler Jews had a larger audience of their peers before whom to contest honor and status. In this growing, yet amorphous and unstratified world of the humble, defending oneself and one's family against dishonor and insult was essential for winning and maintaining the esteem of one's peers. For the lower classes, challenging the prevailing fiscal and political regime in the aljama had become less important; what mattered increasingly was one's place in the pecking order of the ill-defined *mans menor e mitjana* (lower and middle classes).

Thus in the latter half of the fifteenth century more incidents of violence between lower-class Jews were recorded by royal officials penalizing the aggressors. Salamó Artato, for example, was fined 250 sous for having pulled a dagger on Mossé Abenrabo in the synagogue.[44] In a hostel in the suburb of Morvedre Isaac Cania and Sahul Levi wounded one another with daggers.[45]

---

[41] ARV: B 1296: 348r (1477/4/29) [Hinojosa Montalvo 1993a, no. 769]. The Jew was Jahudà Cohen from Monzón; he had to promise the society's officers that he would reimburse them. Meyerson 2004a for the fourteenth century.

[42] ARV: B 1152: 1259r (1456/6/1) [Hinojosa Montalvo 1993a, no. 559]. This legislation was renewed in 1458 and 1459, though, as the bailiff general noted in 1459, some women were not observing it (B 1152: 1595v [1/23]). Cf. Orfali Levi 1993, 83–85.

[43] Archivo Municipal de Alcoy: P, Pere Benavent: n.f. (1492/7/11) [Hinojosa Montalvo 1993a, no. 585].

[44] ARV: MR 82: 178v (1472/5/21) [Hinojosa Montalvo 1993a, no. 706]. I am not suggesting that violence among the Jews of Morvedre, or specifically within the lower class, was unknown before the fifteenth century. See Assis 1985; or, for Morvedre, ARV: MR 3985: M. 1, 2r (1382), regarding a brawl between two Jewish "vagabonds." I am arguing that violence has a history, and that its perpetrators and victims, frequency, and style must be viewed in a local context. The world of lower-class Jews in Morvedre changed meaningfully in the fifteenth century, in terms of demography and political consciousness and objectives. Cf. Meyerson 1991, chap. 6, and 2004b.

[45] ARV: MR 86: 175v (1476/8/30) [Hinojosa Montalvo 1993a, no. 764]. In another example,

The community's enlarged population had increased the likelihood of Jews' resorting to arms to resolve disputes. Communal officials seem to have understood as much. In 1459, in addition to the sumptuary legislation, they passed an ordinance "over the arms that Jews should bear."[46] The officials' concern was not to prevent the lower classes from taking arms against them but to address and regulate a widespread and growing social phenomenon.

No longer subject to the grinding and inflammatory taxation that had antagonized them in the past, the lower and middle classes were less inclined to question the authority of communal officials, most of whom came from well-to-do families. The stability of aljama government was consequently enhanced. Though not challenged from below by the mass of poorer families demanding institutional and fiscal reform, officials nonetheless had their hands full with the moral reform and correction of their charges. Gambling and sexual impropriety were perennial concerns, the former warranting repeated prohibitions on the part of officials.[47] The lavish dress of affluent women and the arms-bearing of men had become problems demanding official attention only in the larger and more complex community of fifteenth-century Morvedre. Violators of communal ordinances were duly penalized. None impugned the adelantats' power to punish them for such infractions.

One of the most serious challenges to the adelantats' authority lay in the realm of judicial affairs. The struggle to maintain Jewish juridical autonomy against the encroachments of Christian officialdom was long-standing. Excessive Christian interference in matters properly pertaining to the jurisdiction of Jewish law threatened to undermine the authority of Jewish magistrates who administered the law and the sanctity of the law itself in the eyes of individual Jews. Disregard for halakhic standards weakened the cohesiveness of the Jewish community and struck at the very heart of Jewish identity. The danger was probably no more dire in the fifteenth century than in earlier times, but the political and religious elites in the aljama of Morvedre may well have perceived it to be so. Even if their community was increasing in size and prosperity, it was, after the demise of the great aljama in Valencia, more isolated. In the place of the aljama in the capital was a large converso population the extent of whose conformity to Jewish law ranged from the most scrupulous observance possible to outright rejection in favor of Catholicism or a confused

---

the brothers Jahudà and Abraham Allolayhas drew their weapons after having words with Levi Arroti on the royal road near Almenara (B 1155: 244v [1474/6/10]).

[46] ARV: B 1152: 1595v (1459/1/23): "sobre les armes que los juheus deven portar."

[47] ARV: MR 3986: 7r (1394); MR 3992: 24v (1413); MR 3995: 11v (1424); B 1150: 379r (1449/4/4) [Hinojosa Montalvo 1993a, no. 504] all concern the collection of fines from Jews caught gambling in violation of communal ordinances. See above regarding the harsh punishment of sexual transgressors when Jacob Façan was adelantat. Along these lines, ARV: MR 4015: 6r (1476) records the 45-sous fine collected from Jucef Barbut "per tant com fou trobat dins casa de una juhia de la juheria."

agnosticism. For aljama authorities in Morvedre, the conversos sat at the bottom of the slippery slope down which their community might slide if they did not defend the dominion of Jewish law and Jewish courts.[48]

Aljama officials were fairly successful in this endeavor. Jewish litigants did not flock to Christian tribunals. Most civil suits between Jews were adjudicated by the adelantats or Jewish arbitrators without any involvement of royal officials; hence they were not recorded. In a good number of cases, however, the royal authorities did play a role. Yet even in these cases Jewish and Christian magistrates usually divided their labors in such a way that both halakhic standards and the authority of Jewish officials were upheld.[49]

Recourse to the Crown proved most useful in criminal cases in which the Jewish offender had taken flight or was deemed dangerous. In 1434 the adelantats relied on Christian officials for "the capture of the person of Mossé Levi," and in 1467 they encouraged the royal prosecutor to proceed against Jucef Quatorze and other Jews who had assaulted Cadias Agí.[50] Individual Jews with complaints against the members of other aljamas sometimes needed the aid of the bailiff general to secure the cooperation of their adelantats, as did Salamó Comte, when he accused Jews from another community of theft.[51] Some Jews appealed to the bailiff when the adelantats of their own aljama chose, for whatever reason, to ignore their pleas. One "David, son of Mossé," was stonewalled by the adelantats after his two brothers-in-law entered his house and punched him out. If David was a notorious wife-beater or philanderer, the adelantats may well have sanctioned this form of private justice.[52]

Potentially more damaging to Jewish legal autonomy were those cases in which Jews involved in civil litigation with coreligionists resorted to royal bailiffs. That Jewish litigants would occasionally do so was inevitable. After all, due to their kinship and political ties, the adelantats who were supposed to administer justice fairly could not always be impartial. The bailiffs intervening in Jewish civil suits at the behest of one of the litigants nonetheless had a carefully circumscribed role. They acted merely as supervisors, ensuring that a fair sentence was handed down and properly executed. Jewish judges — usually but not always the adelantats — rendered the decision and did so in accordance

---

[48] A related response, treated in chap. 6, was to work to drag conversos back up that same slope.

[49] Cf. Meyerson 1991, 185–202.

[50] ARV: C 264: 29r (1434/6/7): "in captione persone de Mose Levi." Levi was a pretty tough customer; he had once been fined for drawing arms in a brawl with Jahudà Abenardut (MR 3992: 108r [1417]). B 1154: 56v (1467/5/14) [Hinojosa Montalvo 1993a, no. 669], for the case against Quatorze, alias Cuberet, and others. Quatorze was initially sentenced to death, a frequent procedure in cases in which the assailant had fled. B 1154: 406v–407r (1469/7/7) shows that he was ultimately fined for his crimes. Another example is the death sentence passed by the royal prosecutor in 1492 against the fugitive Jucef Najari, at the instance of Bonadona, the wife of Samuel Adzoni (B 1160: 430r-v [Hinojosa Montalvo 1993a, no. 839].

[51] ARV: B 1151: 322v (1451/10/13) [Hinojosa Montalvo 1993a, no. 521].

[52] ARV: B 1150: 323v (1448/12/23).

with Jewish law. When Samuel Bonet and Samuel Agí litigated over the ownership of a house, for example, the bailiff general directed Pere Berenguer, the lieutenant bailiff of Morvedre, to rule on the case "with the counsel of the adelantats . . . according to the law of the Jews."[53] Indeed, in certain cases, like those concerning the disposition of synagogue seats, the presumption was that the reigning adelantats could not be unbiased. The bailiff would then act without their counsel and rely only on the advice of upright and impartial members of the Jewish community well versed in Jewish law.[54] The same procedure was followed when a Jewish litigant appealed a sentence handed down by the adelantats. When Samuel Agí or his opponent, a certain Jamila, filed an appeal with the bailiff general, the latter instructed his subordinate in Morvedre to find two Jewish legal experts who were unaffiliated with either party, that is, "not Çaporta, Xamblell, Façan, [or] Jacob Legem the rabbi."[55] In all such cases the jurisdiction of the *halakhah* was preserved, since Jews conversant with Jewish law were in fact adjudicating.

Christian bailiffs and Jewish judges proceeded in much the same fashion when handling difficult and more sensitive cases of family law. The bailiff general, for instance, delegated Isaac Arrondi to act as judge when, after the betrothal of Astruga, the daughter of the late Isaac Abnajub, to Samuel Legem Jr., Astruga's stepfather and mother refused to deliver her to Samuel.[56]

Even though this modus operandi effectively preserved Jewish legal autonomy in most cases, the adelantats were never complacent. Constantly vigilant, they took preventive, occasionally aggressive, measures when they deemed the role of Christians in Jewish lawsuits problematic or felt that Jewish litigants were resorting to Crown officials too frequently. In 1454 they reissued a communal ordinance forbidding Jews litigating with coreligionists to have Chris-

[53] ARV: B 1152: 985r (1455/3/10) [Hinojosa Montalvo 1993a, no. 544]. B 1155: 126r (1473/9/16) [Hinojosa Montalvo 1993a, no. 724], treating the suit pitting Salamó Çaporta against Mossé Ardit, more specifically instructs Berenguer to judge in accordance "with the law of master Moyses of Egypt . . . with the counsel of the adelantats . . . and of other Jews expert in the law who are not suspected by either party." The "law" in question was the *Mishneh Torah* of Maimonides, a work on which Jewish authorities in the kingdom of Valencia heavily relied — see Hershman 1943, 21, 68–69. Other examples of similar legal procedures are B 1151: 735r (1453/6/12); B 1153: 251r (1462/1/7); B 1155: 254v (1474/6/27); B 1157: 334r (1482/11/5); B 1159: 172v–173r (1489/3/11) [Hinojosa Montalvo 1993a, nos. 530, 613, 731, 799, 826].

[54] ARV: B 1152: 994r (1455/4/11), regarding the suit over a synagogue seat between Abraham Adzoni and Astruga, the ex-wife of Abraham Legem, which Berenguer was to handle with the counsel of Astruc Çaporta. B 1152: 1002v (1455/4/15) [Hinojosa Montalvo 1993a, no. 545] is a similar case.

[55] ARV: B 1152: 904v (1454/10/10) [Hinojosa Montalvo 1993a, no. 538].

[56] ARV: B 1147: 615r (1434/4/21), 688r-v (12/22); B 1148: 45v (1435/6/10), 57r-v (6/17), 308v (1436/12/24) [Hinojosa Montalvo 1993a, nos. 412, 427, 432, 433, 450]. Samuel was the son of Jacob Legem. Astruga's stepfather was Abraham Legem; her mother was Mira. Another example is B 1150: 445r (1449/11/19), in which the bailiff general supervises the adelantats and other leading men of the community in partitioning a house between Isaac Façan and his nephew Samuel.

tians stand surety for them.[57] The adelantats also found disquieting the few cases in which Christian magistrates rendered final decisions in lawsuits between Jews without the assistance of Jewish legal counselors. Yet because Jewish judges or arbitrators had at least initially attempted to resolve these disputes, the adelantats, confident in the bailiffs' good intentions, kept quiet in the interests of communal harmony. They were silent, for instance, when the suit between the widows of Vidal and Gento Abenjamin was "left" to Jacme Munyós, the local bailiff, to arbitrate.[58]

Intolerable, however, were those cases in which Jewish litigants resorted to the courts of royal bailiffs and the jurisdiction of the *Furs* in the first instance, as if they were beyond the jurisdiction of Jewish law and Jewish courts. The adelantats took a stand on this issue a few times between 1464 and 1480. The dramatic growth of the Jewish community in the latter half of the century may well have inspired the adelantats to take more vigorous action, lest the immoderate intrusion of Crown officials erode their authority and hinder their large and vital community from governing itself.

The most explosive case, in 1464, involved Mossé Xamblell and his stepson Jucef Gracia, who were battling over the division of the assets of their failed cloth-production venture. Perhaps because Xamblell was himself an adelantat that year, Jucef immediately turned to the bailiff general in March for a fair hearing.[59] This did not sit well with the aljama authorities, who imposed a ban on Jucef and threatened to jail him. The perplexed bailiff general then asked Pere Berenguer, the local lieutenant bailiff, to seek the opinions of two upstanding Jews on the legitimacy of the ban.[60] Meanwhile, Xamblell, who regarded the bailiff general's decisions in the lawsuit as illegitimate, refused to divide the assets in accordance with the bailiff's ruling.[61]

[57] ARV: B 1152: 881v (1454/6/?). Lest the Jewish community misinterpret their resolve to end this practice, the adelantats and the bailiff general decided that the local bailiff should be present for the proclamation of the ordinance. The bailiff was to direct all Jews who had any questions to his superior in Valencia. See also chap. 2.

[58] ARV: B 1153: 9r (1460/1/14) [Hinojosa Montalvo 1993a, no. 598]. Another example is B 1153: 224r-v (1461/11/16), 277r (1462/3/4), 303v (5/12), 302v (5/14) [Hinojosa Montalvo 1993a, nos. 608, 614, 623, 624], in which the bailiff general intervened and ruled in favor of Cincha, the widow of Jucef Astori, who encountered difficulties in recovering her dowry from her brothers-in-law Jahudà and Vidal. In 1462 he intervened in another inheritance dispute between the daughters and sons-in-law of the deceased Samuel Cap. Problems arose owing to irregularities in Samuel's will and to the preemptive seizure of some of his property by one son-in-law, Abraham Adzoni (B 1153: 277r-v, 277v–278r, 283r, 331v–332r [Hinojosa Montalvo 1993a, nos. 615, 616, 618, 629]).

[59] ARV: B 1153: 513r (1464/3/?), 552v (5/18) [Hinojosa Montalvo 1993a, nos. 643, 646]. Later, in August 1465, the bailiff general would inform Berenguer that when he asked Jucef whether he wished to be judged by Jewish or Christian law, Jucef said "that I was his judge" (B 1153: 639v–640r [Hinojosa Montalvo 1993a, no. 656]).

[60] ARV: B 1153: 513r.

[61] ARV: B 1153: 557r, 558r (1464/6/22) [Hinojosa Montalvo 1993a, nos. 648, 649].

Because of his stepfather's recalcitrance, Jucef denounced him to the Christian authorities. Jewish officials regarded Jucef as little more than an informer and so jailed him. Berenguer sought the advice of his superior "as the said Xamblell is judge and party [to the case]." The bailiff general instructed Berenguer to remove Jucef from jail and place him under house arrest. Because Jucef had initiated the suit before him in his court, he did not feel that the Jewish authorities had the right to punish him as an informer.[62]

A long stalemate ensued. Finally, in August 1465, Berenguer jailed Xamblell, who was no longer an adelantat, and held him until he paid his debts to his stepson and fines to the Crown, as stipulated by the bailiff general. Once satisfied, Jucef asked Berenguer to release Xamblell.[63] The reigning adelantats, however, were extremely dissatisfied. Regardless of the merits of the bailiff general's decision in the case, they were horrified that Jucef had successfully defied the authority of communal government and had completely escaped halakhic jurisdiction. Jucef had set a dangerous example for other Jews. Jucef, moreover, seems to have been enjoying his victory a little too much and was causing "scandals." The adelantats informed Berenguer that they would resign in protest if Jucef were not punished.[64] The bailiff general sought more information, but before he could act the adelantats and councillors banished Jucef from the Jewish community. Responding to this violation of his prerogatives, the bailiff fined the aljama 500 gold florins.[65] Jewish officials obviously thought their reaffirmation of Jewish legal autonomy to be well worth the penalty. Jucef Gracia died in exile in 1469. An admonishment from the bailiff, at the behest of Jucef's father-in-law, Mossé Gallego, was needed to persuade the adelantats to use the 500 sous the dying Jucef had bequeathed to the community for a Torah crown.[66] The adelantats and councillors had made their point loudly and clearly to the Jewish community.

Nevertheless, the bailiff general did not, on principle, accept the position of the Jewish authorities that Jews wishing to pursue civil suits against other Jews could not in the first instance file suit in his court, or in that of the local bailiff, where decision would be rendered in accordance with the *Furs*.[67] The point

---

[62] ARV: B 1153: 698r (1464/9/13) [Hinojosa Montalvo 1993a, no. 651].

[63] ARV: B 1153: 639v (1465/8/28) [Hinojosa Montalvo 1993a, no. 655].

[64] ARV: B 1153: 639v–640r [Hinojosa Montalvo 1993a, no. 656].

[65] ARV: B 1153: 644v–646r (1465/9/10).

[66] ARV: B 1154: 466r-v [Hinojosa Montalvo 1993a, no. 693, though the folio numbers given are incorrect], 466v (1469/10/26).

[67] ARV: B 1155: 524r-v (1475/11/8) [Hinojosa Montalvo 1993a, no. 754] concerns an apparently theoretical discussion that started when some Jews showed Jacme Garcia, a lawyer and lord of Alaquàs, a "privilege" asserting that only the adelantats had the power to adjudicate Jewish civil suits. The lieutenant bailiff general, Pere Garro, then insisted on the bailiff's supreme jurisdiction over all Jewish cases, civil and criminal. Similar discussion had arisen in 1398. On 18 May Queen María granted the adelantats the right to handle all civil suits between Jews (ACA: C 2335: 88r-v). On 25 July, however, she revoked this privilege in response to the complaint of the local bailiff

was usually moot, for few Jews dared to brave the wrath of the communal authorities and suffer the fate of a Jucef Gracia.[68] The great commotion that the adelantats raised over Jucef's case indicates just how unusual his course of legal action was. The preeminence of Jewish law and Jewish judges in civil suits between Jews was secured. The community could continue to grow and prosper and preserve its identity within this essential legal framework.

While the ruling families governed the aljama with little concerted opposition from the lower classes and communal officials endeavored with a large measure of success to maintain their judicial and moral authority over the rest of the community, the families comprising the governing elite changed somewhat over the decades. The openness of the ruling group to newcomers, and its ability to absorb and, in effect, coopt them contributed to the general stability of class relations and to the durability of the electoral regime. Through a combination of economic success, a reputation for probity, and useful marital and political alliances, middling families could rise into the oligarchy. At the same time powerful families declined as a result of economic, political, and biological misfortune. The oligarchy, then, was neither closed nor static. If political struggles on a vertical plane were minimal, those on the horizontal plane were vigorous. The stable electoral and fiscal regime of the fifteenth century, which would have collapsed under the strain of intense and prolonged class struggle, accommodated the fierce and fractious politics of elite and would-be elite families.

The rotation of individuals through aljama government, which can be traced only partially through fragmentary sources, reflected to a significant degree the shifting alignment of power within the community. Until the 1450s, the Legem and Façan families were both major players in communal politics. They were joined in aljama government by their respective allies Jahudà Arrami and the Xamblells, and by an old, established Morvedre family, the Bonets. Members of families of more recent success also held government

---

(C 2335: 125r-v). Bailiffs were anxious to maintain civil as well as criminal jurisdiction over the Jews so as not to lose the additional income thus earned. Yet, as has been seen, in practice Jewish judges usually rendered decision according to the halakhah; the bailiff supervised the proceedings "with the counsel" of his Jewish counterparts, ensuring fair play and moving appeals through the legal system.

[68] In 1478 Isaac Abenrabi filed suit against Salamó Astori and Mossé Abusach in the court of the bailiff general. The adelantats then threatened him with a communal ban and exclusion from the synagogue if he did not withdraw his suit. The bailiff general naturally objected (ARV: B 1156: 263r-v [Hinojosa Montalvo 1993a, no. 776]), but whether he finally tried the case is not known. The Abenrabi family had several enemies in the aljama besides Astori and Abusach. In 1477 "Benrabi, alias Sardet" was fined 20 sous "per unes bastonades havia donat a un juheu de Nules," and another 40 sous as "composicio per una coltellada havia donada a Mosse Roderich juheu" (MR 4015: 16v). In 1482, Salamó Abenrabi, perhaps the brother of Isaac, and "those who accompany him" were licensed to bear arms for protection against their enemies (B 1157: 270v–271r [6/2]).

posts in these years: Salamó Fanduix, Mossé Gallego, Astruc Malequi, Haim Vinaig, Astruc Çaporta, Salamó Astori, Salamó Tarfon, and Jucef, Gento, and Vidal Abenjamin. A decade of transition, the 1450s saw the Legems pass from the scene; they would return as a political force only in the late 1480s. The Arramis, Fanduix, Gallegos, Malequis, and Abenjamins fell from power as well, though they never returned. The descendants of Jacob Façan, however, remained influential in communal government. The Astoris, Çaportas, Vinaigs, Xamblells, and Tarfons—families who had risen in the 1420s, 1430s, and 1440s — continued to serve in the latter half of the century. Among their colleagues were members of families whose political and economic advance in Morvedre was more recent: the Adzonis, Comtes, Alateffis, Jabbas, Toledanos, Agís, Rodrichs, Castillos, Avincanes, and Asseyos.

The nature of the politics largely responsible for these changes in the corps of aljama officials was subtly different from what the community had known in the later thirteenth and fourteenth centuries. True, powerful and influential men possessed attributes much like those of their ancestors. Wealth, and therefore birth for some, remained crucial. Wealth enabled one to acquire the religious and legal education required of an adelantat and respected arbitrator; to employ, offer charity to, and exercise patronage over the less fortunate, including lower-class aljama councillors; to obtain the material possessions and enjoy the lifestyle long associated with the powerful; to cultivate relations with the Christian ruling classes that had long been fundamental to Jewish survival and prosperity; and to win, one way or another, sufficient respect and esteem among one's fellows to get elected to office. Election to office itself placed one in a position to serve the community, which enhanced one's prestige and moral authority, or perhaps to do harm to enemies.

Yet if affluence and office holding still characterized Morvedre's elite Jewish families, taxation, the question that had perennially divided them and that had been the focus of aljama politics, ceased to be a major source of contention after 1416. Jews from Morvedre no longer bombarded the king with complaints about the excessive taxation to which aljama officials were subjecting them, complaints that had been the stuff of the community's intense fiscal politics. The pleas that Crown officials received now related mainly to fiscal negotiations between aljamas, as the Jews of Borriana, Castelló, and Vila-real reacted against possible subjugation to the aljama of Morvedre.[69] Within the aljama of Morvedre politics took on a different tenor.

The Jews' political and economic life had been organized to an unusual if not abnormal degree (by contemporary Christian and Muslim standards) around the necessary production of massive fiscal revenues for the Crown. Families jockeying for power had devised strategies, behaviors, and modes of self-presentation

---

[69] See chap. 2; and Meyerson 2004a for politics in earlier centuries.

that suited the community's uncommon brand of fiscal politics. Attaining and maintaining high social status had entailed serving the community as a "big tax-payer" while retaining significant wealth and avoiding ruination; defeating political opponents had involved taking advantage of a term of office in aljama government to overtax them and thus reduce them or bring them closer to "the disgrace of poverty." With the end to the monarchy's incessant demands for exorbitant extraordinary subsidies and with the institution of a more moderate fiscal regime, the significance of taxation as a determinant of social promotion or demotion diminished. Elite families still contributed plenty to the community's financial well-being through rendering the peita and through guaranteeing the censals that the aljama assumed, but taxation no longer loomed as a threat to their social prominence. Burdened less by royal taxes, they more effectively consolidated their position in the community vis-à-vis their economic and social inferiors. When contesting power with their social peers elite families channeled some of the energy they had once invested in fiscal politics into the violent politics of the feud. The communal legislation of 1459 regarding "the arms that Jews should bear" against one another was a sign of the times.

Violent status competition had always been normative among the Christian and Muslim populations of the kingdom of Valencia, feuding key for determining the allocation of power within the Christian and Muslim communities. Violence and aggression had by no means been unknown among the Jews in earlier centuries — far from it. But now, with the weapons of tax assessment blunted, Jews resorted more frequently to verbal and physical aggression to degrade their enemies. Jews were not simply emulating Christians and Muslims in this regard; rather, Jews were giving freer rein to forms of status competition that they had, like Christians and Muslims, practiced to some degree but that an obsessive and consuming fiscal politics had limited.

Elite Jewish belligerents embroiled in blood feuds, or in heated contests that threatened to spiral into feud, sometimes turned to or attracted the attention of the Christian authorities. The latter would intervene to limit, regulate, or penalize Jewish violence, much as they had once and occasionally still mediated between Jews squabbling over tax rates. Members of leading families, like the Façans and the Xamblells, made assurances (*assegurament*, or *assecuramentum*) before royal bailiffs in which they swore not to assault or insult one another on pain of monetary fine.[70] When such sworn assurances proved inadequate for maintaining peace, Jews, like feuding Christian or Muslim families, were party to the Crown-sponsored "peace and truce," adherence to which

---

[70] ARV: B 1152: 1259v (1456/6/7) [Hinojosa Montalvo 1993a, no. 561] for the sworn assurances between Mossé Façan "and other Jews" and their opponent Salamó Xamblell. (The editor misinterprets this document.) B 1152: 1705v–1705r bis (1459/11/19) concerns those between Salamó Astori and a certain Maymonet.

the threat of heavier penalties encouraged.[71] Royal bailiffs also promoted peace between Jews by licensing certain individuals, as well as their friends and family, to carry arms for protection against their enemies.[72] The very request for such a license alerted the bailiff to the fact that the applicant lived in serious danger of attack by his enemies; licensing the applicant to bear and use arms — in effect, to shed blood without penalty — helped deter the potential assailants. Outside royal lands, Christian nobles known and respected by the Jews, like the Pròixidas, effected compromises between Jewish belligerents.[73]

Violence within the Jewish upper class, which might also involve upwardly mobile middle-class families, paralleled violence within the Jewish lower class. As in the case of the latter, the growing incidence of violence between members of the Jewish elite was partly a function of the demographic expansion of the community. More families contested power and the audience judging the contest was larger; the possibilities for friction and conflict increased while communal officials found it more difficult to keep the peace within a burgeoning community.

The use of violence in defense of individual and family honor had become, and probably had always been to some extent, socially prescribed behavior. If elite Jews did not usually resort to violence in order to achieve power, they nonetheless had to be prepared to respond to verbal and physical affronts in like manner if they hoped to earn or preserve the esteem of their fellows. Elections, not feuds, determined who held aljama office, but performance in feuds — making an honorable showing — affected a family's reputation and therefore had a bearing on its prospects in communal elections. An ability and willingness to employ violence when necessary was, then, one of the several attributes of the Jewish elite, one that the changed circumstances of the fifteenth century allowed to develop more fully.

Morvedre's elite Jewish families demonstrated how accustomed they were to compete aggressively for status in a blood feud that reached a critical point — but not an end point — in 1430, when Mossé Maymó and some Muslim accomplices murdered the converso Pau de Sant Martí.[74] The main parties to the feud were all silversmiths: on one side, the brothers Jahudà and Mossé

[71] ARV: B 1147: 469v-470r (1433/2/5) [Hinojosa Montalvo 1993a, no. 402] concerns the violation of a truce between Jahudà Maymó and his allies and Abraham and Samuel Agí and their allies. For assurances, public truces, and the efforts of Valencian authorities to regulate violence among Christians, see Ferrer Micó 1982; Narbona Vizcaíno 1990; Pérez García 1990, 233–253; for the Muslims, Meyerson 1991, 238–254.

[72] ARV: B 1147: 375r (1432/3/17): license to Jahudà Maymó to bear arms for self-defense against the Agí brothers; B 1157: 270v–271r (1482/6/2): license to Salamó Abenrabi [Hinojosa Montalvo 1993a, nos. 395, 797]; and see n. 76.

[73] See n. 77.

[74] Mossé Maymó was hanged in Valencia for his crime, which gave the Sant Martís and the Agís at least partial satisfaction. Jahudà Maymó and his allies later wounded Abraham Agí. The feud seems not to have drawn to a close until 1436, if even then. See Meyerson 2003b, and chap. 6.

Maymó, and, on the other side, the brothers Abraham and Samuel Agí. Silversmiths were the most affluent Jewish artisans and frequently served in aljama government. In addition to converso relatives and friends, each side had among its allies prominent members of the community. The Maymós, themselves descendants of an old and once powerful family, had the support of their maternal uncle and future treasurer Salamó Tarfon, and of Mossé Xamblell, member of an influential family. The Agís were backed by Jucef Bonet, member of an officeholding family, and by the then important Fanduix family, including the adelantat Salamó. The individuals involved, then, were neither sociopaths nor criminals but respected members of the Jewish community.

Another feud involving elite, officeholding families occurred in the 1470s and pitted the Xamblells against the Rodrichs, their in-laws the Comtes, and the Toledanos.[75] The permit to bear arms that the bailiff general granted to Astruc Rodrich and Jacob Toledano in 1473 seems to have deterred the Xamblells for a time.[76] The "compromise" Isaac Xamblell and Astruc Rodrich reached in 1475 under the sponsorship of the noble Elionor de Pròixida proved less effective, however.[77] Little more than a week later one of the Xamblells struck Vidal Comte, the father-in-law of Astruc (or Pastor) Rodrich, in the face outside his house in the Jewish quarter. Then, after fleeing to Almenara, the same Xamblell, along with Christian accomplices, assaulted and attacked Rodrich on the royal road.[78] Although Salamó Xamblell had served as adelantat in 1469,[79] no other member of the family seems to have been elected to office thereafter. The Xamblells made too many enemies among the political elite in the 1470s. In 1479 Mossé Xamblell complained that his name was not even included in the sack of names of Jews being considered for election to aljama office.[80] Small surprise that that very year Vidal Comte was elected adelantat and Isaac Toledano councillor.[81]

---

[75] Tensions between the Comtes and the Xamblells were long-standing. In 1456 Vidal Comte and Salamó Xamblell clashed over Comte's daughter. For an unknown reason, she was "en poder" of Xamblell who would not return her to her father (ARV: B 1152: 1236r, 1259v [Hinojosa Montalvo 1993a, nos. 556, 560]). The Xamblells may well have been the allies of Jucef Quatorze, who with "other Jews" assaulted Cadias Agí in 1467 (B 1154: 56v [Hinojosa Montalvo 1993a, no. 669]). The latter was represented in court by Abraham Agí and Abraham Comte. In 1471 Quatorze robbed Vidal Comte on the royal road (ARV: MR 81: 174v [Hinojosa Montalvo 1993a, no. 701]).

[76] ARV: B 1155: 46r (1473/3/9) [Hinojosa Montalvo 1993a, no. 715].

[77] APPV: P 25226, J. Argenti: n.f. (1475/9/25). Pere Esparça, a knight from Morvedre, was also present.

[78] ARV: B 1155: 498v–499r (1475/10/7) [Hinojosa Montalvo 1993a, no. 750]. Pastor and Astruc Rodrich must be the same person, for in 1489 Astruc Rodrich represented the widow of Vidal Comte — his mother-in-law — in her lawsuit with Abraham Agí (B 1159: 172v–173r [Hinojosa Montalvo 1993a, no. 826]).

[79] Along with Cresques Façan: ARV: MR 79: 262v (1469/6/6).

[80] ARV: B 1156: 368r (1479/2/5) [Hinojosa Montalvo 1993a, no. 779]. Vidal Abenjamin was another complainant; he had no luck either.

[81] APPV: P 17861, L. Miralles: n.f. (1479/10/13).

Such spectacular sanguinary exploits were far less frequent among the Jews of Morvedre than the trading of insults and occasional blows, acts that community members tallied on the communal scorecard of honor but with which royal officials hardly bothered. An uneasy balance of power and shifting of alliances between rival families kept most serious violence in check, their fear of the escalation of violence itself acting as a deterrent. Though the most overt and dangerous way of flexing political muscle, engaging the enemy in a blood feud was neither the most common nor the most effective method of vying for and winning political power. When a feud erupted it sometimes, as in the case of the Xamblells and their rivals, grew out of or was bound up with behind-the-scenes electoral politics. For the most part, votes were more decisive than swordplay.

As fragmentary election results indicate, no one family or faction of families was able to dominate aljama politics in the decades after 1416. The community was suspicious of any family or faction arrogating too much power to itself. The prosperity and socioeconomic mobility of a good number of families, and the flexibility of an electoral regime that facilitated their entry, with the right backing, into communal government, presented potential kingpins with several new challengers besides their old opponents. Rising families and newcomers to aljama office formed a pool of potential allies for existing factions to draw on. The oligarchy's openness to replenishment from below consistently fragmented and reallocated power at the upper reaches of Jewish society, thereby preserving a rough balance between families and factions.

This balance of power is obvious in some years from the first half of the century. In 1429, for example, members of old rival families, the Legems and the Façans, were both elected as adelantats; or in 1440, Salamó Fanduix and Salamó Tarfon, who had backed opposite sides in the Agí-Maymó feud in the 1430s, were both elected to the aljama executive. For most years, however, the paucity of ancillary evidence makes it difficult to determine precisely how families were aligned and power distributed. Still, the absence of complaint regarding electoral issues in this period indicates that most of the community was indeed satisfied with how power was shared, in contrast to the misgivings some Jews expressed in the late 1440s and 1450s.

Owing in part to the rapid growth of the community after 1445, the 1450s saw considerable political upheaval and failed attempts at hegemony by certain families. Some influential families experienced but survived the frustration of their schemes and ambitions; others declined precipitously.

The first casualties among the latter were the Gallegos and the Abenjamins. The fall of the Gallegos from the ruling elite was attributable to a noticeable worsening of their economic status and their feeble performance in a feud with powerful rivals. Highly regarded by his fellows, Mossé Gallego had been elected adelantat as early as 1425 and held the post as late as 1444.[82] But fi-

---

[82] ARV: MR 44: 242r (1425/4/18); MR 46: 111r (1427/28); MR 59: 255r (1444) [Hinojosa Montalvo 1993a, no. 472].

nancial difficulties forced him, at the end of the 1440s, to borrow money from and mortgage his houses to Jacob Vinaig, member of an officeholding family and community treasurer in 1456. Gallego's debt became public knowledge and a source of humiliation when a Christian creditor attempted to place a lien on the same houses and thus butted heads with Vinaig.[83] Around the same time the Gallegos fell afoul of the Bonet family. In February 1452 Jucef Gallego fled to the bailiff general to complain that Isaac Bonet had come to "attack [his] house in order to injure him." In the Valencian feuding tradition, forcibly entering the home of an enemy and assaulting him or his womenfolk was an effective means of publicly dishonoring him.[84] Gallego's pusillanimous appeal to the bailiff, instead of violent retaliation, damaged the reputation of his family among the Jews of Morvedre. The Gallegos never again held office. As for Isaac Bonet, neither the bailiff's warrant for his arrest nor his violent conduct hurt his chances in aljama politics: he was elected adelantat in 1454 and 1456.[85]

As for the Abenjamins, Jucef was the first of three brothers from that family to serve the aljama in an official capacity. His death in 1442 did not hamper the ascent of the other two, Vidal and Gento: Vidal was elected adelantat in 1445 and Gento in 1448.[86] The brothers had been so effective at collecting allies and votes that they could count on Vidal's election as adelantat in 1449.[87] Vidal swept into office after thwarting enemies' efforts to prevent his election by tampering with the electoral system.[88] He may well have been the ally of the other adelantat chosen that year, Salamó Xamblell.[89] After this, however, the electorate balked, concerned that the Abenjamins had grown too powerful. Neither brother was chosen as adelantat in 1450, 1451, or 1455, the years for which there is extant evidence. Vidal died in 1455. Mossé Façan quickly moved to appropriate his synagogue seat, as if to mark publicly the Abenjamins' decline.[90] Gento Abenjamin was certainly weaker without his brother. He was

---

[83] ARV: B 1151: 202r-v (1451/5/17), 202v–203r (5/18) [Hinojosa Montalvo 1993a, nos. 514–515]; and see chap. 2. MR 67: 273r (1456/4/13) for Vinaig.

[84] ARV: B 1151: 464v (1452/2/9) [Hinojosa Montalvo 1993a, no. 526]; Meyerson 2004b.

[85] ARV: MR 66: 268v (1454/7/16); MR 68: 267v (1456/4/13).

[86] ARV: MR 50: 94r-v (April–June 1431): Jucef, Salamó Xamblell, and Astruc Çaporta render payment to the bailiff on behalf of the aljama. ARV: B 1149: 231v–232r (1442/10/6) [Hinojosa Montalvo 1993a, no. 545] for Jucef's death. MR 60: 124r (1445/11/17), MR 63: 259v (1448/6/27) for the activities of Vidal and Gento as adelantats.

[87] On the eve of aljama elections Gento thus appeared before the bailiff general, on behalf of the aljama, to request that the current electoral system — that instituted by Queen María in 1403 — be continued (ARV: B 1150: 356v [Hinojosa Montalvo 1993a, no. 502]).

[88] ARV: B 1150: 362v (1449/2/19) [Hinojosa Montalvo 1993a, no. 503]. MR 64: 257r (1449/6/10) shows that Vidal and Salamó Xamblell were adelantats.

[89] This is suggested by the joint complaint of the Xamblells and the Abenjamins regarding their exclusion from the sack of nominees in 1479 (ARV: B 1156: 368r [Hinojosa Montalvo 1993a, no. 779] and the Xamblells' immediate reaction to the Façans' success in 1455.

[90] ARV: B 1152: 1002v (1455/4/15) [Hinojosa Montalvo 1993a, no. 545].

never again elected adelantat before his own death in 1460. A combination of too much success and bad luck ruined the Abenjamins.

The political success of families like the Abenjamins had been facilitated by the weakening of the formidable Legem and Façan families. In the 1420s, 1430s, and 1440s, both families branched out to Castelló and Borriana in pursuit of economic opportunities. Though weaker, they both remained a presence in aljama government until 1450: the Legems represented mainly by Jacob and the Façans by Isaac. The expansion of the Morvedre community after 1445 presented each family with the choice of either concentrating more energy on aljama politics in Morvedre in order to secure its position there or withdrawing, politically, to the smaller Jewish communities in the north. The Legems decided on the latter option, maintaining investments in Morvedre but not returning to aljama government until the 1480s.[91]

The Façans, in contrast, chose to fight for political power in Morvedre. In the late 1440s Samuel Façan and his son Mossé returned from Castelló to join forces with Samuel's uncle Isaac. They were probably key members of the faction opposing the Abenjamins between 1449 and 1455. They triumphed at the Abenjamins' expense. Samuel Façan was elected adelantat in 1454 while the Abenjamins were shut out; in 1455 his son Mossé appropriated the synagogue seat of the deceased Vidal Abenjamin.

In 1455 the Façans' victory was nearly complete. Not only was Mossé himself elected clavari but, thus emboldened, he chose his own father as one of the councillors. Such blatant nepotism provoked other elite families, especially the Xamblells, allies of the Abenjamins. The Xamblells were in a good position to frustrate the Façans, for that year one of them, Mossé Xamblell, was elected adelantat. He and his fellow adelantat, Abraham Adzoni, immediately ejected Samuel Façan from the community council. Samuel appealed to the bailiff general, pointing out that in the past outgoing adelantats had been designated as councillors by the incoming adelantats and clavari. This was true enough. Samuel neglected to mention, however, that in 1455 his own son was clavari. It was highly irregular for father and son or brothers to serve together the same year.[92]

The Façans were incensed. By the summer there was so much ill will between them and the Xamblells that the bailiff general advised his counterpart in Morvedre to look into the dispute and to take such measures "that the said aljama remains in peace and tranquillity."[93] The bailiff managed to cool tem-

[91] When Abraham Legem definitively left Morvedre in 1455 there were no Legem men in Morvedre to inherit his synagogue seat. Only his divorced wife Astruga (muller quondam) and some unnamed supporters opposed the ultimately successful attempt of Abraham Adzoni to obtain it—ARV: B 1152: 994r (1455/4/11). Abraham was in Castelló in 1456.

[92] ARV: B 1152: 979v (1455/2/11) [Hinojosa Montalvo 1993a, no. 543].

[93] ARV: B 1152: 1060v (1455/8/14): "que'en façats segons vos sia benvist remetent ho a vostre bon arbitre per manera que la dita aljama reste ab pau e asosech."

pers temporarily, until the next election in February 1456. Just before it took place, Samuel Façan informed the bailiff general of the Xamblells' machinations: "the father finding himself adelantat"—that is, Mossé Xamblell—"is nominating and putting his son forward for adelantat."[94] In order to avert a donnybrook between the Façans and the Xamblells and the breakdown of aljama government, the bailiff and his subordinate in Morvedre convened with leading members of the community. They agreed that one of the adelantats should be Astruc Çaporta, a righteous individual whom most of the elite families could accept and on whom they could depend to thwart questionable political tactics.[95] Wisely excluding both the Xamblells and the Façans from the executive, the community then elected Isaac Bonet as adelantat and Jacob Vinaig as treasurer to serve alongside Çaporta.[96]

Either the Xamblells or the Façans were sore losers. In March "some" Jews abused and dishonored the adelantats when they collected the peita.[97] The Xamblells appear the most likely suspects, since by June Abraham Xamblell still had not paid the peita.[98] In any case, the Xamblells and the Façans reserved most of their spleen for each other. With the families on the verge of drawing daggers, Mossé Façan and "other Jews" stepped forward and expressed their willingness to swear to assurances with "Salamó Xamblell and his supporters." The local bailiff prevailed upon Xamblell to meet Façan halfway.[99] Violence was prevented.

The Façans and the Xamblells may well have engaged in another test of strength in 1459 by backing opposing candidates for the post of communal rabbi, Isaac Soriano and Vidal Addaix. The community chose Soriano, the favorite of the Façans, but, as Soriano complained in March, some dissenters "who wish him ill want to have him ejected from [the post of] rabbi."[100] Even if the Xamblells were among the ill-wishers, the majority's choice of Soriano was determined less by the effective politicking of the Façans than by its principled opposition to royal interference in the community's religious affairs. Vidal Addaix was a relative of the queen's tailor, Mossé Abuzmael, and King

---

[94] ARV: B 1152: 1215v (1456/1/21) [Hinojosa Montalvo 1993a, no. 553].

[95] ARV: B 1152: 1217r (1456/1/24) [Hinojosa Montalvo 1993a, no. 552].

[96] ARV: B 1152: 1240r-v (1456/4/1).

[97] ARV: B 1152: 1236r (1456/3/4) [Hinojosa Montalvo 1993a, no. 557].

[98] ARV: B 1152: 1259v (1456/6/7) [Hinojosa Montalvo 1993a, no. 562]. B 1152: 1180v (1455/11/13) describes Abraham as "habitant en la vila de Onda," but he still would have been a member of the aljama of Morvedre. Considering the mobility of the Morvedre Jews, he may well have been back in Morvedre by election time in 1456.

[99] ARV: B 1152: 1259v (1456/6/7) [Hinojosa Montalvo 1993a, no. 561].

[100] ARV: B 1152: 1608r (1459/3/14): "Per part de Ysach Soriano, juheu de aqueixa juheria, es stat suplicat lo senyor Rey dihent que alguns de la dita aliama per que'l volen mal, volen fer llançar de rabi." B 1153: 411r (1463/3/9) [Hinojosa Montalvo 1993a, no. 633] clearly demonstrates the association of the Façans to Soriano. On communal rabbis, see Assis 1997, 139–141; Hershman 1943, 116–120.

Juan had therefore urged the aljama in February to appoint him to the rab-binate.[101] Despite the king's suggestion and the continued interference of the royal treasurer, Soriano was not abandoned by the Façans or his other sup-porters. He ultimately acceded to the rabbinate.[102]

Both the Façans and the Xamblells continued to hold aljama offices through the 1460s, sometimes serving in alternate years, other times serving together. The Façans, however, probably had the upper hand. Their initiation of peace-making with the Xamblells and their bold leadership of the Jews in their bat-tle with the municipality over taxation must have earned them the respect and gratitude of much of the community.[103] Yet, as has been seen, the final defeat of the Xamblells in aljama politics was not the work of the Façans but resulted from their feud with the Comtes, the Rodrichs, and the Toledanos. The Façans could just stand by as the Xamblells intemperately antagonized other families and spoiled their political chances.

The decline of the Xamblells did not lead to the hegemony of the Façans. The Façans were influential until the end, but they faced too much competi-tion from other powerful individuals and families, such as Salamó Çaporta, Gento Avincanes, the Comtes, the Toledanos, the Adzonis, and the Bonets. The community instinctively avoided allowing any one family to acquire too much power. Not even royal favorites like Salamó Çaporta and Vidal Astori were able to use their court connections and economic clout to lord it over the rest of the community. Çaporta was chosen as adelantat a few times prior to his exile in 1488 but he did not dominate his fellows. Although King Fernando nearly appointed Astori chief judge and rabbi over various Jewish aljamas in Castile, Astori's political influence in Morvedre was not great.[104]

In 1479 the bailiff general instituted a new electoral regime for the aljama of Morvedre, a reform Fernando II confirmed in 1481. The new system, *in-saculació*, was modeled on the system the monarchy was then imposing on var-ious municipalities. Every four years the names of upper-, middle-, and lower-class Jews worthy of holding aljama office were to be placed in separate sacks according to class. Then each year at election time the names of the three ex-ecutives and seven councillors were to be drawn by lot from the sacks as fol-

[101] ARV: C 90: 19v (1459/2/28) [Hinojosa Montalvo 1993a, no. 583]. In C 283: 86r (1459/7/26) the king commands his vicar general to hand over to Mossé Abuzmael "una de aquexes dues biblies ebraiques" that the queen wanted him to have.

[102] ARV: B 1152: 1626v–1627r (1459/3/24). B 1153: 644v–646r (1465/9/10) lists Isaac Sori-ano as community rabbi.

[103] E.g., in 1464 Mossé Xamblell was an adelantat (ARV: MR 75: 256v); in 1465 Mossé Façan was elected to this office (B 1153: 644v–646r). In 1469 Salamó Xamblell and Cresques Façan were both adelantats (MR 79: 262v). See chap. 2 for the struggles with the municipality in the 1450s.

[104] Baer 1929–36, 2: no. 329 (1476/3/12): Fernando informs the Castilian aljamas that he is withdrawing his appointment of Astori because it conflicts with the prior appointment of Abraham Seneor as chief judge and rabbi in Castile. On Seneor, Gutwirth 1989a.

lows: the two adelantats and two councillors from the upper-class sack; the clavari and two councillors from the middle-class sack; and three councillors from the lower-class sack.

According to King Fernando, the bailiff general's aim had been "to remove the differences that were in our jueria . . . for reason of its governance."[105] The new system certainly would have reduced the likelihood of grave political controversies at election time. Yet since 1463, when the community seems not to have managed to elect any adelantats, elections had not been the source of serious conflict.[106] Moreover, the process of choosing which names belonged in the sacks was open to manipulation and might cause some discontent.[107] The main reason for the electoral reform was not dangerous upheaval in the aljama but King Fernando's preference for municipal regimes in which political stability and royal authority were enhanced through consolidating the power of reliable oligarchs.[108] This reform kept upper-class Jews in a dominant position while leaving middle- and lower-class Jews with some voice in aljama government. In dealing with the aljama thus, King Fernando was looking toward the future he then supposed it would have.

---

[105] ACA: C 3663: 104v–105r (1481/12/24): "En dies passats per ordinacio feta per lo tunc batle general nostre en aquest regne per levar les differencies que eren en la nostra jueria de la vila de Morvedre per causa del regiment de aquella."

[106] ARV: B 1153: 459r (1463/9/5) [Hinojosa Montalvo 1993a, no. 639].

[107] Recall the complaint of the Xamblells and Abenjamins about the exclusion of their names from the sacks of nominees in 1479.

[108] On the *sistema insaculatorio*, see Torras i Ribé 1994; Bernabé Gil 1994; and Motis Dolader 1996, 939–944, regarding its diffusion among Jewish aljamas and Christian municipalities in the kingdom of Aragon.

Chapter Six

CONVERTS AND KINSFOLK

THE FAMILIES dominating the aljama of Morvedre in the fifteenth century were also, because of the destruction of the Jewish community in Valencia in 1391, the leading Jewish families of the entire kingdom. Yet the fruits of their newfound status were bittersweet. They were painfully aware of the absence of the large and thriving aljama in the capital, an absence made palpable each time they traveled to the city, each time they wandered into the parishes of Sant Andreu, Sant Thomàs, and Sant Esteve, which had once housed so many Jewish families, and saw the churches that had once been sites of Jewish prayer and Torah study. The Jews of Morvedre knew that they flourished in a smaller and impoverished Jewish world.

It was not just façades of former synagogues and Jewish homes that evoked memories of the capital's Jewish past and of a larger and richer Valencian Jewish world. The conversos who now occupied many of these homes and who attended the new parish churches also kindled such memories among the Jews of Morvedre. At the same time, many conversos of Valencia or Morvedre itself, whether themselves once Jews or the children or grandchildren of baptized Jews, chose not to forget who they were and whence they had come and deliberately cultivated memories of their Jewish past. Even when conversos opted to obliterate their Jewish heritage, some Old Christians would not let them forget it. For conversos of both kinds, the Judaizers and the assimilationist Catholics, the Jews of Morvedre were living reminders of their Jewish past, either sources of inspiration or sources of shame. The conversos of Valencia and the Jews of Morvedre regarded each other with longing or with purposeful contempt. Under the circumstances, indifference was hardly possible.

The Jews of Morvedre could never fully detach themselves from the conversos in Valencia because members of their own families had received baptism and moved there. Blood ties only intensified the wistfulness or the bitterness with which even unrelated Jews and conversos viewed each other. Kinship functioned either to sustain and strengthen the religious bonds between Jews and conversos or to bring about divisive disputes over property and inheritance.

Some of Morvedre's Jews were motivated by a deep sense of religious commitment to the conversos that had little to do with kinship ties. These Jews did not imagine that they could ever recreate the Jewish world that had existed prior to 1391, but they found it impossible to remain unresponsive to the needs of conversos determined to cling to their Jewish past and to make that past somehow part of their present and future. The conversos became a focus for Jewish piety. Aiding the conversos was a positive act of faith and an affirmation of Jewish identity. Jews and Judaizing conversos lived in a fruitful and dangerous symbiosis. The conversos who served as a spiritual stimulus for some Jews of Morvedre were ultimately the cause of the entire community's undoing.

FAITH, FAMILY, AND FEUDING

The Jews of Morvedre were fortunate to have escaped the violence that engulfed the kingdom's other Jewish communities in the summer of 1391. Yet, even if forced baptisms and murder had not obviously transformed the socioreligious landscape of Morvedre itself, when the Jews emerged from the local castle in the winter of 1392 to return to their homes in the jueria, they reentered a wider Valencian world that was irrevocably altered, now peopled by thousands of baptized Jews. For the rest of their days in Iberia, the Jews of Morvedre would have to respond to the question of how they, as Jews, should deal with the converso population. Their answers at any given moment varied, but also changed over the ensuing century. The Jews' responses depended on a range of variables, including their kinship ties to individual converts, the conversos' motives for accepting baptism, the conversos' religious identity, their own personal piety, economic interest, and the actions of royal and ecclesiastical authorities.

The Jews of the kingdom of Valencia who converted during the summer of 1391 acted under the threat of death or under great psychological duress. In Morvedre itself, the handful of Jews who received baptism were not physically coerced but succumbed to the fear and panic that gripped the Jewish community when news of the violent happenings in other towns reached it. The only sure victim of forced baptism from Morvedre was David, the son of Jacob Façan, though his conversion took place in Gandia. The baptism of one son of David el Rau may also have been coerced.

Whatever had possessed these Jews of Morvedre at the moment of their conversion, once the atmosphere of terror dissipated they regretted their decision. Their erstwhile coreligionists, who had themselves lived through the terrible summer and fall of 1391, sympathized and were inclined to clemency. The Jewish relatives of these remorseful converts were especially forgiving, regarding them as members of the family as well as of the Jewish community. Thus during the Passover of 1393 Jews welcomed their baptized children, parents, and cousins to their seder table, where, together, they could pray for redemption. Jacob Façan and David el Rau wanted their converso sons to celebrate the Passover that year as Jews unambiguously and without fear. Using their financial clout and connections, and despite the likelihood of never seeing their sons again, they shipped them off to Jewish communities in North Africa.[1] Wherever their newly baptized relations celebrated the Passover in 1393, the Jews of Morvedre considered them Jews.

The web of kinship and friendship in which the Jews and conversos of Morvedre were enmeshed quickly expanded to include the converso community of Valencia, as a result of the flight to Morvedre of Jewish refugees from the capital who stayed in contact with their baptized relatives there.[2] The Suxens and the Xamblells were the most notable of such additions to the Morvedre community. Furthermore, both the old and new Jewish inhabitants of Morvedre maintained economic relations with conversos in Valencia. Çahadia Haçon, for example, arranged to provide the converso bookbinder Simó de Carcassona with glass and silverwork valuing 15 florins, while Astruc Addet requited the converso tailor Martí de Sayas for certain services.[3] The frequency of Jewish visits to the conversos of the capital, for commercial or other purposes, moved Valencia's officials in 1400 to demand from King Martí legislation prohibiting Jewish travel to their city as a means of safeguarding the Christian faith of the neophytes.[4] Martí eventually responded in the Corts of 1403 with legislation that limited the length of the Jews' sojourns in Valencia to ten days and the places of their lodging to Old Christian parishes. The Jews, however, were not denied entry to the city.[5] Far from it: in 1410 and 1411 the bailiff general licensed Jews from Morvedre, such as the brothers Jucef and Mossé Gallego, as well as Castilian Jews to reside in Valencia for periods of one month or longer, sometimes in the houses of converso relatives.[6]

[1] Assaf 1933, 29; Bokser 1984, 72–79, 85–87; Fredman 1981, 95–103; and see chap. 1.

[2] ARV: P 2810; n.f. (1391/11/13) [Hinojosa Montalvo 1993a, no. 56] records the expenses of the conversos Gabriel Ballester and Roger de Montcada, who "went to Morvedre to speak with the Jews who are there and who went there from here." See also chap. 1.

[3] ARV: P 1445, B. de la Mata; 74r-v (1399/2/27) for Çahadia Haçon; 201r (7/23) for Astruc Addet. P 1446, B. de la Mata: n.f. (1401/2/8) is another example, in which Gabriel de Montcada, a converso jeweler, acknowledges that Astruga, the wife of Isaac Morcat (her second husband) and Salamó and Jucef Abencabal, her sons from her first marriage, have paid him the 440 sous they had confessed to owe him "cum publico instrumento, acto Valencie, in posse Mosse Cap, judei scribe juddarie olim Valencie." Conversos also traveled to Morvedre for business purposes. In 1408 the Valencian conversos Nicolau de Valldaura and Pere de Conqua farmed Crown taxes in Morvedre (ARV: MR 3991: 7r).

[4] AMV: LM g3–7: M. 2, n.f. (1400/9/18) [Hinojosa Montalvo 1993a, no. 262].

[5] ACA: 2322: 43r (1403/9/28); ARV: C 630: 350r-v [Hinojosa Montalvo 1993a, no. 270]; chap. 1.

[6] ARV: B 1219: 210r (1411/6/5): license to the Gallegos for a one-month stay; 63v (1409/12/4), 117v (1410/8/1): to Samuel and Jamila Suxen for one-month stays; 68v (1409/12/20): to Astruc Abenjarin, Jew of Lorca, to stay in Valencia for two months in the home of the converso tailor Francesc Castellar; 108v (1410/7/14): to Isaac Frances, Jew of Toledo, for a one-month stay in the house of the converso Johan Palomar or in the house of the converso Lop Rodríguez; 217r (1411/6/30): to Cresques Nasci, Jew of "Calaf del Comdat de Cardona," for a four-month stay in the house of his conversa sister Saura, the widow of Pasqual Maçana. (In ARV: C 394: 100v [1426/8/3] King Alfonso licenses Nasci, now described as a Jew of Morvedre, to reside in Valencia, in

The ties of blood and trade linking the Jews of Morvedre to the conversos of Morvedre, Valencia, and other towns, the forced, insincere conversion of the great majority of the neophytes, and the openness of the Jews to their baptized brethren created conditions propitious for perpetuating Judaism among the conversos. The latter did not require religious instruction or inspiration from the Jews, though deliveries of matzah on Passover certainly helped.[7] What they most needed and got from their Jewish friends and family was acceptance and the assurance that they were still deemed members of the Jewish community. In Morvedre this sense of community was expressed and strengthened through joint prayer, commensality, and even cohabitation.

Over the nineteen years between the violence of 1391 and the death of Martí I, royal officials, inquisitors, and bishops prosecuted and monetarily penalized Jews in Morvedre in order to discourage them from rolling out their welcome mats to conversos. Their successes were only temporary; whenever official pressure subsided, Jews and conversos would again gravitate toward one another. The excesses of the inquisitors, who habitually harassed the Jews far more than was necessary, inhibited long-term success by provoking royal intervention and thereby affording the Jews and conversos some breathing room. In 1394, for instance, the Jews' threat to move elsewhere because of the inquisitors' "daily" and expensive investigations into their activities elicited a quick royal response in favor of the Jews.[8] Clearly there were not enough conversos in Morvedre to have kept the inquisitors so busy. In the event, after the king compelled the inquisitors to relent, the Jews and conversos resumed their fraternizing. Hence in 1396 King Joan had to require the Jews of Morvedre to wear red badges so that local officials could easily identify them and prevent them from eating, drinking, and praying with conversos.[9] The inquisitorial and episcopal officials whom his successor Martí unleashed in 1398 found conversos in Morvedre still living in the Jewish quarter, consorting with Jews, and performing Jewish rituals.[10] Yet the clerics' abuse of power and their terrorizing of the Jewish women Mira and Astruga, the daughter of Samuel and Jamila Suxen, again prompted royal intervention and cast doubt on even the more legitimate procedures against Judaizing conversos and their Jewish accomplices in Morve-

---

any parish, for a period of four years.) In contrast, Jews who visited Valencia without a license could be arrested. Such was the case of one "Donna, juhia de Morvedre," whom the converso tailors Bernat Castellà and Guillem Ramon represented in the bailiff's court (B 1219: 282v–283r [1411/7/27]); she was at the same time licensed for a one-month stay (283r).

[7] E.g., Jacob Façan's alleged sending of matzah to conversos in Sogorb — see chap. 1.

[8] ACA: C 1906: 213v–214v (1394/3/1) [Hinojosa Montalvo 1993a, no. 209]; CR Joan I, caixa 7, no. 797, for the original letter.

[9] ACA: C 1911: 46r (1396/4/4) [Chabret Fraga 1979, 2: 341–342 n. 1].

[10] *Visitas pastorales*, no. 242, for the converso Guillem de Blanes (1398/7/15), and letters 227, 231 for the general problem. ACA: C 2233: 76v–77r (1401/12/9) concerns the converso Jaume de Lorde. See also chap. 1.

dre.[11] As royal and ecclesiastical officials clashed over the prosecution of Jews — the king's treasure — some Judaizing conversos could slip painlessly between the competing jurisdictions.

In these first decades after 1391, the most effective means of putting a stop to the conversos' Judaizing and mingling with Jews would have been a thorough and systematic education of the converts in Catholic doctrine, the strict physical separation of Jews from conversos, and the full cooperation of the royal and ecclesiastical authorities in carrying out these tasks. The first was barely attempted; the second, owing to Crown interest in fostering Jewish business, was pursued only halfheartedly; and the third was impeded by the inveterate, mutual mistrust of Crown and church. What indoctrination, segregation, and prosecution could not achieve, time eventually would, though only in part.

Prior to the reign of Fernando I, then, the Jews of Morvedre did not doubt that the conversos were still part of the wider Valencian Jewish community and therefore, circumstances permitting, natural participants in its ritual and social life. Kinship enhanced Jewish reception of the conversos and the latter's identification with their natal community. Indeed, because the baptisms had been so obviously coerced, because the converts had only yesterday been Jews, and because the sense of community among Jews and conversos was thus spontaneous and natural, social relations — and machinations — among Jews and conversos were, in several respects, continuous with those obtaining among just Jews before 1391. In other words, the communal feeling that created the conditions for Jews and conversos to sit together at the seder table, or for conversos to reside in Morvedre's Jewish quarter, also allowed Jews and their baptized relatives to conspire and compete for status as a family unit against other Jews and conversos. The new conglomerate community of Jews and conversos was no less riven by conflict than the homogeneous Jewish community had been. Since the conversos were still part of the Jewish community, they remained embroiled in Jewish politics. The welcome and assistance that Jews instinctively extended to their baptized brethren did not preclude but in fact encouraged the participation of the latter in the contest for wealth and power within the Jewish community.

The religious, family, and communal ties between Jews and conversos thus did not guarantee peaceful interaction and altruism. On the contrary, the new legal and social problems produced by the baptism of so many Jews sometimes made social competition within the conglomerate community of Jews and conversos that much more vicious. Questions of property, inheritance, and marriage acquired an added complexity that rival families and relatives, baptized and unbaptized, could exploit.

In 1396, for example, the whole aljama of Morvedre filed suit against Joan

---

[11] See chap. 1.

de Natera, a converso of Valencia, to whom the now deceased converso of Morvedre Manuel de Villafrancha had bequeathed all his property. Back in 1393 Manuel, né Isaac, the son of Meora Avinaçara (d.), and his Jewish mother, Sol, had been fined for celebrating Passover together. Consequently deeming Manuel, for all intents and purposes, a member of the aljama at the time when he followed his parents to the grave, aljama officials laid claim to those of his properties that were liable to communal taxation. Manuel's heir Natera did not take these communal obligations of Manuel's parents and of Manuel into account when he immediately appropriated the property. Despite the Christian status of both Manuel and Natera, Queen María instructed the bailiff to sequester the disputed property until a final decision could be rendered in the suit between Natera and the Jewish aljama.[12]

The Façan family of Morvedre had a wide range of contacts with conversos in Morvedre, Valencia, Sogorb, and Teruel. Jacob, the family patriarch, acted energetically on behalf of a number of forced converts, spiriting his own son off to a Jewish community in North Africa, provisioning conversos in Sogorb with matzah, and doing in Sogorb other "things touching the Catholic faith" — of the conversos no doubt — which got him in hot water with the local bishop.[13] Having married their daughter Jamila to Isaac Xamblell, a refugee from Valencia whose mother and brother had been coerced to convert, Jacob and his wife, Ceti, did not hesitate to agree to back Isaac's conversa mother, Beatriu, in any lawsuits possibly arising from her sale of a domicile to the converso Ramon de Vilanova.[14] Nor did Isaac Façan, Jacob's son, have any qualms about designating Isaac Xamblell and Beatriu as his legal agents for certain affairs.[15] Baptized relatives were naturally included in the affinal relationship between the Façan and Xamblell families.

Notwithstanding Jacob Façan's sympathy for the baptized Jews and their predicament, his relations with them were not always so smooth. Political differences with David el Rau inspired Jacob to insult David's converso grandson before the Jewish community by calling him "renegade."[16] The charity Jacob showed the baptized kin of his Jewish allies did not extend to the converted relatives of his Jewish enemies. Jacob and Ceti litigated for many years with the converso Gabriel de Najari and his Jewish son Samuel. Najari was originally

---

[12] ACA: C 2330: 58v (1396/12/1); MR 393: 38v (1393); chap. 1.

[13] ACA: C 1906: 64r–66r (1393/5/10) [Hinojosa Montalvo 1993a, no. 164]; C 2335: 89v–90r (1398/5/18); chap. 1.

[14] ARV: P 25915, G. de Ponte: n.f. (1399/9/24). Beatriu was the widow of Jacob (or Salamó, as he is sometimes named [ACA: C 2143: 50r (1404/7/21)]) Xamblell. ACA: C 1906: 64r–66r mentions the marriage of Jamila and Isaac Xamblell. Isaac's converted brother was Manuel Pardo, as indicated in ARV: P 1446, B. de la Mata: n.f. (1401/10/3), where the silkweaver Joan Pardo, Manuel's son, acknowledges his debt of 100 florins to Isaac, "avunculo meo, judeo Muriveteris."

[15] ARV: P 1445, B. de la Mata: 280r-v (1399/10/16).

[16] ACA: C 1906: 64r–66r (1393/5/10); chap. 5.

from Teruel, the Façans' hometown, but had since moved to Sogorb, whence he sued for money and goods in the hands of the Façans.[17] In 1436 the heirs of Jacob and Gabriel were still disputing the matter.[18]

The most prominent Valencian refugees to settle in Morvedre were Samuel Suxen and his wife, Jamila, daughter of the late Jahudà Alatzar. They came to Morvedre with money and connections — connections with converso relatives. From the time of his emigration to Morvedre in 1392 until at least 1401 Samuel worked closely with his converso brother Manuel Salvador. Manuel, formerly Mahir Suxen, was a citizen of Xàtiva, Samuel's home prior to his marriage to Jamila, and a frequent visitor to Valencia.[19] From the moment of his baptism in the summer of 1391, Manuel had been busy trying to prevent the inquisitors from exhuming and burning the bones of their father, Mossé Mahir Suxen, on the charge of having fashioned and worshiped an image of metal and mandrake.[20] As a result of his encounters with the inquisitors, Manuel was compelled to render 725 florins to the Crown in 1393.[21] The payment was probably a settlement related to his father's case or perhaps a penalty arising from his own prosecution for Judaizing.

Whatever scruples Manuel evinced in protecting the bones of his father were not on display when he and his brother Samuel dealt with their widowed sister-in-law, Haluha, and her father, Saçon de Quatorze of Teruel. With the passing of her husband, Salamó Suxen, in 1392, Haluha, a childless widow, was obliged, according to the laws of levirate marriage, to marry her brother-in-law. She could not receive her dowry or marry another man unless her brother-in-law released her from the obligation through the ceremony of *halitzah*. Since Manuel was a converso with a Christian wife and child and Samuel was already married with children, they ought immediately to have ritually freed Haluha from the levirate requirement. The responsibility was first incumbent on Manuel since he, presumably, was the elder of the two. Manuel and Samuel had other ideas, however, and conspired to profit from Haluha's misfortune at the expense of her father. Relations between the Suxen and Qua-

[17] ACA: C 2339: 152r (1404/8/14); C 2340: 35v–36r (12/3); ARV: B 1144: 107v–108r, 109r-v (1405/10/16, 11/20) [Hinojosa Montalvo 1993a, nos. 271, 278]; ACA: C 2159: 102v–103r (1408/9/26); C 2186: 22r-v (7/9) all treat this case and arbitrators' failed efforts to reach a settlement. The father Gabriel had been named Saçon before his baptism; his son Samuel, who converted in 1416, took the name Gil Ruiz. On this family, see Vendrell 1948; Edwards 1984b, 345–346.

[18] ARV: C 64: 66v (1436/11/14). Jacob's heir was Isaac Façan, and Gabriel's Gabriel de Najari, now of Valencia (C 33: 150v–151r [1425/3/20]). Gabriel Jr. must have been Gento, the brother of Samuel — see Edwards 1984b, 345.

[19] By July 1406 Manuel had moved from Xàtiva to Valencia — ACA: C 2151: 19r. Hinojosa Montalvo 1999 offers useful, though sometimes misinterpreted, data on this family.

[20] ACA: C 1850: 40r-v (1391/8/30, 9/8) [Hinojosa Montalvo 1993a, nos. 49–50]. The exhumation of the bones was merely stayed until royal officials had the chance to review the records from Suxen's trial. The results of the judicial review are unknown. See also chap. 1.

[21] ACA: MR 393: 29v (March 1393).

torze families had in any case been strained on account of the disastrous marriage of Haluha and Salamó. Shortly after the nuptials Salamó had gone mad and had to be kept in chains in his father's house in Xàtiva until his death ten years later. Leaving her dowry in the hands of her father-in-law, Haluha had in the meantime returned to the house of her father, Saçon, in Teruel. Saçon's pleas to the Suxens to provide support for Haluha from her dowry or from Salamó's property had fallen on deaf ears. Consistent with their family's earlier treatment of Haluha and Saçon, Manuel and Samuel determined to extort a "redemption" price from Saçon before Manuel journeyed to Teruel to perform ḥalitzah. In order to keep up appearances while pressuring Saçon, the brothers induced the governor of the kingdom of Valencia to issue a formal prohibition of Manuel's travel to the kingdom of Aragon, and to Teruel in particular. The queen, however, saw through the subterfuge — Manuel's *malicia*, as she called it — reprimanded the governor for his complicity, and ordered Manuel to Teruel to do right by Haluha. Saçon was nonetheless required to pay Manuel's travel expenses.[22]

Samuel's subsequent dealings with his converso brother were more mundane. On several occasions Samuel acted as the procurator of Manuel and his adult son, Manuel Jr. (formerly Samuel Suxen), collecting, for instance, money from peasants of Torrent indebted to his brother.[23] Manuel and another converso, Thomàs de Montcada, acted as arbitrators in a lawsuit between Samuel and Vicent Orriols, a citizen of Valencia.[24]

Samuel and his brother Manuel had a parting of the ways sometime after the summer of 1401, probably owing to religious differences. The death in August of Manuel's once Jewish son, Manuel Jr., the offspring from his first marriage to a Jewish woman, pushed Manuel further away from Judaism. He had already started to drift away when he married an Old Christian woman and had a child with her. Without Manuel Jr. around to remind him of his former

[22] ACA: C 2039: 129r-v (1392/8/19), 130r, 131r-v [Baer 1929–36, 1: no. 449; Hinojosa Montalvo 1993a, no. 79]. Though it is not clear from these letters whether Manuel's *muller cristiana* was an Old Christian or a conversa, she was almost certainly an Old Christian. At this early date her conversa status would have been noted. ACA: C 1904: 221v–222r (1393/2/6) [Hinojosa Montalvo 1993a, no. 147] is a royal safe-conduct issued to Manuel for his trip to Teruel. On the law of levirate marriage, see Wegner 1991, 70–72; Adelman 1991, 151. In 1393 Rabbi Isaac ben Sheshet Perfet addressed the case of an anonymous Jewish widow of Morvedre who asked to be freed from the obligation to marry her brother-in-law, a convert to Christianity (*She'elot u-teshuvot*, no. 1).
[23] ARV: P 1445, B. de la Mata: 177r-v (1399/7/1), 313v (11/17). In P 1446, B. de la Mata: n.f. (1401/7/8) Manuel Jr. designates Samuel his procurator "ad petendum penssionum . . . violariorum nostrorum et penas." An incomplete entry in the same register, dated 1 July, describes Manuel Jr. as "olim vocati Samuel Suxen, civis Xative." He died around a month later, and on 5 August the same notary recorded Manuel Sr. and Joan de Natera as "tutores et curatores testimentarii filii et heredis Manuelis Salvador."
[24] ARV: P 1445, B. de la Mata: 129v (1399/4/23). On 31 October the arbitrators decided in favor of Orriols, requiring Samuel to pay him 2,400 sous (295r).

Jewish life, and with an Old Christian wife nudging him ever further down the assimilative path, Manuel could slash at the last kinship ties binding him to his Jewish past: his ties to Samuel and his family. He turned on Samuel, using tactics that, in their wickedness, surpassed those he had employed when exploiting the plight of his erstwhile sister-in-law Haluha. Manuel whispered to the bishop of Valencia that Samuel's daughter Astruga had been baptized but had returned to Judaism at the inducement of Samuel's wife, Jamila, and of Jamila's aunt Astruga. As a consequence of Manuel's charges, the three women were thrown in the episcopal jail. Manuel hoped that his niece would be terrorized into accepting baptism and then into marrying his widowed converso brother-in-law, the former husband of his, and Samuel's, deceased sister. He and the new husband could divvy up Astruga's large dowry. Manuel's plot failed and Astruga eventually wed a Jewish man. But his subconscious goal of breaking with Samuel and his family succeeded.

Even though Samuel and his family understandably wanted nothing further to do with Manuel Salvador, they did not cease all contact with conversos. On the contrary, they aided and abetted conversos in their Judaizing, which led, in 1407, to their prosecution and penalization by the inquisition. As usual, however, the inquisitors got carried away, and in 1408 they indicted Samuel, Jamila, and her aunt, Astruga, for being relapsed converts. The accusation was spurious. It may well have originated with Manuel Salvador.[25]

Manuel Salvador's efforts to distance himself from Judaism so rapidly and to obliterate his connections with his Jewish relatives were not characteristic of the forced converts of 1391. Most did not immediately intermarry with Old Christians and most were not as calculating and malicious as Manuel. However, the Jews who converted between 1413 and 1416, as a result of the Disputation of Tortosa, the preaching of Vicent Ferrer, and the anti-Jewish legislation of 1415, were more like Manuel Salvador than like the other converts of 1391. Even if they were not possessed of the same Machiavellian talents as Manuel, they were more apt to share his desire to deny their Jewish roots and dissociate themselves from Jewish relatives and acquaintances.

The preachments of the charismatic Dominican, the vituperation and threats of his Christian hangers-on, and the bad news from Tortosa fell on the ears of Jews in Morvedre who were acquainted, intimately in some cases, with conversos from the generation of 1391 and who therefore had a good understanding of the opportunities and dangers involved in opting for baptism. Conversion had become a less forbidding option, less of a leap into the unknown. This time Christians did not have to menace Jews with death; the experience of living in a Jewish world transformed by the violence of 1391 and the despair evoked by the policies of King Fernando and Pope Benedict XIII were sufficient to move some Jews to contemplate baptism seriously and ultimately to

---

[25] See chap. 1.

take the plunge. The vicissitudes of family and communal politics also helped push Jews toward the baptismal font. For some Jews in Morvedre, personal disgruntlement, general Jewish demoralization, and familiarity with conversos proved a combination too powerful to resist.

Not yet at the age of majority (twenty) when he sought baptism in 1415, David el Rau — soon-to-be Pere de Pomar — had had a childhood experience that left him more vulnerable to the proselytizing pressure exerted during the reign of Fernando I. He was the grandson and namesake of the wealthy and powerful David el Rau, and the son of Haim el Rau and Oro, the daughter of Salamó Abenardut, who both passed away in 1401. Haim had died intestate and had not made any provisions for the guardianship of David and his sister Conort. The paternal grandparents, David el Rau and Regina, became the orphans' guardians, but the tranquillity of their grandparents' household was soon disrupted when their grandfather David, desirous of a direct male heir, took a young second wife, Jamila, since their grandmother Regina was beyond the age of childbearing. The birth of Davinet, or "little David," to Jamila deprived David ben Haim of his status as his grandfather's namesake and principal heir. He and Conort were not disinherited but their economic future was now dimmer; their maternal uncle, Alatzar Abenardut of Teruel, had already confiscated their mother's dowry by virtue of a *donatio inter vivos* Oro had made to him.[26] After their grandfather's death in July 1404, young David and Conort remained in the house of the bitter Regina, who battled Jamila and Davinet in court for months over the division of David's property.[27] Besides being an interested party in the quarrels between his grandmother and his grandfather's second wife, David witnessed the bickering between grandmother Regina and his maternal grandfather, Salamó Abenardut. As a consequence of David el Rau's death, Queen María had appointed Salamó and Isaac Xamblell as David and Conort's guardians, though the two wards stayed with their grandmother.[28] Regina's efforts to obstruct the marriage Salamó was arranging between Conort and his own son Jahudà resulted in the Crown-mandated removal of Conort from Regina's house in December 1406.[29] Whether David joined Conort in the house of grandfather Salamó is unclear.

[26] For more on David el Rau's family affairs and the relevant documentation, see chap. 5 at nn. 26–27.

[27] ACA: C 2339: 178v (1404/9/30); C 2340: 30r (12/1), which notes that Maymó Pardo and Abraham Gallego were the executors of the will of David el Rau; CR Martí I, caixa 7, no. 810 (1405/8/10). By order of the queen, Jewish sages were to render decision in accordance with Jewish law. The outcome is unknown.

[28] ACA: C 2339: 155r-v (1401/8/18). The adelantats, with the counsel of one Rabbi Jahudà, modified this arrangement somewhat; on 29 September they made Abraham Gallego the other guardian along with Abenardut. The instrument was redacted in Hebrew by the aljama scribe, Salamó Caxo, on the same day; a second version, translated from Hebrew into "romanicum vulgare," was redacted by the notary Ximino de Taraçona on 13 October 1404 (C 2340: 31v [1404/12/4]).

[29] ACA: C 2150: 100r (1406/9/9); C 2152: 94r (12/2). Regina must have been particularly an-

Young David, then, occupied an uncertain position in an unhappy family. However the el Raus managed to resolve their internal disputes or those with their affines, the Abenarduts, it was clear to all in Morvedre's Jewish quarter that with the death of the patriarch David el Rau the power of the family had declined precipitously, if it was not totally extinguished. One forcibly baptized son of the patriarch had been shipped off to North Africa in 1392; he had left behind one son, Daniel, who converted and took the name Jaume de Lorde; Haim el Rau, another son of the patriarch and David's father, was dead; and the patriarch's last son, Davinet, was but a child whose future was apparently being secured at David's expense. The prospects of David ben Haim in Jewish society were not bright when Fernando I succeeded to the Crown of Aragon. The king and his clerical accomplices persuaded him that he would be better-off in Christian society. David was baptized in 1415 and took the name Pere de Pomar.[30]

Pere's conversion precipitated a break between him and his still Jewish sister, Conort, by then the wife of Jahudà Abenardut. Conort and Jahudà seem to have regarded Pere as "dead" for all Jewish purposes, and thus unfit to inherit any of the property of his grandfather, David, and his father, Haim, who had both died as Jews. Whether they acted out of religious scruples or simply out of greed, Conort and Jahudà spread a rumor that Pere was actually deceased. With the connivance of a local Christian notary, Berenguer Centelles, the couple managed to secure from the unwitting and newly crowned King Alfonso one-half of Pere's inheritance in October 1416.[31] By the following month, however, the king had been given reason to be "doubtful" and "uncertain" about Pere's death. Were Pere alive, the king instructed, his inheritance should be placed in the hands of his *tutor*, the notary Jaume Rull.[32]

Retaining at least part of his inheritance, the still animate Pere reached the age of majority and managed to marry fairly well. In September 1418 he wed Beatriu, the daughter of Arnau Castellar, a converso broker of Valencia. Beatriu brought a substantial dowry of 5,000 sous to the marriage; Pere contributed an *augmentum* of 2,500 sous.[33] With the help of his father-in-law, Pere ham-

---

tagonized on learning that the marriage contract between Conort and Jahudà had been confirmed by Conort's paternal uncle, the infant Davinet el Rau. Jahudà Abenardut, who resided in Jaca, feared that Regina was going to marry Conort to someone else; hence her removal from Regina's house.

[30] ACA: C 2375: 173r-v (1415/8/23): Jaume Rull, a notary of Morvedre, is appointed *tutor* of Pere de Pomar. C 2378: 21v–22r (same date) states that the previous Jewish *tutores*, Salamó Abenardut and Abraham Gallego, cannot act as such on account of the baptism of David/Pere; the king ruled thus in accordance with a sentence of the pope regarding the administration of the *tutelas* of converts.

[31] ACA: CR Alfonso IV, caixa 3, no. 297 (1416/9/3); C 2458: 111r-v (10/15).

[32] ACA: C 2585: 171v–172v (1416/11/19) [Baer 1929–36, 1: no. 522].

[33] APPV: P 25970, P. Castellar: n.f. (1418/9/7). The entry of 15 November lists Arnau Castellar as a witness to the purchase of sheep by two Jews of Morvedre, possibly an indication of long-standing contacts with the Jews.

mered out a final agreement with Conort and Jahudà regarding the el Rau inheritance. Pere's sister and brother-in-law probably eventually returned to Aragon, the Abenarduts' kingdom of origin; his own future was among the conversos of Valencia.[34]

Neither turbulent childhoods nor poor political and economic prospects in the Jewish community influenced Samuel Legem and his son Abraham when they converted to Christianity in 1414 and 1415, respectively. On the contrary, Samuel was the son of the wealthy tax farmer Jahudà Legem, and himself a tax farmer and elected adelantat on at least three occasions. Scion of one of the most powerful Jewish families in Morvedre, which was at least holding its own with the rival Façans, Abraham Legem had reason to expect a bright future — as a Jew.

The Legems' wide-ranging economic activities had brought them into contact with conversos in the capital by at least 1401, interaction that may have paved the way for their dramatic decision to abandon Judaism. Samuel Legem employed a converso agent to lend money to Christian farmers in Torrent, and Joan Sentpol, a converso dyer and silkweaver, acted as Samuel's guarantor when he purchased goods on credit from a Valencian merchant.[35] Abraham Legem and his son Jacob used the services of a converso broker from Valencia, Pere Clausells, to buy silk and pearls from one Miquel Rull of Morvedre.[36] Through such contacts the Legems learned that conversion need not entail ruination and that the conversos of Valencia, with whom they had connections, were in fact economically vigorous and upwardly mobile.

The Legems were also linked to some conversos through their common adherence to Judaism. In 1407 the inquisitors prosecuted Samuel along with other Jews and conversos, most likely in relation to the Judaizing of the latter. Samuel was technically "absolved," but for a price, which meant that the inquisitors were neither proclaiming his innocence nor guaranteeing that they would not harass him and his fellows again.[37] Even though Samuel's prosecution by the inquisition resulted from his identification with Judaizing conversos, it, and the rest of the inquisitorial offensive during these years, may have aroused in him a profound pessimism about the future of the Jews in the Crown of Aragon. The anti-Jewish activities that ensued after Fernando I's ac-

---

[34] APPV: P 25970, P. Castellar: n.f. (1418/12/16). Unfortunately the terms (*capitula*) of the agreement are not listed here. After this date, there is no indication of an Abenardut presence in Morvedre. ARV: B 1221: M. 1, 23v (1444/5/7) mentions Jucef Abenardut, Jew of Jaca, then visiting Valencia.

[35] ARV: P 1446, B. de la Mata: n.f. (1401/11/9), where Samuel makes loans "per manus Johannis de Bordils, olim Fahim Homeraig"; B 1219: 89v (1410/5/29): Sentpol stands surety as Samuel acknowledges his debt of 675 sous to the merchant Anthoni Ros.

[36] ARV: B 1219: 246v (1411/11/26). In B 1219: 132r (1410/9/24) Pere Stheve, converso tanner and tailor, posts bail for Abraham, who had been arrested at the instance of Pere Forcadell of Morvedre.

[37] ACA: C 2150: 137r (1407/2/4).

cession would have changed Samuel's pessimism into utter despair. Hence his
baptism in 1414.

The conversion of such a prominent Jew greatly interested King Fernando,
who, as has been seen, did all he could to persuade Samuel's wife, Bonafilla,
and their children to follow their husband and father—now Joan de Sant
Feliu—into the church.[38] Abraham joined his father, taking the name Francesc
Suau. The king licensed both father and son to become brokers, careers that
were potentially lucrative and consistent with the Legems' activities prior to
1415.[39] Still, it would have been difficult to improve much on the economic
standing Joan/Samuel had achieved as a Jew. In fact, within thirteen years of
his baptism Joan had sunk to the status of "pauper," not in absolute terms but
relative to his former lofty position. He had profited little from partnerships with
old converso acquaintances, such as the silkweaver Joan Sentpol.[40] His son
Francesc, however, had better luck. In 1429, in his capacity as a broker, he
worked with the bailiff to farm out the Crown's fiscal revenues in Morvedre.[41]
In 1437 Francesc moved to Valencia, a sign of his hope and ambition.[42]

Another member of the Legem clan, Jahudà, possibly a son of Samuel,
sought baptism in 1422 along with his wife and four children. His converso relatives must have swayed him. Oddly enough, he too took the name Francesc
Suau. The jurats of Valencia urged their counterparts in Morvedre to provide
the new convert with a stall in the town abattoir, which would contribute to
the sustenance of his family.[43]

Bonafilla, Joan's spouse, clung to Judaism, despite the financial benefits offered by the king and the arguments of her husband, who still lived with her
and the children with the express permission of the king.[44] Just how long Joan
and Bonafilla continued to cohabit after 1415 is unknown. Relations between
them were, surprisingly, not too acrimonious. Rather than abandoning Bonafilla, Joan gave her some of his property—at least a house and a vineyard of
which he was the *senyor*. In 1419 Bonafilla, still described as Joan's "wife," empowered her converso husband to lease the house and vineyard; the rent was
to be used to pay the annuities that Joan, or Samuel, had sold to Joan de Natera, honored citizen of Valencia, and his wife, Mari Ferrández in 1398.[45] In

---

[38] See chap. 1.

[39] ACA: C 2374: 190r-v (1415/7/15) for Francesc; C 2396: 196r-v (8/23) for Joan.

[40] ARV: C 43: 141r-v (1428/12/7), which treats Joan's lawsuit with Bernat Guerau of Morvedre and Pere Gaya of Valencia, describes him as "pauperem et miserabilem personam." C 44: 143r-
v (1428/12/15) concerns the suit between Sant Feliu and Sentpol, "ratione certorum compoto-
rum," which indicates a prior partnership.

[41] ARV: MR 3996: 19r (1429).

[42] Piles Ros 1978, 255, no. 1086.

[43] AMV: LM 15: 209v–210r (1422/3/24) [*Epistolari*, 2: no. 132].

[44] ACA: C 2394: 83v–84r (1415/6/22).

[45] ARV: B 1145: 246v (1419/7/6): "en Johan Sent Feliu, axi com a procurador de la dita na
Bonafilla, muller de aquell." B 318: M. 2, 48r-v (1421/9/10).

1427 Joan and his "wife" Bonafilla were still working together, in this case litigating with the converso Lupo Martínez de Najari, the guardian of Caterina, conversa and daughter of the Jew Todroç Abendavit. The couple was represented by a Jewish relative, Abraham Legem (not Joan's son), then resident in Castelló.[46]

Few of the converts who accepted baptism during the reign of Fernando I maintained relations with their former coreligionists as amicable as those Joan de Sant Feliu seems to have had with his Jewish spouse, Bonafilla. On the contrary, in 1414–15 some of these newer conversos plotted with Old Christians to make trouble for and harm the Jews of Morvedre.[47] Their deliberate decision to convert had, after all, involved arguing against and denying Judaism; living near Jews required further self-justification. Demonstrating the sincerity of their conversion to Old Christians and distinguishing themselves from the more suspect conversos of 1391 necessitated attacking and vilifying Jews and Judaism. By acting in an overtly anti-Jewish manner — like so many Jerónimo de Santa Fés in their own town — these proselytes could calm their own unease, counter the reproach of Jewish relatives and friends, and more fully remake themselves as Christians.

Yet in the kingdom of Valencia the conversos who sought baptism during the reign of Fernando I were few, a minor fraction of the total converso population, almost all of whom had converted in 1391 as a result of physical coercion or outright terror. There were not enough new converts to become a source of persistent problems for the Jews. Besides, even King Fernando (d. 1416) but especially his successor Alfonso IV made it clear that such harassment of the Jews would not be tolerated. After 1415, then, the Jews of Morvedre were not troubled by the abuse or conspiracies of new converts with something to prove. The conversos who continued to vex Jews acted not as the enemies of Jews or Judaism per se but as the antagonists of particular Jewish families by virtue of their kinship or friendship to others. For some Jews in Morvedre the most dangerous conversos were those most heavily involved in Jewish politics, those who in several respects still identified themselves as Jews.

The aggressive status competition within the aljama of Morvedre, which before 1391 had concerned only Jewish families, for several decades afterward included the converso relatives and allies of these same families. Ties of kinship and friendship between Morvedre's Jews and Valencia's conversos in fact remained strong into the 1430s and were fundamental to the formation of factions that cut across official religious boundaries. For example, in the blood feud that erupted in Morvedre in 1430 between the Jewish Maymó and Agí families, both families enjoyed the support of converso allies from Valencia. The principal victim of the feud, the Valencian converso Pau de Sant Martí,

---

whom Mossé Maymó ambushed and murdered, was the first cousin of the
brothers Abraham and Samuel Agí. Jahudà Maymó, the brother of Mossé, had
previously been assaulted by Samuel Agí, Pau de Sant Martí, and other Jews
and conversos. When Cinha, the sister of Jahudà and Mossé Maymó, learned
of this attack on her brother, she was staying at the home of her converso
brother-in-law, one Mossèn Pujades, in Valencia's converso neighborhood.
One of the witnesses for the prosecution in the trial of Salamó Tarfon, uncle
and alleged accomplice of the Maymó brothers, was Jacme Català, a converso
quiltmaker from Valencia and cousin of the Agís and Sant Martís. In attempting to disqualify the evidence presented by Català on the grounds of his willingness to lie under oath on behalf of his Jewish and converso kin, Tarfon's defense attorney, Berenguer de Tolosa, presented the testimony of Johan Just, a
converso shoemaker of Valencia acquainted with Català:

> he had heard them [Català and the Agí brothers] call each other cousins all the
> time . . . and had seen the said Agís, Jewish brothers, entering and leaving, and
> staying at the house of the said En Jacme Català [and they were] hidden there . . .
> in the time when the wounds were inflicted on the person of Jahudà [Maymó] . . .
> and there they stayed eating and drinking.[48]

The Jews and conversos implicated in the Maymó-Agí feud performed their
bloody deeds before an audience composed of Jews from Morvedre and conversos from Valencia. They acted in accordance with the informal code of a
Jewish honor culture, "Jewish" because its participants were all Jews or of Jewish origin. What mattered most to the actors was how other Jews and conversos evaluated their conduct. There was ample opportunity for such collective
appraisal, since the news of reciprocal acts of violence spread rapidly through
both the Jewish quarter of Morvedre and the converso neighborhood of Valencia. Jacme Català, for instance, heard other conversos talking about the assault of Samuel Agí and company on Jahudà Maymó and the reason for it:
Jahudà's prior slashing of the face of Abraham Agí, a mark of dishonor Abraham could not hide. When Jahudà's sister Cinha was informed of the attack
on her brother, she stood at the door of the house of her converso brother-in-
law, located on the Carrer Nou, the main street in Valencia's converso neighborhood, and loudly proclaimed her family's intention to get revenge on the
Agís and the Sant Martís. Obviously many conversos heard her threats; Jews in
Morvedre would, too, soon enough.[49]

Blood ties and religious ties between Jews and conversos were not necessarily coextensive, but the willingness of these Jews and their converso kin to shed
blood on behalf of one another suggests a level of social intimacy that made
the Judaizing of the latter more than possible. When Jews from Morvedre, like

---

[48] ARV: B Procesos, P. 2618: 108r-v [transcribed in Meyerson 2003b, n. 34].
[49] Meyerson 2003b.

the Agí brothers and the Maymós' sister Cinha, lodged and ate in the homes of converso relatives in Valencia, they could do so presumably because their converso kin observed the laws of kashrut. If in Christian Valencia Jews and conversos could partake of kasher meat and wine behind closed doors, they were also capable of celebrating — and probably did occasionally celebrate — the Jewish Sabbath or other Jewish holidays together.[50] In 1430, then, the Jews of Morvedre and a portion — perhaps a large portion — of the converso population of Valencia still constituted a larger Jewish-converso cultural entity held together by bonds of kinship and friendship and in at least some cases by a common observance of Jewish customs and rituals.

By the time of the Agí-Maymó feud, however, the kinship ties between Jews and conversos were weakening and the conglomerate honor culture, which was galvanized by competition between family and faction, was beginning to disintegrate. Forty years after 1391 blood ties were inevitably more tenuous, and the Jews and conversos guarding the memories that sustained them and lent them meaning were fewer in number. The converso Guillem de Reig, for instance, was able to pinpoint the relationship between the converso Jacme Català and the Agí brothers: the Agís' mother was the first cousin of Català's grandmother. But Reig, who said that he knew "the aforesaid and their generation for a long time" and that, when a Jew, he had been raised among them, was already more than sixty years old in 1430.[51] The descendants of Guillem de Reig, Jacme Català, the Agí brothers, and their Jewish and converso fellows were not likely to give such bonds of kinship the same significance; nor could they very well perpetuate them, for the simple reason that Jews and conversos could not intermarry. The family circles within which Jews and conversos situated themselves would overlap less and less, moving ever closer to mutual exclusivity.

After 1430 there were a few cases of apostasy in the Jewish community of Morvedre. The conversion and subsequent transfer of these individuals to Valencia had the potential to create new kinship ties, or to reinforce old ones, between Jewish families in Morvedre and converso families in Valencia. This indeed occurred in certain cases, as will be seen. Yet the voluntary baptism of the new converts also, and perhaps more frequently, embittered their Jewish relatives and led to the severance of family ties.

After witnessing his two sisters and widowed mother convert and move to the capital, the place of residence of their new husbands, the rancorous Haim

---

[50] However, the witnesses Francesc Stheve, a silversmith, and Johan Salvador, a converso tailor, both described Jacme Català, the Agís' converso cousin and host, as a "good Christian" who goes to Mass (ARV: B Procesos, P. 2618: 122v–123r, 125r-v). This of course says nothing of what Català did at home. In subsequent decades there was certainly a connection between Jewish-converso commensality and converso Judaizing. See below.

[51] ARV: B Procesos, P. 2618: 110v–111r: "per ço com coneix per antiquitat los dessus dits e lur generacio e ell havia pus de LX anys e s'es criat entre lurs paretats."

Vinaig washed his hands of them and appropriated whatever property his mother had left behind in Morvedre. As long as the women had husbands to support them, they had no need of further contact with Haim. When her husband, the converso tailor Jacme Miquel, died, however, Haim's mother, Maria, turned to him for assistance. Haim refused her request; only the help of her daughters kept her from begging. In order to prevent his mother from getting her hands on any of his — or her own — property, Haim resorted to the artifice of conveying the property to the dowry of his wife Astruga. Orders from the bailiff general and Queen María in 1440 were necessary to compel Haim to provide his mother with a certain amount of wheat and other essentials annually. But Haim respected the agreement for only two years; afterward, according to his brother-in-law, the tailor Alfonso de Borja, "the said Vinaig stopped giving the said food to his said mother, and he [Alfonso] saw much dismay between them until she [Maria] died."[52]

Even if Haim Vinaig's rejection of his mother and sisters was an atypical Jewish response to the apostasy of relatives, in the decades after 1416 there simply were not enough Jewish conversions in Morvedre to have perpetuated much beyond 1430 the sort of conglomerate Jewish-converso honor culture wherein family loyalty had moved Jews and conversos to take up arms to defend and avenge one another. After the Maymó-Agí feud, Jewish families did not recruit converso friends and relatives to combat their rivals. With the passing of a kin-based Jewish-converso honor culture, the ties that bound Jews to conversos were primarily religious.

JEWS AND JUDAIZERS

Without family feeling drawing them together, there was little more than spiritual kinship to tie the Jews of Morvedre to the conversos of Valencia. The conversos' religious identification with Jews and Judaism, however, was not automatic. As the generations passed, a growing number of conversos naturally felt

[52] ARV: B Procesos, P. 36: n.f. (1463) records the lawsuit pitting Astruga, the widow of the now deceased Haim Vinaig, against her widowed daughter-in-law Horo, formerly the spouse of her son Jacob Vinaig, and her son Haim, still a minor. The suit concerned the status of the property Haim Sr. had once conveyed to Astruga's dowry and whether it now properly belonged to Astruga or Haim Jr. as his grandfather's heir. (The suit, decided in favor of Astruga in 1463, was still in the courts as late as January 1482 [ACA: C 3637: 154v–155r]). The trial record includes the testimonies of a few witnesses regarding Haim's break with his mother; among them is that of Alfonso de Borja (1463/4/21), which concludes: "e apres lo dit Vinag cessa de dar los dits aliments a la dita mare sua e veu entre aquells molta congoixa fins que aquella mori." ARV: B 1149: 16r (1440/2/20) treats the initial decision of the bailiff general that Haim must give 15 sous annually to his widowed mother. B 320: 104v (1451/6/17): after Maria cedes to the tailor Galceran de Montagut the amount of wheat Haim still owes her, Montagut sues for ten years' worth of wheat. This confirms the statement of Alfonso de Borja.

estranged from the Jewish faith of their ancestors. Accepting the faith into which they were baptized, intermarrying with Old Christians, and assiduously climbing the rungs of the ladder of Christian society, such conversos spared little thought for Jewish law and ritual or for the Jews down the road in Morvedre. Aldonça, a conversa who had married an Old Christian, Pere de Penyafel, thus sat at her window spinning one Friday (Jewish Sabbath) evening in 1475. Her conversa neighbor from across the street, Angelina, the wife of the broker Berthomeu de Leó, called out and motioned to her to come over. "Because she knew she was a conversa," Angelina reprimanded Aldonça for violating the Jewish Sabbath, saying, "Have you no conscience or shame that you would spin on this holy Friday night? To our Lord there is nothing so corrupt as to spin on Friday night or on Saturday." Aldonça retorted, "Save your words for the Jewish women of Morvedre!" Later, when Aldonça told her husband Pere about this exchange with Angelina, he admonished her, "You keep away from that one."[53]

Two conversas with opposing views of Jews and Judaism: unlike the assimilating Aldonça, Angelina was married to a Judaizing converso, with whom she observed the Jewish Sabbath, Passover, Yom Kippur, and other holy days. She had a brother Alfonso who at the age of seventeen returned to Judaism in Jerusalem; he later visited her in Valencia "in the clothes of a Jew" and gave her a piece of black stone from the Temple in Jerusalem. Angelina herself was "much praised" by other conversos for her knowledge of Jewish rituals. She gave alms to the Jews of Morvedre and visited their synagogue.[54] There was, then, a real basis for the remark of Aldonça, who associated Angelina's Jewish practices with her connections to the Jews of Morvedre.

Of course, a good number of Judaizing conversos had minimal or no demonstrable contact with the Jews of Morvedre. Converso families intent on maintaining a Jewish lifestyle and adhering to Judaism were capable of passing on a knowledge of Jewish law and ritual from one generation to the next without the help of unbaptized Jews. Nor did all Jews in Morvedre feel impelled to teach, provide kasher foodstuffs for, and otherwise assist those conversos who

---

[53] AHN: Inq., leg. 541, caja 1, no. 8: 14r (1485/10/13): the testimony of Aldonça, in which she recounts Angelina's reprimand: "'no teniu conciencia ni vergonya que fileu en [e]sta nit santa de divendres a vespre, que a nostre senyor no es cosa tant corrupta com filar lo divendres a vespre e en lo dia del dissabte,' y aquestes paraules digue la dita Angelina a ella dita testimoni perque sabia que era convessa." Aldonça's retort: "'que aquelles paraules digues a les juyes de Morvedre.'" Pere's admonishment: "'que's apartas de la companyia d'aquella.'"

[54] AHN: Inq., leg. 541, caja 1, no. 8: 20r–26r for the Jewish observances of Angelina and her spouse; 26r-v, 28v, regarding Angelina's brother, who returned to Judaism ca. 1472, his visit "en habit del juheu," and the "pedra del temple de Jerusalem . . . de color negra"; 20v bis, regarding how "Angelina era molt loada . . . per que sabia molt de les ceremonies judayques"; 29r-v, 20v bis for her contacts with the Jews of Morvedre. For more on the prominent role of conversas in preserving and passing on a knowledge of Jewish traditions, see Assaf 1933, 40; Levine Melammed 1986 and 1999, esp. 16–30.

somehow clung to Judaism. Still, many Jews did; many incorporated positive religious acts — "good deeds" — on behalf of conversos into their Jewish way of life, just as many conversos looked to the Morvedre Jews as living guides to the Jewish life they strove to follow. For the Jews in Morvedre, the Jewish community included Judaizing conversos, and the performance of meritorious acts entailed addressing the special needs of these conversos. The Jewish community thus conceived was necessarily changeable and unstable, but making room for conversos wishing to belong brought the Jews spiritual and material rewards.

In the latter half of the fifteenth century a wide range of commercial relationships between Jews and conversos contributed to this sense of community. Converso merchants exported the product of Morvedre's Jewish winegrowers; Jewish and converso silkweavers and merchants collaborated; converso wholesalers sold merchandise to Jewish retailers; and converso artisans and shopkeepers had Jewish clients.[55] Opportunities for Jews visiting Valencia on business to communicate with conversos, for diverse reasons, were ample. The Jewish visitors perforce lodged outside the three converso parishes and sometimes stayed in the local Muslim quarter; a member of the Façan family even owned a house in the moreria that other Jews used. Their movements outside their lodgings, however, were hardly restricted.[56]

The conversos trading with Jews were not all curious or enthusiastic about Judaism, but for those who were, business dealings facilitated the pursuit of Jewish interests. The converso clients and partners of the entreprenuer Salamó Çaporta must have been among the conversos to whom Salamó read the Torah and taught Hebrew.[57] Pere Alfonso, a converso notary who would only admit to his "inclination" for the Law of Moses, acted as the legal agent for some Jews in Morvedre. When he visited the town for this purpose, the Jews sent him wine and fruit at his lodging, and sometimes they even invited him to sleep at their house, where he ate food "prepared in the Jewish fashion." Pere otherwise expressed his Jewish "inclination" by reading Hebrew books, saying Hebrew prayers, irregularly observing some Jewish holy days, and visiting the synagogue in Morvedre.[58]

[55] See chap. 3; also AHN: Inq., leg. 537, caja 1, no. 5: 24r-v, 61v–62r (1464), regarding the Jewish customers of the converso silversmiths Joan Pardo and Gonzalo de Córdova; leg. 541, caja 2, no. 27: 54v (1492/8/20), regarding the Jewish woman from Morvedre who purchased hats from the shop of the conversa Ursula, the wife of Bernat Macip.

[56] ARV: B Procesos, P. 52: n.f. (1470/8/12) mentions that Quatorze, Crespi, and other Jews from Morvedre stayed in Façan's house in the moreria; P 2785, J. de Campos Jr.: n.f. (1474/1/19), regarding Isaac Crespi "moram trahens in moreria civitatis Valencie." ARV: B 1154: 420r-v (1469/7/26) is a license granted by Prince Fernando to Salamó Zameron, a Jewish cordmaker and "fidelis servus camere nostre" to reside in Valencia. Jews were fined for residing in the converso parishes and for working in the city for an extended period without a license — ARV: MR 86: 176v (1476/12/19), MR 87: 176r (1477/3/26) [Hinojosa Montalvo 1993a, nos. 765, 768].

[57] AHN: Inq., leg. 536, caja 2, no. 19: 1v (1488/5/12).

[58] AHN: Inq., leg. 534, caja 1, no. 10: 14r (1487/8/7), where Pere confesses to his contacts with

Despite the greatly diminished importance of kinship as an adhesive holding the community of Jews and Judaizing conversos together, there were still
a few conversos whose Jewish identity and way of life were enriched by communication with Jewish relatives. Jewish relations in Morvedre, for example,
sent matzah to the converso Gaspar Sayes on Passover.[59] Abraham and Jacob
Adzoni, kin of the conversa Clara Fuster, also made matzah for Clara and her
family. Owing to this family connection, the Fusters "had a lot of contact with
Jews from Morvedre." A rabbi even officiated at the wedding of one of Clara's
daughters, Beatriu.[60]

Yet within the families of Judaizing conversos there could be differences of
opinion as to the degree of contact that ought to be maintained with Jewish
relatives. Desiring to have, if possible, the best of both worlds, the Christian
and the Jewish, and therefore concerned to appear honorable and "Christian"
in the eyes of Old Christians, some conversos did not want to draw too much
attention to their Jewish roots. They desired to keep their Judaism secret or
even relegated to the realm of family traditions. Less assiduous in practicing
Judaism than his wife, Ursula, though willing enough to join her in quiet observances, the converso merchant Bernat Macip was discomforted and angered
by the frequent visits of her Jewish relatives from Morvedre, members of the
Quatorze family. Bernat quarreled with Ursula and threw the Jews out of his
house.[61] Beatriu, the daughter of the aforementioned Clara Fuster, was "much
displeased" when the rabbi presided at her wedding, and she argued with her
father about it. Her spouse, Joan de Berra, however, was content, feeling that
the rabbi's blessings gave the marriage "greater stability." As it turned out, Beatriu and Joan observed the Jewish Sabbath and some holy days in their own
home, though not as consistently and thoroughly as Beatriu's parents had.[62]

<hr/>

Jews in Morvedre. The record of this trial is incomplete. Nevertheless, it is clear that Pere Alfonso
was much interested in Judaism and performed Jewish rituals many times, though not consistently.
He was, however, a converso who hedged his bets, practicing and believing at least some tenets of
Catholicism at the same time.

[59] AHN: Inq., leg. 545, caja 1, no. 7: 39r-v bis (1489/10/15).

[60] AHN: Inq., leg. 539, caja 3, no. 16: 69r, 70r (1518/3/21–22), where Enric Fuster, the son of
Clara and Andreu, confesses about the Adzonis' matzah, how "tenien molta conversacio ab juheus
de Morvedre," and his sister's wedding with "hun juheu Rabi que'ls esposas segons la lley de Moyses." The testimonies of Enric's sisters, Aldonça, the wife of Perot Boïl (2v [1491/5/30]), and Beatriu (4r [same date]) provide additional information on Abraham Adzoni's visits to their parents'
house, his slaughtering of poultry for them, and Beatriu's Jewish wedding. Assaf 1933, 32, treats
the converso practice of having two Jews witness their betrothals before going to church for marriage before a priest.

[61] AHN: Inq., leg. 541, caja 2, no. 27: 21r (1492/6/30), the testimony of Catherina, wife of Pere
Johan, once maidservant to the Macips. In his own confessions, Macip asserted that he had never
performed Jewish ceremonies before his marriage to Ursula in 1475 or 1476 (70v [1492/8/29]).
In any case, the inquisitors sentenced Macip to death and relaxed him to the secular arm on 3–4
January 1493.

[62] AHN: Inq., leg. 539, caja 3, no. 15: 3v–4r (1489/11/12), Beatriu's confession: "la qual cosa
. . . fonch feta desplague molt a ella confessant e tantost devalla al dit son pare, dient li lo dit son

The Jews of Morvedre who chose to assist conversos with Jewish leanings seem implicitly to have held opinions akin to those of Jewish authorities like Rabbi Isaac Abarbanel. Abarbanel viewed the forced converts and those of their descendants who still in some way clung to Judaism as part of the Jewish people, as sinners who would be redeemed along with other Jews with the advent of the Messiah. Even if not moved, like Abarbanel, by a belief that the coming of the Messiah was imminent, these Jews of Morvedre seem to have shared a view like his that, ultimately, the conversos would fully return to Judaism and "take part in the process of the 'ingathering of the exiles'."[63] Hence the Jews took it upon themselves to educate conversos in Judaism and to persuade them to adhere to it. They worked for the salvation of the conversos, believing that their benevolent acts on behalf of the conversos would hasten the redemption of all, Jews as well as Judaizers.

Occasionally Jews assumed the role of missionary, proselytizing conversos vacillating between Christianity and Judaism. One of the Adzonis persuaded the converso doublet-maker Pere de la Rosa "that the Law of Moses was the true one" and that he would achieve salvation through performing Jewish ceremonies. Other already convinced conversos, like Joan Aldomar and Jaume Scrivà, then told Pere more about Jewish life and ritual.[64] The conversa Elionor Canella also succumbed to the religious arguments of an elderly Jew named Civello, which were seconded by a fervent Judaizing conversa, Ursula Forcadell. Elionor confessed that "a Jew induced her to believe in the Law of Moses, telling her that it is the only law, and that she should not believe that there is a Trinity but [should believe] that there is only one God who created the heavens, stars, sea, and sands." Ursula assured her that "the Jew had told her the truth."[65] Thus persuaded, Elionor and her husband, the converso barber Pere Moreno, attended the Forcadells' Passover seder. As well, they once observed Yom Kippur "at the induction of the rabbi of Morvedre, who is the father-in-law of Mossé Asseyo."[66]

---

pare 'que es aço Beatriu?'" The wedding took place in 1480. Leg. 539, caja 3, no. 16: 70r (1518/3/22) is the account of Enric, Beatriu's brother, regarding the opinion of Joan de Berra, who "dix que'n era content perque tengues major firmetat lo dit matrimoni."

[63] Regev 1997, 122–128; Silver 1959, 117–130; but cf. Lawee 2001, esp. 7–8.

[64] AHN: Inq., leg. 536, caja 1, no. 1: 6r (1483/2/3): "E mes dit e confesse que hun juheu de Morvedre, lo qual dien Pastor [Adzoni] lo pare, induy a ell confessant que la ley de Moyses era la verdadera." This apparently took place in the 1450s.

[65] AHN: Inq., leg. 538, caja 1, no. 2: 7r (1509/2/20). Here Elionor describes events occurring before 1482: "un jueu la induy a que cregues en la ley de Moyses, dient li que no havia altra ley sino aquella e que no cregues que hagues trinitat sino hun sol deu que fou lo cel, estelles, la mar e les arenes e que fes ceremonies judayques . . . e poch dies apres Na Forcadella . . . li dix que lo jueu li havia dita la veritat." In her first confession, made on 23 October 1482, Elionor said that she performed various Jewish ceremonies—the Sabbath, Yom Kippur, Passover—"a induccio de hun juheu vellet qui anava per ciutat, lo qual havia nom Civello." I have not been able to identify this individual or link him specifically to Morvedre.

[66] AHN: Inq., leg. 546, caja 2, no. 23: n.f. (1482/10/12), from the confession of Pere Moreno; see chap. 7, n. 17.

Normally Jews from Morvedre offered religious instruction to conversos who had already declared their interest in and loyalty to the Jewish faith. Members of some of the town's leading Jewish families were active as teachers among such conversos. Salamó Çaporta read the Bible and another book with conversos on the Jewish Sabbath. He also taught them how to read Hebrew. He allegedly kept a Torah scroll in the home of a converso for these purposes.[67] Mossé Xamblell went to the house of Franci de Calatayut, a converso silk-weaver, to speak with him about Jewish law.[68] Jacob Toledano and one of the Rodrichs frequently visited the home of the converso lawyer Francesc Palau and were even willing, according to a nanny who had worked in the Palau household, to eat the meat and poultry slaughtered by Palau. They apparently supplied Palau with Hebrew books, which Pere Vicent, a Valencian citizen, found on a desk in a secluded area of Palau's study. His curiosity aroused, Vicent mounted a spiral staircase leading from the secluded spot to another chamber, outside the door of which he heard a Jew — either Toledano or Rodrich — speaking in Hebrew to Palau's wife and other conversas.[69] For such Jews, educating the conversos was consonant with their status as upright, influential members of the Jewish community; it was what their poorer and less educated fellows expected of them.

Other Jews of unknown family affiliation acted as teachers and guides for conversos. A "bearded Jew" was espied on the roof of the house of a converso silkweaver, Bernat Guimerà, reading a Hebrew parchment to him. Guimerà bowed his head and uttered "Lord" in response to the Jew's words.[70] A certain Rabbi Abraham taught the sons and daughters of another converso silkweaver, Joan Francés, to read and write Hebrew at the request of their father.[71] The

[67] AHN: Inq., leg. 536, caja 2, no. 19: 1v (1488/5/12). This incomplete trial record provides only the charges against Salamó and the sentence — two years in exile and a monetary fine — that the inquisitors passed against him. Given Salamó's prominence and position as a royal favorite, it is unlikely that King Fernando would have approved such a sentence were the charges against him not credible.

[68] AHN: Inq., leg. 544, caja 1, no. 1: 11v (1488/8/7), from the testimony of Perot Joan, who was an apprentice living in the house of Calatayut between 1475 and 1484.

[69] AHN: Inq., leg. 545, caja 1, no. 6: 2r (1482/2/4), the testimony of Damiata, wife of the farmer Joan Loça, who had "criat" the daughter of Luys Palau, the brother of Francesc; 4v (9/27), the testimony of Pere Vicent.

[70] AHN: Inq., leg. 545, caja 1, no. 7: 13r-v (1482/1/28), the testimony of Anthoni Miquel. The incident with the "juheu barbut" took place in 1477 or 1478.

[71] AHN: Inq., leg. 538, caja 1, no. 6: 3v (1486/12/12). According to the witness Joan Aguilaret, who had converted to Christianity in 1476 or 1477, this Rabbi Abraham later received baptism and practiced alchemy as "master Luis." (This testimony is recorded again in leg. 540, caja 1, no. 12: 28r.) Other examples of Jews providing instruction to or reading texts with conversos are leg. 539, caja 3, no. 15: 2v (1489/11/10), where Clara Fuster confesses to having been "advised" about the festival of Sukkot by a Jew; leg. 540, caja 2, no. 21: 2r (1495), the sentence of Beatriu Guimerà, the wife of Manuel Çabata, who was said to have read "en hun saltiri sens *gloria patri* e alguna bolta en la biblia ab cert jueu"; leg. 542, caja 2, no. 22: 1r-v (1487/8/7), the sentence of Beatriu de Mur, in which she is sentenced to death for, among other things, "ser instruyda per un jueu en

visits of learned Jews left a great impression on converso children. Looking
back on her youth in her mother's house, in 1509 Violant Natera recounted
the following incident to Coloma Sanchis, her fellow prisoner in the inquisition's jail:

> many Jews used to come to the house of her mother; they taught many things.
> Once there came a Jew very learned in that law; it was a marvel to hear the things
> he said and knew about the law. And he gave amulets to her and her sisters. And
> that Jew and her mother debated about that law, and it was a blessing to hear how
> many good things and how many prayers and devotions he knew.[72]

Besides providing religious instruction and Hebrew texts to interested conversos,[73] Jews from Morvedre also supplied them with kasher foodstuffs, understanding that through the deliberate consumption of kasher food the conversos would internalize their identification with the Jewish people.[74] Since
many in their own community were involved in the production of kasher wine
on a large scale, obtaining some for the conversos' ritual purposes would not
have been difficult. Salamó Çaporta, who himself farmed the royal tax on wine
in Morvedre, gave kasher wine to conversos.[75] Abraham Adzoni sometimes
brought it with him on his frequent visits to his converso relations, the Fusters.[76] When he ran out of kasher wine, the converso Pere Alfonso would simply — or so it was alleged — "send for it at the tavern of the Jews [in Morvedre]."[77]
Provisioning conversos with meat slaughtered in accordance with the rules

---

les dites cirimonies judayques"; leg. 543, caja 1, no. 3: 2r, the incomplete sentence of Bernat Pin-
tor, merchant of Valencia, according to which a Jew taught him certain prayers and to read certain psalms.

[72] AHN: Inq., leg. 542, caja 2, no. 24: 17v–18r (1509/8/8), the confession of Coloma: "venien
a casa de sa mare molts juheus, los quals mostraren moltes cosses, e que una volta vingue hun
juheu molt sabent en aquella ley que era una maravella hoyr aquelles coses que deya e sabia de la
ley, y que'ls dona sengles nomines a ella e a ses jermanes, e que aquell juheu e sa mare disputaven
de aquella ley, e que era una benediccio hoyr los quantes bones coses deyen e quantes oracions e
devocions sabia." The Jew, later identified as one "Rabi Ysayas" (21v–22r), is said to have emigrated to Naples (most likely in 1492), where he became a favorite of the king there.

[73] The testimony of Luis Jaffer de Loriz, from the trial of the converso notary Pere Alfonso, is
of interest with respect to the circulation of Hebrew texts in Valencia. When he was in the house
of the notary Monsoriu, a Jew from Xàtiva, Salamó Zalmati, came bearing some gatherings printed
with Hebrew letters. Jaffer asked the Jew if he could read the Hebrew. The Jew said yes, adding
that "havia alguns christians [conversos] en la present ciutat de Valencia que la sabessen legir dita
letra" and that Pere Alfonso "conoxia be les letres ebrayques." See AHN: Inq., leg. 534, caja 1, no.
10: 5v (1486/10/9).

[74] Beinart 1981, 259–264; Brumberg-Kraus 1999, 230–231.

[75] AHN: Inq., leg. 536, caja 2, no. 19: 1v (1488/5/12); chap. 3.

[76] AHN: Inq., leg. 539, caja 3, no. 16: 14r (1491/6/4), the testimony of Aldonça Boïl, the daughter of Andreu and Clara Fuster.

[77] AHN: Inq., leg. 534, caja 1, no. 10: 9v (1487/8/1): "y quando no'n [kasher wine] tenia, em-
biava por ella a la taverna de los jodios."

of kashrut was a somewhat more difficult proposition. Jews visiting the homes of converso friends and relatives slaughtered poultry for them or brought meat to them as a matter of course.[78] The Old Christian servants working in these households were thus sometimes left in an uncomfortable position. When a Jew from Morvedre slaughtered "hens or capons" for the converso Manuel Ça-bata, his maidservant Caterina asked her colleague Brigida, "How are we going to eat what the Jew slaughtered?" Brigida answered resignedly, "There's nothing else for us."[79] Conversos themselves occasionally made the short trip to Morvedre to get kasher meat or dishes prepared by Jews.[80] One converso even asked his Jewish uncle, Gento Tarfon, to butcher an entire cow for him and to help him salt the meat "in Jewish fashion."[81]

The special dietary requirements of the Jewish Passover presented challenges to conversos determined to celebrate the holiday. Fortunately Jews in Morvedre were ready to assist the conversos in overcoming them. In response to the request of the conversa Ursula Forcadell, a Jew sent her from Morvedre a supply of ḥaroset, the mixture of nuts, fruit, spices, and wine symbolizing the mortar used by Jewish slaves in Egypt to make bricks. Ursula was well known among the Jews of Morvedre, for when they came to Valencia she welcomed them into her home "and showed them much honor."[82] Jews more commonly brought or had matzah delivered to the homes of converso friends and relatives.[83] Not all were quite so altruistic. One Jew from Morvedre wandered around the capital with a sack of matzah, selling it to conversos.[84]

[78] AHN: Inq., leg. 536, caja 2, no. 19: 1v, where Salamó Çaporta is punished for, among other acts, giving conversos ritually slaughtered meat; leg. 539, caja 3, no. 16: 4r, regarding Abraham Adzoni's slaughtering poultry for the Fusters; leg. 538, caja 1, no. 17: 1v, from the sentence against Joan Domènech, according to which he "mengat moltes vegades carn degollada de jueus." Domènech was relaxed to the secular arm for execution in 1492.

[79] AHN: Inq., leg. 540, caja 2, no. 19: 24v (1493/7/27), the testimony of Caterina: "E mes dix que la dita Brigida . . . li dix a ella testimoni que una volta era vengut hun juheu de Morvedre y havia degollat gallines o capons . . . , y ella testimoni li respos 'ay mezquina, com de lo que degolla lo jueu menjarem?' Y que la dicha Brigida li respos 'no que alre [sic] ay pera nosaltres.'"

[80] E.g., AHN: Inq., leg. 540, caja 1, no. 12: 32r (1491); leg. 546, caja 2, no. 23: n.f. (1482/10/12); chap. 7, n. 17.

[81] AHN: Inq., leg. 538, caja 2, no. 27: 38r (1491/1/31): "carn salada al modo judaych." The converso was Guillem Ramon Splugues.

[82] AHN: Inq., leg. 539, caja 1, no. 11: 1r-v, from the sentence against Ursula, relaxed to the secular arm for execution in 1506: "E per semblant havia fet moltes e diverses vegades la pascua del pa alis, me[n]gant pa alis, appi e lecugues e salsa de harocet, e hun any pera celebrar la dita pascua tramete a Morvedre a un jueu que li trametes de dita salsa e axi la'y tramete . . . e que quant venian jueus a la present ciutat los acullia a dormir e mengar en casa sua y'ls feya molta honrra."

[83] E.g., AHN: Inq., leg. 536, caja 2, no. 19: 1v (1488/5/12); leg. 544, caja 1, no. 1: 26r (1487/1/27); also n. 59. One converso, Joan Sanchis, a merchant of Valencia who happened to be staying at a Muslim's house in Paterna during the Passover, baked matzah in the oven of the local moreria (leg. 540, caja 2, no. 25: 7v–8r [1489/6/15]).

[84] AHN: Inq., leg. 536, caja 1, no. 1: 6r (1483/2/3), the testimony of Pere de la Rosa regarding his Jewish observances with his first wife, Ursula Vilanova: "lo qual pa [matzah] compraven de

Just as important as the Jews' efforts to provision conversos with kasher food for their own consumption were the invitations the Jews extended to conversos visiting Morvedre to eat with them in their homes. If by eating specially Jewish fare and avoiding food prohibited to Jews conversos consciously distinguished themselves from Old Christians and identified with Judaism, actually eating at a Jew's table in a Jewish home powerfully enhanced the conversos' sense of belonging to the Jewish community. Here conversos could witness a Jewish family eating, talking, and praying together — real flesh-and-blood people, more tangible than the archetypal guardians of the Law of Moses of the conversos' imagination. Commensality bound the conversos of Valencia more closely to the Jews of Morvedre.[85]

Jews could make a big impression on conversos by welcoming them into their homes on Jewish holidays. In sentencing Salamó Çaporta, the inquisitors asserted: "You have invited some Christian persons on your festivals, giving them food to eat prepared by Jews with Jewish ceremonies."[86] On Sukkot, the Feast of Tabernacles, Jews feted conversos in the booths built in the courtyards of their houses. As Aldonça, the widow of the merchant Francesc Esparça, recalled: "I ate in the home of a certain Jew, and at a table we ate chicken and other viands slaughtered and prepared by him. The Jew made a great festivity, adorning the whole house [or booth] with green reeds and other things."[87] The conversa Beatriu Guimerà fasted "together with a certain Jew" on the Ninth of Ab, in commemoration of the destruction of the Temple in Jerusalem. She then joined the Jew in breaking the fast, "supping with him at a table and from the same food; and at the beginning of the supper the Jew blessed the table in Jewish fashion."[88]

The rituals of the Passover seder, which were intended to break down social barriers between Jews, particularly strengthened the converso participants' feelings of connection with a Jewish community still bound to God by an ever-

---

hun juheu de Morvedre que anava venent per ciutat ab una talequa." This happened in 1453 or 1454.

[85] E.g., AHN: Inq., leg. 538, caja 1, no. 17: 1v (1492); leg. 538, caja 1, no. 25: 12v (1492); leg. 540, caja 2, no. 20: n.f. (1495); leg. 542, caja 2, no. 22: 1v (1487); leg. 543, caja 1, no. 3: 2r (1489).

[86] AHN: Inq., leg. 536, caja 2, no. 19: 1v: "has convidat en les tues festes algunes presones chris-tianes, donantlos a menjar de les viandes aparellades per juheus ab les ceremonies judayques."

[87] AHN: Inq., leg. 538, caja 1, no. 19: 4v: "E per lo semblant en casa de cert jueu mengi ab aquell en sa casa y en una taula menjant ab aquell gallines e altres viandes degollades y aparel-lades per aquell, lo qual jueu feu grant festa enramant tota la casa de canyes verdes e altres coses." Gostança, the widow of Guillem Ramon Splugues, also confessed to observing Sukkot with her husband's uncle, Gento Tarfon, a Jew of Morvedre then staying in Nules (leg. 538, caja 1, no. 25: 8v [1492/5/15]).

[88] AHN: Inq., leg. 540, caja 2, no. 21: 2r (1495), from the sentence of Beatriu: "E mes que feu hun dejuni de la destruccio de Jerusalem ensemps ab cert jueu, sopant ab ell en una taula e de unes matexes viandes, e al principi del sopar lo dit jueu beney la taula a modo judaych." Beatriu was penalized with a year of household imprisonment and a fine of 1,000 sous.

lasting covenant. That conversos were consuming matzah and kasher wine, instead of partaking of the Eucharist, greatly disturbed church authorities. In sentencing the converso marriage-broker Joan Domènech to death by burning, the inquisitors claimed that

> he has made and celebrated the Jewish Passover with Jews, eating matzah for eight days consecutively; and at the head of the table they ate celery and lettuce in the Jewish fashion, and before eating a Jew took bread [matzah] and a cup of wine and he blessed it in the Jewish fashion, and then he gave a piece of matzah and a sip of wine to the said Joan Domènech and to the others who were there with him celebrating the said Passover.[89]

Meals at the homes of Jews in Morvedre were sometimes followed by visits to the local synagogue. In June 1478 the conversos Bernat Guimerà and his wife, Violant, their two daughters and sons-in-law, Manuel Çabata and Perot Sanchis, and Galceran Ferrandis all enjoyed both the midday meal and supper in the home of the Jew Jacob and his wife, Perla. They ate well: beef and duckling at midday, beef and chicken for supper. At both meals Jacob said blessings in Hebrew, which Galceran Ferrandis, at least, "could not understand," and then passed around the wine cup from which they all drank. After supper,

> they all went to the synagogue, but they found that it was locked. The said Jew, Jacob, went to look for the Jew who had the key to the synagogue, and he returned with him and they opened the synagogue. The Jew who had the synagogue key was a little, old man . . . and he showed all the aforesaid [conversos] the synagogue . . . and they looked at a pool which they had covered there with some planks [the *miqveh*, the ritual bath]. They opened a cabinet where the Torah was kept, and the said old Jew took the Torah in his hands, and it seemed to the witness [Galceran Ferrandis] that he raised it [the Torah] above the heads of all the aforesaid [conversos], of whom some were kneeling and others were still on their feet. Afterward, the witness saw how the said Çabata opened his purse and took out a piece of gold . . . and with the said Guimerà, his wife, and all others present and watching, he gave the said gold piece to the said Jew who had shown them the Torah, telling him that he was giving him the said gold piece for oil for the lamp of the synagogue.[90]

---

[89] AHN: Inq., leg. 538, caja 1, no. 17: 1v (1492): "E axi mateix ha feta y celebrada la pasqua dels jueus del pa alis ensemps ab jueus, menjant pa alis per vuyt dies arreu e al principi de la taula menjaven api e lacugues al modo judaych, y ans de menjar un jueu prenia pa y una taça de vi e benehia aquell al modo judaych y apres donava un boci de pa y un glop de vi al dit Johan Domenech y als altres qui ensemps ab ell feyen la dita pasqua." Bokser 1984, 80–84; Fredman 1981, 10–11, 75–93.

[90] AHN: Inq., leg. 545, caja 1, no. 7: 15r-v (1489/8/28), from the testimony of Galceran in the trial of Violant, the wife of Bernat Guimerà, sentenced to death by the inquisition on 24 April

The Jews often led interested conversos on tours of the synagogue. Angelina, the wife of Berthomeu de Leó, confessed that on her first trip to Morvedre "she entered in the said *scoles* [synagogue] with other people [conversos]. . . . She saw the Torahs of the Jews, which they showed to her, the said confessant and witness, within a cabinet, just as they used to show them to other people."[91] Adolescents were included in these converso tour, or pilgrimage, groups. They were mature enough to comprehend what was being shown them but young and impressionable enough to be influenced by the true guardians of the Law of Moses, the Jewish friends of their Judaizing elders. Joan Guimerà, the son of Bernat and Violant, remembered that "with my said father and mother and others I entered there [the synagogue] many times and with many youths, among whom I recall there were the two sons of the late Pere Sanchis—the older was named Joan and the younger Miqualet."[92] In 1516 the older son, Joan, recalled one of these visits, which had taken place some forty years earlier: "they went to the synagogue of Morvedre, where they knelt and said a prayer, and they ate in the home of a Jew from whom he [Joan] sought penance and forgiveness."[93]

Perhaps not all conversos found their visits to the synagogue as affecting as did Joan Sanchis, who was moved to beg forgiveness from a Jew for the error of his Christian ways. Violant Guimerà asserted, when the inquisitors interrogated her in July 1489, "that she did not enter the synagogue for Jewish cere-

---

1490: "tots anaren a la sinagoga y trobaren la dita sinagoga tancada e lo dit Jacob, juheu, ana a cercar lo juheu qui tenia la clau de la sinagoga, e torna ab ell e obriren la sinagoga; e lo dit juheu qui tenia la clau de la dita sinagoga era hun home petit juheu vell . . . e amostra tota la sinagoga a tots los sobredits . . . e miraren una bassa quey havia cuberta ab unes posts e obriren un armari a hon stava la tora, e lo dit juheu vell trague la thora en la ma e que al parer del testimoni li semble que la posa damunt lo cap de tots los sobredits, dels quals ni havia alguns que stavan ajonoyllats, altres que staven de peus; e apres veu ell testimoni com lo dit Sabata obri la boça e trague una peça d'or . . . e present e vehent los dit Guimera, sa muller e tots los altres, dona la dita pessa d'or al dit juheu que mostrava la thora, dihentli que li donava la dita peça d'or per oli per a la lantia de la sinagoga." Galceran offers a shorter version of the same incident in his testimony of 24 January 1482 (13v–14r; also recorded in leg. 540, caja 2, no. 19: 7v–8r, the trial of Graciosa Guimerà, another daughter of Bernat and Violant). The confessions of Bernat Guimerà (29r-v, 44r) and Violant (31r-v, 42v bis) confirm Galceran's version of the synagogue visit.

[91] AHN: Inq., leg. 541, caja 1, no. 8: 29v (1486/7/14): "una volta entra en les dites scoles ab altres gents e que fou la primera vegada que ana a Morvedre . . . que veu les tores dels jueus que mostraren a ella confessant e testimoni dins un armari axi com les mostraven a altres gents." Angelina's assertion here that she nonetheless neither kissed nor made any other show of reverence to the Torah belies her later fuller confessions and the testimonies of other witnesses about her wide range of Jewish practices and knowledge of Judaism. See n. 54.

[92] AHN: Inq., leg. 544, caja 1, no. 18: 3r (1494/12/10): "ab los dits mon pare e mare y altres y entri molts vegades e ab molts fadrins, entre los quals so recordant hi eren los dos fills d'en Pere Sanchis, quondam, apellats lo major Johan e lo chich Miqualet."

[93] AHN: Inq., leg. 544, caja 1, no. 18: 5r (1516/5/23): "E mes dix que . . . foren a la sinoga de Morvedre, en la qual se agenolaren e feren oracio, e menjaren en casa de hun jueu del que s'en penit e demana misericordia."

mony but only to see what a Jewish synagogue was." A few months later, however, Violant admitted that she had knelt before the Torah; she had been, moreover, according to her own son Joan, a frequent visitor.[94] The reluctance of
conversos like Violant to disclose to the inquisitors the nature and depth of
their own spiritual experience in the synagogue of Morvedre is understand-
able, as is their willingness, under pressure, to recount the experiences of others.[95] Enric Fuster told the inquisitors about his encounter with the converso
Borriges and his wife on their return from Morvedre.

> he [Borriges] told me that they came from Morvedre, where they had gone under
> the pretext of the [running of] the bulls, [and] that they had entered the synagogue
> of the jueria of Morvedre and that they had prayed in the said synagogue, praying
> before the Torah, and that it was a meaningful experience.[96]

Indeed, most visitors to the synagogue would not have been just casual or curious tourists, but Judaizers intent on apprehending the symbols and texts of a
faith from which they were unavoidably distanced. When sentencing the Judaizer Ursula Forcadell in 1506, the inquisitors captured the spirit of her activities in Morvedre's synagogue:

> she went two other times to Morvedre . . . in the time when there were Jews there
> with the intention of seeing the synagogue and praying in it. She stayed in the

---

[94] AHN: Inq., leg. 545, caja 1, no. 7: 31v: "Empero dix ella confessant que no es entrada en la
dita sinagoga per cerimonia judayca sino per veure quina cosa era sinagoga dels juheus." On 21
October 1489, Violant conceded that when "hun home jueu . . . los posa la dit tora sobre lo cap
. . . ells feu ajonollar en terra." For the testimony of her son Joan, see n. 92. The lengthy record of
Violant's trial leaves little doubt that prior to her first abjuration before the inquisitors in 1482 —
that is, during the years when she had visited the synagogue — she and her husband, Bernat, had
been fervent Judaizers. Whether or not she was justly condemned to death as a relapsed heretic
for Judaizing after 1482 is another matter.

[95] Other Judaizing conversos confessed laconically, and sometimes disingenuously, about their
visits to Morvedre's synagogue. The notary Pere Alfonso said that he entered the synagogue "only
to look." He admitted viewing the Torah, but styling himself a free-thinker with only an "inclination" for Judaism, he pointed out that he had also visited some mosques (AHN: Inq., leg. 534, caja
1, no. 10: 14v). Joan Pardo admitted seeing the Torah but maintained that he did not pray in the
synagogue, since "at that time he [Joan] only believed in the things of our holy Catholic faith"
(leg. 542, caja 2, no. 32: 2v). Aldonça, the widow of Pere Manbrell (or Mambella), confessed that
she and Violant, the wife of Francès Çelma, only looked "and did not perform any ceremony" (leg.
544, caja 1, no. 2: 2r). Anthoni Tença admitted entering the synagogue with his wife and giving
alms to an old Jew, but nothing else (leg. 544, caja 2, no. 36: 4v–5r). Yet every one of these conversos was, judging by the evidence presented in their trials, a Judaizer. Pere Alfonso, Joan Pardo,
Pere Manbrell, and Anthoni Tença and his wife were all sentenced to death by the inquisition for
Judaizing (García Cárcel 1976a, 239–304). It is difficult to believe that their visits to the synagogue
were as dispassionate as they portrayed them.

[96] AHN: Inq., leg. 539, caja 3, no. 16: 70r (1518/3/22): "que'm dix que venien de Morvedre y
que en enscuses dels bous eren anats a Morvedre, que eren entrats en la sinoga de la juhiria de
Morvedre y que havien fet oracio en la dita sinoga e que feyen oracio a la tora y que era riqua cosa."

house of Jews and entered the synagogue, and she kissed the Torah, bowing down
before it with great devotion; and she gave money for oil for the lamp.[97]

The Jews who brought conversos into the synagogue and showed them the
Torah were engaged in missionary work, shoring up the Jewish faith of the ir-
resolute and deepening that of the committed. In some years at least, the Jews
made the point of inviting the conversos around the time of Shavuot, which,
according to tradition, was the anniversary of the giving of the Ten Commandments on Mount Sinai. For Judaizing conversos the first revelation of
the Torah in the synagogue of Morvedre was the most powerful moment in
their lives as Jews. Conversos had been born and baptized into a church where
they were told repeatedly that the New or Evangelical Law of the Christians
had superseded the Old Law of the Jews, the Law of Moses. The Judaizers
among them had decided to adhere to the Law of Moses; others still hedged
their bets, leaning toward Judaism while believing in some elements of
Catholic doctrine. But it was one thing to ponder the Law of Moses and follow some of its precepts, quite another to see it and hear it read in its ancient
and holy tongue. When the Jew removed the Torah from the cabinet, or Holy
Ark, and raised it over their heads, the conversos experienced something akin
to a reenactment of the revelation at Sinai. Displaying the Torah scrolls to the
Guimerà family and their friends, the Jew Jacob declared, "These parchments
are the Ten Commandments!"[98] For the first time in their lives, the conversos were seeing *the* Law of Moses. No wonder some of them fell to their knees
in admiration and devotion. Adolescent conversos sharing the moment with
their parents realized that they, too, were linked to the Jewish people and its
representatives in Morvedre through common adherence to the Law of
Moses, and that the continuation of the Old Law and its people was somehow
incumbent on them.

The conversos' genuflection before the raised Torah was more than an emo-
tional reaction to a potent Jewish symbol; it was a manifest denial of Christianity that physically paralleled the Catholic rituals they performed in church
but psychologically and spiritually differed from them. In church conversos
had to kneel like the rest of the congregation when the priest raised the con-

<hr/>

[97] AHN: Inq., leg. 539, caja 1, no. 11: 1r-v: "E que havia anat dos otres vegades a Morvedre . . .
en lo temps que havia jueus ab intencio de veure la sinagoga e fer oracio en aquella; e posava en
casa de jueus y entra dins la sinoga e besa la tora, inclinantse a d'aquella ab molta devocio e dona
dines pera oli a la llantia."

[98] AHN: Inq., leg. 545, caja 1, no. 7: 31r (1489/7/18), from the confessions of Violant Guimerà:
"E lo dit juheu Jacob qui los mostra tota lo sinogoga dix 'aquestes cartes son los deu manaments.'"
In her attempt to downplay the significance of her visit to the synagogue, Violant offhandedly re-
ferred to the Torah as a "sack full of parchments" and disingenuously recounted having asked
Jacob, "I also have parchment in my house, so should I adore it?" According to her, Jacob replied,
"Be quiet! You are sinning. These are the Ten Commandments!" See also n. 94. This visit and that
of the Borriges (n. 96) occurred around the time of Shavuot.

secrated host, the body of Christ, who was the Word. In Morvedre's synagogue conversos knelt before what they believed to be the Word of God: the Torah revealed to Moses at Sinai. When Joan Sanchis instinctively sought "penance and forgiveness" from a local Jew after genuflecting in the synagogue, he was influenced by, and at the same time reacting against, his earlier Catholic practices. The conversos who entered the synagogue of Morvedre and viewed the Torah were pledging allegiance to Judaism. For them the Torah, the synagogue, and the Jewish worshipers within were not museum pieces, artifacts of a dead Old Law, but living symbols of and custodians of a vital faith, the Law of Moses.[99]

One way in which Judaizing conversos expressed their devotion to Judaism and their fundamental conviction that through observing it they would ensure the salvation of their souls was to give alms to the Jews of Morvedre. The conversos believed that such charity was spiritually meritorious and that, in return, the Jews would pray for the souls of their dead loved ones and for the health of the ill. Among the charges the inquisition's prosecutor presented against Pere Alfonso was that "when he or his children or wife were sick, he received the consolations and good wishes of Jews, and he had oil and alms given to Jews so that they would pray and fast for them."[100] Clara Fuster donated a glass lamp to the synagogue but had to ask a Jewish woman to deliver it there for her. Clara told the woman that they would share the "merit"—that is, of the Jews' prayers.[101] Her daughter Aldonça, both as a maiden and as a married woman, often gave money to her Jewish relative, Abraham Adzoni, so that Abraham would distribute it among poor Jews on her behalf "for the love of God."[102]

The donations conversos offered the Jews of Morvedre often had specific ends. Conversos provided money for the oil that was burned in the lamps of

[99] My interpretation of the conversos' synagogue visits has benefited from Marcus 1996, 9–13, 74–101; Brumberg-Kraus 1999, 260–262. The assertion of Goldberg 1987, 113, that the adornment of the Torah with silver crowns led Jews to equate the Torah with a royal personage supports the view that for the conversos the raised Torah was like the embodied Word of God, similar yet superior to the raised host, the embodied Christ/Word.

[100] AHN: Inq., leg. 534, caja 1, no. 10: 9v (1487/8/1): "y quando el o sus figos o muger stavan mal recebia consolaciones e salutaciones de jodios, e fazia dar olio e limosna a jodios porque rezassen e ayunassen por ellos." Pere's response to this charge was rather disingenuous. Not willing to admit to more than an "inclination" for Judaism, and at times presenting himself as a person interested in all religions, he maintained that he would give charity to anyone seeking alms whether the person was "juheu, moro o christia o vergonyat o mendicant" (11r). Pere may well have been so liberal. Even so, there can be no doubt that his attachment to Judaism was greater than that to Christianity (or to Islam) and that the alms he gave to Jews, and the prayers he hoped to get from Jews, meant more to him.

[101] AHN: Inq., leg. 539, caja 3, no. 16: 7v (1482/3/12), from the confession of Clara: "li dix que la volia donar a una sinogua de juheus y que hauria part del merit."

[102] AHN: Inq., leg. 539, caja 3, no. 16: 2v (1491/5/30), from the confession of Aldonça: "dines que donas per mi per amor de deu . . . es a saber per que donas a juheus o a persones de manacio."

the synagogue for the souls of the deceased.[103] They no doubt had in mind the souls of departed conversos as well as of Jews. Sometimes, as in the case of Clara Fuster, they even contributed the lamps.[104]

Conversas, in particular, were active collecting alms for poor Jewish girls. The money was used to provide the girls with dowries. Damiata, the wife of Francès Ramayo, was one of the main organizers of this dowry fund. She would send her maidservant "to go collecting for a certain charity among the conversa ladies, which served for marrying [poor] Jewish girls." Normally the conversas donated money, but sometimes they gave articles of clothing as well.[105]

The impulse of Valencia's conversos to give charity to the Jewish community of Morvedre originated in their profound sense of belonging to it and sharing its devotion to the Law of Moses. The alms given were but a small compensation for all that the Jews of Morvedre did for them: providing religious instruction, supplying kasher food, and including them and their loved ones in their prayers. The Jews, however, neither sought nor expected reward — at least not from the conversos and not immediately in this world. In assisting the conversos the Jews of Morvedre saw themselves to be performing so many *mitzvot*, positive acts that ultimately would bring about the redemption of the Jewish people, which, in their eyes, consisted of Jews and Judaizers.

THE PASSIONS OF GUILLEM RAMON SPLUGUES

Participation in this tightly knit community of Jews and Judaizing conversos, however, presented certain dangers to the Jews. Through their association with conversos, who were all, to varying degrees, "Christian," the Jews were exposed more frequently than they had been before 1391 to Catholic doctrine and practice. Contact with the committed Judaizers among the conversos was, paradoxically, perhaps the riskiest thing for the Jews, since the Jews saw that one could, at least until the advent of the Spanish Inquisition in 1482, convert and enjoy the social and economic rewards of Christian society and yet still practice Judaism with relative impunity and even retain the fellowship of Jews.

[103] E.g., AHN: Inq., leg. 541, caja 2, no. 31: 1v; leg. 541, caja 2, no. 37: 2r; also nn. 90, 97.

[104] E.g., AHN: Inq., leg. 534, caja 1, no. 10: 9v; leg. 538, caja 2, no. 27: 14v–15r (1482/2/26). See also Assis 1997, 218; Toaff 1996, 89–94.

[105] AHN: Inq., leg. 541, caja 1, no. 8: 20v bis (1486/7/20), the testimony of Magdalena Aronoz in the trial of Berthomeu de Leó: "estant en casa del dit Ramayo, acostumava de anar acaptar certa almoyna entre les dones convesses que servia pera maridar juhies." She further notes that Angelina, Berthomeu's wife, contributed to the charity. This same organized caritative work on behalf of poor Jewish women, and occasionally men, is attested to in numerous other trials: leg. 540, caja 2, no. 25: 7r; leg. 541, caja 2, no. 27: 11v–12r ("pera les pobres donzelles juhies de Morvedre"), 20v–21r ("clochetes y capellets pera les dites juhies pobres"), 45v; leg. 544, caja 2, no. 25: 9r, 18v–19r; leg. 545, caja 1, no. 7: 27v, 43v bis.

Whether because of religious conviction or a cynical aspiration to have their cake and eat it too, some Jews from Morvedre did seek baptism in the years after 1416. The converts were, however, very few and far between, never sufficiently numerous at any given time to have alarmed the Jewish community. Jahudà Maymó, who knew conversos and enjoyed the support of some of them during his family's feud with the Agís, converted in 1433. His decision was more political than religious, prompted by the need to escape the ascendant Agís and the local bailiff who favored them. Life as a Christian in the capital was safer.[106] In 1476 the livestock broker Joan Gerònim de Vallterra, "once Jew, resident of the town of Morvedre, and now newly made Christian," married Johanna, the widow of Berthomeu Abat, a farmer of Valencia. Love or religious beliefs must have drawn Joan into the church; it was almost certainly not greed, for Johanna came with a dowry of only 30 pounds.[107] Two other Jews, perhaps from Morvedre, converted around the same time. One, who took the name Joan Aguilaret, was knifed by the converso Guillem Ramon Splugues. The other, the "Rabbi Abraham" who taught Hebrew to the children of the converso Joan Francès, became "master Luis" and practiced alchemy.[108]

Guillem Ramon Splugues, a broker in Valencia, was baptized in Morvedre in 1463 at the age of thirty-five. The son of Gento del Castillo and Cinha, the sister of Jahudà and Mossé Maymó, he was born in 1428, not in Morvedre but in a Jewish settlement on the "Quart road" in the terme of Valencia. His parents, however, had come from Morvedre and still resided there at least part-time. On account of their involvement in the Maymó-Agí feud and their prosecution for possible complicity in the murder of the Agís' converso cousin, Pau de Sant Martí, Gento and Cinha left the kingdom in the early 1430s and moved to Algiers, where Splugues was raised. When Splugues was a young man he returned with his parents and three siblings to the kingdom and to Morvedre.[109]

---

[106] Meyerson 2003b.

[107] APPV: P 21593, J. de Carci: n.f. (1476/5/5): acknowledgment of the receipt of the dowry by "Johanne Geronimo de Vallterra, olim judeo, vicino ville Muriveteris, nunc vero noviter facto christiano, bestiarum cursore ac etiam potrero civitatis predicte presente."

[108] AHN: Inq., leg. 538, caja 2, no. 27: 79r (1491/10/27); see n. 71.

[109] AHN: Inq., leg. 538, caja 2, no. 27: 10v (1482/2/13), 70v (1491/9/22), where Splugues provides detail on his early life and age. Although Gento had perhaps come from Xàtiva, he settled in his wife's hometown. ARV: B Procesos, P. 2618 shows, through the testimonies of Jacob Legem (78r–79r) and Mossé Gallego (84r-v), that the couple lived in Morvedre from at least 1424 until 1430. Splugues's three siblings were Mossé del Castillo, who remained in Morvedre and became a silversmith; a sister whose name is unknown but who also lived and married in Morvedre; and the Kabbalist Rabbi Yosef Alcastiel (or "del Castillo") of Xàtiva, on whom see Scholem 1955, 169–170. Scholem, however, does not assert that Alcastiel and Splugues were brothers, only relatives. Even though the Kabbalist moved to Xàtiva, there is no reason to doubt that Splugues himself had lived in Morvedre when a Jew. He states (10v) that he converted in "the town of the archdeacon,"

There Splugues became an administrator of the synagogue; he drew on his religious erudition to deliver sermons to the other Jews.[110]

A respected member of the Jewish community and a scholar of local note,
Splugues was not a likely convert. But in addition to his passion for Jewish
learning, Splugues had another fatal passion: a passion for Christian women.
As he told Cathalina Ortíz, his Old Christian lover during the months between
his second public reconciliation by the inquisition in September 1487 and his
final arrest by the inquisition at the end of 1490, "among Christian women I
was very worldly."[111] Splugues further confessed to Cathalina, while recount-
ing the story of his conversion, that he had fathered a son with one of these
women. Despite the woman's desire to have the child baptized, Splugues saw
to it that he was raised as "a good Jew."[112] The bastard son of a Jewish father
and a Christian mother could not easily have gained acceptance from the Jewish community. Splugues's parents, Gento and Cinha, were not terribly impressed by his efforts to make the child Jewish. They were in fact so disgusted
by their son's dissolute behavior that they refused to invite him to his own sister's wedding, mentioning him "neither at the beginning nor at the end of the
marriage ceremony."[113] This deliberate snub deeply wounded and outraged
Splugues. In order to strike back at his family, Splugues informed Cathalina,
"I immediately received baptism."[114]

When Splugues added, "[But] first I had a dispute with [Christian] masters
in theology," Cathalina asked, "Then did they persuade you that the Christian
law is the true law and yours the false law?" Splugues replied by disdainfully
thrusting back his shoulders, dismissing the very notion that Christian theologians could have bested him in a religious debate.[115] He stuck to his story of
the conversion. Cathalina was incredulous: "I can't believe that you became a

---

that is, Morvedre. As the evidence from his trial demonstrates, Splugues continued to maintain
connections with Jewish relatives — his maternal uncle Gento Tarfon, his brother Mossé, and his
sister — and friends in Morvedre. His contact with Xàtiva was, by comparison, minimal. Baer 1961,
2: 360, who offers a brief account of the trial of Splugues, implies (496, n. 33) that Splugues was
from Xàtiva because the inquisitors interrogated witnesses there in February 1482. These witnesses, however, were Castilians who had met Splugues in Alacant (see n. 148).

[110] AHN: Inq., leg. 538, caja 2, no. 27: 34v (1491/1/28); also n. 116.

[111] AHN: Inq., leg. 538, caja 2, no. 27: 34r: "'yo fuy molt mundanal entre christianes.'"

[112] AHN: Inq., leg. 538, caja 2, no. 27: 34r: "e respos lo dit Splugues a ella testimoni, 'encara
que digues la mare que'l batejassen, yo havieu de fer ell es bon juheu.'" This moved Cathalina to
ask, "How is it that he is a good Jew while you are a Christian?" (34v)

[113] AHN: Inq., leg. 538, caja 2, no. 27: 34v: "Respos lo dit Splugues, 'no't dich que per deu y
per aquell deu que yo y tu creem esser deu que no'n he fet sino per ontes, que no me convidaren
a les bodes ni feren mencio de mi al començ ni a la fi del matrimoni.'"

[114] AHN: Inq., leg. 538, caja 2, no. 27: 34v: "'ple d'iniquitat y de malicia pensieu que los fore
ontes e digui donchs "yo mudare de ley" e de continent yo'm bategi.'"

[115] AHN: Inq., leg. 538, caja 2, no. 27: 34v: "'e primer tingui una disputa ab mestres en the-
ologia.' E ella testimoni li respongue, 'donchs feran te conexer que la ley christiana era verdadera
e la tua ley era falsa?' E lo dit Splugues respos lançant ho atras les spatles."

Christian over such a little thing, you who were administrator of the synagogue, such a good preacher of the Jewish law, and, as you say, such a good biblical scholar."[116] Splugues insisted,

> I cannot make you believe what you don't want to believe, but I swear to you by the God who created heaven and earth that I have not become a Christian for any other reason. Just as soon as I did it I regretted it.[117]

Later, in a desperate attempt to avoid conviction and execution by the inquisition as a relapsed heretic, Splugues would maintain that he had converted because the rabbis could not resolve certain doubts he had regarding the coming of the Messiah.[118] Yet difficult as Cathalina found it to credit his account of the postwedding baptism, this new story was even more improbable. A converso like Splugues who persistently practiced Judaism during the twenty-seven-year interval between his baptism and final arrest by the inquisition could not have harbored any serious doubts about the legitimacy of the Jewish faith and rabbinic interpretations of the Messiah's future advent. On the contrary, as Splugues told Cathalina on more than one occasion, "I am what I used to be; I am a Jew."[119] Once he wept openly before her as he related "the miracles and other things of Queen Esther, and other miracles of the Old Law."[120]

Cathalina's efforts to loosen his attachment to Judaism proved fruitless. She argued with Splugues, asserting that because of the Jews' refusal to accept Jesus as the Messiah,

> you [Jews] have never had honor but are dishonored throughout the world; you are the most vile of all people. All dishonor you and have you under their foot, and they spit in your face. The Moors say that they would rather be Christians than Jews.[121]

[116] AHN: Inq., leg. 538, caja 2, no. 27: 34v: "'no puch creure que tu te hajas fet christia per tant poca cosa e que si es estat administrador de la sinoga e tan bon sermonador de la ley judayca e esser tan bon biblista, com tu dius.'"

[117] AHN: Inq., leg. 538, caja 2, no. 27: 34v: "E lo dit Splugues respos, 'e dir yo no vos poria fer creure lo que no voleu creure, mes jur vos en deu que ha fet lo cel y la terra que yo no'n me he fet per altra cosa christia; e tant prest com ho hagui fet tant prest me has penedit.'"

[118] AHN: Inq., leg. 538, caja 2, no. 27: 45r (February 1491), where Splugues responds to the list of accusations against him: "per quant demanava certs duptes al juheus rabins de la venguda del messies y perço no li saberen donar solucio als dits dubtes ell confessant, lavors conexent que era vengut lo messies, se feu christia." Some Jews of course had such doubts — on which see Lawee 1996 — but Splugues was not one of them.

[119] AHN: Inq., leg. 538, caja 2, no. 27: 32v: "'yo so aquell que solia esser y juheu so.'" Cathalina recounts other conversations (34v, 35v) with Splugues in which he says the same thing.

[120] AHN: Inq., leg. 538, caja 2, no. 27: 32v: "lo dit Splugues contava a ella testimoni los miracles y coses de la Reyna Ester y altres miracles de la ley vella, y quant contava les dites histories vehia ella dita testimoni que lo dit Splugues plorava." See Walfish 1993, 125, on the significance of this text for crypto-Jewish conversos.

[121] AHN: Inq., leg. 538, caja 2, no. 27: 36r: "'mirau si may haveu tengut honor sino que sou

Splugues replied scornfully, saying that were any Jew to believe that Jesus was the true Messiah, other Jews would excommunicate and stone him. He went on to call Jesus a "thief" and "a man of evil life."[122] When Cathalina tried to frighten him with the spectre of the inquisition, Splugues stated, "if they were burning me" for being a relapsed Judaizer, "I would say 'since I have to be burned, I want to die as a Jew.'" "Truly," Splugues continued, "I would much prefer to die as a Jew than as a Christian."[123] In the event, he got his wish. Meanwhile, Splugues carried on his stormy relationship with Cathalina. He spent his last night of freedom, before his final arrest by the inquisition, in her bed.[124]

Cathalina Ortíz was not the only woman in the postbaptismal life of Guillem Ramon Splugues. Before her there had been several others. In February 1491 the inquisitorial prosecutor accused Splugues of having persuaded seven or eight Christian women to become Jews, and of sleeping with such women "with the intention of producing Jewish offspring, in order to spread the Law of Moses."[125] These charges, which seem to have originated in some inquisitor's nightmare, were not without substance.

Splugues's first wife after his conversion was an Old Christian from Valencia named Barbara, the sister of the carter Berthomeu Castell. By all accounts, Splugues induced Barbara to share his Jewish way of life. Together they observed the Sabbath, Passover, Yom Kippur, Sukkot, and Purim.[126] According

---

[122] AHN: Inq., leg. 538, caja 2, no. 27: 36r: "Respos lo dit Splugues e dix a ella testimoni que si los juheus creguessen que si algun juheu cregues que Jhesu Christ . . . fos lo verdader messies los juheus lo tendrien per excomunicat e'l pedregarien. . . . Dix lo dit Splugues que fos hun ladre . . . hun home de mala vida."

[123] AHN: Inq., leg. 538, caja 2, no. 27: 36v: "de la Inquisicio lo dit Splugues respos, 'si a mi me cremaven . . . yo diria "puix cremat tinch estar, yo vull morir com a juheu" . . . de veritat . . . que mes amaria morir com a juheu que no com a christia.'"

[124] In his appearance before the inquisitors on 28 April 1491, Splugues attempted to defame Cathalina and thus disqualify her testimony against him (AHN: Inq., leg. 538, caja 2, no. 27: 53r-v). On 22 September he contradicted his previous suggestions that Cathalina was his enemy by admitting to having slept in her house the night before his arrest (70v). Their relationship, however, was volatile. The mason Joan Fortuny, for instance, attested to one of their arguments in which Splugues blasphemed Jesus and the Virgin Mary and Cathalina threatened to rat on him to the inquisition (73v).

[125] AHN: Inq., leg. 538, caja 2, no. 27: 38r–42r (1491/2/5) is the list of charges against Splugues. No. 26 asserts that he "ha persuadit . . . a moltes persones christianes que's fossen juhies . . . set o huyt persones christianes qui ara per ell se eran fetes juhies" (41r); no. 20 states that "quant se acosta ab dones . . . les diu que es jueu, e com jueu ha carnal ajustament ab aquelles, volent ho dir ab intencio de engendrar jueu per augmentar la ley mosayca" (40v). With regard to conversos having liaisons with Old Christian women, Splugues was not unique — see Assaf 1933, 35–36.

[126] AHN: Inq., leg. 538, caja 1, no. 25: 8r–9v (1492/5/15), the confessions of Gostança, the second wife of Splugues, who, before her marriage to Splugues, lived with him and Barbara and practiced Judaism with them. Leg. 538, caja 2, no. 27: 3r, 12r–15r, 19r-v is all relevant evidence from the trial of Splugues.

to Ursula Trilles, an Old Christian who entered the Splugues household in 1467 at the age of five and worked there as a maidservant for twelve years, Barbara was just as active as her master in the performance of Jewish rituals. The two of them persuaded Ursula to join them in their Jewish observances, telling her, for instance, that the Jewish Passover was just like the Last Supper of Jesus, or that they did the same things as all Christians and that it was all in "the service of God." Ursula knew better. Even so, Splugues managed to marry her off to the recently baptized converso Joan Aguilaret, whom the inquisitors later burned for Judaizing.[127] In a vain effort to avoid the same fate, Splugues and another converso, Jaume Viabrera, attempted to bribe Ursula to reveal nothing about their Judaizing to the inquisition.[128]

Barbara died sometime in 1479. Ursula left Splugues's house three months later. In 1482 Splugues married Gostança, a member of his household and his lover since at least 1476. Gostança, a conversa, had entered Splugues's service along with her husband Gonçalbo de Carmona, around 1470. After Gonçalbo's death some eighteen months later, Gostança had stayed on and eventually became the object of Splugues's affections.[129] By 1477 she was pregnant. Splugues sent her to Almenara for the birth. While in Almenara Gostança was visited by a Jewish physician from Xàtiva, one master Vidal, who gave her an amulet, or piece of parchment, inscribed with Hebrew letters. As intended, the amulet helped effect a speedy and safe delivery. News of Splugues's marvelous birthing amulet spread quickly in Valencia. Old Christians and conversos borrowed it to assist their own wives and lovers.[130]

The entrance of a Jew, master Vidal, into the comfortable world of Splugues some fourteen years after his baptism was not wholly fortuitous, an anomaly in the life of a converso who had abandoned the Jewish community. Splugues may well have asked his brother in Xàtiva, the Kabbalist Yosef Alcastiel, to send Vidal with the Hebrew amulet to Gostança.[131] Despite his painful and abrupt break with his family in Morvedre, Splugues had not severed all ties with the Jewish community. In fact, the rift between Splugues and his relatives had not

---

[127] AHN: Inq., leg. 538, caja 2, no. 27: 71r–73r (1491/9/24). Ursula recalled Splugues and Barbara's telling her, "'Ursola fes quant nosaltres fem, que tots los christians ho fan y es servey de deu'" (72r). Ursula told the inquisitors, "que be conexia que no eran coses de christians."

[128] AHN: Inq., leg. 538, caja 2, no. 27: 74r–77r (1491/9/30).

[129] AHN: Inq., leg. 538, caja 2, no. 27: 72v–73r.

[130] AHN: Inq., leg. 538, caja 1, no. 25: the testimonies of Gostança (4v–5r [1492/3/7]) and Splugues (5r–6v [1492/1/25, 3/7]). One of the Old Christians who borrowed the amulet was the notable Perot de Castellvi. The parchment amulet is reproduced in the record of Splugues's trial (leg. 538, caja 2, no. 27: 3r). The inquisitors asked Maymó Zalmati, a Jew of Xàtiva, to translate the words inscribed on the amulet. He said that they were "the names of angels and that the Jews are accustomed to give them to Jewish women who are giving birth." See also Scholem 1955, 170, who relates the inscriptions on this amulet to books of "practical Kabbalah."

[131] Scholem 1955, 170, is not willing to go so far as to assert that Vidal received the amulet from Alcastiel because of the errors in the inscriptions on the amulet.

been left gaping for long. Realizing that his conversion was a momentary act of madness and seeing that he still lived as a Jew, Splugues's parents and siblings had taken him back into the fold. His father bequeathed at least part of his library to him. Splugues frequently read these Hebrew books, but when the Spanish Inquisition set up shop in Valencia in 1482, he delivered them to one of his brothers, most likely to Yosef in Xàtiva.[132]

The other brother, the silversmith Mossé del Castillo, came from Morvedre with their sister to dine with Splugues, Barbara, and Gostança on at least one occasion.[133] When he took ill, Mossé occupied a bed in Splugues's house for seven months. For five of those months Splugues was away on business in Alacant, but when he was at home Splugues arranged to have Jews supply his brother with kasher meat.[134] The two brothers also did some business together; they were perhaps partners in Splugues's leasing of the butcher shops in Nules. Their dealings, however, eventuated in a dispute that the lawyer Gabriel de Riusech arbitrated in 1477.[135] During his final trial before the inquisition in 1491, Splugues would, out of sheer desperation, blame Mossé for having "perverted" his Old Christian wife Barbara "to the Law of Moses."[136] Ten months in the inquisition's jail was enough to leave most anyone grasping at straws.

Splugues remained on good terms with his maternal uncle in Morvedre, the Jewish silversmith Gento Tarfon. He commissioned Tarfon and other Jews to produce large quantities of kasher wine for export to Jewish communities in North Africa.[137] At his request, his uncle also ritually slaughtered a cow.[138] Splugues even received an invitation from Jewish kin or friends to attend a

[132] AHN: Inq., leg. 538, caja 2, no. 27: the testimonies of Joan Trilles, 2v (1490/12/7), and Ursula Dezpina, 5r, marginalia (1491/2/7). Splugues confessed to possessing alchemical works and a scroll of the Book of Esther in Hebrew (31r, 70r).

[133] AHN: Inq., leg. 538, caja 2, no. 27: 14v–15r (1482/2/26), the testimony of Elisabet, daughter of Pere Beltran, who lived in Splugues's house for three months in 1480.

[134] AHN: Inq., leg. 538, caja 2, no. 27: 44v, from the confessions of Splugues.

[135] APPV: P 13415, J. Calaforra: n.f. (1477/8/23). In the course of his confessions to the inquisitors on 3 January 1491 Splugues mentioned that in 1476 or 1477 he was lessee of "les carniceries de Nules" (AHN: Inq., leg. 538, caja 2, no. 27: 38r). Splugues's litigation with Abraham Aluleyço, Jew of Morvedre, and Ramon Sparech, butcher, may also be related to the leasing of the butcheries of Nules (ACA: C 3633: 41r-v [1479/3/3]).

[136] AHN: Inq., leg. 538, caja 2, no. 27: 69r (1491/9/22). Splugues asserts here that he went to Naples, leaving his sick brother in his house, and that when he returned, Mossé "havia pervertida" Barbara "a la ley de Moyses." Splugues continues to claim, quite implausibly, that he then became angry with Barbara on account of her Judaizing and that he had held Jewish rituals in abhorrence since his own baptism. None of Splugues's assertions here accord with the abundance of evidence about his own postbaptismal Judaizing, to which many witnesses and he himself attested.

[137] AHN: Inq., leg. 538, caja 2, no. 27: 37v (1491/1/31); chap. 3, n. 26. Splugues was also involved in the production of liquor (aygues forts). He had a Jew from Vitoria named Cahon living in his house and distilling the liquor for a salary (12r-v, 14v–15r, 44v).

[138] See n. 81.

wedding in the jueria of Morvedre, this some fourteen years after his exclusion, while still a Jew, from his sister's wedding.[139]

In the eyes of the inquisitors, and of all those who feared that a Judaizing cancer was eating away at the Catholic church from the inside, Guillem Ramon Splugues was a very dangerous man. He was like a wolf among the flock of New and Old Christians. In contrast to almost all the conversos resident in Valencia, who were the second- or third-generation descendants of Jews, Splugues had himself been a Jew, and a learned one at that. His conversion, moreover, had been insincere, a step taken in the heat of anger and near insanity. Once he recovered his senses, he saw himself as a Jew, endeavored to live like one, and reestablished close relations with the Jews in Morvedre. Worse still, he was a ladies' man, one capable of coaxing Christian women not just into his bed but also into his Jewish religion.

Neither of his wives could resist him. Barbara, the Old Christian, spent her married life with him as a Jew. Gostança, the conversa, had apparently known little of Judaism prior to entering Splugues's household. Splugues and Barbara soon convinced her that she would be saved through observing the Law of Moses. Before and after Barbara's death, and before and after she and Splugues first abjured their Jewish errors before the inquisition, Gostança practiced Judaism with Splugues. Her love for her husband and devotion to the Law of Moses would earn her the same terrible end as him.[140]

Restless, combative, and self-assured, Splugues spread his corruptive influence beyond the confines of his house. Groups of conversos would gather to listen to him read "the stories of Queen Esther." Using Hebrew texts in his possession, Splugues would translate extemporaneously from Hebrew into the "Valencian tongue."[141] He also led conversos in Jewish prayers. On "one day of the year" — perhaps Rosh Hashanah or Yom Kippur — "he read to many persons nodding."[142]

---

[139] AHN: Inq., leg. 538, caja 2, no. 27: 13r-v (1482/2/25). His brother-in-law, Berthomeu Castell, testifies how in 1477 or 1478 "ell dit testimoni veu al dit Splugues en Murvedre a casa de un juheu a les sposalles e bodes de un juheu. E aqui menjava e bevia e stava ab los juheus."

[140] AHN: Inq., leg. 538, caja 1, no. 25: the trial of Gostança.

[141] AHN: Inq., leg. 538, caja 2, no. 27: 31v (1491/1/24). Splugues confesses that in 1478 a number of conversos, whose names he provides, "pregaren a ell confessant que los legis les istories de la Reyna 'Ster y (..) y ell confessant tenia hun libre ebraych en lo qual ell confessant los legi e los splanava del ebraych en la present lengua valenciana les dites histories y com ell confessant los hague lestes y declarades les dites histories."

[142] AHN: Inq., leg. 538, caja 2, no. 27: 78v–79r (1491/10/27). Here Splugues responds to the testimony of specific witnesses: "Mes anant diu lo dit testimoni que lo dit en Splugues los divendres al vespre legia cabotegant e que hun dia en l'any legi a moltes persones cabotegant, les quals cosses lo dit en Splugues ja ha confessat." Splugues then explains why Jews nod their heads when they pray, though he asserts that the nodding itself is not a Jewish ceremony. The inquisitors, needless to say, were hardly swayed by such an argument.

Before the Spanish Inquisition established itself in Valencia, Splugues was more than willing to use his knowledge of the Torah to debate theological questions with Old Christians. One day, in the bookstore of the converso Francesc Castellar, which was located on the plaza of the cathedral, Splugues held forth on the matter of the messianic advent. A number of people were there. He started off by declaring that since the ingathering of the exiles that the prophets foretold had not taken place, then the Messiah had not yet come. Joan Cirera, an educated Old Christian maker of clogs, interjected that the prophesies had indeed been fulfilled when the exiles returned from Babylonia and the Temple in Jerusalem was rebuilt. Splugues countered by reminding Cirera that not all of the exiles returned; rather "many of them remained in Babylonia." He further pointed out, referring to Isaiah 11:11–12, that it was the task of the Messiah to gather Judah and Israel "from all four corners of the world." This prophesey was still unfulfilled.[143]

Cirera then cited Haggay, 2:6–10, as proof that the Messiah, Jesus, had come. He asserted that since the "last house," or second Temple, mentioned in Haggay had been destroyed, then the coming of "the one desired by all the nations" must refer to the Messiah. Furthermore, Cirera averred, when the prophet states "in this place I will give peace," by "peace" he means Jesus' "redemption of human nature." Splugues argued that this text had nothing to do with the Messiah, and that the thing "desired by the nations" was, as the text reads, silver and gold. Cirera grumbled, "This gloss is Jewish and corrupts the Holy Scripture."[144]

Cirera finally tried Isaiah 7:14, maintaining that where the prophet says "*Ecce virgo concipiet*," he was "clearly speaking of the advent of the Messiah and of the incarnation." Splugues shot back with the traditional Jewish response to this Christological interpretation: "Jerome mistranslated . . . for in

---

[143] AHN: Inq., leg. 538, caja 2, no. 27: 16v–17v (1482/2/26), the testimony of Joan Cirera, which provides a detailed account of the "disputation" with Splugues. Splugues's response to Cirera's assertion that "aquell repleguament del qual parlaven los prophetes . . . ja era stat fet per Esdras e per Zorobabel en la reedificacio del segon temple quant tornaren de Babilonia": "que no'y tornaren tots, que molts romangueren en Babilonia. E los prophetes dien que serien ajustats de totes les quatre parts del mon. . . . Donchs dix lo dit Splugues aquesta condicio no es complida, solament es axo de una partida e no [en] general segons que parlen los prophetes" (17r). For other Jewish responses to Christological interpretations of Isaiah, 11:11–14, see Berger 1996, 108–109; Chazan 1989, 109–111; Maccoby 1982, 132–133.

[144] AHN: Inq., leg. 538, caja 2, no. 27: 17r: "E ell dit testimoni [Cirera] respos e dix que la prophecia de Aggeu mostra que ja era complit lo replegament, perço com diu 'e vendra lo desigat de totes les gents e sera la gloria de aquests casa darrera . . . e dare en aquest lloch pau,' e per conseguent com la casa darrera sia ja destrohida la prophecia complida es; del desijat de totes les gents lo es del mesies, perço com deya en aquest lloch donare pau ço es la redempcio de natura humana. E lo dit Splugues respos que lo test no deya axi sino que vendria lo disig o la cupdiçia de les gents, ço es or e argent. E axi lo test no's entenia del messies, ans se entenia del or e del argent. E ell testimoni li respos e dix 'aquexa glosa es judayqua e corrompeu la scriptura sancta.'"

Hebrew [the text] does not state thus [i.e., "virgin"] but says *'almah*, which is to say 'young woman.'"[145] When the exasperated Cirera asked Splugues which text speaks most clearly about the Messiah, "since in the aforesaid [texts] he is not spoken of," Splugues referred him to the seventh chapter of the Book of Daniel.[146]

Consistent with the evident delight he took in theological disputation, Splugues told Cathalina Ortíz that he wished to mount the pulpit and debate publicly with preaching friars and masters of theology. He was confident that he could defeat them because "they do not understand the texts." In this way, he would "die for the people, just as those Gentiles did who upheld the public good."[147]

These dreams, uttered by Splugues sometime during his last months of freedom, paled in comparison to those he had allegedly revealed in Alacant to a Castilian widow named Anthona in 1482. Anthona had followed Splugues to Alacant to seek his help in freeing her son from captivity in Muslim Granada. (Splugues, it seems, was acquainted with a converso merchant named Alfonso Dies, who was active in arranging prisoner exchanges in Granada.) When she found Splugues she pretended to be a conversa. Splugues then told her of his plans to emigrate to Muslim Almería via Alacant; there he would openly return to Judaism. After that, he went on, he would return to Valencia and, with converso accomplices, murder the chief inquisitor of the new Spanish Inquisition, Juan Cristóbal de Gualbes.[148]

Splugues never moved to Almería; nor did he ever make an attempt on the inquisitor's life. The inquisitors seem not to have taken Splugues's dreams of vengeance too seriously. In 1482 they accepted his repentance and reconciled

---

[145] AHN: Inq., leg. 538, caja 2, no. 27: 17r: "E mes dix ell testimoni que Ysayes clarament parlava del adveniment del mesies e de la incarnacio quant dix *Ecce virgo concipiet*. E lo dit Splugues li respos que Sant Geronim havia mal trelladat, que en lo test no stava axi, car en lo abrahich no deya axi sino *alma*, que vol dir 'jove.'" See also Berger 1996, 100.

[146] AHN: Inq., leg. 538, caja 2, no. 27: 17r-v: "E ell dit testimoni dix mes a Splugues, 'En quin test se parlava pus clar del messies, puix que en lo dessus dit no'n parlava?' Respos lo dit Splugues, 'En Daniel a set capitols en aquell que parla dels quatre vents e dels quatre besties e del corn pent, que alli parlava pus clarament que no parlava en tota la scriptura sancta.'" The passage to which Splugues referred is Daniel 7:25. For rabbinic and medieval Jewish discussions of this text, see Klausner 1955, 228–231; Silver 1959, 83–86, 94–97, 107–108, 117–125, 243; Chazan 1992, 179–180; and Gutwirth 1998, for the fifteenth-century context — Jewish, converso, and Old Christian.

[147] AHN: Inq., leg. 538, caja 2, no. 27: 36v: "que plagues a deu que ell pogues parlar e pujar en trona, que ell volria morir per lo poble axi com feyan aquells gentils que mantenien lo be publich, que encara no's desconfiava de pujar hi . . . y tornava a dir, 'si lo temps me ajudava que yo pogues parlar, yo'ls faria a conexer als pedagochs que no saben dar palada,' dient ho dels sermonadors dels christians, 'que no entenien en los tests.'"

[148] AHN: Inq., leg. 538, caja 2, no. 27: 9r–10r (1482/2/8). The testimony of Anthona's other son, Martín (10r-v), who was present at her meeting with Splugues, reads like a summary of her own.

him to the church. What troubled the inquisitors in 1482 and later in 1491 was Splugues's persistent Judaizing and promulgation of the Jewish faith among conversos and even Old Christians. As far as they were concerned, Splugues imperiled the souls of New Christians in the same way that an unbaptized Jewish missionary might were he permitted to live in their midst. Splugues was like Salamó Çaporta in disguise. At least Çaporta lived in Morvedre.

On 15 February 1492 the judges of the Valencian tribunal of the Spanish Inquisition convicted Guillem Ramon Splugues as a relapsed heretic. They sentenced him to be burnt at the stake and relaxed him to the secular arm. On 16 March 1492 Splugues suffered his final passion.[149]

As a baptized Christian, Splugues fell under the jurisdiction of the Spanish Inquisition. The new institution was designed to eradicate Judaizing heretics like him; it was not meant to deal with unbaptized Jews like Salamó Çaporta. Even so, the inquisitors could hardly ignore the Jewish abettors of the Judaizing conversos. They and the Catholic Monarchs, Fernando of Aragon and Isabel of Castile, would have to come up with a solution to the problem of the Jews. When Splugues ascended to the scaffold, not to preach but to die, the wheels were already in motion.

[149] AHN: Inq., leg. 538, caja 2, no. 27: 83v–86v.

Chapter Seven

CHILL WIND FROM CASTILE

WHEN FERNANDO II ascended the throne in 1479 the Jewish community in Morvedre was prosperous and secure. Its population was growing and its constituent families were engaged in a wide range of economic activities: wine production and export, tax farming, moneylending, cloth production, silverwork, and retail commerce. Relations with Christians in Morvedre itself, in Valencia, and in the wider region extending from Valencia to Castelló were, on the whole, stable and mutually beneficial. To all appearances, times were good for the Jews.

Initially King Fernando did nothing to alter this state of affairs. In October 1479 he confirmed all royal privileges previously granted to the aljama of Morvedre, and, as further recognition of its importance, conferred on it all privileges that the aljamas of Zaragoza and Valencia enjoyed or, in the latter case, had once enjoyed. He insisted that the Jews pertained only to the jurisdiction of the Crown and its bailiffs. Seigneurs were not permitted any jurisdiction over Jews and were admonished not to exploit or vex Jews trading on their estates.[1] News that Anthoni Rull, the bailiff of Morvedre, had acted "in our disservice and to the damage and detriment of our revenue and of the public good of the said town and of its Jewish aljama, which is our property," elicited a prompt response from Fernando: Rull was to be removed from office and replaced by Francesc Munyós.[2]

At the same time, the king tightened his grip on aljama government by imposing on it the new electoral regime of insaculació, which consolidated the power of oligarchs on whom the monarchy could rely.[3] Fernando indeed had Jewish favorites in Morvedre. Salamó Çaporta purchased silk in Italy for Fernando, and, at the king's behest, was permitted to farm all royal taxes in Morvedre. Vidal Astori was the royal silversmith; Fernando also employed him as his envoy in Portugal and Castile.[4] Fernando's benevolent treatment of the Jewish

---

[1] ARV: C 303: 80v–82r (1479/10/10).

[2] ARV: C 304: 192v (1481/3/17): "in deservicium nostrum atque damnum et detrimentum jurium nostrorum reique publice dicte ville et aliame judeorum illius que pecculium nostrum est."

[3] ACA: C 3633: 104v–105r (1481/12/24); see chap. 5.

[4] See chap. 3 on these figures. In 1480 royal officials made various payments to Çaporta. Fernando himself instructed the maestre racional and the royal treasurer Luis Sánchez to pay Salamó 100 sous, "quos eidem elargiri volumus gratiose" (ACA: C 3615: 35v [3/15]). Anthoni Rotla, the royal castellan in Xixona, acknowledged owing Salamó 323 sous, a sum he was supposed to pay "pro Johanne Sanchiz, tesaurari domini regis certis causis" (ARV: P 443, J. de Campos Jr.: n.f. [6/

community was not modified when charges were laid against three Jews of
Morvedre for tampering with the royal coinage. The king simply proceeded in
the traditional manner: he "pardoned" the accused for the hefty sum of 635
florins.[5]

Fernando, of course, expected something in return for the privileges, protection, and favor he gave the Jews of Morvedre: loyal service and tax revenue.
He made greater fiscal demands of the Jews of Morvedre than had Alfonso IV
and Juan II. The aljama, however, did not find the tax burden to be inordinately large or insupportable.[6] The fundamental logic guiding Fernando's policy in the initial years of his reign was that the more Jews there were in a royal
town like Morvedre the better it would be for the local economy and the royal
treasury.[7] Following this line, the bailiff general granted a safe-conduct in 1480
to Salamó Zamero to return with his wife from Algiers, where they had gone
to collect an inheritance, and to live in Morvedre "as vassal[s] of the said lord
king."[8]

Judging by the treatment King Fernando accorded them and their coreligionists in the Crown of Aragon during the first two years of his reign, the Jews
of Morvedre had little to fear. Fernando, however, was more than just the ruler
of the Crown of Aragon; he was also, by virtue of his marriage to Isabel I of
Castile, the king of Castile. If any Jews in Morvedre were cognizant of certain
initiatives already taken by Fernando and Isabel in Castile, they might have
seen some reason for trepidation. Yet it would have been difficult for even the
most farsighted of them to have fathomed the long-term implications of the es-

---

27]). As for Astori, in 1480 royal officials were more concerned to recover the gold remaining from
the quantity Fernando had given the silversmith for making a gold harness for him (ARV: B 1156:
768r-v [4/30]). At this juncture, Astori was in Castile in the king's service.

[5] ARV: C 304: 159v–161r (1481/1/23). The three accused were Salamó Tarfon, *maior*, Gento
Tarfon, and Gento Çalema. Later that year Fernando placed under royal protection Jucef Quatorze, alleged *falsador de moneda* (B 1157: 89v [8/21]); royal officials then made sure that Jucef
could collect all debts owed him so that he might pay his fine to the Crown (B 1157: 164r [Hino-
josa Montalvo 1993a, no. 796]). In the fall of the previous year, similar charges had been laid
against Mossé Asseyo, which resulted in his arrest by agents of the governor. The bailiff general intervened on Mossé's behalf after the adelantats complained that Mossé had been arrested on the
Jewish Sabbath, in violation of the privilege that "juheus neguns no puxen esser en dissabte presos." More importantly, the bailiff general pointed out, the governor had infringed on his jurisdiction over the Jews (B 1156: 852r-v [1480/9/2]). It was, in other words, business as usual.

[6] See chap. 2.

[7] The monarchy's concern to promote prosperity in Morvedre at least partly in order to keep
revenue flowing into its treasury emerges clearly in a letter from the bailiff general to the bailiff of
Morvedre—ARV: B, Apendice 205: n.f. (July 1482). He orders the local bailiff to make a register
(*capbreu*) of all properties and utilities leased by the Crown in Morvedre, and notes the need to
establish rent-paying subjects on those properties that are vacant and abandoned. The Jews are not
mentioned here, but they obviously played an important role as lessees of royal utilities and real
estate. Cf. Meyerson 1991, chap. 1.

[8] ARV: B 1156: 729r-v (1480/3/1) [Hinojosa Montalvo 1993a, no. 788].

tablishment of the first provincial tribunal of the new Castilian inquisition —
or Spanish Inquisition — in Seville in January 1481.

The founding of the tribunal in Seville occurred more than two years after
Pope Sixtus IV issued a bull authorizing Fernando and Isabel to appoint inquisitors in Castile. Castile had not had a Dominican-controlled papal inquisition like that which had long been operating in the territories of the Crown
of Aragon. This was a deficiency the monarchs had wished to correct, but in
such a way as to enhance royal power while battling the Judaizing heresy
threatening the Castilian church. The papal bull thus afforded Fernando and
Isabel an unusual degree of control over the new Castilian inquisition, far ex-
ceeding whatever influence Aragon's kings might have had on the papal inquisitors working in their realms.

In Castile the problem of the conversos had assumed dangerous proportions
by the time Fernando and Isabel secured the throne. In the cities and towns of
New Castile and Andalucía the conversos had frequently, since 1449, been at
the center of bitter religious debate and sociopolitical unrest. There were serious outbreaks of violence against conversos in Andalucían cities as late as the
1470s. Powerful conversos had acquired equally powerful enemies, and politics
indeed lay at the root of much of the anticonverso violence. Yet what lent the
conflict between conversos and Old Christians such virulence in Castile was
the especially volatile mixture of religion and politics there. The knowledge that
many conversos were still practicing Judaism further embittered their Old
Christian political enemies and enabled them to label the conversos as "Jews"
and "heretics" as a means of drumming up popular support against them.[9]

On both scores, the political and the religious, the converso problem deeply
troubled the new rulers of Castile. Determined as they were to quell disorder
in and establish firm control over their cities, Fernando and Isabel could hardly
avoid wading into the upheavals involving the conversos. The monarchs were
also, and more importantly as far as the conversos were concerned, intent on
reforming the Castilian church.[10] The reform of Catholic laypeople could not
advance too far if Judaizing conversos were permitted to remain among them
spreading their noxious ideas and practices. A new inquisition, which they
themselves controlled, was well suited for addressing both the religious and sociopolitical aspects of the converso problem. It would eradicate the Judaizers
from among the Catholic faithful, of Old and New Christian origin, and thus
promote the church's spiritual welfare. At the same time, it would remove from
the scene at least some of the individuals embroiled in urban factionalism and
also deprive the conversos' political opponents of the religious ammunition
they used against them.

[9] See Benito Ruano 1961; Márquez Villanueva 1957; MacKay 1972 and 1985; Beinart 1981,
48–87; Edwards 1984a, 142–187; Ladero Quesada 1984.
[10] Hillgarth 1976–78, 2: 394–410.

In the urban centers of the Crown of Aragon the existence of substantial and frequently successful converso populations had not generated nearly the same level of turbulence, violence, and religious polemic that Castilian cities had been experiencing. At the end of Juan II's reign, however, the jurats of Valencia did attempt to ban the conversos from holding public office. The jurats and their allies viewed converso officials as agents of a centralizing monarchy. In 1478, in order to sway King Juan to agree to such a ban — unsuccessfully, as it turned out — the jurats played the religious card, instructing their ambassador at the royal court to inform the king that "it is very true that the conversos practice the Jewish law so much . . . among the Christians that in their entire way of life they are Jewish and not Christian." Referring to the growing "pride" of "these rats of Pharaoh," the jurats vented their bitterness. The jurats were not alone in resenting the political and social ascent of some conversos.[11] Nevertheless, this political opposition and religious hostility did not translate into social unrest and political violence. Hence King Juan's son and successor, Fernando II, did not feel compelled to introduce in Valencia a new institution like the Castilian inquisition for the purpose of restoring political order.

Yet Fernando did see a necessity — a religious necessity — for bringing the new royally controlled Castilian inquisition into the lands of his own Crown of Aragon. Reports of converso Judaizing may not have greatly bothered Juan, but they deeply disturbed Fernando and Isabel, who viewed the cells of Judaizers, wherever they lived, as so many threats to their project to reform the Catholic church, both clergy and laity, inside their realms. The monarchs and their Castilian advisors were more than prepared to disregard "national" boundaries as well as regional laws and privileges in the interest of ecclesiastical reform. They appointed Castilian clergy to prosecute the reform of the religious orders in the Crown of Aragon, notwithstanding the protests of local convents. Believing that they could make a better job of it than the papacy, Fernando and Isabel preferred to direct the reform of the Catholic church in both Castile and the Crown of Aragon themselves. Since they had no qualms about sending, for instance, Castilian Observant Dominicans to reform Dominican houses in Aragon and Catalonia, small surprise that they extended the new Castilian inquisition to Aragon, Catalonia, and Valencia to eradicate the Judaizing New Christians who lived in these territories just as they did in Castile.[12]

True, there already was a papal inquisition in the Crown of Aragon that could have dealt with the conversos who still stubbornly adhered to Judaism,

[11] AMV: LM 29: 34v–35v (1478/7/30) [*Epistolari*, 2: no. 134]. Rubio Vela 1998, 88. See also chap. 2.

[12] Meyerson 1995a, 102–104, 110–111. Haliczer 1990, 12, notes that Miguel de Morillo, appointed inquisitor of the new tribunal in Seville in 1481, was also appointed provincial of the reformed Dominicans of Aragon.

but its various regional tribunals had been, in this regard, largely inactive since the reign of Fernando I or had at best made desultory attempts to prosecute the Judaizers.[13] During the 1460s the papal inquisitors in Valencia tried fifteen conversos whose efforts to travel to the East under the inspiration of Jewish messianism had attracted considerable local attention. Yet even though the few Judaizers prosecuted in these trials constituted merely the tip of an iceberg, the papal inquisitors proceeded no further and did not pursue a thoroughgoing investigation of the extensive network of Judaizers in the capital and other Valencian towns. By the time King Fernando took steps toward establishing the new inquisitorial apparatus in the Crown of Aragon, the papal inquisitors in Valencia had not prosecuted a Judaizing converso for some fourteen years.[14] In the eyes of Fernando and Isabel, papal appointees were neither determined enough nor painstaking enough for the task at hand, whether it was reforming the religious orders or eradicating heresy.

In November 1481 Fernando instructed his ambassador in Rome to seek from Pope Sixtus a bull authorizing the establishment of the new inquisition in his own realms. Despite the pope's unwillingness to issue such a bull, Fernando had Juan Orts and Juan Cristóbal de Gualbes appointed as inquisitors of the new inquisitorial tribunal in Valencia. Orts and Gualbes entered Valencia in December and set to work. By May 1482 they had proclaimed an "edict of grace," though they did not actually receive papal confirmation of their appointments until the following December. Complaints about Gualbes's irregular procedures and his clashes with episcopal officials, however, soon reached the pope, who beseeched Fernando to remove Gualbes from office. The king acceded to the pope's request in August 1483. The pope, in turn, ceased all overt resistance to the institution of the new inquisition in the Crown of Aragon. On 17 October 1483 he named Fernando's nominee, Fray Tomás de Torquemada, inquisitor general of the Crown of Aragon. Torquemada already held the same post in Castile. The new, "modern," Castilian-run inquisition was now in operation in the lands of the Crown of Aragon.[15]

During this period of institutional uncertainty stretching from the arrival of the inquisitor Gualbes in Valencia in December 1481 until the appointment of Torquemada as inquisitor general of the Crown of Aragon, the Jews of Morvedre had their first encounters with the new inquisition. However questionable some of his methods, by the fall of 1482 Gualbes had reached the correct conclusion that at least some Jews in Morvedre had an intimate knowledge of the Judaizing activities of Valencian conversos, in part because they

[13] Sánchez Moya and Monasterio Aspiri 1972, 105; Vicens Vives 1936–37, 1: 367, 373–375; Fort i Cogull 1973, 113–119, 134–139.

[14] Baer 1929–36, 2: 437–444 and 1961, 2: 292–295; García Cárcel 1976a, 38. I disagree, however, with García Cárcel's suggestion that the papal inquisition in Valencia had been operating with "efficacy" when Fernando established the new inquisition there.

[15] García Cárcel 1976a, 39–46; Haliczer 1990, 12–13; Rubio Vela 1998, 77–81.

themselves had been encouraging and helping conversos lead a Jewish life. He therefore commanded that "certain Jews of the . . . jueria of Morvedre" be delivered into his custody so that he could extract from them "full information of that which was necessary for the exercise of the said office of the Inquisition."[16] Among the Jews brought before Gualbes for interrogation were Mossé Asseyo and his wife, Dolçina. Testimony like that given by the converso barber Pere Moreno in October 1482 must have led the inquisitor to the Asseyos:

> he, the confessant, along with a youth named Alfonset, who lived in the house of the said master Andreu [Forcadell], went to Morvedre and brought back from there a pot with a rice dish, which rice dish was given to them in the house of Na Dolçina, wife of Mossé Asseu [Asseyo], Jew of Morvedre, so that they would give the said rice dish to the wife of the said master Andreu. And the said confessant also says and confesses to have performed "the fast of pardon" [Yom Kippur] once, and [he did] this at the inducement of the rabbi of Morvedre, who is the father-in-law of Mossé Asseu.[17]

Initially, the bailiff general, guardian of the royal patrimony and therefore of the Jews, did not object to the inquisitor's merely questioning Jews about their knowledge of and contacts with Judaizing conversos. Logically, Gualbes might require the testimony of Jews in order to perform more effectively the task King Fernando had assigned him — uprooting the Judaizing heresy.[18] In mid-October 1482, however, the bailiff's lieutenant, Berenguer Mercader, protested that Gualbes had "overstepped the limits of [his] office" and infringed on the Crown's jurisdiction over Jews. The inquisitor had tortured one Jew and was imprisoning others, even after he had finished interrogating them.[19]

Mercader took a stand on behalf of the Asseyos. Gualbes held Mossé in a "very cramped jail" and kept Dolçina in the episcopal prison. Apparently he intended to punish them. Mercader marched over to the house of the episcopal vicar and compelled him to release Dolçina into his custody. He then rejected the inquisitor's demands that he hand Dolçina over. Mercader was not

[16] ARV: B 1157: 323r–324v (1482/10/16), a letter from the lieutenant bailiff general to Gualbes: "Car en dies passats principiantse la dita Inquisicio, havent mester certs juheus de la dita juheria de Morvedre, vos foren de continent remesos perque de aquells poguesseu haver complida informacio del que era necesari pera'l exercico del dit offici de la Inquisicio."

[17] AHN: Inq., leg. 546, caja 2, no. 23: n.f. (1482/10/12): "E mes dix e confessa star en veritat que ell confessant ensemps ab un jove qui ha nom Alfonset, qui stava en casa del dit mestre Andreu, anam [sic] a Morvedre e portaren de alla una olleta de aroçet, lo qual aroçet los fonch donat en casa de na Dolçina, muller de Mosse Asseu, jeu de Murvedre, per que donasen dit aroçet a la muller del dit mestre Andreu. E axi matex dix e confessa ell confessant haver fet lo dejuni del perdo una vegada e aço a induccio del rabi de Morvedre qui es sogre de Mosse Asseu."

[18] Cf. Edwards 1984b; Beinart 1978.

[19] ARV: B 1157: 323r–324v: "encara que apres se sia hauda noticia verdadera de haver procehit contra hu dels dits juheus a actes de tortura e a altres actes molt prejudicials a la reyal jurisdiccio, excidunt los limits de vostre offici."

impressed by Gualbes's arguments and fulminations that he was disobeying
"Holy Mother Church, impeding and disobeying the authority of our holy office," and violating an old order of King Martí requiring royal officials to cooperate with the (Dominican) inquisitors. The lieutenant bailiff replied that
jurisdiction over and punishment of the Jews "pertains to his royal majesty and
to the court of the bailiff general."[20]

King Fernando would have sympathized with Mercader's efforts to protect
the Jews and to maintain the inviolability of the Crown's jurisdiction over
them, since the true objects of inquisitorial prosecution were Judaizing conversos and other Christian heretics, not unbaptized Jews. Gualbes's successors
in the Valencian tribunal, in fact, never engaged in such illicit and wanton mis-
treatment of the Jews. They sometimes subpoenaed Jews to testify and in one
unusual case even put a Jew on trial, but they did not torture and jail Jews as
had Gualbes.

Still, Fernando's dismissal of Gualbes from the post of inquisitor was meant
to placate the pope, not to hamstring the new inquisition or do the Jews any
special favors. As events would soon show, the arguments of a Berenguer Mercader or of a Macià Mercader, the episcopal vicar general who had frequently
been at odds with Gualbes, about traditional rights and jurisdictions and the
time-honored way of doing things would sway neither the successors of Gualbes nor the king who promoted their activities. The appointment of Torquemada as inquisitor general of the Crown of Aragon after the removal of Gualbes
only strengthened the hands of the new inquisitors in Valencia.

King Fernando was determined to establish the new inquisition in his own
realms and to eliminate all opposition to it. In Valencia, for instance, the king
saw to it that Martí Trigo replaced Macià Mercader as episcopal vicar when it
became clear that Mercader was antagonizing Gualbes's successor Juan Epila
as much as he had Gualbes.[21] For Fernando, the inquisition's eradication of
the Judaizing heresy was a priority. None of the arguments advanced by his
Catalan, Aragonese, and Valencian subjects against the new institution swayed
him. A popular king greeted with nearly messianic expectations at the time of

---

[20] ARV: B 1157: 323r–324v: "E axi ara novament . . . vos son estats tramesos hun juheu ap-
pellat Mosse Asseo e Dolçina, juhia muller de aquell . . . E per quant per vos apres de haver re-
buda la dita informacio, es estat procehit a incarceracio del dit Mosse Asseo, juheu, lo qual huy
en dia deteniu pres e incarcerat en preso molt estreta, continuant e volent procehir contra los dits
juheu e juhia a cogniscio e punicio de crims, pretenent la conexenca e jurisdiccio e punicio de
aquells vos pertany. . . . E com la conexenca e jurisdiccio e punicio dels dits juheus en los dits cas-
sos pertany a sa reyal magestat e a la sua cort de la batlia general." B 1157: 322r-v (1482/10/16) is
Gualbes's letter to Mercader describing and objecting to his liberation of Dolçina: "e com vosaltres . . . sien venguts personalment a la casa del dit vicari general a hon manavam detenir dita
juhia, e vosaltres menyspreant la obediencia de Santa Mare Esglesia e la auctoritat de nostre sacre
offici empaixant e perturbant aquell, vos haiau portada presa dita juhia." The order of King Martí
to which Gualbes next refers was issued on 15 September 1400 (see chap. 1).
[21] García Cárcel 1976a, 58–59.

his accession, Fernando did not need the new inquisition to enhance royal authority. On the contrary, by introducing a Castilian-run institution, which violated the laws and liberties of his realms, he consciously risked angering his
subjects and creating a constitutional crisis. But protecting the Catholic
church and its members against the Judaizing cancer was, for him, worth the
risk. The economic arguments of his subjects proved no more effective than
their constitutional protests. Even though Fernando had been working to revive the Catalan economy after the debilitating civil war and hoping to profit
from the kingdom of Valencia's general economic vigor, he informed Catalans
and Valencians in no uncertain terms of his willingness to damage local
economies, by causing the flight of conversos and their capital or by allowing
the inquisitors to confiscate the assets of condemned conversos, if the inquisition could better the spiritual health of the Catholic body social.[22]

Small surprise, then, that King Fernando, having some inkling of the influence Jews exercised over conversos in the kingdom of Valencia and other regions, soon took steps to discourage Jewish contact and cooperation with conversos. If he was resolute enough to provoke a constitutional crisis in all Crown
territories or to endanger Catalonia's economic recovery with the new inquisition, he was not, in the case of the Jews of Morvedre, going to agonize much
over enacting measures that contravened the letter or spirit of the privileges
and favors he had recently granted them. As early as March 1483, while
Gualbes was still inquisitor, the king specifically revoked all licenses that officials had given Jews not to wear the Jewish badge or to stay in the city of Valencia for more than ten days at a time, the limitation stipulated in the legislation of 1403 but often enough honored in the breach.[23] If Jews wore their
badges, then the authorities could more easily distinguish them from conversos and prevent the two groups from mingling. Shorter stays in Valencia would
reduce the Jews' opportunities for communicating with conversos. The information gathered by Gualbes in 1482 may well have inspired Fernando to take
a more rigorous approach. Although these restrictions were hardly drastic, and
in fact amounted to enforcing existing laws, wearing the badge potentially exposed the Jews to ridicule and harassment, while limiting the Jews' visits to the
capital might have economic drawbacks. But the most important—and troubling—thing about these restrictions was what they implied: that the necessi-

[22] García Cárcel 1976a, 47–67; Haliczer 1990, 13–17; Vicens Vives 1936–37, 1: 92–105,
365–424; Rubio Vela 1998, 90–110.
[23] ACA: C 3684: 10r (1483/3/6) [Baer 1929–36, 1: no. 557]. On 18 August 1487 the bailiff
general reiterated this order and had it publicly proclaimed—ARV: B 1220: M. 2, 24r-v (1487).
For the legislation of 1403, see chap. 1. These measures, however, pale beside those that the monarchs, in conjunction with the Cortes of Toledo, took against the Jews of Castile in 1480 and subsequent years. With the exception, perhaps, of the Jewish communities in Zaragoza and Calatayud, far less seems to have been done to separate the Jews of the Crown of Aragon from
Christians. See Beinart 1986, 70–84, and 1994, 19–26.

ties of the new Spanish Inquisition in its war on converso Judaizing were increasingly shaping the king's Jewish policy.

Gualbes had compiled some damning evidence of the corrupting influence certain Jews of Morvedre, such as the Asseyos, exerted on Judaizing conversos, but it was only a fraction of the information collected by the next team of inquisitors, the Aragonese Dominican Juan Epila and the theologian and canon of Valencia Martí Enyego. After Gualbes read the "edict of grace" in May 1482, only eleven conversos had come forth to confess their errors.[24] During the term in office of Epila and Enyego, which extended from August 1484 to March 1487, many more conversos took advantage of the terms of grace to confess and abjure their Judaizing heresies. As the Spanish Inquisition's procedures became more familiar to them, they realized that if they confessed voluntarily during the term of grace, they could be reconciled to the church without having their property confiscated and without suffering more than a monetary fine or penance. After the first edict was proclaimed in November 1484, only five individuals were reconciled during the one-month period of grace; fourteen abjured after its expiration. However, in the summer of 1485, when there were, in effect, two periods of grace, 354 conversos came forward to confess. The final period of grace initiated by Epila and Enyego lasted from February to August 1486; 265 conversos abjured during it and another 44 after it expired.

The conversos who confessed during these early years of the new inquisition's operation in Valencia thought that after their abjurations the inquisitors would be through with them, hardly imagining how relentless and frighteningly efficient this inquisition was. The inquisitors scoured and organized the evidence contained in their voluntary confessions so that they could identify and then watch the Judaizers in the converso community. Conversos who had not confessed fully to all their own Jewish practices and to what they knew about the Judaizing of others were deemed by the inquisitors to have deliberately concealed information and were therefore subsequently prosecuted as heretics. Conversos who continued their Jewish observances after their initial abjuration were indicted by the inquisitors as relapsed heretics. Few conversos evaded inquisitorial surveillance. Only 12 percent of the conversos who had come forward during these first periods of grace escaped subsequent trial by the Spanish Inquisition.[25]

As Epila and Enyego painstakingly scrutinized the Jewish observances, social networks, and movements of Valencia's Judaizers, one thing emerged clearly: the important role of the Jews of Morvedre in abetting a good number of Judaizers in their heretical activities. The inquisitors informed King Fernando of their findings, which more than substantiated the evidence Gualbes had uncovered. In March 1486 Fernando wrote to the bailiff general calling

[24] García Cárcel 1976a, 44.
[25] García Cárcel 1976a, 63–67, 179–180; Haliczer 1990, 59–61.

for the imposition of greater restrictions on the Jews and for the bailiff's full co-operation with the inquisition. Fernando was convinced that "many Jews" were staying in the city of Valencia for extended periods with the bailiff general's per-mission. This was "against the form of the *fur* [of 1403] and in great disservice of our Lord and in great offense to the Catholic faith." The king insisted that the bailiff prohibit the Jews from staying in Valencia for more than three days — one week less than the legislation of 1403 had allowed them. Jews who violated this limitation or who traveled without displaying their badges were to be "rig-orously punished." For economic reasons, Fernando was not ready to deny the Jews of Morvedre all access to Valencia. He hoped that, together, the more con-certed offensive of the Spanish Inquisition against the Judaizers and the tighter restrictions on the movements of the Jews would serve to keep the two groups apart.

Considering the evidence of the religious and social bonds that united Jews in Morvedre to conversos in Valencia, the king and the inquisitors concluded that the inquisition still might need "to constrain some Jew" of Morvedre to tes-tify before it "in order to know the truth of some matter." Fernando, however, saw a potential obstacle to the inquisition's use of Jewish witnesses: the laws against informing. Royal privileges had empowered aljama officials "to kill as a malsin" any Jew who reveals "secrets of the Jewish community (*juderia*) touch-ing Jews and conversos, whence some damage might befall them." Fernando therefore instructed the bailiff general to send him a copy of these privileges for his inspection. Fernando would have found that the aljama's legislation against informing did not specifically cover the conversos, but, given the sense of com-munity shared by Jews and Judaizers, he logically thought that it might.[26] In any case, a king who disregarded the constitutional arguments of his Christian sub-jects was not about to let the aljama's laws and privileges impede the progress of the Spanish Inquisition. Indeed, he demanded that the bailiff general give the inquisitors "all the favor and aid that they need, and finally you must honor [and] favor them."[27] The stand Berenguer Mercader had taken against the in-

---

[26] For earlier royal measures empowering officials of the aljama of Morvedre to proceed against and punish informers, see chap. 5. Sometime after the advent of Gualbes and the new inquisi-tion, aljama officials possibly attempted to prohibit Jews from testifying to the inquisition about the conversos by threatening them with a communal ban. On 6 August 1487 Jacob Bernabes, a Jewish broker who had been living in Morvedre for seven or eight years, gave testimony to the in-quisition about the visits of the Guimerà family to Jews in Morvedre in 1481 or perhaps 1480. He pointed out that what he was presently saying he had already told the inquisitor Gualbes, and then asserted, "E per lo ve e alam [*alatma*, or communal ban] no dix saber pus de neguns christians convessos de la ciudat e regne de Valencia" (AHN: Inq., leg. 545, caja 1, no. 7: 25r-v). This rather cryptic reference to a possible communal ban is difficult to interpret. Aljama officials could not have easily upheld it or enforced it in the face of pressure from a determined King Fernando and his inquisitors.

[27] ACA: C 3684: 91r-v (1486/3/20): "e perque som certificats que contra forma del fur e en gran deservey de nostre Senyor e en gran offensa de la fe catholica ab guatges [*sic*] stan en aquexa

quisitor Gualbes in 1482 probably would not have earned him royal approval in 1486. The evidence of widespread Judaizing in Valencia that Epila and Enyego had since uncovered was too massive, too disturbing. Nothing could be allowed to hinder the inquisitors from putting an end to the Judaizing of Christians in the Crown of Aragon's largest and wealthiest city.

The bailiff general, Diego de Torre, did not mistake the gravity of the king's orders. Besides enforcing them, in September 1486 the bailiff decreed that all Jews must vacate the city of Valencia at least three days before the start of any Jewish holy day or festival. He specifically mentioned Rosh Hashanah, Yom Kippur, Sukkot, and Passover—all holidays on which the conversos had enjoyed the instruction, companionship, and kasher supplies of Morvedre's Jews.[28] The next year the bailiff had King Fernando's orders of March 1483 proclaimed again throughout the city of Valencia.[29] The Jews of Morvedre were the principal Jewish visitors to Valencia and the bailiff general was thus advising the city's Christian population to identify the Jews and follow their movements.

The bailiff general further obeyed the king by fully cooperating with the inquisitors, even when, in the winter of 1487, they initiated procedures against Salamó Çaporta, royal favorite and farmer of the Crown's rents in Morvedre. The inquisitors' prosecution of a Jew was highly irregular; Judaizing Christian heretics fell under their jurisdiction but not Jews. The inquisitors apparently intended to make an example of Çaporta. Since he was such a prominent member of the Jewish community and also well known and respected among both New and Old Christians, the inquisitors hoped that their trial of Çaporta would discourage other Jews from assisting the Judaizers and the conversos from turning to the Jews. Clearly, if a Jew of Çaporta's stature could not claim immunity from inquisitorial prosecution, then nobody could.

---

ciutat molts jueus, vos manam que no consintau que degu hi estiga mes de tres dies e aquells no vaien sen[se] senyals e los contrafaents sien rigorosament castigats. E perque aximatex havem sabut que los jueus de Molvedre [sic] e los altres tenen certs privilegis hon les es donada facultat que a qualsevol que denunciara alguns secrets de la juderia tocants a jueus e a conversos de hon dan algun a les pogues seguir al aquest tal lo puxen matar per malsin, vos manam que tantost nos ne trametau trellat de dit privilegi que per algunes causes satisfa a nostre servey fer lo veure e regonexer; e per algun cas volran los inquisidors de la heretica pravidat strenyer algun jueu per saber la veritat de algun negoci, vos manam en fer ho, los doneu tot lo favor e ajuda que mester hauran, e finalment los honreu, favorexcau." Edwards 1984b, 350, points out that as early as 10 December 1484 Fernando had ordered that the Jews of the kingdom of Aragon "be compelled to give testimony 'for the successful pursuit of the Inquisition.'"

[28] ARV: B 1220: M. 3, 15v–16v (1486/9/19). This order followed one forbidding Muslims and Jews to purchase black Muslim slaves from "Guinea" and other places, lest the slaves be prevented by such infidel masters from coming to a recognition of Christian truth and being instructed in the Catholic faith (B 1220: M. 3, 5v–6r [8/29]). Taken together, the two orders reflect a mounting anxiety in official circles over the orthodoxy and orthopraxy of New Christians, whether conversos or baptized slaves. For the Jews' contacts with the conversos on Jewish holidays, see chap. 6.

[29] ARV: B 1220: M. 2 , 24r-v (1487/8/18).

King Fernando appreciated the inquisitors' strategy and was prepared to allow them to punish his Jewish favorite, as long as they uncovered firm evidence of the offenses he had committed against the Catholic church. Fernando himself, however, did not presume that Çaporta was guilty. He therefore made sure that the Jew received a fair trial by the inquisition's standards. When Çaporta complained to Fernando that the inquisitors were not providing him with a proper defense counsel, the king issued instructions to the inquisitors enjoining them to "give to the said Çaporta defense, advocate and procurator, those whom he will want and choose." The inquisitors, moreover, were not to pressure or hinder the Jew's defenders in any way; they should be able to work on his behalf "without any fear."[30] At the same time, Fernando angrily warned the maestre racional not to touch any of Çaporta's property, for, after all, the trial might result in his acquittal.[31]

The king was disappointed when the inquisitors reached a verdict on 12 May 1488. After considering the arguments of the prosecution and the defense and the testimonies of witnesses presented by both sides, the inquisitors concluded that "you Salamó Çaporta have offended against the holy Catholic faith." His transgressions included provisioning conversos with kasher foodstuffs; celebrating Jewish holidays with conversos and inviting them to his table on such days; reading the Torah and other Hebrew texts to conversos and teaching them to read Hebrew. Çaporta abjured his errors and promised not to perpetrate such offenses in the future. The inquisitors nevertheless sentenced him to pay a fine of 200 gold castellans and to two years of exile from the kingdom.[32]

Çaporta's exile, which was supposed to have started on 1 June 1488, did not begin until 1489. King Fernando gave him time to arrange his affairs before going into exile. Fernando himself seems to have believed the sincerity of his favorite's abjuration and to have expected his rehabilitation.[33] The king probably had plans for Çaporta when he returned from exile in 1491. Çaporta unfortunately died abroad.

The new inquisition's offensive against the Judaizing conversos of Valencia and the trial and exile of a leading light of their own community must have made the Jews of Morvedre nervous and caused them to limit their contacts with the converso population, or at the very least to have exercised far greater caution when they communicated with conversos. Both Jews and conversos knew that they possessed much incriminating evidence about one another, evidence in which the inquisitors would be keenly interested. At times members

---

[30] ACA: C 3665: 51r (1487/3/5): "deys al dicho Çaporta defiensas, advocado e procurador, aquellos que el querra e sleria. Los quales . . . sin miedo alguno . . . advoquen, procuren e razonen a el e su causa."

[31] ACA: C 3665: 51r (1487/3/5); see also chap. 3.

[32] AHN: Inq., leg. 536, caja 2, no. 19: 1v (1488/5/12): "tu Salamo Çaporta haver delinquit contra la sancta ffe catholica." See chap. 6.

[33] See chap. 3.

of each group must have wondered whether they could rely on acquaintances in the other group to maintain a guarded silence about what they knew. The conversos who counted on the Jews to keep their lips sealed were not disillusioned. Very few Jews from Morvedre testified before the inquisitorial tribunal. The inquisitors compiled plenty of evidence against the Judaizers from the confessions and interrogations of conversos and Old Christians; they did not need to subpoena many Jews. Only Gualbes briefly took this tack. Most importantly, hardly any Jews of Morvedre came forward voluntarily to testify against conversos.

The one exceptional case in which a Jew deliberately informed against conversos was the result of unusual circumstances. It involved the Jew Jacob who, with his wife, Perla, had maintained particularly close relations with the Guimeràs, a family of Judaizers from Valencia. At the beginning of 1482, just after Gualbes had started working in Valencia, Jacob and Perla visited the homes of Bernat Guimerà and his son-in-law Manuel Çabata in Valencia. When Çabata discovered that some articles were missing from his house, he accused Jacob of theft and had the authorities arrest Jacob. According to Vicent Domènech, an acquaintance of Çabata who witnessed the arrest in Morvedre,

> as they were taking away the said Jew under arrest, the said Jew demanded that the said Bernat Guimerà and his son-in-law be arrested, saying that they were neither Jews nor Christians and that they merited going to the flames, and among other things the said Jew said that the said Manuel Çabata had given money for oil for the lamps of the synagogue.[34]

The Spanish Inquisition had become a factor in the lives of Jews and conversos. A misunderstanding or worse between them could have disastrous consequences. Fortunately for the conversos, few if any other Jews had reason to be as antagonized as Jacob.

Yet such was the weight of evidence against Judaizing conversos from Old and New Christian sources that additional evidence extracted from the Jews would not have made a great deal of difference in the inquisition's determination of their fate. Indeed, it was precisely this evidence that convinced the inquisitors that some action had to be taken against the Jews of Morvedre, even if they did not properly pertain to their jurisdiction, and that motivated them to risk angering the king by prosecuting and exiling his favorite Salamó Çaporta. Still, the inquisitors knew that, beyond making an example of a Jew like Çaporta, the king would not permit them to try a large segment of the Morve-

---

[34] AHN: Inq., leg. 545, caja 1, no. 7: 19r-v (1482/2/12): "com portaven pres lo dit juheu, e lo dit juheu requeria que lo dit Bernat Guimera ab son gendre fossen presos, dient que no eren ni juheus ni christians e que marexien anar al foc, e que entre les altres coses dix lo dit juheu que lo dit Manuel Çabata havia donats certs diners pera oli a les lanties de la sinogoga."

dre community. King Fernando was certainly aware of the connection between
converso Judaizing and the Jewish presence, but at the time of Çaporta's exile
he and Isabel still had not arrived at a final solution to the problem.

Unable to put the Jews of Morvedre on trial, the inquisitors — in this case
the friars Miguel de Montemunio and Diego Magdaleno — had another card
up their sleeves, another means of further pressuring and marginalizing them.
On 24 April 1490, instead of holding the auto de fe in the capital as usual, they
conducted it in the main plaza of Morvedre. On a scaffold erected in the plaza
the inquisitors read the sentences against conversas like Johana Blanes, the wife
of Martí Sentpol, a converso dyer and silkweaver, and Violant, the wife of
Bernat Guimerà. Both of these women were sentenced to burning and "relaxed to the secular arm." Among those specifically listed by the inquisition's
scribe as having witnessed these public condemnations were the noble Joan
de Pròixida, the knight Luis Aguiló, and Francesc de Sant Feliu, the bailiff of
Morvedre. All three were members of powerful families with a long history of
close relations with the Jews of Morvedre, families who in the past had acted
as the Jews' patrons and protectors. Pròixida, Aguilo, and Sant Feliu were not
alone:

> and gathered there were many other notable persons and the majority of the pop-
> ulation of the said town who were summoned by the reverend lord inquisitors to
> hear the sermon and acts of faith in favor and exaltation of the holy Catholic
> faith.[35]

The message was clear: local Jews who aided and abetted Judaizing conversos were enemies of the Catholic church. The Jews' most powerful friends and
patrons together with the greater part of the local Christian population were,
in effect, advised to regard their Jewish neighbors with suspicion and to be wary
of excessive contact with them. Huddled behind the walls of the Jewish quarter, the Jews heard the commotion and the inquisitors thundering from the
scaffold in the plaza nearby. The Jews would have noticed the unease and discomfort pervading their relations with local Christians in the days, weeks, and
months following the auto de fe. They felt the chill wind from Castile.

When the Jews and Christians of Morvedre received word of the edict of expulsion, which the Catholic Monarchs had issued on 31 March 1492, they
may well have thought back to that auto de fe held in the town square two years
before and concluded that even then the inquisitors had been preparing them
for the expulsion. If so, they would have been reading too much into the past.
Still, the role of the Spanish Inquisition and the inquisitor general Torquemada
in the monarchs' final decision to expel the Jews was crucial. Among the Jews

---

[35] AHN: Inq., leg. 544, caja 2, no. 25: 30r: "ac multis aliis notabilibus personis et maxima parte
populi dicte ville ibidem congregata, qui ad audiendum sermonem et acta fidey in favorem et ex-
altationem sancte fidey catholice per reverendos dominos inquisitores fuerunt vocati."

of Castile and the Crown of Aragon the Jews of Morvedre were not unique in the amount of moral and material support they offered to Judaizing conversos. Evidence gathered by inquisitors sitting on the tribunals established throughout both realms pointed to the same conclusion: that Jews exercised a negative influence on conversos, and that if there were to be any hope of the conversos becoming sincere Catholics, then this noxious Jewish influence had to be removed.[36]

Thus, like the Jews of other towns in Castile and the Crown of Aragon, the Jews of Morvedre were ultimately forced to take the path of exile, the path where they had been led by their sense of identity as Jews, their sense of duty as Jews, and their sense of just who belonged to the Jewish community. In his own commitment to the Jewish community — the community of Jews and Judaizers — and in his exile, Salamó Çaporta set the standard for other Jews in Morvedre.[37]

In the eyes of Jews, conversos, Old Christians, and King Fernando, Salamó Çaporta had indeed been a model Jew: a pious and upright communal official, a trustworthy businessman, and a loyal servant of the Crown. But in abetting converso Judaizing, he had sinned grievously. As far as the king and the inquisitors were concerned, Salamó had committed an offense far worse than violating Jewish law, business ethics, or even royal law. He had threatened the well-being of the Catholic church.

A brutal and ineluctable logic guided the rulers of Castile and the Crown of Aragon in this age of Catholic reform. No matter how much the municipal officials of Morvedre and Valencia preferred the presence of a flourishing Jewish community in Morvedre; no matter how much local lay and clerical elites favored the Jews; no matter how much the Christians and Muslims of the region relied on the Jews for small "gratuitous" loans, retail merchandise, silverware, and wine, the Jews still had to go. The Jews endangered the cause of Catholic reform in a way that only the inquisitors, Fernando and Isabel, and the conversos really understood. By affixing his signature to the edict of expulsion, Fernando the Catholic brought 244 years of Jewish existence in Morvedre to an abrupt end. But in the minds of the Jewish exiles and of the Old and New Christians of Morvedre the memories of what was and what might have been lingered, perhaps for generations. They knew much better than we can just what was lost, a loss almost unfathomable were it not so awfully familiar.

[36] Beinart 1994, 28–56; Kriegel 1978.

[37] Of course, not all Jews opted for exile; some chose to stay and thus had to convert. See Meyerson 1992; Baer 1961, 2: 436–437; Cantera Montenegro 1979. I have not, however, encountered any evidence of Jews from Morvedre converting in 1492 or returning to Morvedre, as Christians, in subsequent years.

RENAISSANCE, then expulsion; a revival snuffed out. The reader may well wonder what significance a Jewish renaissance in fifteenth-century Morvedre could possibly have when this town's Jews, like all other Iberian Jews, were ultimately thrust into exile. The Jews of Morvedre who were living through this period of rebirth might answer that this was simply their reality, that for them terms like "renaissance" and, before the late 1480s, "expulsion" had no meaning, that they and the Christians of their town were just going about the business of earning their bread, which entailed cooperation and compromise across the age-old religious divide. The Jews might say that, true, there were a lot more of them in town now and the community on the whole was prospering, but this was a result of hard work, a little luck, and perhaps — were they so bold to suggest it — divine favor. Really, it was nothing extraordinary.

Indeed, it was not. Neither Jew nor Christian ventured any enlightened opinions about the religion of the other; neither made any astonishing gestures of goodwill toward the other. This was, after all, the fifteenth century. What is meaningful to us more than five hundred years later is the sheer ordinariness and mundanity of so much of this Jewish revival in Morvedre: that the Jews could rebuild and carry on after the disasters of 1391; that they could adjust, when necessary, to new economic, social, and religious circumstances; and that they and their Christian neighbors could cope, however imperfectly, with ideological antagonism. The silence of the records concerning fifteenth-century Morvedre is just as, if not more, striking than anything that was said or done. These records tell us nothing about vicious anti-Judaism, nothing about frequent or systematic harassment of the Jewish community, nothing about Christian mob violence against Jews or even common interpersonal violence between individual Christians and Jews. The records, in other words, tell us nothing about the kinds of behavior we might expect to find during the decades preceding the expulsion.

The revival of the Jews of Morvedre in the fifteenth century has implications for the understanding of the three intertwined histories mentioned at the beginning of this book: the local, the Spanish, and the Jewish. In regard to the history of Morvedre — or Sagunto — the demographic and economic facts speak eloquently: the Jews comprised more than one-quarter of the town's population; municipality and aljama were fiscally interdependent; the Jews had an integral role in the local and regional economy. The history of fifteenth-century Morvedre is, in this basic way, incomprehensible without giving due attention to the history of its Jews. But one might want to go further and ponder the relatively peaceful coexistence of Christian and Jew in a century so often characterized by inquisition and expulsion, and thus realize, in human terms, what Morvedre lost in 1492.

The history of the Jews of Morvedre after 1391 is as well an emphatic validation of local history as a methodology for grasping the complexity of premodern plural societies. It demonstrates that it is problematic to structure a historical narrative around the views expressed in polemical texts, acts of mob violence, and state-engineered expulsions alone; that once uncovered and interpreted, the minutiae of social and economic interchange may well lend themselves to the construction of a very different narrative, and not just of the history of one town or region. The significance of Morvedre's history extends far beyond the municipal terme and the borders of the kingdom of Valencia, because it forces us to rethink the intertwined narratives of Spanish history and Jewish history.

In regard to the history of interfaith relations in later medieval Spain, it is patent that one region or kingdom — say, Andalucía or Castile — cannot stand for all of Spain, and that even those regions whose histories are taken as established demand closer investigation with a different set of questions.[1] The Jewish renaissance in fifteenth-century Morvedre argues against writing the history of the years between the midfourteenth century and 1492 as a history of exponentially increasing anti-Judaism, persecution, and victimization, in which Christians and Jews everywhere staggered mechanically down the same path of hatred and violence that their fathers and grandfathers supposedly set. Presenting later medieval Spanish history as a monolithic and monotonous narrative of persecution may be politically useful for some, but it is a gross distortion of the historical experience of Christians, Jews, and Muslims in many places; it rips events out of context and subsumes everything under the rubric of 1492.

In light of the success of the Jews of Morvedre in the fifteenth century, the history of the Jews of southern Europe gains more nuance, particularly if we inquire into the conditions for a revival such as the Jews of Morvedre experienced — if we ask, in other words, what made it all work. With glances at the rest of the Crown of Aragon, Castile, and Italy, some suggestions can be made.

First of all, the small or medium-sized town environment of Morvedre was crucial to the flourishing of its Jewish community. Scholars have noted the geographical shift of Jewish communities in post-1391 Spain from major cities to towns, villages, and seigneurial domains, and have seen this shift as fundamental to the communities' reconstruction.[2] They have not, however, explained why the existence of Jewish aljamas became increasingly difficult in some cities before and after 1391. One reason is that the development of civic identity on the basis of civic religion and religious propaganda raised serious

---

[1] E.g. Castaño González 1995 and 1998, for Castile.
[2] E.g., Baer 1961, 2: 246–247; MacKay 1972, 36–38.

questions about the presence and function of non-Christians. Thus Valencia's city fathers beseeched King Martí not to reestablish an aljama in their city; yet they subsequently found the prosperous aljama in Morvedre, a town under their jurisdiction but outside their city's walls, to be most convenient. Italian cities, which styled themselves as "most Christian," also could not easily justify ideologically the presence of Jews whom they felt they needed for economic purposes; hence many of them, most notably Venice, ghettoized their Jews over the course of the sixteenth century.[3]

The ruling elites of smaller urban centers, in contrast, often could not afford the luxury of ejecting their Jews, of somehow making the composition of local society conform with what was, at best, a poorly articulated civic identity. Or, if they did feel that they could remove the Jews, as in the cases of Borriana and Vila-real, it was because the Jews had neither the demographic weight nor the economic importance to make their continuance seem essential. In Morvedre, as has been seen, the Jews had both; the town fathers acted accordingly. The history of Castilian towns and villages shows that the outlook of the Christians of Morvedre was not unique.[4] The movement of most Jews in fifteenth-century Spain to smaller centers, then, warrants much greater attention in any reconsideration of the history of Spanish Jewry, for the large majority of the Christian population resided in villages and small towns. Its commonplace interaction with Jews should be a central theme and should be given at least as much weight as the statements and actions of city-dwellers.

In linking the religious homogenization of Spain to the rise of the early modern state — that is, in arguing that the more authoritarian monarchical state required adherence to one (Catholic) faith by all its subjects — many historians have therefore been looking in the wrong place. It was the governing classes of the cities, not the monarchs, who placed the greatest premium on ideological uniformity; the tension between this ideal and a pluralistic social reality was most often created in the cities and fostered by civic ritual and propaganda. The monarchical state, if it did anything, protected the religious minorities; in the kingdom of Valencia at least, its new and more efficient institutions improved the conditions of Jewish life. True, Isabel and Fernando made the final decision to expel the Jews, but they took this step in order to solve a particular socioreligious problem — that of heretical, Judaizing conversos — which was a problem internal to the Catholic church.[5] They were not ideologically motivated to make Spain religiously uniform. Fernando certainly was keen to protect his many, many thousands of Muslim subjects.[6]

The politics of kings, cities, and great nobles figure importantly, in a differ-

---

[3] Ravid 2001, 7–16, 20–26; Crouzet-Pavan 1992; Toaff 1996, 187–194.
[4] E.g., León Tello 1963; Rodríguez Fernández 1976.
[5] Kriegel 1978.
[6] Meyerson 1991.

ent way, into the explanation of why the Jews of Morvedre experienced fewer problems with their Christian neighbors than did the Jews of a number of Castilian and Catalan towns in the fifteenth century. The public discourse generated by political action at the highest levels of society tended to shape attitudes and stimulate anti-Jewish behavior at the lower levels. In Castile the political dynamics that had caused anti-Jewish violence during the Castilian civil war and had led to the conflagration of 1391 persisted through much of the fifteenth century. Noble factions continued to oppose the monarchy and to employ anti-Jewish and anticonverso propaganda to drum up support; their domination of urban politics greatly influenced local attitudes toward Jews. The vicious and explosive politics involving noble-led factions and powerful conversos, many of whom served the Crown, did not so much deflect attention away from the Jews as cast more aspersions on them. The enemies of converso officials attributed their alleged abuses and malfeasance to their Jewish roots and real or imagined Judaizing. Whatever the religious beliefs and practices of these influential conversos, in this type of public discourse Jews and Judaism were represented as the root of all evil. Thus in some Castilian cities elite conversos made a point of distancing themselves from Jews and even of harassing them. The heated political environment of several cities in Andalucía and New Castile made them unpropitious for Jewish communities and for conversos with Jewish connections.[7]

In the kingdom of Valencia, as has been seen, conversos were not at the center of social and political upheaval as they were in Castile; thus it did not witness the same kind of strident anticonverso activity that reflected so negatively on the Jews of Castile. The firm relationship between the Jews of Morvedre and Judaizing conversos in Valencia therefore did not translate into grave social and political problems for the former. The Jews' role in fostering "heresy" became the source of serious difficulties for them only when the Spanish Inquisition arrived and publicly labeled such activity a crime.

Politically motivated action against Jews and conversos, however, was not absent from the Crown of Aragon. In Catalonia consistent constitutional opposition to the kings of the new Trastámara dynasty included agitation against Jews and conversos, the perceived and real allies of the monarchy. In 1419–20 the Catalan Corts not only objected to Alfonso IV's revocation of the anti-Jewish ordinances of Benedict XIII and Fernando I but attempted to make them part of the "constitutions" of the principality. The small Jewish communities — some of them, like the one in Girona, the remnants of once great aljamas — suffered from the molestations of municipal officials who did not fear to challenge the Crown or to lose aljamas whose economic weight had considerably diminished since 1391. During the Catalan civil war (1462–72)

---

[7] Benito Ruano 1961; MacKay 1972 and 1985; Monsalvo Antón 1985, 277–336; Haliczer 1973 and 1997.

Catalan troops sacked the Jewish quarter of Cervera and threatened to do the same in Tárrega. Fearing rebel aggression, affluent converso families fled from Barcelona. In the kingdom of Aragon Jews and conversos encountered fewer difficulties of this sort, in part because Aragonese opposition to the Trastámaras was less fierce. True, the Aragonese and their Cortes often proved uncooperative, but they did not violently rebel against the monarchy. In fact, Zaragoza, the capital and home of the largest Jewish community, offered Juan II much assistance during the Catalan civil war.[8] Valencians, as has been noted, cooperated for the most part with Alfonso IV and Juan II, and provided both kings with substantial revenue. The Jews and conversos of the kingdom were therefore not put in a dangerous position by virtue of their ties to the monarchy.

Besides being in a propitious town environment and in a kingdom that was not plagued by the kind of political strife that caused so many problems for the Jews and conversos of Castile and Catalonia, the Jews' revival in Morvedre was facilitated and their relations with Christians ameliorated by a third key factor. This was the introduction of new credit mechanisms — the censal and violari — and the rise of the purchasers of these annuities, the censalistas, to a position of dominance in the kingdom's credit markets, a position the Jews had occupied until the later fourteenth century. When combined with the development of a more elaborate and efficient royal fiscal regime that taxed the Jews more moderately and regularly, the restructuring of regional credit markets released Jews from the necessity of lending money and then pressuring Christian debtors in order to render huge subsidies to the king. Well-to-do Jews diversified their investments and the Jewish community as a whole engaged in a wider range of economic activities, often, as has been seen, with considerable success. Even though Jews still loaned small amounts to farmers and artisans, Jewish usury — now illegal but in fact disguised — ceased to be a subject about which bishops and friars fulminated and Christian debtors protested. The censalistas were now the wielders of financial power. The use of the censals was widespread: not only did municipalities and aljamas sell these annuities to creditors to raise funds in the public interest; individuals of all faiths sold them in order to obtain money for private purposes. The censal became the credit instrument of choice at all levels of society. Jewish usury, a perennial source of tension between Christian and Jew in the thirteenth and fourteenth centuries, was no longer one in the kingdom of Valencia in the fifteenth century.

The kingdom of Aragon saw similar developments. There too municipalities and Jewish aljamas, such as those of Zaragoza and Huesca, were in debt to censalistas.[9] There too Jewish economic activity was highly diversified. There too relations between Christians and Jews were stable, unmarked by outbreaks

---

[8] Riera i Sans 1993b, 74–79, 83–90; Falcón Pérez and Palacios Martín 1982, 588–589.
[9] Falcón Pérez 1997, 267–270; Motis Dolader 1990, 1: 165–179; Durán Gudiol 1984, 130–132.

of violence. There too, although Jews still loaned small sums to Christians and Muslims, "Jewish usury" ceased to be a major topic of public discussion. As Motis Dolader puts it, "Officially, [Jewish] loans seemed to vanish."[10]

In their recourse to the annuity as an instrument of credit for both public and private purposes, the lands of the Crown of Aragon were precocious.[11] The same cannot be said for either Castile or Italy, where in the fifteenth century Jewish usury consequently remained a topic of public debate, Christian complaint, and a reason for anti-Jewish agitation. The Castilian Cortes often complained about it; sometimes they reduced the rate of interest Jewish lenders could charge, other times they outlawed all interest. Whatever the legislation passed, and regardless of the fact that in Castile, like everywhere else, there were many Christian usurers, Jews remained, in the public perception, the usurers par excellence.[12] Private recourse to the sale of annuities did not become widespread in Castile until well into the sixteenth century; hence credit markets could not be restructured in such a way as to reduce and obscure the Jews' role.[13]

As for Italy, Tirosh-Rothschild neatly characterizes the Jews' situation: "Ironically, the major focus of anti-Jewish sentiment and legislation in Western Europe — moneylending — became the catalyst for the growth and creativity of Jews in fifteenth-century Italy."[14] Growth and creativity, indeed, but the price the Jews paid was living an insecure existence — from one residence charter to another — and becoming the targets of Franciscan preachers who endeavored to establish charity funds (*monti di pieta*) in order to drive Jews out of the credit business and even out of town. The Jews of Morvedre could flourish without living this kind of paradox. They managed to get out from under the yoke of usury.

These social, political, and economic conditions were sufficient for the Jewish community in Morvedre to grow and prosper and to enjoy reasonably good relations with the Christians and Muslims of the region, perhaps as good as one could hope for in the fifteenth century. The word "renaissance" perhaps suggests something more, something that looks and feels like real progress, something that seems like the dawn of a new age. But between 1391 and 1492 Jews and Christians were a long way — centuries away — from putting their relationship on an entirely new footing. Considering that we are, after all, talking about a medieval Jewish community, we should not expect too much when

---

[10] Motis Dolader 1997a, 89.

[11] Schnapper 1965, 978–983; Sánchez Martínez 1995, 126–129.

[12] Monsalvo Antón 1985, 177–179, 186–187, 295, 308–310, 321; Haliczer 1997, 248; Fernández Bilbao 1997, 267–270.

[13] Bennassar 1960. The use of *juros* for public purposes, however, began earlier (Castillo Pintado 1963, 44–46).

[14] Tirosh-Rothschild 1991, 12; also, Molho 1971, 38–40, 150–152; Gow and Griffiths 1994; and sources cited in introduction, n. 25.

wondering about the appropriateness of the term "renaissance." Nor, when we consider humanity and the ability of communities of different faiths and backgrounds to get along and get on with life, should we expect too little. No great leap of the imagination is needed to place the words of the twentieth-century Catalan poet Salvador Espriu in the mouth of a Jew in Morvedre circa 1470, a Jew all too aware of his community's past, optimistic about its present circumstances, but ignorant about its future:

> So, when someone
> asks us,
> sometimes,
> in a harsh voice:
>> "Why have you stayed
>> here in this hard, dry land,
>> this land soaked in blood?
>> This is surely not
>> the best of the lands you came upon
>> in the long
>> trial
>> of your Exile." —
> with a small smile
> that remembers our fathers,
> and our grandfathers,
> we only say:
>> "In our dreams, yes, it is."[15]

[15] Espriu 1977, verse 7.

GLOSSARY

adelantat — an executive official in a Jewish or Muslim community

aljama — a legally constituted Jewish or Muslim community, analogous to a Christian municipality

alqueria — hamlet; small agricultural settlement

amīn — an official in a Muslim community with fiscal and policing functions

cena de presencia — a hospitality tax paid by each municipality or *aljama* to support the visiting royal court

censal — a mortgaged loan, widely used in the Crown of Aragon from the mid–fourteenth century

censalista — purchaser of a *censal* and recipient of the annuity

cisa — indirect tax on the sale of foodstuffs and on other transactions

clavari — treasurer in the Jewish *aljama*

consell — municipal or communal council

converso — Jewish convert to Christianity, especially after 1391

cotum — official rate of interest for Jewish lenders set by the Crown

fanecada — unit of measure equal to 831 square meters

Furs — the law code of the kingdom of Valencia

halakhah — Jewish law

jueria — Jewish quarter

jurat — an executive official of a Christian municipality

kasher — ritually fit according to Jewish law

maestre racional — auditor of the royal accounts

malshin, malsin — an informer

malshinut — the act of informing

matzah — unleavened bread eaten by Jews on Passover

morabatí — a tax originally granted to Jaume I in exchange for his promise not to tamper with the coinage; normally collected every seven years from all households at a rate of 1 morabatí (7 sous) per household

moreria — Muslim quarter

mossèn — an honorific form of address, literally "my sir"

Mudejar — a Muslim living under Christian rule in Iberia

mustaçaff — municipal official in charge of the market

peita — property tax

pena del quart — a fine collected from a dilatory debtor equivalent to one-quarter of the sum owed

prohomens — the leading men of a town

qāḍī — judge in an Islamic court

seder — the Passover meal

terç de delme — one-third of the ecclesiastical tithe that the papacy had originally granted Jaume I the right to collect in all territories under direct royal lordship

terme — municipal district

violari — like the *censal*, a mortgaged loan repaid in the form of annuities; usually automatically extinguished on the death of the creditor, it carried a higher rate of interest than the *censal*

BIBLIOGRAPHY

Abulafia, D. 1994. *A Mediterranean Emporium: The Catalan Kingdom of Majorca* (Cambridge).

Adelman, H. 1991. "Italian Jewish Women," in *Jewish Women in Historical Perspective*, ed. J. R. Baskin, pp. 135–158 (Detroit).

Ainaud de Lasarte, J. 1972. "Alfonso the Magnanimous and the Plastic Arts of His Time," in *Spain in the Fifteenth Century*, ed. R. Highfield, pp. 193–225 (New York).

Archivo Histórico Municipal de Segorbe, 1286–1910, ed. F. J. Guerrero Carot (Valencia, 1986).

Assaf, S. 1933. "The *Conversos* of Spain and Portugal in Responsa Literature" (in Hebrew), *Me'assef Zion* 5: 19–60.

Assis, Y. 1981. "The 'Ordinance of Rabbenu Gershom' and Polygamous Marriages in Spain" (in Hebrew), *Zion* 46: 251–277.

———. 1985. "Crime and Violence in Jewish Society in Spain (13th–14th Centuries)" (in Hebrew), *Zion* 50: 221–240.

———. 1988. "Sexual Behaviour in Mediaeval Hispano-Jewish Society," in *Jewish History: Essays in Honour of Chimen Abramsky*, ed. A. Rapaport-Albert and S. Zipperstein, pp. 25–59 (London).

———. 1997. *The Golden Age of Aragonese Jewry: Community and Society in the Crown of Aragon, 1213–1327* (London).

Aureum opus regalium privilegiorum civitatis et regni Valentie, ed. L. Alanya (Valencia, 1515; facsimile ed., 1972).

Baer, Y. (F.) 1929–36. *Die Juden im Christlichen Spanien: Urkunden und Regesten*, 2 vols. (Berlin).

———. 1961. *A History of the Jews in Christian Spain*, trans. L. Schoffman, 2 vols. (Philadelphia).

Barceló Torres, M. C. 1984. *Minorías islámicas en el País Valenciano: Historia y dialecto* (Valencia).

Barrio-Barrio, J. A. 1993. "El señorío de los Daya y el municipio de Orihuela en el siglo XV," in *Señorío y feudalismo*, vol. 3, pp. 259–270.

Beinart, H. 1978. "Jewish Witnesses for the Prosecution of the Spanish Inquisition," in *Essays in Honour of Ben Beinart: Acta Juridica*, pp. 37–46 (Capetown).

———. 1981. *Conversos on Trial: The Inquisition in Ciudad Real*, trans. Y. Guiladi (Jerusalem).

———. 1986. "The Separation of Living Quarters between Jews and Christians in Fifteenth-Century Spain" (in Hebrew), *Zion* 51: 61–85.

———. 1994. *The Expulsion of the Jews from Spain* (in Hebrew; Jerusalem).

Belenguer Cebrià, E. 1976. *València en la crisi del segle XV* (Barcelona).

———. 1989. "Els trets institucionals," in *Història del País Valencià*, pp. 351–373.

Beltrán de Heredia, V. 1961. "Las bulas de Nicolas V acerca de los conversos de Castilla," *Sefarad* 21: 22–47.

Benito Ruano, E. 1961. *Toledo en el siglo XV: Vida política* (Madrid).

Bennassar, B. 1960. "En Vieille-Castille: Les ventes de rentes perpétuelles, première moitié du XVIe siècle," *Annales ESC* 15: 1115–1126.

Berger, D. 1996. *The Jewish-Christian Debate in the High Middle Ages: A Critical Edition of the Nizzahon vetus*, 2d ed. (Northvale, N.J.).

Bernabé Gil, D. 1994. "Las oligarquías urbanas del reino de Valencia en el tránsito a la Edad Moderna," in *1490 — En el umbral de la modernidad: El Mediterráneo europeo y las ciudades en el tránsito de los siglos XV–XVI*, ed. J. Hinojosa Montalvo and J. Pradells Nadal, vol. 1, pp. 205–231 (Valencia).

Blumenthal, D. 2000. "Implements of Labor, Instruments of Honor: Muslim, Eastern, and Black African Slaves in Fifteenth-Century Valencia" (Ph.D. dissertation; University of Toronto).

Bokser, B. M. 1984. *The Origins of the Seder: The Passover Rite and Early Rabbinic Judaism* (Berkeley).

Bonfil, R. 1984. "The Historian's Perception of the Jews in the Italian Renaissance: Towards a Reappraisal," *Revue des Etudes Juives* 143: 59–82.

———. 1994. *Jewish Life in Renaissance Italy*, trans. A. Oldcorn (Berkeley).

Boswell, J. 1977. *The Royal Treasure: Muslim Communities under the Crown of Aragon in the Fourteenth Century* (New Haven).

Brumberg-Kraus, J. 1999. "Meat-Eating and Jewish Identity: Ritualization of the Priestly 'Torah of Beast and Fowl' (Lev. 11:46) in Rabbinic Judaism and Medieval Kabbalah," *Association for Jewish Studies Review* 24: 227–262.

Burns, R. I. 1996. *Jews in the Notarial Culture: Latinate Wills in Mediterranean Spain, 1250–1350* (Berkeley).

Cantera Montenegro, E. 1979. "Judíos de Torrelaguna: Retorno de algunos expulsados entre 1493 y 1495," *Sefarad* 39: 333–346.

Cárcel Ortí, M. M. 1998. "Casa, corte y cancillería del obispo de Valencia Hug de Llupià, 1398–1427," *Anuario de Estudios Medievales* 28: 635–659.

Carmen Peris, M. 1990. "La prostitución valenciana en la segunda mitad del siglo XIV," *Revista d'Història Medieval* 1: 179–199.

Carrete Parrondo, C. 1992. *El judaísmo español y la Inquisición* (Madrid).

Castaño González, J. 1995. "Las aljamas judías de Castilla a mediados del siglo XV: La Carta Real de 1450," *En la España Medieval* 18: 183–205.

———. 1998. "Tensiones entre las comunidades judías y la monarquía en Castilla, c. 1447–1474: El nombramiento del Juez Mayor de las aljamas," in *Creencias y culturas: Cristianos, judíos y musulmanes en la España medieval*, ed. C. Carrete Parrondo and A. Meyuhas Ginio, pp. 11–20 (Salamanca).

Castillo Pintado, A. 1963. "Los juros de Castilla: Apogeo y fin de un instrumento de crédito," *Hispania* 23: 43–70.

Castillo Sainz, J. 1993. "De solidaritats jueves a confraries de conversos: Entre la fossilització i la integració d'una minoria religiosa," *Revista d'Història Medieval* 4: 183–205.

Catlos, B. 2003. *The Victors and the Vanquished: Christians and Muslims in the Ebro Valley* (Cambridge).

Chabret Fraga, A. 1979. *Sagunto: Su historia y sus monumentos*, 2 vols. (reprint of 1888 ed.; Sagunto).

Chazan, R. 1989. *Daggers of Faith: Thirteenth-Century Christian Missionizing and Jewish Response* (Berkeley).

———. 1992. *Barcelona and Beyond: The Disputation of 1263 and Its Aftermath* (Berkeley).

Císcar Pallarés, E. 1977. *Tierra y señorío en el País Valenciano, 1570–1620* (Valencia).

Cohen, G. D. 1967. Review of B. Netanyahu, *The Marranos of Spain*, in *Jewish Social Studies* 29: 178–184.

Cohen, J. 1982. *The Friars and the Jews: The Evolution of Medieval Anti-Judaism* (Ithaca).

Col.loqui Corona, municipis i fiscalitat a la baixa Edat Mitjana, ed. M. Sánchez and A. Furió (Lleida, 1997).

Crouzet-Pavan, E. 1992. "Venice between Jerusalem, Byzantium, and Divine Retribution: The Origins of the Ghetto," in *Jews, Christians, and Muslims in the Mediterranean World after 1492*, ed. A. Meyuhas Ginio, pp. 163–179 (London).

Cruselles, E. 1992. "'Todo es cerrazón y noche:' La sociedad urbana valenciana en la encrucijada a los tiempos modernos," *Revista d'Història Medieval* 3: 117–141.

Cueves Granero, M. A. 1959. "Problemas valencianos de los primeros años del reinado de Alfonso el Magnánimo," in *IV Congreso de Historia de la Corona de Aragón*, vol. 1, pp. 447–465 (Palma de Mallorca).

Danvila, F. 1886. "El robo de la judería de Valencia en 1391," *Boletín de la Real Academia de la Historia* 8: 358–397.

———. 1891. "Clausura y delimitación de la judería de Valencia en 1390 á 91," *Boletín de la Real Academia de la Historia* 18: 142–158.

Díaz de Rábago, C. 1994. *La morería de Castelló de la Plana, 1462–1527: Estudio socioeconómico de una aljama musulmana medieval* (Castellón).

Dinur, B. 1967. "A Wave of Emigration from Spain to Eretz Yisrael after the Persecutions of 1391" (in Hebrew), *Zion* 32: 161–174.

Doñate Sebastià, J., and J. R. Magdalena Nom de Déu. 1990. *Three Jewish Communities in Medieval Valencia: Castellón de la Plana, Burriana, Villarreal*, trans. S. Nakache and E. Gutwirth (Jerusalem).

Duran, E. 1982. *Les Germanies als Paisos Catalans* (Barcelona).

Duran, Simon ben Ẓemaḥ. *She'elot u-teshuvot* (Amsterdam, 1741).

Durán Gudiol, A. 1984. *La Judería de Huesca* (Zaragoza).

Edwards, J. 1984a. *Christian Córdoba: The City and Its Region in the Late Middle Ages* (Cambridge).

———. 1984b. "Jewish Testimony to the Spanish Inquisition: Teruel, 1484–7," *Revue des Etudes Juives* 143: 333–350.

Eimeric, N., and F. Peña. 1983. *El manual de los inquisidores*, trans. L. Sala-Molins and F. Martín (Barcelona).

Emery, R. 1959. *The Jews of Perpignan in the Thirteenth Century* (New York).

Epistolari de la València medieval, ed. A. Rubio Vela, 2 vols. (Valencia, 1985–98).

Epstein, I. 1968. *The Responsa of Rabbi Simon B. Ẓemaḥ Duran: A Source of the History of the Jews in North Africa*, in *Studies in the Communal Life of the Jews of Spain, As Reflected in the Responsa of Rabbi Solomon ben Adreth and Rabbi Simon ben Zemach Duran*, 2d ed. (New York).

Espriu, S. 1977. *La Pell de Brau* (Madrid); trans. as *The Bull-Hide* by B. Raffel (Calcutta).

Falcón Pérez, M. I. 1997. "Finanzas y fiscalidad de ciudades, villas y comunidades de aldeas aragonesas," in *Finanzas y fiscalidad municipal: V Congreso de Estudios Medievales*, pp. 239–273 (Avila).

Falcón Pérez, M. I., and B. Palacios Martín. 1982. "Las haciendas municipales de
    Zaragoza, a mediados del siglo XV," in *Historia de la hacienda española, épocas an-
    tigua y medieval: Homenaje al Profesor García de Valdeavellano*, pp. 539–606
    (Madrid).
Fellous, S. 1998. "La Biblia de Alba: L'iconographie ambiguë," in *Creencias y culturas:
    Cristianos, judíos y musulmanes en la España medieval*, ed. C. Carrete Parrondo and
    A. Meyuhas Ginio, pp. 41–96 (Salamanca).
Fernández Bilbao, L. 1997. "News about the Jewish Community upon its Departure,"
    in *The Jews of Spain and the Expulsion of 1492*, ed. M. Lazar and S. Haliczer, pp.
    263–276 (Lancaster, Calif.).
Ferrer i Mallol, M. T. 1970–71. "El patrimoni reial i la recuperació dels senyorius ju-
    risdiccionals en els estats catalano-aragonesos a la fi del segle XIV," *Anuario de Es-
    tudios Medievales* 7: 351–491.
Ferrer Micó, R. 1982. "Pau e Treua en Valencia," in *Estudios dedicados a Juan Peset
    Aleixandre*, vol. 3, pp. 1–15 (Valencia).
———. 1997. "Los beneficiarios del municipio: Arrendatarios y censualistas de la ciu-
    dad de Valencia," in *Col.loqui Corona*, pp. 643–674.
Ferrer Navarro, R. 1980. "Los judíos en el comercio valenciano durante el siglo XIV,"
    in *Primer Congreso de Historia del País Valenciano*, vol. 2, pp. 811–820 (Valencia).
Foa, A. 2000. *The Jews of Europe after the Black Death*, trans. A. Grover (Berkeley).
Fort i Cogull, E. 1973. *Catalunya i la Inquisició* (Barcelona).
Fredman, R. G. 1981. *The Passover Seder: Afikoman in Exile* (Philadelphia).
Furió, A. 1982. *Camperols del País Valencià: Sueca, una comunitat rural a la tardor de
    l'Edat Mitjana* (Valencia).
———. 1993a. "Crédito y endeudamiento: El censal en la sociedad rural valenciana,
    siglos XIV–XV," in *Señorío y feudalismo*, vol. 1, pp. 501–534.
———. 1993b. "Diners i crèdit: Els jueus d'Alzira en la segona meitat del segle XIV,"
    Revista d'Història Medieval 4: 127–160.
———. 1995. *Història del País Valencià* (Valencia).
———. 1997a. "Senyors i senyories al País Valencià al final de l'Edat Mitjana," *Re-
    vista d'Història Medieval* 8: 109–151.
———. 1997b. "Estructures fiscals, pressió impositiva i reproducció econòmica al País
    Valencià en la baixa Edat Mitjana," in *Col.loqui Corona*, pp. 495–525.
Furs de València, ed. G. Colón and A. Garcia, 9 vols. (Barcelona, 1970–2002).
Gampel, B. 1989. *The Last Jews on Iberian Soil: Navarrese Jewry, 1479/1498* (Berkeley).
———. 1998. "Does Medieval Navarrese Jewry Salvage Our Notion of *Convivencia*?"
    in *In Iberia and Beyond: Hispanic Jews between Cultures*, ed. B. Cooperman, pp. 97–
    122 (London).
Garcia, A. 1987. *Els Vives: Una família de jueus valencians* (Valencia).
García Ballester, L. 1988. *La medicina a la València medieval* (Valencia).
———. 1994. "A Marginal Learned Medical World: Jewish, Muslim, and Christian
    Medical Practitioners and the Use of Arabic Medical Sources in Medieval Spain," in
    Practical Medicine from Salerno to the Black Death, ed. L. García Ballester, R.
    French, J. Arrizabalaga, and Andrew Cunningham, pp. 353–394 (Cambridge).
García Cárcel, R. 1976a. *Orígenes de la Inquisición Española. El tribunal de Valencia,
    1478–1530* (Barcelona).
———. 1976b. "El censo de 1510 y la población valenciana de la primera mitad del
    siglo XVI," *Saitabi* 26: 171–188.

————. 1981. *Las Germanías de Valencia*, 2d ed. (Barcelona).

García Marsilla, J. V. 1993. *La jerarquía de la mesa: Los sistemas alimentarios en la Valencia bajomedieval* (Valencia).

García Marsilla, J. V. and J. Sáiz Serrano. 1997. "De la peita al censal: Finanzas municipales y clases dirigentes en la Valencia de los siglos XIV y XV," in *Col.loqui Corona*, pp. 307–334.

Garcia Oliver, F. 1991. *Terra de feudals: El País Valencià en la tardor de l'Edat Mitjana* (Valencia).

————. 1994. "De Perpinyà a Elx: Desenvolupament económic i geografia de les aljames," in *Xudeus e conversos na historia*, ed. C. Barros, vol. 2, pp. 247–261 (Santiago de Compostela).

————. 1997a. "El censal en el senyoriu: Valldigna, 1393–1530," *Revista d'Història Medieval* 8: 153–173.

————. 1997b. "Estructura agrària i crisi rural. La Corona d'Aragó en el tombant de l'Edat Mitjana," in *La Corona de Aragón y el Mediterráneo, siglos XV–XVI*, ed. E. Sarasa Sánchez and E. Serrano Martín, pp. 41–61 (Zaragoza).

García Sanz, A. 1961. "El censal," *Boletín de la Sociedad Castellonense de Cultura* 37: 281–310.

Gerber, J. 1992. *The Jews of Spain: A History of the Sephardic Experience* (New York).

Gitlitz, D. 1996. *Secrecy and Deceit: The Religion of the Crypto-Jews* (Philadelphia).

Glick, T. F. 1979. *Islamic and Christian Spain in the Early Middle Ages: Comparative Perspectives on Social and Cultural Formation* (Princeton).

Goldberg, H. 1987. "Torah and Children: Some Symbolic Aspects of the Reproduction of Jews and Judaism," in *Judaism Viewed from Within and Without: Anthropological Studies*, ed. H. Goldberg, pp. 107–124 (Albany).

Gow, A., and G. Griffiths. 1994. "Pope Eugenius IV and Jewish Money-Lending in Florence: The Case of Salomone di Bonaventura during the Chancellorship of Leonardo Bruni," *Renaissance Quarterly* 47: 282–329.

Grayzel, S. 1989. *The Church and the Jews in the XIIIth Century*, vol 2, *1254–1314*, ed. K. Stow (Detroit).

Guinot Rodríguez, E. 1986. "Un precedent en la recuperació del patrimoni reial al País Valencià: La jurisdicció d'Onda, 1393," *Saitabi* 36: 137–153.

Guiral, J. 1974. "Les relations commerciales du royaume de Valence avec la Berbérie au XVe siècle," *Mélanges de la Casa de Velázquez* 10: 99–121.

————. 1975. "Convers à Valence à la fin du XVe siècle," *Mélanges de la Casa de Velázquez* 11:81–98.

————. 1986. *Valence, port méditerranéen au XVe siècle, 1410–1525* (Paris).

Gutwirth, E. 1985. "El comercio hispano-magrebi y los judíos, 1391–1444," *Hispania* 45: 199–205.

————. 1989a. "Abraham Seneor: Social Tensions and the Court Jew," *Michael* 11: 169–229.

————. 1989b. "Hispano-Jewish Attitudes to the Moors in the Fifteenth Century," *Sefarad* 49: 237–261.

————. 1992. "Towards Expulsion, 1391–1492," in *Spain and the Jews: The Sephardi Experience 1492 and After*, ed. E. Kedourie, pp. 51–73 (London).

————. 1998. "Jewish and Christian Messianism in XVth Century Spain," in *The Expulsion of the Jews and Their Emigration to the Southern Low Countries, 15th–16th c.*, ed. L. Dequeker and W. Verbeke, pp. 1–22 (Leuven).

———. 1999. "History and Intertextuality in Late Medieval Spain," in *Christians, Muslims, and Jews in Medieval and Early Modern Spain: Interaction and Cultural Change*, ed. M. Meyerson and E. English, pp. 161–178 (Notre Dame, Ind.).

Hacker, J. 1985. "Links between Spanish Jewry and Palestine, 1391–1492," in *Vision and Conflict in the Holy Land*, ed. R. I. Cohen, pp. 111–139 (New York).

———. 1992. "'If We Have Forgotten the Name of Our God' (Psalm 44:21): Interpretation in Light of the Realities in Medieval Spain" (in Hebrew), *Zion* 57: 247–274.

Haliczer, S. 1973. "The Castilian Urban Patriciate and the Jewish Expulsions of 1480–92," *American Historical Review* 78: 35–58.

———. 1990. *Inquisition and Society in the Kingdom of Valencia, 1478–1834* (Berkeley).

———. 1997. "The Expulsion of the Jews as Social Process," in *The Jews of Spain and the Expulsion of 1492*, ed. M. Lazar and S. Haliczer, pp. 237–251 (Lancaster, Calif.).

Hershman, A. M. 1943. *Rabbi Isaac Ben Sheshet Perfet and His Times* (New York).

Hillgarth, J. N. 1976–78. *The Spanish Kingdoms, 1250–1516*, 2 vols. (Oxford).

———. 1985. "Spanish Historiography and Iberian Reality," *History and Theory* 24: 23–43.

Hinojosa Montalvo, J. 1976. "Sobre mercaderes extrapeninsulares en la Valencia del siglo XV," *Saitabi* 26: 64–77.

———. 1979. "Actividades comerciales de los judíos en Valencia, 1391–1492," *Saitabi* 29: 21–42.

———. 1981. "La comunidad hebrea en Valencia: Del esplendor a la nada, 1377–1391," *Saitabi* 31: 47–72.

———. 1983. "Solidaridad judía ante la expulsión: Contratos de embarque, Valencia, 1492," *Saitabi* 33: 105–124.

———. 1985. "Actividades judías en la Valencia del siglo XIV," in *La ciudad hispánica durante los siglos XIII al XVI*, vol. 2, pp. 1547–1566 (Madrid).

———. 1993a. *The Jews of the Kingdom of Valencia: From Persecution to Expulsion, 1391–1492*, trans. S. Nakache (Jerusalem).

———. 1993b. "La inserció de la minoria hebrea en la formació social valenciana," *Revista d'Història Medieval* 4: 45–64.

———. 1995. "Apuntes para la demografía de la aljama judía de Sagunto en los siglos bajomedievales," *Sefarad* 55: 273–284.

———. 1999. "From Suxén to Salvador: The Saga of a Jewish Valencian Lineage," *Hispania Judaica Bulletin* 2: 17–33.

Hirschberg, H. Z. 1974–81. *A History of the Jews of North Africa*, 2 vols. (Leiden).

Història del País Valencià, vol. 2, *De la conquesta a la federació hispànica* (Barcelona, 1989).

Hughes, D. O. 1986. "Distinguishing Signs: Ear-rings, Jews, and Franciscan Rhetoric in the Italian Renaissance City," *Past and Present* 112: 3–59.

Iborra Lerma, J. M. 1981. *Realengo y señorío en el Camp de Morvedre* (Sagunto).

Idel, M. 1999. "Chronicle of an Exile: R. Isaac ben Hayim Ha-Kohen from Xàtiva" (in Hebrew), in *Jews and Conversos at the Time of the Expulsion*, ed. Y. Assis and Y. Kaplan, pp. 259–272 (Jerusalem).

Igual Luis, D. 1994. "Las galeras mercantiles venecianas y el puerto de Valencia, 1391–1534," *Anuario de Estudios Medievales* 24: 179–200.

Iradiel, P. 1986. "Familia y función económica de la mujer en actividades no agrarias," in *La condición de la mujer en la Edad Media*, pp. 223–259 (Madrid).

———. 1989. "L'evolució econòmica," in *Història del País Valencià*, pp. 267–324.

Iradiel, P., and G. Navarro. 1996. "La seda en Valencia en la Edad Media," in *España y Portugal en las rutas de la seda: Diez siglos de producción y comercio entre Oriente y Occidente*, pp. 183–200 (Barcelona).

Iradiel, P., D. Igual, G. Navarro, and J. Aparici. 1995. *Oficios artesanales y comercio en Castelló de la Plana, 1371–1527* (Castelló).

Jiménez Jiménez, M. R. 1959. "La política judaizante de Alfonso V a la luz de las concesiones otorgadas en 1419 a la aljama de Murviedro," in *IV Congreso de Historia de la Corona de Aragón*, vol. 1, pp. 251–262 (Palma de Mallorca).

Klausner, J. 1955. *The Messianic Idea in Israel: From Its Beginning to the Completion of the Mishnah*, trans. W. F. Stinespring, 3d ed. (New York).

Kriegel, M. 1978. "La prise d'une décision: L'expulsion des juifs d'Espagne," *Revue Historique* 260: 49–90.

———. 1979. *Les juifs à la fin du Moyen Age dans l'Europe méditerranéenne* (Paris).

Küchler, W. 1963. "Mosse Mahir Suxen: Ein Beitrag zur Inquisition und zum Judenregal in den Ländern der Aragonischen Krone," *Gesammelte Aufsätze zur Kulturgeschichte Spaniens* 21: 175–186.

———. 1968. "Besteuerung der Juden und Mauren in den Ländern der Krone Aragons während des 15. Jahrhunderts," *Gesammelte Aufsätze zur Kulturgeschichte Spaniens* 24: 227–256.

———. 1997. *Les finances de la Corona d'Aragó al segle XV, regnats d'Alfons V i Joan II*, trans. V. Farías Zurita (Valencia).

Ladero Quesada, M. A. 1984. "Judeoconversos andaluces en el siglo XV," in *Actas del III Coloquio de Historia Medieval Andaluza: La sociedad medieval andaluza, grupos no privilegiados*, pp. 27–55 (Jaén).

Lawee, E. 1995. "On the Threshold of the Renaissance: New Methods and Sensibilities in the Biblical Commentaries of Isaac Abarbanel," *Viator* 26: 283–319.

———. 1996. "'Israel Has No Messiah' in Late Medieval Spain," *Journal of Jewish Thought and Philosophy* 5: 245–279.

———. 2001. "The Messianism of Isaac Abarbanel, 'Father of the (Jewish) Messianic Movements of the Sixteenth and Seventeenth Centuries,'" in *Millenarianism and Messianism in Early Modern European Culture: Jewish Messianism in the Early Modern World*, ed. M. Goldish and R. H. Popkin, pp. 1–39 (Leiden).

León Tello, P. 1963. *Judíos de Avila* (Avila).

Lesley, A. M. 1988. "Jewish Adaptation of Humanist Concepts in Fifteenth- and Sixteenth-Century Italy," in *Renaissance Rereadings: Intertext and Context*, ed. M. Cline Horowitz, pp. 51–66 (Urbana).

Levine Melammed, R. 1986. "The Ultimate Challenge: Safeguarding the Crypto-Judaic Heritage," *Proceedings of the American Academy for Jewish Research* 53: 91–109.

———. 1999. *Heretics or Daughters of Israel? The Crypto-Jewish Women of Castile* (Oxford).

Llop Català, M. 1995. *San Vicente Ferrer y los aspectos socioeconómicos del mundo medieval* (Valencia).

Llorens, P. 1967. "Los sarracenos de la Sierra de Eslida y Vall d'Uxó a fines del siglo XV," *Boletín de la Sociedad Castellonense de Cultura* 43: 53–67.

López Elum, P. 1974. "Proceso de incorporación a la Corona Real de Vall de Uxó, Sierra de Eslida y Segorbe en 1445," *Boletín de la Sociedad Castellonense de Cultura* 50: 50–65.

Lourie, E. 1989. "Jewish Moneylenders in the Local Catalan Community, c. 1300: Vilafranca del Penedés, Besalú and Montblanc," *Michael* 11: 33–98.

Maccoby, H. 1982. *Judaism on Trial* (East Brunswick, N.J.).

MacKay, A. 1972. "Popular Movements and Pogroms in Fifteenth-Century Castile," *Past and Present* 55: 33–67.

———. 1985. "The Hispanic-*Converso* Predicament," *Transactions of the Royal Historical Society*, 5th series, 35: 159–179.

Magdalena Nom de Déu, J. R. 1972. "Estructura socio-económica de las aljamas castellonenses a finales del siglo XV," *Sefarad* 32: 341–370.

———. 1974. "Población, propriedades e impuestos de los judíos de Castellón de la Plana durante la Baja Edad Media," *Sefarad* 34: 273–288.

———. 1988. *Judíos y cristianos ante la "Cort del Justícia" de Castellón* (Castelló).

———. 1988–89. "Aspectes de la vida dels jueus valencians a la llum d'unes fonts hebràiques: Les respostes de Rabí Yishaq Ben Séset Perfet, segona meitat del segle XIV," *Afers* 4: 189–205.

Maravall, J. A. 1969. "Franciscanismo, burguesía y mentalidad precapitalista: La obra de Eiximenis," in *VIII Congreso de Historia de la Corona de Aragón*, pp. 285–306 (Valencia).

Marcus, I. 1996. *Rituals of Childhood: Jewish Acculturation in Medieval Europe* (New Haven).

Mardurell, J. M. 1965. "El arte de la seda en Barcelona entre judíos y conversos: Notas para su historia," *Sefarad* 25: 247–281.

Márquez Villanueva, F. 1957. "Conversos y cargos concejiles en el siglo XV," *Revista de Archivos, Bibliotecas y Museos* 63: 503–540.

Meyerson, M. D. 1988. "Prostitution of Muslim Women in the Kingdom of Valencia: Religious and Sexual Discrimination in a Medieval Plural Society," in *The Medieval Mediterranean: Cross-Cultural Contacts*, ed. M. J. Chiat and K. Reyerson, pp. 87–95 (St. Cloud, Minn.).

———. 1991. *The Muslims of Valencia in the Age of Fernando and Isabel: Between Coexistence and Crusade* (Berkeley).

———. 1992. "Aragonese and Catalan Jewish Converts at the Time of the Expulsion," *Jewish History* 6: 131–149.

———. 1995a. "Religious Change, Regionalism, and Royal Power in the Spain of Fernando and Isabel," in *Iberia and the Mediterranean World of the Middle Ages: Studies in Honor of Robert I. Burns, S. J.*, ed. L. Simon, pp. 96–112 (Leiden).

———. 1995b. "Slavery and the Social Order: Mudejars and Christians in the Kingdom of Valencia," *Medieval Encounters* 1: 144–173.

———. 1996. "Slavery and Solidarity: Mudejars and Foreign Muslim Captives in the Kingdom of Valencia," *Medieval Encounters* 2: 286–343.

———. 1997. "The Jewish Community in Murviedro, 1391–1492," in *The Jews of Spain and the Expulsion of 1492*, ed. M. Lazar and S. Haliczer, pp. 129–146 (Lancaster, Calif.).

———. 1998. "The Economic Life of the Jews of Murviedro in the Fifteenth Century," in *In Iberia and Beyond: Hispanic Jews between Cultures*, ed. B. Cooperman, pp. 67–95 (London).

———. 2002. "Victims and Players: The Attack of the Union of Valencia on the Jews of Morvedre," in *Religion, Text, and Society in Medieval Spain and Northern Europe: Studies in Honor of J. N. Hillgarth*, ed. T. Burman, M. D. Meyerson, L. Shopkow, pp. 70–102 (Toronto).

———. 2003a. "Samuel of Granada and the Dominican Inquisitor: Jewish Magic and Jewish Heresy in Post-1391 Valencia," in *The Friars and the Jews in the Middle Ages and the Renaissance*, ed. S. McMichael and L. Simon (Leiden).

———. 2003b. "The Murder of Pau de Sant Martí: Jews, *Conversos*, and the Feud in Fifteenth-Century Valencia," in *"A Great Effusion of Blood"? Interpreting Medieval Violence*, ed. O. Falk, M. D. Meyerson, and D. Thiery (Toronto).

———. 2004a. *Jews in an Iberian Frontier Kingdom: Society, Economy, and Politics in Morvedre, 1248–1391* (Leiden).

———. 2004b. "'Assaulting the House': Interpreting Christian, Muslim, and Jewish Violence in Late Medieval Valencia," in *The Children of Abraham: Judaism, Christianity, and Islam in the Middle Ages*, ed. A. Dykman and M. Taccioni (University Park, Pa.).

———. 2004c. "Defending Their Jewish Subjects: Elionor of Sicily, María de Luna, and the Jews of Morvedre," in *Partners in Politics: Queens and Kings in Medieval and Early Modern Spain*, ed. T. Earenfight (Ashgate).

Mira Jódar, A. J. 1993. "Els diners dels jueus: Activitats econòmiques d'una família hebrea al món rural valencià," *Revista d'Història Medieval* 4: 108–125.

———. 1997. "*Administrar los drets al senyor rey pertanyents*: La gestión de la fiscalidad real en el País Valenciano en la Baja Edad Media," in *Col.loqui Corona*, pp. 527–553.

Mira Jódar, A. J. and P. Viciano Navarro. 1996. "La construcció d'un sistema fiscal: Municipis i impost al País Valencià," *Revista d'Història Medieval* 7: 135–148.

Miret y Sans, J. 1911–12. "El proces de les hosties contra.ls jueus d'Osca en 1377," *Anuari del Institut d'Estudis Catalans* 4: 59–80.

Mitre Fernández, E. 1994. *Los judíos de Castilla en tiempo de Enrique III: El pogrom de 1391* (Valladolid).

Molho, A. 1971. *Florentine Public Finances in the Early Renaissance, 1400–1433* (Cambridge, Mass.).

Monsalvo Antón, J. M. 1985. *Teoría y evolución de un conflicto social: El antisemitismo en la Corona de Castilla en la Baja Edad Media* (Madrid).

Motis Dolader, M. A. 1985. "Explotaciones agrarias de los judíos de Tarazona (Zaragoza) a fines del siglo XV," *Sefarad* 45: 353–390.

———. 1988. "Régimen de explotación de las propiedades agrarias judías en el noroeste del reino de Aragón en el siglo XV," *Hispania* 48: 405–492.

———. 1990. *La expulsión de los judíos del Reino de Aragón*, 2 vols. (Zaragoza).

———. 1996. "Población, urbanismo y estructura política de las aljamas judías de Aragón en el siglo XV," *Hispania* 56: 885–944.

———. 1997a. "The Socio-Economic Structures of the Jewish *Aljamas* in the Kingdom of Aragon, 1391–1492," in *The Jews of Spain and the Expulsion of 1492*, ed. M. Lazar and S. Haliczer, pp. 65–127 (Lancaster, Calif.).

———. 1997b. "Quiebra de la estructura multiconfesional en la Corona de Aragón y nacimiento del 'Estado Moderno'," in *La Corona de Aragón y el Mediterráneo, siglos XV–XVI*, ed. E. Sarasa Sánchez and E. Serrano Martín, pp. 155–230 (Zaragoza).

Muñoz Pomer, R. 1987. *Orígenes de la Generalitat Valenciana* (Valencia).

————. 1992. "Las Cortes valencianas y el cambio de las estructuras fiscales en el tránsito del siglo XIV al XV," *Anuario de Estudios Medievales* 22: 463–483.

Myers, D. N. 1995. *Re-Inventing the Jewish Past: European Jewish Intellectuals and the Zionist Return to History* (Oxford).

Narbona Vizcaíno, R. 1990. *Malhechores, violencia y justicia ciudadana en la Valencia bajomedieval* (Valencia).

————. 1992a. *Pueblo, poder y sexo: Valencia medieval, 1306–1420* (Valencia).

————. 1992b. "Finanzas municipales y patriciado urbano: Valencia a finales del Trescientos," *Anuario de Estudios Medievales* 22: 485–512.

————. 1994. "El nueve de octubre: Reseña histórica de una fiesta valenciana, siglos XIV–XX," *Revista d'Història Medieval* 5: 231–290.

————. 1995a. *Valencia, municipio medieval: Poder político y luchas ciudadanas, 1239–1418* (Valencia).

————. 1995b. "Marrades, un partit patrici," in *L'univers dels prohoms: Perfils socials a València baix-medieval*, pp. 17–55 (Valencia).

Navarro, G. 1992. *El despegue de la industría sedera en la Valencia del siglo XV* (Valencia).

Netanyahu, B. 1973. *The Marranos of Spain from the Late XIVth to the Early XVIth Century According to Contemporary Hebrew Sources*, 2d ed. (New York).

————. 1995. *The Origins of the Inquisition in Fifteenth-Century Spain* (New York).

Nirenberg, D. 1996. *Communities of Violence: Persecution of Minorities in the Middle Ages* (Princeton).

Orfali Levi, M. 1982. *Los conversos españoles en la literatura rabínica: Problemas jurídicos y opiniones legales durante los siglos XII–XVI* (Salamanca).

————. 1993. "Influencia de las sociedades cristiana y musulmana en la condición de la mujer judía," in *Arabes, judías y cristianas: Mujeres en Europa medieval*, ed. C. del Moral, pp. 77–89 (Granada).

Pacios López, A. 1957. *La Disputa de Tortosa: Estudio histórico-critico-doctrinal*, 2 vols. (Madrid).

Pastor Zapata, L. 1984. "Censales y propriedad feudal: El Real de Gandía, 1407–1550," *En la España Medieval* 4: 733–766.

Perarnau i Espelt, J. 1982. "El *Tractatus brevis super iurisdictione inquisitorum contra infideles fidem catholicam agitantes* de Nicolau Eimeric: Edició i estudi del text," *Arxiu de Textos Catalans Antics* 1: 79–126.

Pérez García, P. 1990. *La comparsa de los malhechores: Valencia, 1479–1518* (Valencia).

Perfet, R. Isaac ben Sheshet. *She'elot u-teshuvot* (Jerusalem, 1968).

Peris, M. C. 1990. "La prostitución valenciana en la segunda mitad del siglo XIV," *Revista d' Història Medieval* 1: 179–199.

Piles Ros, L. 1957. "La judería de Sagunto: Sus restos actuales," *Sefarad* 17: 352–373.

————. 1969. *Apuntes para la historia económica-social de Valencia durante el siglo XV* (Valencia).

————. 1970. *Estudio documental sobre el Bayle General de Valencia, su autoridad y jurisdicción* (Valencia).

———. 1978. *La población de Valencia a través de los "Llibres de Avehinament,"* *1400–1449* (Valencia).

———. 1984. "El dret del XXe e XXXXe: Para favorecer las relaciones comerciales de los judíos nor-africanos con el Reino de Valencia, 1393–1495," *Sefarad* 44: 217–282.

———. 1990. "El final de la aljama de los judíos de Burriana," *Sefarad* 50: 129–166, 373–411.

Puig i Oliver, J. 1980. "El procés dels lul.listes valencians contra Nicolau Eimeric en el marc del Cisma d'Occident," *Boletín de la Sociedad Castellonense de Cultura* 56: 319–463.

———. 1982. "El *Tractatus de haeresi et de infidelium incredulitate et de horum criminum iudice*, de Felip Ribot, O. Carm: Edició i estudi," *Arxiu de Textos Catalans Antics* 1: 127–190.

Pullan, B. 1971. *Rich and Poor in Renaissance Venice: The Social Institutions of a Catholic State, to 1620* (Oxford).

———. 1983. *The Jews of Europe and the Inquisition of Venice, 1550–1670* (New York).

Ravid, B. 2001. "The Venetian Government and the Jews," in *The Jews of Early Modern Venice*, ed. R. C. Davis and B. Ravid, pp. 3–30 (Baltimore).

Regev, S. 1997. "The Attitude Towards the *Conversos* in 15th-16th Century Jewish Thought," *Revue des Etudes Juives* 156: 117–134.

Rembaum, J. 1982. "The Talmud and the Popes: Reflections on the Talmud Trials in the 1240s," *Viator* 13: 203–221.

Riera i Sans, J. 1974. *La crònica en hebreu de la Disputa de Tortosa* (Barcelona).

———. 1977. "Los tumultos contra las juderías de la Corona de Aragón en 1391," *Cuadernos de Historia: Anexos de la Revista "Hispania"* 8: 213–225.

———. 1980. "Estrangers participants als avalots contra les jueries de la Corona d'Aragó el 1391," *Anuario de Estudios Medievales* 10: 577–583.

———. 1987. "Els avalots del 1391 a Girona," in *Jornades d'història dels jueus a Catalunya*, pp. 95–159 (Girona).

———. 1988. "La conflictivitat de l'alimentació dels jueus medievals, segles XII–XV," in *Alimentació i societat a la Catalunya medieval*, pp. 295–312 (Barcelona).

———. 1993a. "Jafudà Alatzar: Jueu de València," *Revista d'Història Medieval* 4: 65–100.

———. 1993b. "Judíos y conversos en los reinos de la Corona de Aragón durante el siglo XV," in *La expulsión de los judíos de España: II Curso de cultura hispano-judía y sefardí de la Universidad de Castilla–La Mancha*, pp. 71–90 (Toledo).

Roca, J. M. 1929. *Johan I d'Aragó* (Barcelona).

Rodríguez Fernández, J. 1976. *Las juderías de la provincia de León* (León).

Romano, D. 1991. "Cortesanos judíos en la Corona de Aragón," in *De historia judía hispánica*, pp. 401–413 (Barcelona).

Roth, C. 1959. *The Jews in the Renaissance* (Philadelphia).

Roth, N. 1995. *Conversos, Inquisition, and the Expulsion of the Jews from Spain* (Madison).

Rubin, M. 1999. *Gentile Tales: The Narrative Assault on Late Medieval Jews* (New Haven).

Rubio Vela, A. 1979. *Peste negra, crisis y comportamientos sociales en la España del siglo XIV: La ciudad de Valencia, 1348–1401* (Granada).

————. 1981. "Ideologia burguesa i progrés material a la València del Trescents," *L'Espill* 9: 11–38.

————. 1989. "La lenta recuperació, 1375–1410," in *Història del País Valencià*, pp. 235–264.

————. 1998. "Valencia y Torquemada: En torno a los comienzos de la Inquisición española, 1482–1489," *Boletín de la Sociedad Castellonense de Cultura* 74: 77–139.

Ruderman, D. 1981. *The World of a Renaissance Jew: The Life and Thought of Abraham ben Mordecai Farissol* (Cincinnati).

Ruzafa García, M. 1988. "Las relaciones económicas entre los mudéjares valencianos y el reino de Granada en el siglo XV," in *Relaciones exteriores del Reino de Granada*, ed. C. Segura Graiño, pp. 343–381 (Almería).

————. 1990. "Façen-se cristians los moros o muyren!" *Revista d'Història Medieval* 1: 87–110.

Ryder, A. 1990. *Alfonso the Magnanimous: King of Aragon, Naples and Sicily, 1396–1458* (Oxford).

Sánchez Martínez, M. 1995. *El naixement de la fiscalitat d'Estat a Catalunya, segles XII–XIV* (Girona).

Sánchez Moya, M. and J. Monasterio Aspiri. 1972–73. "Los judaizantes turolenses en el siglo XV," *Sefarad* 32: 105–140, 307–340; 33: 111–143, 325–356.

Sanchis Guarner, M. 1980. "Les raons de la discrepància entre Francesc Eiximenis i Sant Vicent Ferrer," in *Primer Congreso de Historia del País Valenciano*, vol. 2, pp. 665–670 (Valencia).

Schnapper, B. 1965. "Les rentes chez les théologiens et les canonistes du XIIIe au XVIe siècle," in *Etudes d'histoire du droit canonique dédiées à Gabriel le Bras*, vol. 1, pp. 965–995 (Paris).

Scholem, G. 1955. "The Kabbalistic Responsa of R. Yosef Alcastiel to R. Yehuda Hayyat" (in Hebrew), *Tarbiz* 24: 166–207.

Schwartz, D. 1991a. "The Spiritual-Intellectual Decline of the Jewish Community in Spain at the End of the Fourteenth Century" (in Hebrew), *Pe'amim* 46–47: 92–114.

————. 1991b. "A Study of Philosophical Variety in Spain and Provence before the Expulsion" (in Hebrew), *Pe'amim* 49: 3–23.

Señorío y feudalismo en la Península Ibérica, ss. XII–XIX, ed. E. Sarasa Sánchez and E. Serrano Martín, 4 vols. (Zaragoza, 1993).

Sevillano Colom, F. 1951. *Préstamos de la ciudad de Valencia a los reyes Alfonso V y Juan II, 1426–72* (Valencia).

Shmueli, E. 1986. "The Jerusalem School of History: A Critical Evaluation," *Proceedings of the American Academy for Jewish Research* 53: 147–178.

Silver, A. H. 1959. *A History of Messianic Speculation in Israel: From the First through the Seventeenth Centuries*, 2d ed. (Boston).

Simonsohn, S. 1988–91. *The Apostolic See and the Jews*, 8 vols. (Toronto).

————. 1991. *The Apostolic See and the Jews: History* (Toronto).

Soloveitchik, H. 1978. "Can Halakhic Texts Talk History?" *Association for Jewish Studies Review* 3: 153–196.

Talmage, F. 1985. "Trauma at Tortosa: The Testimony of Abraham Rimoch," *Mediaeval Studies* 47: 379–415.

Tasis i Marca, R. 1980. *Pere el Ceremoniós i els seus fills*, 2d ed. (Barcelona).

Thrupp, S. 1981. "Medieval Industry, 1000–1500," in *The Fontana Economic History of Europe: The Middle Ages*, ed. C. Cipolla, pp. 221–273 (Glasgow).

Tirosh-Rothschild, H. 1991. *Between Worlds: The Life and Thought of Rabbi David ben Judah Messer Leon* (Albany).

Toaff, A. 1979. *The Jews of Medieval Assisi, 1305–1487* (Florence).

———. 1996. *Love, Work, and Death: Jewish Life in Medieval Umbria*, trans. J. Landry (London).

Torras i Ribé, J. M. 1994. "La política municipal de Fernando el Católico en los reinos de la Corona de Aragón," in *1490 — En el umbral de la modernidad: El Mediterráneo europeo y las ciudades en el tránsito de los siglos XV–XVI*, ed. J. Hinojosa Montalvo and J. Pradells Nadal, vol. 1, pp. 233–256 (Valencia).

Valdeón Baruque, J. 1968. *Los judíos de Castilla y la revolución Trastámara* (Valladolid).

Vendrell, F. 1948. "Concesión de nobleza a un converso," *Sefarad* 8: 397–401.

———. 1950. "La política proselitista del rey D. Fernando I de Aragón," *Sefarad* 10: 349–366.

———. 1953. "La actividad proselitista de San Vicente Ferrer durante el reinado de Fernando I de Aragón,"*Sefarad* 13: 87–104.

———. 1960. "En torno a la confirmación real, en Aragón, de la pragmatica de Benedicto XIII," *Sefarad* 20: 319–351.

Vicens Vives, J. 1936–37. *Ferran II i la ciutat de Barcelona*, 3 vols. (Barcelona).

Viciano Navarro, P. 1989. *Catarroja: Una senyoria de l'Horta de València en l'època tardomedieval* (Catarroja).

———. 1990. "Ingrés i despesa d'una vila valenciana del Quatrecents: Les finances municipals de Castelló de la Plana, 1426–1427," *Boletín de la Sociedad Castellonense de Cultura* 66: 635–664.

———. 1992. "Fiscalitat local i deute públic al País Valencià: L'administració de la vila de Borriana a mitjan segle XV," *Anuario de Estudios Medievales* 22: 513–533.

———. 1995. "Francesc Agramunt, un home de vila," in *L'univers dels prohoms: Perfils socials a la València baix-medieval*, pp. 175–215 (Valencia).

———. 1997. "Entre la coerció i el mercat: Els inversors en la gestió de la fiscalitat reial i municipal al País Valencià," in *Col.loqui Corona*, pp. 603–621.

Vidal Beltrán, E. 1974. *Valencia en la época de Juan I* (Valencia).

Viera, D. 1985. "The Treatment of the Jew and the Moor in the Catalan Works of Francesc Eiximenis," *Revista Canadiense de Estudios Hispánicos* 9: 203–213.

———. 1992. "Sant Vicent Ferrer, Francesc Eiximenis i el pogrom de 1391," in *Actes del Sisè Col.loqui d'Estudis Catalans a Nord-Amèrica*, pp. 243–254 (Barcelona).

Vincke, J. 1941. *Zur Vorgeschichte der Spanischen Inquisition: Die Inquisition in Aragon, Katalonien, Mallorca und Valencia während des 13. und 14. Jahrhunderts* (Bonn).

Visitas pastorales de Valencia, siglos XIV–XV, ed. M. M. Cárcel Ortí and J. V. Boscá Codina (Valencia, 1996).

Voltes Bou, P. 1968. "Les associacions de seders medievals barcelonins," *Anuario de Estudios Medievales* 5: 483–494.

Walfish, B. 1993. *Esther in Medieval Garb: Jewish Interpretation of the Book of Esther in the Middle Ages* (Albany).

Wegner, J. R. 1991. "The Image and Status of Women in Classical Rabbinic Judaism,"
    in *Jewish Women in Historical Perspective*, ed. J. R. Baskin, pp. 68–93 (Detroit).
Wolff, P. 1971. "The 1391 Pogroms in Spain: Social Crisis or Not?" *Past and Present*
    50: 4–18.
Yerushalmi, Y. H. 1971. *From Spanish Court to Italian Ghetto: Isaac Cardoso, a Study
    in Seventeenth-Century Marranism and Jewish Apologetics* (New York).

INDEX

Lightning Source UK Ltd.
Milton Keynes UK
UKOW051026130613

212205UK00002B/65/P